A straightforward, honest, hard-hitting account of one of America's most creative entrepreneurs. James Sorenson's story is one which absolutely must be told.

—JON HUNTSMAN, SR., *American industrialist*

Equipped with grit, determination, and his own peculiar brand of genius, Jim defied all odds, including poverty, dyslexia, and the expectations of others, to become one of the world's greatest inventors of medical devices.

—MILES WHITE, *CEO, Abbott Laboratories*

He'd take a common situation and notice [it was] not ideal, and then innovate. That was his genius. And that courage to go forward and trust your ideas, develop, and convince other people it was worthwhile, was the other part of his genius.

—DR. JEFFREY L. ANDERSON, *associate chief of cardiology, LDS Hospital*

Jim had the greatest mind I've ever been around in terms of ideas. He would bury us with ideas. His mind just raced. He would call somebody, then forget why he called them.

—JAMES LARSON, *longtime COO, Sorenson Development Inc.*

He made a contribution to the well-being and happiness of millions of people by virtue of his inventions. He cared about his community, his culture, his faith, about his family.

—MITT ROMNEY, *former presidential candidate and governor of Massachusetts*

Front cover: Jim in 1979, one year before selling Sorenson Research to Abbott Labs for $100 million ($290 million in 2015 dollars).

# TRUE WEALTH

# TRUE
# WEALTH

## The Vision and Genius of Innovator
## James LeVoy Sorenson

## LEE RODERICK

Probitas Press

Published in the United States by
Probitas Press LLC., Los Angeles
www.probitaspress.com
800-616-8081

LIBRARY OF CONGRESS CATALOGING-IN-PUBLICATION DATA
Roderick, Lee
True wealth: the vision and genius of innovator James LeVoy Sorenson / Lee Roderick.
— First edition.
p. cm
Includes biographical references, patent appendix, and index.
1. Sorenson, James LeVoy 1921-2008. 2. Medical instruments
and apparatus industry--United States--History.
3. Businesspeople--Utah--Biography.
4. Medical innovations--United States--History. I. Title.
HD9994.U5R63 2014   338.7'681761092--dc23
[B]
Summary: Biography of the late James LeVoy Sorenson, who rose from
poverty to one of the world's richest men by inventing medical devices
and founding some 40 companies.
ISBN 978-0-9673432-8-0
ISBN 978-0-9961850-0-4
eISBN 978-0-9961850-7-3

Also by Lee Roderick:
*Voices Behind the Voice of America*
*Leading the Charge*
*Television Tightrope*
*Gentleman of the Senate*
*Bridge Builder*
*Courage*

For Beverley

Jim's Steadfast Anchor

# CONTENTS

# ACKNOWLEDGEMENTS

Early in 1998 I approached Jim Sorenson with a proposal to write a book on him. Also prodded by a mutual friend, the late Washington columnist Jack Anderson, Jim agreed to cooperate, and the book began. About six months later, however, other priorities pressed, and Jim ended our project.

That was not a total surprise. Among the elusive billionaire's papers are a handful of other unfinished manuscripts by previous writers who also tried to tell his story. In the end all of their efforts were aborted or shelved by Jim. He was a loner by nature and not comfortable revealing himself.

Jim subsequently died in 2008. Three years later his widow, Beverley Taylor Sorenson, gave me renewed access to Jim's files. She and other family members and professional colleagues made themselves available to shed new light on her late husband. Most of Jim's papers were well organized into large black binders by his longtime assistant Gloria Smith. Beverley's own special assistant Lisa Cluff helped facilitate access to research sources. Tom and Alison Armstrong Taylor supplied some of the photos.

Family members who were especially helpful included James Lee Sorenson, Carol Sorenson Smith, Gary Crocker, Gail Sorenson Williamsen, Joan

Sorenson Fenton, and Gloria Backman. Family historian David Sorenson researched the early history of the Sorenson family from the time they lived in Norway.

Two journeyman inventors, K. Pannier and Gordon Reynolds, helped Jim create most of his medical devices that are now used in hospitals around the world. With both men deceased, their families cooperated in explaining the work of K. and Gordon. They also loaned the author medical devices the men helped invent. Two sons, Scott Pannier and Val Reynolds, were especially cooperative.

Medical and academic professionals who helped invent, test, and employ Sorenson medical devices included Dr. Homer Warner, the father of medical informatics; Dr. Reed Gardner, a close colleague of Warner's, and Dr. Robert Hitchcock, currently a professor in the Department of Bioengineering at the University of Utah. Each gave in-depth interviews, including Dr. Warner who died in August 2012, months after our discussion.

Many former or current Sorenson employees gave freely of their time in interviews and guided tours of facilities. Jim Larson showed the author around the White Sage Ranch and Farm in Kanosh, Utah. Don Wallace, head of Jim Sorenson's far-flung real estate operations, patiently explained the most important developments and holdings.

Other key employees who were especially helpful include West Price and John Brophy, Sorenson Bioscience; LeVoy Haight, Sorenson Medical; Scott Woodward, Sorenson Molecular Genealogy Foundation; Doug Fogg and Lars Mouritsen, Sorenson Forensics; and Ben Smith, LeVoy's. Also: financial assistant Duane Toney, attorney and patent specialist Reed Winterton, and public relations advisors David Parkinson and John Ward.

My photographer son, Eric Roderick, shot key photos and assisted in other ways as the manuscript was written. Graphic artist Elizabeth Shaw designed *True Wealth*.

Finally, and most importantly, my wife Yvonne was and is forever encouraging. A true book professional in her own right, she is also my best editor and best friend.

To each of you, and others unnamed who also helped, my deepest thanks.

# PROLOGUE

On a spring morning in 1955 Jim Sorenson was making his rounds of Salt Lake City hospitals as a drug salesman for the Upjohn Company.

While in Holy Cross Hospital, emergency doors flew open and he saw a young accident victim, bleeding profusely, trundled in. Doctors and nurses sprinted to the emergency room in a frantic effort to save the blond 11-year-old boy.

Some tried to find and stem the sources of bleeding. Others inserted an intravenous line and began to pump in blood expanders and replacement fluids as fast as possible. Concentrating on those tasks, the medical team failed to see that a glass bottle of replacement fluid ran dry. Before it could be replaced, an air bubble moved to the boy's heart. His heart spasmed and he died almost instantly.

Sorenson left the hospital emotionally drained. "As I drove my car from the parking lot, I began asking myself, 'Isn't there a better way? There's got to be a better way!'"

There was—and he would invent it.

Mankind's march through history has been painful. Disease, irreparable injury, and early death have marched lock-step with him and her from the dawn of civilization.

Major conflicts provide benchmarks of suffering. The American Civil War resulted in 93,000 deaths of Union soldiers from combat and another 210,000 from disease. Southern losses were similar. Three decades later, 289 Americans died in combat or from wounds in the Spanish-American War. For every soldier laid low in battle, another thirteen died of disease.

The start of the twentieth century was scarcely more hopeful. World War I unleashed unprecedented havoc. Ten million soldiers died, along with about 5 million civilians. Hostilities ended in 1918, only to be followed by a devastating pandemic of influenza which, in four months, killed more than had died in four years of war, about 20 million souls, including 450,000 Americans infected by returning troops.

While the 1900s began in an ancient, deadly way, the new century would soon prove to be something entirely different. It ushered in the greatest scientific and technological advances the world had seen. Scientists and medical engineers at last would discover and invent effective ways to prevent or relieve much human suffering.

The medical revolution included X-rays enabling doctors to see inside the human body; the discovery of radium, a powerful weapon against cancer; sulfa drugs and vaccines to fight diseases; and penicillin, the first antibiotic, which arrived one war too late and might have prevented millions of flu-related deaths.

The names of great medical pioneers, Louis Pasteur, Pierre and Marie Curie, Alexander Fleming, and others, are hallowed in history.

Much of the progress in modern medicine has also come from biomedical engineers. Working closely with doctors, they help explain the function of living organisms and provide the tools to diagnose, prevent, and treat diseases or injuries. While these men and women have contributed enormously to human health, they are largely unknown to the public.

James LeVoy Sorenson is one of these unsung heroes.

He was an American original, eccentric and complex, yet perfectly clear when selling an idea; generous with the poor but often tightfisted with peers and family; one who preached teamwork but was utterly incapable of being anything but the leader; insistent on his rules, but indifferent to everyone else's.

One thing not in dispute is his brilliance. A professor and collaborator at the University of Utah called Jim "beyond genius" for his array of abilities. A close thirty-year colleague said Jim had "the greatest mind I've ever been around in terms of ideas...his mind just raced." Another colleague added that "Jim had a unique way of looking at the world. He couldn't shut it off."

An American poet observed that "We look at the world once, in childhood. The rest is memory."[1]

In Jim Sorenson's case, that might help explain a lot. He was reared in poverty in the depths of the Depression. While his father dug ditches by hand and delivered ice, Jim as a small boy hawked newspapers and magazines door-to-door, mostly to older women who found his aw-shucks manner and winsome face irresistible. When wind blew walnuts from neighborhood trees, he gathered and sold them for about fifteen cents a bucket. Young as he was, Jim helped lift his family from poverty.

Soon after starting school, a teacher branded Jim "mentally retarded" for his inability to read. He could not process graphic symbols and reversed the letters on a page. "Saw" became "was," "b" looked like "d"and "p" like "q." The word "OIL" appeared as the number 710.

Ninety years ago there was no name for Jim's learning disorder. Today it is often called "dyslexia" (Greek for disturbed reading). Those affected typically have certain things in common: above-average intelligence, curiosity, creativity, and intuition. They are inventive and often excel at real-world challenges.

Many dyslexics surrender to their fate, have low self-esteem, and live less than full lives. But rich rewards are available to those who reach deeply within themselves and refuse to give in. Albert Einstein was dyslexic, as was Thomas Edison and Alexander Graham Bell. Gen. George Patton had trouble reading, but no trouble leading men into battle. Winston Churchill and Woodrow Wilson rose above the disability to lead nations.

Jim Sorenson joined these and many other notables who have made historic contributions, not in spite of dyslexia but because of it. Inventing medical devices would become his raison d'etre—along with a passion for entrepreneurship wherever he sensed opportunity.

Jim's inventions typically were not the product of endless experimentation, like Edison and the light bulb. Rather, they emerged from astute observation of surgeons and other practitioners at work—and an uncanny ability to conjure what he called "a better way." He saw urgencies that others often failed to notice, and pondered deeply until a possible solution crystallized in his mind. Then he shared his vision with others who helped create it.

In 1956 Jim and two other men founded Deseret Pharmaceutical, to purchase drugs from manufacturers and sell them. Jim's powers of observation soon turned the company in a different direction. From closely watching physicians at work, Jim intuitively knew what tools they lacked—and figured out how to invent them. Two of the tools were the first disposable surgical mask and the first disposable plastic catheter.

These and other innovations proved so profitable that within a dozen years Deseret abandoned drugs altogether and instead developed, manufactured, and sold only medical devices.

Deseret was Utah's first biotechnology firm and a national trendsetter. A half-century later Utah had more than 110 such companies and was recognized as a significant player in the medical-device industry.

Jim was too much of a maverick to work harmoniously and long-term with others he could not command. At the end of 1960 he sold his share of Deseret to his two partners, agreeing not to compete against them for two years. They could stop his making and marketing, but not his mind. The minute the two years were up, Jim opened a desk drawer full of scraps of paper with ideas for new medical devices, and set about to invent them.

He founded Sorenson Research, one of about forty companies he created over his lifetime, and soon showed why Deseret Pharmaceutical had good reason to fear him. Adept at sensing untapped potential in people, he found one man at a metal-stamp shop and another repairing sewing machines. The three became a veritable fountain of innovation, accounting for most of the nearly fifty U.S. patents that carry Jim's name.

Miles White, CEO of Abbott Laboratories, a leading global healthcare company, said of Sorenson: "Equipped with grit, determination, and his own peculiar brand of genius, Jim defied all odds, including poverty, dyslexia, and the expectations of others, to become one of the world's greatest inventors of medical devices."

White added that Jim's inventions "had a monumental impact, and they've stood the test of time. Look in any modern operating room or intensive care unit, and you'll see enduring evidence of Jim's creative solutions to tough medical problems."[2]

Jim was a Renaissance man—an athlete, philosopher, and poet, as well as one of the twentieth century's great inventors and entrepreneurs. During the last years of his life he poured millions into a quixotic quest for global peace.

Jim never lost the common touch. He typically showed more concern for lower-paid individuals than for those better off. He was unfailingly frugal with himself but happy, as a billionaire, to let an aide of modest means pick up the lunch tab, while tipping the waitress with a $100 bill.

Jim personified political incorrectness. His emperor-has-no-clothes candor delighted many observers and mortified others, not infrequently his long-suffering wife.

Beverley Taylor knew from the start that her husband would be difficult to live with, but also that he would make big things happen. She was right on both counts.

### CHAPTER ONE

# TOUGH START

## for Teen Parents

F or Jim Sorenson, tenacity was in the blood.

In the summer of 1849 Hans Olaus Sorenson was born on Goat Island in Norway. His family in fact owned the tiny island, where they indeed raised goats, other livestock, and poultry. They were practicing Lutherans.

Hans' birth coincided with the arrival in Scandinavia of the first missionaries of The Church of Jesus Christ of Latter-day Saints. Seeds planted by Mormon missionaries soon bore fruit among Hans's extended, though not his immediate, family.

Starting in 1852 a number of aunts and uncles were among the first Norwegians to join the Church. At fourteen Hans also began studying with the missionaries, at first in secret. His parents and siblings vehemently opposed his interest in the Church. But he held firm, and was baptized on his twenty-first birthday in 1870, embarking that same day for the American Zion—Utah—with some 350 other recent converts.[1]

Hans likely assumed that, once he got to Utah, fellow believers would help ensure a pleasant life. He was soon disabused of that notion. One of his first jobs was at the Alta silver mine in Little Cottonwood Canyon southeast of Salt Lake City. The town was booming with non-Mormons;

it had twenty-six saloons and a history of violence.

After Hans refused to drink with the miners, four came to his room. Three held him down while the fourth tried to force a bottle of liquor into his mouth. Praying hard, Hans felt a burst of strength. He wrenched his arms free and kicked one burly man onto the floor. As the men were momentarily distracted, Hans fled into the night. He lay in a ditch, unseen as the men sprinted past.

When workers reached a particularly dangerous section of the mine, the boss asked for a volunteer to inspect the tunnel for safety. A miner suggested Hans: "Send the Mormon, it won't cave on him." Hans proceeded down the tunnel. Partway there he stopped to tie his shoes. While on his knees he prayed for protection. Hans rose and was about to walk on when the walls buckled and a massive slide filled the tunnel, starting a couple of steps in front of him.

Hans's close call was one of many encountered by Sorensons through the years, when spiritual promptings likewise saved members of his posterity.

In 1874 two Swedish women LDS converts, good friends, embarked from Denmark for Utah. They were Anna Marie (Hindriksson) Svensson, 31, and Bertha Caroline Rorstrom, 19. An adolescent child born to Anna in Sweden, named Abraham (Abe), was with them. The following year, a time when polygamy was practiced in the Church, 26-year-old Hans married both women in the LDS Endowment House in Salt Lake City.

The family relocated several times in the next few years, finally settling on a homestead in central Utah, a few miles west of the small town of Leamington, Millard County. Hans's church service included thirteen years as superintendent of the local LDS Sunday School. Living in Leamington was very lean. Townspeople built a small schoolhouse but neglected to add a privy. During recess, boys and girls relieved themselves outdoors at opposite ends of a shrub-filled ravine.

The Sorensons raised grain, vegetables, and animals, and sold meat and eggs. Hans was ambitious. He bought a creamery machine and gathered milk from local dairymen to make cream. Later, Hans and five other men, including two sons, bought a thrashing machine, pulled by five teams of horses, with which they thrashed their own grain and, for a fee, the grain of other families in the region.

Long after most other family members left Leamington, the *Millard County Chronicle* saluted Hans for his longevity and patriotism. "People like Mr. Hans Olaus Sorenson, of Leamington, are a credit to our country," began the article, in 1944 when World War II still blazed. "Although almost 95 years of age, Mr. Sorenson has bought a [war] bond during each drive." [2]

Accompanying the article was a photo of Hans, looking dapper in a three-piece suit with white hair and a white walrus mustache. It noted he had outlived his wives. "Asked why he buys bonds, he said 'I am interested in the welfare of our country, and I am also interested in the progress of America. Also I have 12 great-grandchildren in the service of our country.'" He vowed to live long enough "until complete victory and then I am going to sing in the celebration."

Hans didn't quite make it, dying ten months later, in December 1944, five months before the end of war in the European Theater.

Hans and Bertha Rorstrom had six children. Hans adopted Anna Svensson's son, Abe, and they had five others together. Anna's fourth child was Joseph Leonard Sorenson, born in South Jordan on June 26, 1880.

On October 9, 1900 Joseph Sorenson and Annie Elva Johnson were married in the Salt Lake Temple. After forty years of construction, it was completed seven years earlier. Annie was born and reared in Leamington to parents who emigrated from Switzerland. The language of their home was German.

The first of twelve children born to Annie and Joseph was Joseph LeVoy Sorenson. Interestingly, each of their birthdays fell within four days of the same month: Joseph's on June 26, 1880, Annie's on June 30, 1880, and LeVoy's on June 29, 1902. Joseph LeVoy would become the father of James LeVoy Sorenson.

In 1904, Joseph and Annie said goodbye to Leamington. Lured northward by Idaho's fertile soil, the Sorensons worked or owned several farms in the upper Snake River Valley. They built a ten-room home near St. Anthony. LeVoy grew to become a strong, muscular, slow-talking teenager with a great capacity for physical work. LeVoy had an excellent memory but great difficulty reading. "The words always jumble together," wrote LeVoy, who sometimes was threatened or spanked in a vain attempt to force him to untangle them.

The family survived on hard work—and a lot of faith and prayer that produced miracles. In 1915 Joseph was returning home from St. Anthony, driving four horses pulling a hay rack. An electrical storm suddenly erupted. A soft voice told Joseph to pull off the road into a grove of trees. He ignored the prompting. After it came twice more, Joseph turned off the road. Immediately a bolt of lightning struck where he would have been. [3]

When LeVoy was sixteen he was driving six head of horses hitched to a double disc as he plowed a field. It was at the south end of three-hundred acres of waist-high grain. His father Joseph and a young brother, Clayton, were a mile away on the north end.

"Suddenly I heard the roaring of something that sounded like a long freight train," said Joseph. "Looking up I saw a black cloud coming directly toward us." The cloud was a ferocious hail storm, fast bearing down on the precious grain crop—and on LeVoy, tethered to six flighty horses. [4]

"I knew I couldn't reach him in time, so I did the only thing I knew of—that was to call on the Lord. I gathered my little boy in my arms and knelt down on the ground...I asked the Lord to protect LeVoy and turn the hail away from us...When the storm came within a half-mile of where LeVoy was discing it split in two, and half went on each side of our place... For miles on both sides the wheat was beaten to the ground and not a spear of grain remained standing. But on my place there was not a spear knocked down!"

The Sorensons harvested a full crop that year, while a mile south of their farm the hail leveled crops, killed pigs, and broke windows.

But prayer could not protect LeVoy from a storm of the heart. Already well-established in Rexburg when the Sorensons arrived was the Robert and Emma Blaser family. The parents and their first five children emigrated from Switzerland to Idaho in 1900. Unlike most humble Europeans of the era who converted to Mormonism and emigrated to Zion, the Blasers left behind substantial holdings in land, home, income, and, for the father, professional stature.

The Blasers had owned an imposing five-level home in Langnau, a small Swiss village set among rolling hills in a breathtaking valley near Bern. It is one of the sunniest valleys in Switzerland, with almost no fog. Langnau's residents traditionally valued learning; a century later, in 2000, about 70 percent of adult residents had completed non-mandatory, post-secondary education.

Robert Blaser was a master builder and the superintendent of a cement plant, which built cement pipes, troughs, and other infrastructure products. In addition to his native German, he spoke French and Italian. The customary way of doing business was to take clients to establishments where beer flowed freely and the air was thick with smoke.

When Emma gave birth to her third child, Frieda, on March 30, 1895, she became ill with pain and high fever in her chest. A doctor delivered the sobering news: Emma had cancer of the breast. Friends told the Blasers that there were Mormon missionaries in town with the power to heal the sick. Robert contacted the elders—who both had black beards and dressed in dark clothing—and they came to the Blaser home. One was Jacob Metzner from Grant, Idaho.

"...we all knelt down by [Mother's] bed," recalled their eldest child, Ernest, just three and a half at the time. "Dad gave a prayer. The elders prayed, then they took the oil and anointed her breast and then put some on mother's head and administered to her. Through the administration mother was healed." [5]

"Brother Metzner told my mother that if she would investigate the restored gospel with sincerity and prayer, the Lord would bless her...He said 'I promise you that from this time forth, regardless of how many children will come into your family, you will be able to nurse each and every one of those children.'" Emma soon was able to nurse Frieda, as well as the last ten children she later bore.

Like most families in the valley, the Blasers were Lutherans. Profoundly grateful for Emma's miraculous recovery, however, they began a serious study of the LDS Church. They also invited the missionaries into their home, and lodged and fed them at no cost. Such kindnesses to the elders and their message turned townspeople against the Blasers. Their standard of living was threatened, as Robert no longer was comfortable meeting with clients in pub-like settings, and their renters abandoned them.

Late at night on March 28, 1899—two days before the fourth an-
niversary of when the missionaries blessed Emma—church members quietly accompanied her and Robert to the snowy banks of the ice-choked
Ilfis River. There they were baptized into the Church. "They said it never
felt cold because they had such a wonderful feeling," noted the family history book.

Their baptism—to be followed through the years by those of their
children when each reached the age of eight—broke the last tenuous ties
to their neighbors and extended families. "They hated us. They'd pass by
and wouldn't greet you or called you 'Old Mormons.'"

The persecution the Blasers suffered was not new. The Church of
Jesus Christ of Latter-day Saints had been an affront to other religions
and their adherents ever since it was established in 1830. The Church
was not simply another Christian denomination; it claimed to be the only
church on earth fully approved by God.

The LDS saga began a decade earlier, in the spring of 1820, in
upstate New York. The area was experiencing what historians call the
"burned-over district"—religious revivals and Pentecostal movements.
Joseph Smith, a farm boy not yet fifteen, was confused by their competing claims. In reading the Bible he came across a passage that moved him
to action: "If any of you lack wisdom, let him ask of God, that giveth to all
men liberally, and upbraideth [reproach] not; and it shall be given him."
[James 1:5]

"At length I came to the conclusion that I must either remain in
darkness and confusion, or else I must do as James directs, that is ask of
God," Joseph wrote. In the morning of a beautiful spring day, he walked
to a grove of trees near his family's small house outside Palmyra, New
York, and knelt in prayer. After initially experiencing darkness and a
powerful unseen force that alarmed him, Joseph said he was delivered
from it this way:

...I saw a pillar of light exactly over my head, above the brightness of
the sun, which descended gradually until it fell upon me. It no soon-
er appeared than I found myself delivered from the enemy which
held me bound. When the light rested upon me I saw two Person-

ages, whose brightness and glory defy all description, standing above me in the air. One of them spake unto me, calling me by name, and said, pointing to the other—"This is My Beloved Son. Hear Him!" [6]

The two persons, said Joseph, were God the Father and Jesus Christ, who told him not to join any of the churches. He learned that the church established by the Savior during his mortal ministry was taken from the earth after the martyrdom of the early apostles and a general departure from Christ's teachings. Additional revelations followed. Then, on April 6, 1830, Joseph and a handful of followers formally restored Christ's church, organizing it as The Church of Jesus Christ of Latter-day Saints.

In 1823 an angel named Moroni appeared to Joseph and told him of a set of metal plates buried in a nearby hillside. They contained a sacred record of former inhabitants of this continent. The record, covering a thousand years, had been abridged by Moroni's father, named Mormon, and hidden there by Moroni himself. Four years later Joseph was allowed to take the plates. He translated the ancient writing on them into the *Book of Mormon.*

From the earliest days of the Church, LDS (Mormon) missionaries have taken their personal testimonies and copies of the *Book of Mormon* across the globe.

As persecution mounted in Switzerland, less than a year after the Blasers' baptisms, Robert and Emma and their five children boarded the ship *Anchoria,* bound for America and Zion—Salt Lake City. They embarked on January 10, 1900, among about 150 LDS converts. The seventeen-day mid-winter voyage across the north Atlantic was perilous. A terrible storm erupted. The churning sea sickened virtually everyone aboard and broke the ship's rudder. The *Anchoria* floated aimlessly as water flooded the lowest decks and the Blasers scrambled up to the next level.

Robert Blaser helped pump water back into the Atlantic—four hours on and four hours off—around the clock for days. The ship's officers applauded Blaser's strength and endurance, and even more his willingness to spell off lower-class passengers. When the storm abated, an ice breaker and three tugboats appeared over the horizon and pulled the *Anchoria* to Ellis Island.

Once they reached Utah, the Blasers took a train north to Rexburg, Idaho. Other Mormon immigrants also flowed into the fertile Snake River Valley. Rexburg grew from 2,200 in 1914 to 4,000 in 1920. Robert became the area's premier builder. A century later his rock work would continue to stand out on homes, businesses and public edifices including the Tabernacle and the Jacob Spori building on the Ricks school campus.

Robert assured his children they could attend LDS-owned Ricks, which first opened its doors in 1903 as Ricks Academy, offering high school-level classes. A year of college was added in 1917 when the school became Ricks Normal College; it became Ricks College in 1923—a full-fledged two-year college. Today it is a four-year private university known as Brigham Young University-Idaho.

Emma Blaser, her mother's namesake and the eighth of thirteen siblings, was born in 1904. The teenager was spirited and strikingly pretty, with a warm, enigmatic smile. She was a bright student and excellent writer. Emma worked as a proof-reader for the *Rexburg Standard,* where it was said that editor Lloyd Adams' standing rule was that the newspaper was not to be printed until Emma saw it.

She relished the life of the mind, the contest of competing ideas, and was considered gifted by instructors. A teacher read her English themes to the older class as an example of good writing. Among those listening was LeVoy Sorenson, the rough-hewn farm boy from up the road, who liked the prose—and liked its author even more. LeVoy and Emma courted and fell deeply in love.

A thick blanket of snow covered the Snake River Valley and decorative lights shone through windows as Rexburg prepared to celebrate peace on earth in 1920. But there was not a lot of celebrating in the homes of the Sorenson and Blaser families. Two days before Christmas LeVoy, 18, and Emma, 17, quietly wed in a civil ceremony. That same week the *Rexburg Journal* ran a chapter from a serialized novel that seemed a portent of their future. It was about a rancher who suddenly and unexpectedly married a beautiful teen-age girl. Its title: "Comrades of Peril." [7]

LeVoy and Emma moved in with his family, including ten siblings. The atmosphere was tense as well as crowded. His mother Annie, a petite, pretty, normally cheerful woman, was heartbroken and bewildered.

Her dreams for her beloved son dashed. Some family members said cruel things to Emma, accusing her of trapping LeVoy.

The Blasers had strong feelings of their own, apparently believing Emma married below her station. They arrived in the Snake River Valley ahead of the Sorensons, and put down firm roots. While the Sorensons had a minimum of formal education and few work skills beyond farming, Robert Blaser was a highly regarded builder—multi-lingual, skilled mathematician, and a leading citizen who oversaw construction of the Tabernacle and some of the first permanent buildings at Ricks Academy.

A profile in the local newspaper said that back in Switzerland he "had charge of several $200,000 jobs and employed a force of over forty men...the people of Rexburg should be happy to think they have a contractor of his quality here..."[8]

Years later LeVoy and Emma's first child, in the presence of two of her brothers, heard one of them say to the other: "How do you expect him to amount to anything with a father like he has?"[9]

The truth, however, was that LeVoy was an exceptionally hard worker with solid values who set a good example for his family. Though with limited formal schooling, LeVoy was enterprising and, for much of his life, a local leader in both business and church circles.

That winter, working with his father, LeVoy earned $50 for every train car he loaded with potatoes. The work, however, lasted only six weeks. In the early spring LeVoy and Emma moved into a house in nearby Parker. LeVoy then took a job in Island Park, about a hundred miles north of Rexburg, for the Targhee Tie Company. He made $5 a day hauling railroad ties by a horse-drawn wagon to a railhead.

While LeVoy was in Island Park, Emma caught a cold. Her condition deteriorated alarmingly—in a house that probably was not well-heated. She called the Sorensons, asking them to take her to their house. "They wouldn't do it," LeVoy told an interviewer. Emma then contacted her brother Bob, who lived about ten miles away in Plano. He drove to Parker and moved Emma to his family's home.

"That summer I was making pretty good money," said LeVoy. "Then Dad and one or two of my brothers came up to Island Park and got some twenty-foot logs out" for some project. "They charged a handsaw and some boards to me, so when I got ready to go home, I didn't have the money I should have had." He said Emma was pretty upset, but her mother stuck up for him and Emma calmed down. [10]

On July 30, 1921, seven months after their marriage and a month before her eighteenth birthday, Emma and LeVoy's first child was born, entering the world in the Blasers' substantial brick home built by Robert. He was a beautiful, healthy, ten-pound boy. Local newspapers failed to mention the birth. Weeks later, the two families called a truce long enough to gather in a Mormon chapel on the Sabbath for the traditional blessing and naming of a new baby.

Grandfather Joseph Sorenson announced that he would bless the baby and give him his own good name. He swept the infant from Emma's arms and carried him to the front of the congregation, where other adult male members formed a circle in preparation for the ordinance. Before Grandpa could begin, there was a stir in the congregation. Emma rose and hurried to the front. Striding to the far side of the circle, she grabbed the arm of her brother, a recently returned missionary.

"Please, *you* give the blessing," Emma implored her brother. "And don't name him Joseph. His name is to be James LeVoy."

Thus began the mortal journey of James LeVoy Sorenson.

Years later, Emma would teach her children this proverb: "An injustice takes two people—one who will do it to you and one who will let them." Emma, noted a daughter, "had a lot of spunk." It was a quality the young couple would need often as they set about to make a life for their little family.

No matter what others thought, Emma and LeVoy were immensely proud of their handsome new son. LeVoy was clerking in a store in St. Anthony when Jimmy was born. He took the baby out front to show off. "I walked up and down the block many times, and not one person said 'What a fine, beautiful baby,'" he remembered. "I was so disappointed I felt like crying."

In the tight-knit valley where everyday life revolved around the exacting moral standards of the LDS Church, teenagers Emma and LeVoy stood out with their new son.

At first they attended church services with the extended Sorenson

family. When their second child, Eileen, was born fourteen months after Jimmy, the shy young parents joined a different congregation—which
Mormons call a "ward"—in Parker. Three Sundays in a row they went to
services. Each time the greeting was the same. No one stepped forward to
welcome or talk to them. After that, feeling more inadequate and unwel-
come than ever, they stopped attending altogether.

Momentarily discouraged with church, Emma and LeVoy still were
steadfast in their faith in God and in the LDS faith. LeVoy was taught
well from infancy, including by his Grandmother, Anna Maria Sorenson.
When giving LeVoy a cookie she would kneel down, look him in the eye,
and have him repeat after her as she blessed it in her native Swedish. It
was a simple lesson in gratitude that influenced him the rest of his days.

LeVoy's sensitivity to the spirit saved his life while he was working
in Island Park. In an incident similar to the one his father Joseph experienced when driving horses in another storm, LeVoy explained:

> I had to sleep in a boxcar about six feet from the main track. When-
> ever the "Yellowstone Special" went by it shook so bad that it felt
> like it was falling apart, which helped me remember to pray daily for
> protection. One day when I was coming for a load of ties, there was
> a big black cloud overhead with lightning and thunder in a canyon.
> I heard a voice say "Whoa." I automatically tightened the reins and
> the horse stopped. I turned to see if anyone was there. Then that
> same voice said, "Did you not ask for protection today?" Suddenly
> the lightning struck a big tree and it fell across the road, right where
> I would have been had I kept going. It probably would have killed
> me. [11]

LeVoy was reserved, practical, and focused on the here and now,
while Emma loved to debate world events. She cheered the emerging
power of American women, who in 1920 were granted the right to vote
in national elections. While Idaho joined all neighboring states in voting
overwhelmingly for Republican and future President Warren G. Hard-
ing over James M. Cox, Emma was unconvinced and declared herself a
Democrat.

She later applauded a guest column in the *Rexburg Journal* by Mrs.

Philip N. Moore, president of the National Council of Women, who argued that "Women must learn to take part in party politics...We should choose definitely the party with whose principles we are most in sympathy and vote for the candidates of that party. We must vote for principles, not men."

Recalled one of Emma's daughters: "My mother could not stand anything that smacked of unfairness. She was passionate in her beliefs and incredibly focused on all her causes. Mom was a 'women's libber' way before that was fashionable. She fought for children's rights, was anti-racist, and loved being an American. She was exciting and interesting; it was never boring being around her." [12]

The United States and Europe were still trying to recover from the devastation of World War I, which ended in 1918. While those war clouds receded, other clouds formed. A sharp business depression was felt across the U.S. during the closing weeks of 1920.

Sections of the nation competed for in-migration to boost local economies. The *Rexburg Journal,* for one, ran a series of page-one articles touting the wonders of the Snake River Valley and urging "each reader of the paper to mail his copy to friends in distant places." Beginning the series was an article headlined "Rexburg, the Grain Bin of the Rockies." It avowed:

> The soil is a composition of volcanic ash and silt, formed generations and ages ago, when the world was young...The individual who follows agriculture as a life profession is indeed fortunate if he owns a well improved farm in this section of the Snake River Valley. His crop production every year is an assured fact. There has never been a complete failure...The farmer is independent. [13]

Such PR spin, however, could not mask signs of trouble on the farm. In 1920 average wage rates for farm labor reached their highest peaks to that time in U.S. history. Sharp drops in the prices of wheat, cotton, and other commodities brought appeals for assistance. The president of the Idaho Farm Bureau, speaking in Rexburg in February 1921, offered a grim assessment of the outlook for agricultural exports, given America's overstocked warehouses and Europe's enormous debt and depleted credits.

LeVoy helped the Sorenson family on the farm while working at other jobs. Starting in 1922, that family's world started to unravel. Though overshadowed by the Great Depression a decade later, the depression of 1920-21 and its aftermath likewise caused widespread economic dislocation, especially in rural America.

Wrote his father Joseph: "Things were booming [in 1919]. Everything went along nicely for 3 years. Then the 1922 depression hit without warning, and to be sure—I was not prepared...the war had changed everything. Taxes were 4 times higher than they had been, interest was 10% on all loans, there were crop failures, prices tumbled—all in all, life was just one damn thing after another."

Discouraged, Joseph began to make a series of decisions that led to disaster for family fortunes. He leased his 160-acre farm to another family for $6,000 for three years. Strapped for cash, he then sold the notes to a man in Idaho Falls for a deeply discounted $2,500. Things spiraled downward from there and they lost their home.

In a "Little Sketch of My Life," hand-written, apparently in 1944, Joseph talked about "my dealings with the men who helped me lose my farm and left me out in the world without anything except the clothes on my back." He acknowledged placing "too much trust in them," yet continued investing in risky ventures. After losing $500 in a San Francisco deal, Joseph wrote that "Sharpers again stripped me to the bone."

Joseph worked for an implement company and sharecropped for two years. As the Great Depression struck in 1929, Joseph found himself near the bottom rung of the financial ladder—washing dishes in a restaurant one day, sewing socks the next, "moving around a great deal in order to keep out of the bread lines. Thanks to Heavenly Father we never had to except [sic] charity."

Multiple tragedies struck the family. Between 1924 and 1930 four of the Sorenson children died. Annie, pregnant with their twelfth child in 1926, became critically ill. After baby Gloria was born, doctors discovered that Annie, 46, had cancer of the spleen. An agonizing year and a half later, in December 1927, she also died. Emma genuinely grieved for her mother-in-law. Despite their differences, she later told her children, "If Sister Sorenson had lived longer, I think we would have become friends."

In 1935 Joseph made what he later called "the worst mistake ever. I married Laura Johnson, an old girlhood sweetheart. In this I disobeyed the counsel of the Holy Ghost which prompted me many times not to do it." Their marriage lasted three months. "It seems that the spirit of God was greatly displeased, because I have not had the many promptings to guide me since."

Joseph had long considered serving a mission. At 63 he was called by LDS President Heber J. Grant to labor in the Western States Mission. Not an easy man to get along with in the best of times, according to a granddaughter-in-law, he found it very difficult to relate to missionaries a third his age. Nonetheless Joseph fulfilled an honorable mission, often administering to the sick and baptizing a number of converts.

CHAPTER TWO

# "MENTALLY RETARDED"

As the future continued to look bleak in Idaho, Emma and LeVoy set their sights on California, widely regarded as a golden land of opportunity and a place to make a fresh start. States still competed for newcomers, and no state touted its treasures more convincingly than California. In the summer of 1921, even a photo of a west coast rabbit hunt reinforced the image. The photo ran in newspapers across the country, including the *Rexburg Journal,* with this caption: "Out in California everything grows luxuriously, including the Jack Rabbit."

Interstate migration into California was substantial ever since gold was discovered at Sutter's Fort in 1848. First came the Forty-Niners seeking a quick killing in the gold fields. As word spread of California's pleasant climate and abundant natural resources, waves of other vagabond Americans followed, most looking not for gold but for a better life.

The state grew from fewer than 100,000 residents in 1850 to 1.5 million in 1900, a great majority from migration. Even that impressive growth was eclipsed in the following decades, with California's population swelling to 3.4 million by 1920 and 5.6 million by 1930. In the 1900 census it was the twenty-first state in size; by 1920 it was the eighth.

There was an enormous push as well as pull toward California. It included boom and bust cycles in rural America and depleted, overworked farmland from South Dakota to Texas. That uncorked the evil specter, starting in November 1933, of a continuing Dust Bowl that blew across 50 million acres of once-rich land, carrying much of it eastward, darkening the midday sky and dumping prairie dirt off the East Coast into the Atlantic.

The Dust Bowl symbolized the chaos in America's heartland during the Great Depression, and spurred up to 400 thousand dazed and dispirited Americans to California. A Texan spoke for many of them:

> Full well do I remember that good old Texas land,
> Where I lingered on starvation until I was a man...
> Don't let anyone fool you and lead you into harm,
> For you sure can't make a living on a forty acre farm.
> So when I see Old Texas one thing I truly hope. It will
> be from California through a long-range Teliscope. [sic][1]

The mass migration was seared into America's consciousness by author John Steinbeck, born in Salinas, California in 1902—the same year LeVoy was born in Idaho. Steinbeck gave voice to a bewildered nation, and painted the plight of the bedraggled people streaming into his native land with more power than anyone before or since. Although *The Grapes of Wrath* was published in 1939 and focused on that Dust Bowl decade, the flight to California began in the 1920s, before either the Dust Bowl or the Great Depression, which simply accelerated the exodus.[2]

In either decade, the anguish of leaving what was cherished and familiar for what was unknown out in California was the same.

And yet, wrote Steinbeck, "How can you frighten a man whose hunger is not only in his own cramped stomach but in the wretched bellies of his children? You can't scare him—he has known a fear beyond every other."[3]

Emma's brother, Fred Blaser, was the first in the family to abandon the Snake River Valley for California. He settled in Yuba City, about thirty miles north of Sacramento, and wrote home saying there was construction work available.

In 1924 LeVoy left Emma and their two children behind and joined his brother-in-law in Yuba City, a small agricultural community in Sutter County. Decades later the city would earn *Money* magazine's dubious designation as the worst city in America in which to live and rear a family, based on such things as high-crime and unemployment rates and a lack of social services.

Yuba City was founded in 1849 by Sam Brannan, an enterprising Mormon pioneer who got rich provisioning miners heading north to the gold fields. Yuba City and its twin Marysville are on opposite banks at the confluence of the Yuba and Feather Rivers. While attracting honest miners, laborers and settlers, they also got gamblers, thieves and other scoundrels. [4]

One legacy is the violence that has long plagued the area. Some of it has been ethnic in nature, aimed especially at Chinese-Americans whose ancestors came from Canton province to work the gold fields and lay railroad tracks over the Sierra Nevada. They grew prosperous, with a steady work ethic—often laboring for wages lower than their white neighbors would accept—and started dozens of area businesses. One result was fierce resentment that repeatedly boiled over into bloodshed.

Labor unrest also rocked the area early last century, with land owners fiercely opposing attempts by workers to organize. In Wheatland, fifteen miles south of Yuba City, the Durst Ranch raised hops and exploited the migrant workers hired to harvest them at seventy cents to $1.90 a day. A makeshift camp was erected and workers paid seventy-five cents a week to rent tents. Nine toilets located a mile from camp served all 2,800 residents and doubled as the garbage dump. Dysentery, typhoid and malaria raged among the workers.

Finally, led by the few dozen members of the Industrial Workers of the World (IWW) among them, workers struck for better conditions. When a posse burst into a bargaining session with guns and clubs, four men died in the raid, including District Attorney Ray Manwell.

Newspapers railed against the "Communist conspiracy," with a *Marysville Democrat* editorial calling members of the IWW "venomous human snakes preaching the religion of hate, and their weapons are always destruction of property...How long will a civilized community permit them to exist?" [5]

A commission appointed by Governor Hiram Johnson, however, concluded that the community itself was not quite so civilized. Conditions at
Durst Ranch, in fact, were deplorable, and the ranch, under pressure, proceeded to set up a model labor camp in 1914.

Then came the mass exodus from the American heartland to California. The first tourists arriving by automobile in Yuba City and Marysville in
the 1920s were welcomed as sources of tourist income, and local merchants
and civic groups set up auto courts complete with tents, showers, and night
watchmen. The better-heeled among them could get a fine meal at such
places as Kaffen's Grill, which featured private booths, fresh white linen
tablecloths, potted plants, and a player piano.

An artfully done ad in the *Marysville Democrat*—complete with a nubile
maiden displaying a cornucopia of bounties from the soil—beckoned outsiders to the area, much as Rexburg sought to do back in Idaho:

> Yuba and Sutter counties' progress and development has just begun...
> Their climate is unmatched, the fertility of the soil rivals or exceeds
> that of any similar area on earth...[They] are built upon a solid foun-
> dation. The farming lands, orchards, mining, railroad and public util-
> ity interests are investing thousands of dollars on this foundation.
> There is no peak to Yuba and Sutter counties' development. Just as
> long as California continues to progress and prosper, Yuba and Sutter
> counties will go along with it. [6]

Such hospitality, however, did not extend to "Oakies"—the popular
term for most down-on-their-luck outsiders moving to Yuba City-Mar-
ysville in search of work. The fears that earlier made the Chinese an ob-
ject of community concern were now focused on the new wave of workers
who threatened to lower everyone's standard of living by working cheaply.
"Destitute migrants lined river banks and ditches and their hungry children swelled the schools," writes one historian, "while a prosperous, insulated community shuddered at the spectre of homeless hordes." [7]

In December 1924 this environment greeted LeVoy, who arrived in
California in an open-sided Model T Ford with $3.45 in his pocket. An
even worse reception awaited him at the home of Emma's brother, Fred,
and his wife Alice in Yuba City. "It was the coolest reception ever in my

life," LeVoy told an interviewer. "He said I hadn't done right by his sister." This was likely a reflection not of LeVoy himself but of other Sorensons who ostracized her. [8]

LeVoy had no other place to go, so the Blasers put him up and fed him. A few days before Christmas LeVoy bought three small gifts and mailed them to Emma, Jim, and Eileen.

LeVoy still struggled with the written word, and had few skills besides farming. But he was ambitious, with a good head for business, a single-minded instinct for survival, and a powerful body he learned to use efficiently during years of back-breaking labor in Idaho. He carried "mud" for brick work, lugging heavy loads up planks and ladders to skilled bricklayers, the hardest work on the job for the lowest pay.

Fred got LeVoy a job with the Valley Concrete Pipe Company, digging trenches for concrete sewer pipes to replace septic tanks. Trenches were two feet wide and thirty inches deep, with fifteen or more men at a time working on a trench. They were paid by the foot. LeVoy usually was the first man to report for work each day; every cent earned he sent to Emma.

In January Emma, Jim, and Eileen joined LeVoy in Yuba City. He still worked at labor-intensive jobs at low wages. Fred saw LeVoy's work ethic and softened toward his brother-in-law. He talked of them going into business together doing brick and plaster work on homes. Two months later, however, Fred got "quick" pneumonia and died suddenly. They were working on three houses; LeVoy finished all three so Alice would be paid what was owed to her late husband. She remained hostile and did not offer LeVoy a penny of it.

The Sorensons rented a one-bedroom tarpaper shack two blocks from the railroad tracks for $10 a month. It lacked indoor plumbing for a toilet or tub and was in the poorest part of town, except for the teeming river bank near the garbage dump where hobos and fragments of families survived under tin and cardboard shelters.

Their street was one block long; they were at one end, next to an almond orchard. Open fields flanked the other end. The street had no sign but was popularly known as "Bandy Track Alley." Directly across the alley from their house was a brothel.

Most families on Bandy Track Alley had little income. The Sorensons did not often go hungry, however; Emma was a resourceful cook who could take the simplest ingredients and make something palatable—often stew or beans. Decades later Jim and Eileen learned that sometimes their parents missed meals in those lean years to put food on the table for them.

In 1926 Emma gave birth to a second son, Donald. Six months later a flu epidemic swept the region and Donald caught pneumonia. A doctor was summoned but hospitals were full and he arrived too late to help. In a poignant, hurried snapshot taken by Emma on December 18, an anxious LeVoy holds Donald up for the camera. The baby is wrapped in a shawl hand-knitted by Emma's mother; LeVoy is in overalls and a wool Carnaby cap. Donald died the next day.

Donald's death devastated the young couple. "My arms were so empty," wrote Emma. "This was the worst time in my life. I didn't know I could love a baby so much. We were so poor we didn't have the twenty-five dollars to bury our darling baby." Added LeVoy, "I just wanted to quit living."

LeVoy called his father Joseph and asked to borrow $25 to buy a small plot of land and a casket for burial. The money never came. LeVoy perhaps was not surprised. "My father was a big deterrent," he told an interviewer. "He told me a lot of times that I would starve to death if I went out on my own, and that I'd better stay with him." They appealed to one of LeVoy's brothers, but he too turned them down. Finally they contacted Emma's brother Bob Blaser, who sent $35.

While their parents struggled and contemplated a better future, Jim and Eileen explored Bandy Track Alley. They climbed the neighbors' huge black walnut tree and spent hours at a time smashing nuts with rocks and eating the meat inside. They joined other children in the fields at the other end of the alley, playing run sheep run and other games, and digging holes for bonfires where they roasted potatoes until they were charcoal-black outside and milk-white in the center.

The Sorensons were poor in the things of the world, but had a happy home life. LeVoy was still a man of few words and rarely said "I love you" to his children. But he showed it in many ways, having a light-hearted affection for them and patiently kneeling on their level to explain how the world worked and to answer the myriad questions of childhood.

LeVoy tended to internalize concerns, while Emma had a low flash point and vocalized hers. Money often was an issue. On occasion they clashed, and the children looked on in wonderment at the sparring. LeVoy's reputation as a dependable worker was growing in Yuba City, and gradually the family's finances improved.

Emma's domain was their home and street. The stark impacts of the Depression were all around them, and Emma sought ways to be of service. There was no lack of need. Directly across the street were the Harpers, whose lives changed forever on the day an ambulance crept somberly into the alley and took away their polio-stricken father, who never returned. Next door were the Neals, whose mother committed suicide.

Beyond the Neals were the Thomases, with twelve children. When their father lost his job, Emma quietly took a large pot of stew to their family. For Christmas in about 1932, recalled Eileen, Emma went downtown and explained to several merchants the plight of the Thomases and another neighbor family, the Bagleys, who had fifteen children.

"She came home with a turkey, groceries, and all the trimmings for a big dinner for the two families, and a gift for each child for Christmas. It was a lot better food and toys than we had. Mom's example of generosity and encouragement were certainly factors in Jim's generosity." [9]

"We lived close to the railroad tracks on the wrong side of town, and transients were always showing up at our door," recalled Eileen. "Mom fed anyone who came to the house. It was almost like there was an 'X' on the gate saying 'stop here,' because they kept coming. They were usually scruffy looking, but Mom was gracious to everyone.

"Time after time I would come home and there would be some tramp out on our back porch eating ham, eggs, and potatoes. We rarely had ham, but if we had ham, they had ham. They got whatever we got. My mother said, 'You never turn away a hungry person or you could go to hell.'"

One day LeVoy was walking down the street when he heard someone behind him shout "LeVoy!" It was an acquaintance named Winters from back in Idaho. They had been in a high school physical education class together. As they shook hands, the man explained, "We have only thirteen families in our Yuba City [LDS] branch, and we need your family too." At Winters' request, LeVoy went to see him that evening.

"I'm the Sunday School superintendent in the branch," he explained, "and I want you to be my first counselor."

"I can't do that, I'm too bashful," responded LeVoy.

Winters persisted. "Come on Sunday, and sit up front with me. If you don't like it, I won't bother you again."

They went to church the following Sunday. "We couldn't believe how nice they treated us," said LeVoy. It was all the encouragement they needed to return to the faith of their fathers. The Sorensons joined the small congregation of Mormons, and the Church anchored their family's life from then on.

LeVoy became Winters' counselor and, when Winters relocated, took his place as Sunday School superintendent. LeVoy served in that calling, in two congregations, for about twenty years. He then was a bishop—head of the congregation—or a bishop's counselor for another twenty years. Emma held many church positions.

From their first Sunday of renewed activity, LeVoy and Emma considered their most important church function was simply making every person feel wanted. At the end of services they would bolt from their seats and seek out anyone who was a stranger or otherwise looked as though they needed a friend. "My mother often said 'If anybody comes in this church and you haven't made them feel welcome, you have committed a sin,'" recalled Eileen.

Jim started first grade in 1927. Two months later his schooling was interrupted after a telegram arrived from his grandfather Joseph, saying his grandmother Annie Sorenson was dying of cancer in a Salt Lake City hospital. The message told LeVoy that, if he wanted to see his mother alive again, he needed to come to Utah. By then LeVoy was assistant manager of a Safeway in Roseville, thirty miles south of Yuba City. He drove to Safeway's regional office and got a two-week leave of absence.

Because of LeVoy's work schedule the family left Yuba City after midnight, driving a small Chevrolet with a luggage carrier on back. Utah was some 700 miles away. After driving an hour or so, LeVoy could no longer keep his eyes open. The road was so rough that Emma could not hold the steering wheel steady. They pulled off the road, took a seat out of the car, and LeVoy went to sleep on it for a couple of hours.

That was only the start of their nightmare.

It was October and still mild in California—but not in northern Nevada and Utah, where it snowed early that year. Emma and the children, Jimmy, 6, and Eileen, 5, had only light jackets, and Eileen already was sick.

LeVoy filled the car at every opportunity that night, and also carried two extra five-gallon containers of gas. They were getting low on gas when they reached Wendover, on the Nevada-Utah line. A man told them that fifty miles down the road they would reach an all-night gas station. When they got there it was 4 a.m., their gas tank was empty, and it was bitter cold. Worst of all, the gas station was closed.

Eileen had nearly died of pneumonia months earlier, and now was coughing violently. Emma was weeping for fear her children would freeze to death in the car. She climbed into the back seat and covered Eileen and Jim with her body and jacket. LeVoy had long since shed his sweater and put it on the children.

They spotted a small house behind the gas station and LeVoy banged on the door for help. After what seemed like an eternity, a thin, hawk-faced man opened the door a crack.

"Please," implored LeVoy, "we ran out of gas. My children are freezing. Please help us."

"We don't open 'til eight in the morning," came the answer.

Failing to move him with further persuasion, LeVoy also turned hard. "If you don't come out and sell us gas, I'll come in there and drag you out!"

The man disappeared, then reappeared brandishing a shotgun. "I said we don't open 'til eight."

LeVoy slumped forlornly back to the car and walked around trying to keep warm the rest of the night, as a fearful Emma huddled over their children and prayed. At eight o'clock the hawk-faced man appeared and sold them gas. They continued on to Salt Lake City and the hospital where LeVoy's mother lay. She had been in a coma.

Entering her room, LeVoy said "Mother." At the sound of his voice Annie "jumped on the bed like a cricket," he recalled. She pulled little Jimmy close to her and looked intently into his eyes. "You are one of my boys," she wept, wrapping arms around him. "Yes, you are my boy."

Annie then asked LeVoy to kneel at the side of her bed. "Son," she said, "I want you to promise me something."

"What is that, Mother?"

"Promise me that you won't go back to California as long as I'm alive."
LeVoy agreed, canceling his plan otherwise to return within days.

At Joseph's request, LeVoy stayed at the hospital with his mother as
Joseph, Emma and the children drove north to Shelley, Idaho, near Rexburg—the heart of Idaho potato country—where Joseph was renting a
farm with a cellar full of potatoes he needed to ship. Annie had cancer of
the spleen. Doctors operated while LeVoy was there, but the cancer had
spread throughout her spleen. They closed the incision and tried to make
her comfortable.

Annie died in mid-December. By then snow had shut all the passes
over the Sierra Nevada Mountains. The Sorensons remained in Shelley for
the time being.

Emma enrolled Jimmy in first grade. Disoriented, emotionally distraught, and without friends, he found learning extremely difficult. He was
slow of speech and could not learn his ABCs. Weeks later, at a school conference, his teacher gave Emma the devastating news. Jim was so far behind
the other children that he probably was "mentally retarded."

The words struck Emma like a thunderbolt. She refused to accept
them. Having been an exceptionally good student herself, especially with
language, Emma could not fathom how her own flesh and blood could be
otherwise. She resolved to teach Jim to read at home. The harder she tried,
the more frustrated both grew. "You are smart, you can do it," she encouraged. When positive reinforcement didn't work, occasionally Emma would
mete out punishment, including a slap across his rear-end.

"She'd make me sit still to read, and I couldn't do it," Jim recalled.
"When I was alone, rocking in my little red rocking chair, I could. The
rhythm of the rocking helped me with the rhythm of the words. 'The...lit-
tle...dog...went...to...the...neighbor's.' I could seem to read it with rhythm
to help me. But when Mother sat me down and punished me for not being
able to read, I formed an emotional barrier to reading."

Emma fought the idea that Jimmy might be retarded. But she began
to despair that he would ever be able to learn, and her despair fed his own
self-doubt.

Although neither of them could know it at the time, Jim in fact was in
good company. He suffered from what would one day be called the "mother

of learning disabilities": dyslexia. Jim's father LeVoy probably was also dyslexic, as were some of history's greatest geniuses.

Dyslexics by no means are mentally retarded. Quite the opposite.
They begin as early as three months old to develop an unusual capacity for
recognizing objects in their environment and to fill in fragmentary per-
ceptions. Language, which comes along later, in fact slows their learning;
they don't need it to put the puzzle of their world together. Verbal thought
requires an internal monologue of words, while they already think faster in
picture images. [10]

Dyslexics share basic abilities. They typically have a high degree of
curiosity, are highly intuitive and insightful, think and perceive using all the
senses, experience thought as reality, and have vivid imaginations. While
each case of dyslexia is different, the most common disabilities occur in
reading, writing, spelling or math, all of which depend on written symbols
to convey shared, precise meaning.

The dyslexic's problem comes when he starts school. There he often suffers not so much a learning disability as a teaching disability. Many
teachers simply don't know how or don't take the time to present information in a way that children with dyslexia or such related conditions as ADD
(attention deficit disorder) can learn it. Dyslexics may see letters upside
down or in reverse order. Unable to unscramble what his teacher and parents insist is on the page before him, the confused child begins to get upset
and may exhibit behavioral problems. Without sympathetic, effective in-
tervention, his self-esteem will continue to suffer, often to adulthood.

The hopeful news, writes one expert, is that many such people "become highly successful once they escape school. They think they have a
knack for doing something without even realizing that it stems from the
same causes as dyslexia: their ability to mentally combine imaginary and
real-world images in a creative or intuitive way. This talent can play havoc
with reading and writing, but it is highly useful for the arts, engineering,
sports, strategy, salesmanship, and invention." [11]

Eventually those precise traits would describe James L. Sorenson. But
as a dislocated youngster in Shelley, Idaho it was difficult to see beyond his
present awful predicament.

### CHAPTER THREE

# A GIVING HEART

Following the death of Annie in December, the Sorensons returned to their home in Yuba City. LeVoy began working longer hours than ever, delivering beverages and large blocks of ice to homes and businesses for their ice boxes, before the days of electric refrigeration. Soon he became route supervisor. He also moonlighted at other jobs and, a nickel at a time, the family's financial picture began to brighten.

But sometimes at night Jimmy and Eileen overheard urgent, whispered conversations between their parents over money, usually with Emma on the defensive. Eileen agreed with her mother that the family could afford better than they had. Jim defended his father's parsimony——and decades later would follow the same pattern with his own family.

Differences over finances led to a frightful Christmas a few years later. Emma worked outside the home for two weeks to buy gifts, but ran out of money by Christmas Eve before purchasing something for Jimmy. He wanted an erector set, so Emma swallowed hard and charged it at Taylors' Department Store for $5—a day's wage for LeVoy. When gifts were unwrapped around their small tree the next morning, Jim yelled with delight while his father fumed at the extravagance. Emma, holding a sack of eggs, flashed with anger at the destruction of their Christmas spirit.

"You're cute when you're mad...I like your spunk," teased LeVoy.

"I'm leaving you!" she screamed, throwing the bag of eggs at her husband.

With that, Emma was out the door. After awhile LeVoy went to look for her. They were gone several hours, Emma walking along the highway to Live Oak and Gridley. Finally LeVoy returned with Emma and there was an uneasy truce. "Mom reassured Jim and me over and over that she would never really leave us," said Eileen years later, "and she didn't, but we never forgot the fear we felt that day."

Despite differences, there was never any doubt that Emma and LeVoy were still deeply in love." Your mother was something," he would tell his children in later years. "I will never have a daughter more beautiful than Emma."

Jim greatly respected his father's physical prowess and quiet wisdom. Jim never heard his father swear, and he was sure LeVoy was stronger than anyone else he knew. He could carry more ice at a time than any other deliverer. And later, when working for a beverage distributor, his father could stack beer barrels three high—something Jim never saw any other man do.

One day Jim was walking to school past a job site where LeVoy was digging a trench. "The men were paid according to how many feet of trench they were able to dig in a day. My father seemed to be plodding along, much slower than a big, husky guy down the road. I pointed to the larger man and said, 'Dad, he's going to make a lot of money today.' Dad just grinned and said, 'Come back again after school.' Sure enough, when I showed up after school, the big man had worn himself out and was barely working. My father was working at the same pace as in the morning. And he dug a third more than the bigger guy."

Unlike Emma, who was emotional in praise or admonition, LeVoy was methodical and highly self-controlled. Jim disliked working around their house and small yard, and often was reprimanded by his father for laziness. "When my father felt I had stepped out of line, he'd say 'Let's go down and get a willow,'" recalled Jim. "We would whittle it to the right size together and try it. I always had plenty of padding, and the switching wasn't nearly as bad as the mental anguish."

His mother acknowledged Jim was not much good at house work or school work, but she loved his generous heart and invariably was encouraging. "Just try it, Jim, I know you can do it," was a constant refrain. Emma gave him courage to deal with his deficiencies, and the two shared a strong emotional bond.

At least once a year, after tucking the children into bed, Emma would recite again a poem from the old country which reminded her of Jimmy. It was called "Yakob Strauss":

I haf von funny little poy
Vat gomes ust to mine knee.
Der queerest chap, der greatest rogue
Vhatever you didt see.
Ee runs un jumps und smashes tings in all parts of de ouse,
But vot off dot, he ish mine son,
Mine little Yacob Strauss.

He gets der measles und der mumps
Ound everyting vots oud.
He spills mine glass of lager beer,
Puts snuff into mine kraut.
He fills mine pipe mit limberg cheese
Dat vas der greatest chauce,
I dakes dat from no odder poy
But dat young Yacob Strauss!

He asks me questions such as tese:
Vot paints mine nose so red?
Vot iss it cuts der schmood place out
From der air upon mine ead?

Vair doss der glim go from der lamp
Vhen err dere glim I douse?
Ow can I always dese dings esplain
Du dat young Yacob Strauss!

I somedimes tink I shall go vild
Mit such a crazy poy,

Und vish again I could have quiet
Un peaceful dimes enjoy.
But vhen he isch asleep in bed,
So quiet as der mouse,
I pray der Lord "Dakes anydings,
But *leaves* dat Yacob Strauss!"[1]

By the third grade, Jim's life was taking a more hopeful turn. He started doing arithmetic that year and, to everyone's surprise, was remarkably
good at it. Suddenly, the former class dunce was being approached by classmates for help with their arithmetic. "It hit me: If I'm so dumb, why are
the other kids coming to me for help? I really became excited about my
new-found ability. Even at that young age I knew something wonderful was
happening. I had stumbled across something that worked, and my reading
skills started to follow as well."

A main industry in Yuba City was its almond orchards, and at age sev-
en Jim earned money by gathering almonds that fell to the ground. By eight
he was delivering newspapers and hawking magazines across town, canvas
bag slung over his shoulder. He was a handsome little charmer, a street
urchin like Dickens' Oliver Twist, and his impish grin proved irresistible.

"I had my route where my favorite little old ladies would sit on their
porches and wait for me. I'd pet their dogs while I tried to sell them something. I never had a canned sales pitch. I'd just begin, 'I'm a kid from down
the street and I'd like to sell you any magazine you'd like.' If they didn't
want a magazine I'd try to sell them a newspaper. Or I'd just leave a magazine for them to look at. Then I'd check back in a few days and usually make
the sale."

Jim had few friends, leaving him more time to develop his entrepreneurial skills. Success was most likely on King's Row, the wealthy section
of town. Living there was a rich boy whose father was a lawyer. He owned
all the toys Jim could only dream of, but couldn't ride his bicycle or play
football well. So, in addition to selling magazines on King's Row, Jim began
charging the boy to teach him to do those things. Before long the boy had
repaid Jim's efforts by giving him his football, basketball, baseball, bat and
mitt.

Jim took the items home one at a time and hid them under his bed. When everything else was gone, the boy gave Jim his bike. He took it home too and put it in the woodshed. LeVoy discovered the bike there, and it led to the other new toys.

"Where'd these things come from, son?"

"I earned them."

"How?"

"Well, the Harris boy in the big house..."

"You mean Louis Harris' boy? Do you know he's the D.A.? We'd better take these things back, you just don't charge your little friends for playing with them."

With that, the treasures were all returned.

In 1930 the Sorenson household grew by one when LeVoy's youngest sibling, Gloria, 4, whose mother Annie died about three years earlier, moved in. Jim grew to regard her more as a little sister than an aunt, and became Gloria's generous benefactor when both were adults.

With no more space in the tiny house, the three children slept together, Jim's sister Eileen and Gloria on the outside, with Jim in the middle. By then, LeVoy's widowed father and remaining siblings had followed him from Idaho to California, also hoping for a fresh start. Gloria remembers Jim as "a thinker; he didn't seem physical to me."

But Jim inherited his father's strong body and it helped set the course of his life in Yuba City. Unable to compete in the classroom, Jim honed his physical skills and became a fine little athlete. He excelled in the neighborhood's frequent baseball games and occasional fistfights. Poor kids living on or near Bandy Track Alley were tempting targets for town bullies, and Jim organized and led street gangs to defend their turf and each other.

His real nemesis, however, was not a big, tough boy but a beautiful little girl, his sister Eileen. She was, bright, vivacious, and an outstanding student from the start. Jim would begin a sentence and often Eileen would finish it for him. "She could instantly get my adrenalin going," he recalled. "Her quickness overwhelmed me and I could never compete with her on equal terms at any moment. So I was forced to become a long-range planner to survive. Staying ahead of her meant thinking ahead of her."

Jim teased Eileen a lot. He'd hide her candy—after taking the key to the bathroom door to be able to get back at her in the likelihood she'd hit him and take refuge there.

Jim had a giving heart. While he said his little sister was "my number one problem," Eileen regarded him with great affection. Years later, as an adult, Eileen wrote a short essay about him and sent it to other family members. It was called "My Amazing Brother Jim!" She especially loved his generosity. He became expert at marbles, and often shared those he won with Eileen. When he got seventy-five cents working he'd often give Eileen a dime or a quarter for staying home and helping their mother.

Jim won a balloon-tire bicycle selling magazines, and gave his first bike to Eileen instead of selling it. He built her a beautifully detailed, two-story doll house, devoting many days to the project. The children also hulled almonds together for five cents a bucket.

With their earnings, the youngsters often walked several blocks to Forbes Avenue and caught the street car through downtown Yuba City and across the Feather River Bridge to Marysville. There they would enter the fairy land of five-and-dime stores, including Woolworth's and Kress's. "It was wondrous to me what could be purchased for twenty or twenty-five cents," said Eileen, "and I couldn't wait to decide among the treasures. Should I buy candy? A ring or other jewelry? Or how about jacks and a ball or a jump rope?"

More than once, Jim spent his money outside rather than inside the fairy land, helping Depression-era people. Eileen especially recalled one such occasion. Alighting from the street car, they dashed to the stores. Eileen bolted into Woolworth's, shaking with anticipation. Jim didn't follow. His eye caught a man sitting on the sidewalk against a store across the street—a one-legged man holding a tin cup filled with pencils.

Swallowing hard, he crossed the street and dug into his pocket, producing all his money—twenty-five cents—and dropped it into the cup. The man gave him five pencils and said "God bless you, son." Jim wasn't finished. He dashed into Woolworth's and found Eileen, who bought five-cents worth of candy and was about to spend her last dime on a ring.

"No, Eileen!" yelled Jim. "I got something better."

"What's that?"

"Come with me and I'll show you."

They left the store and crossed the street to the one-legged man. In an urgent whisper, Jim tried to persuade Eileen to buy two pencils. But, she whispered back, there were pencils at home, Jim had just bought five more, and, besides, pencils were free in California schools.

"Aw come on, Eileen, he's only got one leg. He needs the money." Jim halfway persuaded her and she bought a single pencil.[2]

As an adult, Eileen wrote that "Our life was hard at times during those early years, but we did have great times we shared. Compassionate service was highly honored and practiced in our home. So it was easy to honor Big Brother for helping the one-legged veteran sell his pencils; for helping the little old lady cross the street, and helping Mom and Dad with money from his cannery earnings, which he shared with them and me."

Jim instinctively knew the value of money. For him, success was bringing home a dollar to give his parents, and receiving a dime or quarter in return. LeVoy provided the necessities and Jim often surprised his family with "luxuries" such as a couch and an electric oscillating fan for their hot home.

Since the death of Donald back in 1926, Emma and LeVoy tried desperately to have another baby, but Emma suffered eight miscarriages in nine years. One problem, she believed, was the sweltering summers in Yuba City, where temperatures often rose above a hundred degrees in the shade. When the Sorensons were finally blessed with another child, Carol, in 1935, Emma credited the fan purchased by Jim with helping her carry the baby to term.

LeVoy improved things on Bandy Track Alley. He bought their tiny house and added two rooms, replaced tarpaper with wood siding and paint, and bought a porcelain tub to replace the round iron tub previously used for bathing, which hung from a nail outside the house when not in use. The new tub was filled with hot water from a faucet just a half-hour after lighting a gas burner. They started out using boxes and orange crates for chairs. One piece at a time, they graduated to modest furniture.

But LeVoy was methodical and conservative to the core, especially after the stock market crash of 1929 plunged the world into depression and cost millions of families their homes and life savings. "He would even have a piece of rope and a nail holding up his pants," recalled Eileen. Emma was impatient for more, and Jim started to side with her.

In 1934, LeVoy was offered an opportunity to pick up the Coca-Cola franchise for all of Sacramento, Sutter, and Placer counties for $2,300. The deal included two trucks, bottles, bottling machines and fixtures, malts and sugar. Although LeVoy had salted away that much in the bank, he didn't have additional money for operating capital. Jim begged him to take a chance and do it anyway, even offering to drop out of school for a while and help him get the business going. But LeVoy declined.

In March 1935 the Sorensons said goodbye to Yuba City and moved about thirty miles southeast to Lincoln, a more upscale community near Sacramento. The future looked promising.

### CHAPTER FOUR

# BOY INNOVATOR

Placer County spans California's Central Valley and climbs the Sierra Nevadas on the east. It is a picturesque region with rolling foothills, rich agricultural land, and forests of the High Sierra. The county was created in 1851, two years after the discovery of gold brought thousands of Forty-Niners pouring into California. Their placer-mining—sifting gold flecks from sand and gravel—gave the county its name.

In 1935 the Sorensons left Yuba City and moved to Placer County in search of a better life. Years earlier, before electric refrigeration was common, LeVoy for two years had a route delivering ice for a man named Malone. Malone fell out of favor with National Ice and Cold Storage, his supplier, when he couldn't pay his ice bill. The company also distributed beverages, including beer.

LeVoy went to National Ice managers and offered to continue delivering ice and barrels of beer, working directly for them. He delivered for another six or eight years. Each year managers said they were going to give him a raise, but never did. Finally he confronted them face-to-face and they offered to make him a regional manager, enabling the Sorensons to relocate and upgrade.

During the intervening years LeVoy steadily salted away money from his various jobs. He did not let Emma know of the secret savings, fearful that otherwise she would spend it all. LeVoy accumulated enough to buy a second house in addition to the one on Bandy Track Alley. In preparation for moving, he put both houses on the market and a woman offered to buy them at a substantially reduced price. When LeVoy refused and said he would take them off the market, the woman bought them at his asking price.

Now with a nest egg, the Sorensons relocated to Lincoln, Placer County, a community with about fifteen-hundred residents. Lincoln supported ranching and farming, especially rice, and was dotted with orchards. It was also home to Gladding McBean, a terra cotta clay manufacturing plant whose several hundred workers made sewer pipe, roofing tile, and decorative facing for the exteriors of public buildings in the West.

LeVoy managed National Ice and Cold Storage and joined the Rotary Club. He and Emma made a down payment on a modest home two blocks from Lincoln Union Elementary School. It had a big kitchen, two bedrooms, a screened-in porch, and a large yard with a garden and chickens. Jim's bedroom was the porch.

When rain blew through the screens and Jim talked of buying canvas to cover them, his father instead brought home a stack of old gunnysacks with "Idaho Potatoes" printed on them and tacked them up over the screens. Jim returned from school, mortified to see the sacks. His mother helped take them down and Jim bought water-repellant canvas to replace them.

"Emma was very, very close to Jim," recalled his Aunt, Gloria, who lived with them. "She told him he could do anything he made up his mind to do." His father, said Gloria, LeVoy's youngest sister, "was a little stern with Jim, telling him 'You do it and you do it now.' My brother was a country farm boy at heart. Emma wanted to rise above it. She was the decision-maker in the house. Emma had good judgment and Joseph would never question her." [1]

Jim's father improvised in other ways, often creating tools to fill particular needs. "He never pampered himself or me," Jim remembered. "In those days, men and boys were expected to be tough. And Dad proved himself by showing, not by telling. He taught me each new task by example and he taught it only once."

While the future looked promising for the Sorensons, the nation was still mired deep in the Depression. The economic tailspin began in October 1929, following an orgy of speculation that drew citizens of almost every economic level into a frenzied rush to risk life savings in the stock market in pursuit of a "fast buck." Banks everywhere made unwise loans, feeding the speculative fever.

Capitalizing on the euphoria sweeping the land, Republican presidential candidate Herbert Hoover predicted in the 1928 campaign, "We shall soon with the help of God be in sight of the day when poverty will be banished from this nation." Hoover was elected and, less than a year later, the bottom fell out of the economy, beginning with the stock market crash, followed by a plunge in prices, production, employment, and foreign trade.[2]

By 1932 about 12 million people—a quarter of the normal U.S. labor force—were out of work. Many of those with rural ties fled to the countryside to help work family farms and wait out the economic storm. In the cities, others were nourished at soup kitchens and in bread lines. Shanty towns, called "Hoovervilles," sprouted from coast to coast. The Depression hit bottom that year and things slowly started to improve. The Sorenson family was largely cushioned from the cruelties of the Depression by LeVoy's careful planning.

But there was great unease elsewhere. The ailing economy spurred the ambitions of demagogues. In Louisiana, Huey P. "Kingfish" Long was elected governor and, promising to make "every man a king," instead made himself king of Louisiana, employing bribery, violence and blackmail to destroy or control state institutions. He moved on to the U.S. Senate and his wider national ambition was ended only by an assassin's bullet in September 1935.

Meanwhile tyrants were preparing to march abroad, including warlords in Japan, Benito Mussolini in Italy, and especially Adolph Hitler, who ominously became president of Germany in August 1934 upon the death of Paul von Hindenburg.

Americans were also mesmerized by personal tragedies. In 1932 the infant son of Charles and Anne Morrow Lindbergh was kidnapped from the family home in New Jersey and murdered. Two years later police arrested a suspect, Bruno Richard Hauptmann, who was found guilty of the heinous crime and sentenced to death in 1935. Also that year, America's favorite over-the-fence philosopher, Will Rogers, was killed, along with famed pilot Wiley Post, in a plane crash in Alaska.

Franklin D. Roosevelt was elected President in 1932 on the promise of doing what his Republican predecessor refused to do: try some new and bold things to lift America out of the Depression. Despite President Hoover's warning that a Democratic victory would mean that "The grass will grow in the streets of a hundred cities," voters took a chance on Roosevelt and helped usher in a pivotal era in the nation's history. Roosevelt, in his inaugural address, insisted that "the only thing we have to fear is fear itself." He also said:

> ...a host of unemployed citizens face the grim problem of existence and an equally great number toil with little return. Only a foolish optimist can deny the dark realities of the moment...The people of the United States...in their need...have registered a mandate that they want direct, vigorous leadership. They have asked for discipline and direction under leadership. They have made me the present instrument of their wishes. In the spirit of the gift I take it....May God guide me in the days to come.

Roosevelt's clarion call thrilled Emma, who supported his array of New Deal initiatives aimed at giving Americans a helping hand and jump-starting the economy. Emma made sure her family followed and debated it all. She devoured books, magazines and newspapers and believed passionately in First Amendment guarantees of free speech and free press. "Mom had her strong views and encouraged us to have ours, and to read both liberal and conservative opinions," said a daughter. "She taught us how to read a newspaper, and the importance of not overlooking the editorial page."

Emma was also devoted to women's causes. "I recall many discussions with her about theology and history," said Jim. "His-story is how Mother used to refer to both because there were so few references to women."

The Sorensons grew produce and distributed it free to less-fortunate neighbors or members of their congregation. "Anyone in need was welcome at our house," recalled a daughter. "I remember one time when it was raining cats and dogs and there were some people huddled on a street corner near our house. Someone said 'Let's take them home to Mom.' That's what we did, knowing she'd dry them off and take care of them."

On another occasion Emma intervened in problems of a family in their neighborhood. Following the father's alleged immoral behavior, the parents divorced and he moved to Colfax, about twenty-five miles distant. One day when the mother Thelma was away, he returned to the family home and took their eight-year-old daughter Mary away to live with him.

"Thelma was distraught and afraid of her husband," Emma remembered. "I felt so sorry for her." Emma drove the two women to Colfax and to Mary's school. "We were worried that we would be caught taking Mary and charged with kidnapping, arrested, or sent to jail," said Emma. She coached Thelma on what to tell the principal, they retrieved Mary, and returned to Yuba City. The father did not take Mary again.[3]

Jim's impact was felt in Lincoln within weeks of moving there in the spring of 1935. Lincoln Elementary was playing Auburn in baseball and had not beaten its arch rival in years. It was the ninth inning, players were on base, and the score was tied when Coach Carl Bayless—also Lincoln's principal—sent 13-year-old Jim to the plate. Eileen remembers the moment: "Jim stepped up to bat and hit the ball so far that we all just stood there in shock. At first, he watched it too and forgot to move until we all started screaming, 'Run, Jim, run!' Then he took off. It was a home run and won the game."

Jim continued to excel in athletics. "We were all excited when he hit town," said William "Willie" Gamboa, a fellow student and star athlete at Lincoln Union High. "We heard he was good at basketball. Jim had a strong body—good legs and shoulders and good coordination. He was a scrappy player."[4]

Lincoln Union had about 200 students in four grades. Jim was one of few Mormons. Four years ahead of him was another Mormon destined to make history: Glen W. Edwards, who went on to U.C. Berkeley and then entered the Army Air Corps. Edwards flew fifty-nine missions in World War II, was heavily decorated, and broke trans-continental speed records. Later he was a test pilot at Muroc Air Base in the Mojave Desert. When he was killed there testing the YB-49 "Flying Wing," it was renamed Edwards Air Force Base.

Basketball was big. The Harlem Globetrotters came annually. Local rivalries were fierce and people from across the valley flocked to games, seeking bragging rights for another year. The Lincoln Zebras—a name that inspired a lot of clever kidding—played their games in a classic old wooden gymnasium which also had climbing ropes, rings, and other exercise equipment.

Ken Bayless, son of the elementary school principal, was a year behind Jim. "I met him playing basketball," said Bayless. "Lincoln Union had an A team and a B team and we both turned out for practice. I could tell from the start he was special. Jim was a good shooter, fast, and aggressive." They were both about five-feet-ten and Jim ended up starting ahead of Bayless in the same position. But Jim tired easily—a trait apparently inherited from his mother—and inevitably the coach would turn to Bayless and yell, "Jim's ass is dragging, get in there for him."

Jim's nickname on the court was "Silver Streak." When he raced the length of the floor with the ball, the crowd—including Eileen, Lincoln's prettiest cheerleader—would scream "Hi Ho Silver Streak!" The star of the team was Gamboa, a Mexican American who was shorter than Jim and Ken but scored most of Lincoln's points and went on to play college ball at San Jose.

Their coach was Richard A. Lee, also the school's principal, who ran a tight ship in classrooms and corridors as well as in athletic competition. A slender, gray-haired man of about 50 who wore three-piece suits, Lee had wrestled for U.C. Berkeley. "Coach Lee was the single most competitive individual I've ever known," said Bayless. "He was not a good loser. If we lost a game he wouldn't walk across the floor to shake hands with the other coach; he'd stomp off the floor. But he really understood the game of basketball and was a wonderful coach."

Coach Lee perhaps had a lasting impact on Jim, who as an adult likewise was known as a fierce competitor and poor loser. Jim had a lot of opportunity to watch his coach stomp off the floor. During his junior year the Zebras won just one regularly scheduled game, and during his senior year they won three and lost four.

Winning was not all Coach Lee expected. In spite of his own behavior his teams played with class. Lincoln usually lost to Auburn, a much-bigger school, but routinely expected to beat Elk Grove, a small school south of Sacramento. In Jim's senior year, his Zebras were trouncing Elk Grove by the end of the first quarter and the starting five—including Jim and Ken Bayless—began celebrating prematurely.

Disgusted, Lee pulled all of his starters and left them on the bench as Elk Grove clawed its way back into the game. Finally, mid-way through the fourth quarter, Lee put Jim, Ken and the rest of his best players back in. But it was too late; they had cooled off, and, as the school's yearbook ruefully reported, "Elk Grove...came from behind to win a 19-18 victory over the Zebras." [5]

Jim and Ken were kindred spirits and would be best friends for life. Both tended to be loners. School and work dominated their teenage years but they found time for hunting, Ken with a ten-gauge double-barrel shotgun and Jim with a sixteen-gauge. Soil in the area was mostly clay, which held water for growing rice. It also provided cover that was ideal for pheasants, a prime quarry for the two young hunters, along with doves and jack rabbits.

On one memorable trip, a group of friends hiked about fifteen miles to Bear River, planning to "live off the land." At dusk, someone was to catch fish and someone else shoot a deer to be roasted over the campfire that night. However, they camped in a manzanita thicket and dark closed in faster than they had reckoned. "To tell the truth, we got a little scared," said Ken. Instead of stalking game they stayed by the campfire and went hungry, hiking back to Lincoln the next morning.

By standard yardsticks, Jim was a poor to mediocre student during his first two years of high school. His report cards were filled with Cs and Ds. He was also lazy at home.

Jim still resisted working around the house and, as in basketball, lacked stamina. His Aunt Gloria recalled Jim's feeble attempts to be of help. "One time Joseph [LeVoy] and I were in the house and Jim was outside," she recalled. "Joseph started laughing and I went to the window to see what was up. There was Jim mowing the lawn. He would cut a single strip with the mower, then sit down and rest. A few minutes later he'd get up and cut one more strip, sit down and rest some more." [6]

When Jim was motivated, however, he was almost unstoppable. Like many others, he looked to the cling peach industry for work. Growers of cling peaches—once the state's most important product—were captive to canneries, which set the price they paid from year to year. A peach orchard normally would bear for about twenty years. Once planted, it didn't start producing for several years and the grower needed four or five seasons of production just to pay off development costs.

During the roaring twenties, with postwar prices high, California cling growers went on a planting binge, adding 6,000 acres in 1921, 10,000 acres in 1922, 12,000 acres in 1923 and 7,000 acres in 1924. After the stock market crash five years later, growers as well as canners lost money and markets were in disarray. [7]

Early in President Roosevelt's first term he addressed farm problems. The Agricultural Adjustment Act (AAA) was an early piece of New Deal legislation, and all food processing came under its rules. Voluntary crop controls gave way to mandatory controls under federal police powers in 1933 and 1934. The 1933 California Cling Marketing Agreement was the first of its kind in the U.S. to be formally approved under the AAA. It regulated maximum and minimum selling prices, which individual canners had to accept to get a license to can. The peach industry did not fully recover until the demands of World War II.

Meanwhile, the peach industry slump was accompanied by worker unrest as both growers and canners sought an edge, sometimes by cutting corners. With so many people clamoring for jobs, owners could pay a tiny wage and provide few amenities.

The nation in the main turned a deaf ear to California farm workers so long as they had brown or yellow skins. It was not until the plight of white migrants into California became a national sensation through Steinbeck's revealing novel *The Grapes of Wrath* and Carey McWilliams's *Factories in the Field,* both published in 1939, that Washington was forced to pay attention.

The Senate Committee on Education and Labor, chaired by crusading Sen. Robert LaFollette, a Wisconsin Democrat, held extensive public hearings at the end of 1939, reporting that "the economic and social plight of California's agricultural labor is miserable beyond belief."

Despite that conclusion, committee member Sen. Elbert Thomas, a Utah Democrat, said the agribusiness complex in California was "impregnable," that its treatment of migratory workers was "traditional in the West" and "so much an ingrained habit that nothing this committee could say would even scratch that empire." Thomas was prophetic and not much changed. [8]

Despite difficult conditions for many agricultural workers, during the Depression jobs were scarce and almost any paying work was highly prized. For hundreds of laborers in Placer County, the most obvious source of employment was the Lincoln Packing Company, located on the Auburn Ravine east of town. It was owned by Harry Gordon and run by his son Pat, and was considered a first-class operation.

The Lincoln cannery included several acres of open buildings. Peaches would arrive by boxcar or truck and be unloaded into reservoirs of water to assure a soft landing with minimal bruising. From there, over a maze of conveyor belts, they were sent through the final processes taking them from tree to sealed container.

The cannery produced canned peaches, fruit cocktail including peaches, and peach jam. Work was seasonal. Tree-ripened peaches usually started arriving at the cannery early in July. They kept coming until early in September. During that peak time, there were about 500 employees, splitting two shifts—7:30 a.m. to 3:30 p.m., and 3:30 until midnight.

At the start of the season in the summer of 1935, when Jim was fourteen, he went to the Lincoln Packing house to witness the excitement of opening day. Hundreds of men approached the gates looking for work but only about one in ten was hired. "I wanted a job too but was too young to get in line," he recalled. Then, while playing with friends, he got an idea.

"I saw that I could get into the cannery by slipping beneath a railroad boxcar that was parked in an opening of the fence. From there, it was a short trip up the tracks to the loading dock, then into the cannery itself. I didn't have much of a plan, but I knew my goal."

Jim slipped into the cannery and saw crews being organized for work. He soon saw where he might fit into the system when he heard a supervisor mention a "pie boy." These bottom-rung workers would pick up peaches that fell from conveyor belts, wash them off, and put them onto another belt to be made into pie filling. "I found an empty pan and acted as if I be-longed there, picking up fruit from the floor." But a foreman spotted Jim and yelled, "What do you think you're doing here? Get back over the fence where you belong. You need to grow up before you start working here!"

"Okay, I understand," Jim answered. "I'll just help you for today. You don't even have to pay me." After an hour or so of watching Jim work, the foreman relented. "Well, kid, maybe you can come in. But you have to be eighteen," he said with a wink.

He gave Jim a card to fill out and invited him to return the next day— to the front gate. Jim had landed his first adult job and worked at the can-nery for the next four years, all the time remaining eighteen years old on his identification card. He returned home that first evening to find that no one else in his household, including some adult uncles, found work that day.

Cannery labor was back-breaking and dangerous; many laborers last-ed only a day or two. A federal government study of canneries in Washing-ton State outlined some of the dangers.

During interviews with women cannery workers and local physicians, says the study, "repeated reference was made to 'fruit poison' and 'fish poison' of various sorts. A burning rash and the loss of fingernails were described as quite common occurrence. Without any known abrasion of the skin tissues, a low-grade infection of the outer skin sets in, resulting frequently in the loss of the fingernail...The workers expect this poisoning and speak of it as if it were a necessary evil..." [9]

While many injuries went unreported, the study documented 168 in-juries in the state in 1923, including 49 wounds that became infected, 42 cases of fruit or fish poison or infection, and three amputations.

The most dangerous job of all in a peach cannery was that of "lye-man." Peaches were first split and pitted, then peeled one of three ways: by hand, by slipping the skins, or by lye, a caustic alkaline solution. Nearly all peaches commercially canned in California were done by lye, which, at the Lincoln cannery, arrived in 55-gallon drums. It was mixed with water, one-half to one pound of concentrated lye per gallon, and heated to a boil in ten-by-twenty-foot vats to produce steam. The vats stretched from pits below ground to about head-high above. All peaches passed through the machine on a conveyor belt.

The lyeman's job was to monitor the process, keeping the right amount of lye, steam and heat flowing. Too little lye and the peaches came out fuzzy; too much and they turned to mush. The job took skill and courage. One man lost an eye when the lye boiled over on his face. Jim knew two others who suffered disfiguring burns on their faces and bodies. Nonetheless, attracted by the great difference in pay—$1 to $1.50 per hour for a lyeman compared to 25 to 35 cents for most other workers—Jim eventually worked his way up to become a lyeman.

"The cannery work tested my ingenuity for the first time," he said. "Instead of simply selling something, I was given assignments that allowed me to see how things work. I examined the way other lyemen worked, at eye level to the lye vats. From that angle it was difficult to judge the air pressure and the level of lye bubbling in the tanks. Then I asked myself the question that I would ask over and over again in the future: 'Isn't there a better way? There's *got* to be a better way!'"

Jim invented a better way. He built a little catwalk and eagle's nest in the rafters, high above the lye vats, from where he could see where the steam was going and watch the level of pressure within the vats before moving in close to where he could be hurt. It was novel, safe, and practical. The ingenious nest began a pattern that would be responsible for much of Jim's future success: His risks were hedged by finding a safer, better way to accomplish a goal. The "better way" emerged following careful observation, and it was kept remarkably simple.

Gloria remembered that, with Jim's first cannery paycheck, he bought the family a large floor-model radio. "It was our entertainment. We'd all gather around it and listen to our favorite shows—"Amos 'n Andy," " Fibber McGee and Molly," "Dick Tracy," "The Shadow." Occasionally Gloria would pack a large lunch and surprise Jim at the cannery with it. Jim would greet Gloria with an endearment he'd teased her with since childhood: "There she is, my little honey bunch—of stink weeds."

### CHAPTER FIVE

# BEVERLEY

## Born in Idyllic Family

The rice fields and orchards of Placer County were far removed from the relatively prosperous east-side neighborhoods of Salt Lake City, Utah. There, at 2020 Lake Street, stood an imposing brick home occupied by Frank and Bessie Taylor and their six children. The second-youngest child, Beverley, would change Jim's life.

The Taylor paternal lineage was as close as one could come to royalty in the state settled by Mormon pioneers. Joseph Smith, first prophet and president of The Church of Jesus Christ of Latter-day Saints, was martyred in Illinois in 1844. He was succeeded by Brigham Young, who sought a refuge from severe persecution and led the saints into Salt Lake Valley three years later. John Taylor, in turn, would succeed Young three decades later.

President Young directed the colonizing of hundreds of communities in the interior mountain region, and sent missionaries throughout North America and across the seas. A leading Church figure, Parley P. Pratt, proselytized in Canada. In Toronto he met the James and Agnes Taylor family, who emigrated from England in 1830.

A son, John, had been uncommonly spiritually sensitive throughout his life. As a small boy he saw "in vision, an angel in the heavens, holding a trumpet to his mouth, sounding a message to the nations." He did not understand its meaning.[1]

Later, as a teenager, "Often when alone, and sometimes in company, I heard sweet, soft, melodious music, as if performed by angelic or supernatural beings."

"Many a time," as a youngster, he explained, "I have gone into the fields and concealing myself behind some bush, would bow before the Lord and call upon Him to guide and direct me. ..He heard my prayer...My spirit was drawn out after God..."[2]

John's countenance was pleasant. His lips curled up at the corners, giving him the appearance of a perpetual smile. He was about six feet tall, with piercing gray eyes, a dark complexion, and a full head of hair that turned prematurely gray and later snow-white.

He was a cooper's apprentice, learning to make and repair barrels. At the age of sixteen he left the Church of England and became a Methodist, convinced the latter more closely followed the Bible. After emigrating to Canada, he became a lay Methodist preacher in Toronto. There, at twenty-seven, he and his first wife, Leonora Cannon, met Elder Pratt. After intensely studying the restored gospel for several weeks, they were baptized in 1836.

Rarely did someone join the Church more uniquely prepared to play a crucial role in its future. John read widely, spoke and debated eloquently, sang beautifully, and had unwavering integrity and courage. He was called to preside over the branches of the Church in upper Canada and, in 1837, met Joseph Smith for the first time in Kirtland, Ohio. The following year he was ordained one of the Church's Twelve Apostles. Years later Taylor wrote:

> I have traveled with [Joseph Smith]. I have been with him in private and in public; I have...listened hundreds of times to his public teachings and his advice to his friends and associates of a more private nature. I have been at his house and seen his deportment with his family...I testify before God, angels, and men, that he was a good, honorable virtuous man... that his private and public character was unimpeachable, that he lived and died as a man of God and a gentleman.[3]

John Taylor's faith in Joseph Smith faced the ultimate test in June 1844. The Prophet was harassed and arrested on various charges throughout his life, but apparently never convicted of wrong-doing. When ordered to surrender to law officers in Carthage, Illinois that summer, Joseph had a strong premonition that his mortal life was coming to an end.

On June 24 Joseph and his brother Hyrum left by horseback from Nauvoo, the city of the saints on the Mississippi, to Carthage. Willard Richards and John Taylor, the only members of the Twelve then in the vicinity, voluntarily went with them. The four were incarcerated in the Carthage Jail, ostensibly to await a judicial hearing.[4]

Three days later, in the afternoon, an uncommon gloom enveloped the four as they sat on the second floor of the jail. One of the men asked John Taylor to sing a song recently introduced in Nauvoo, which Joseph loved: "A Poor Wayfaring Man of Grief." John did so, in a rich tenor voice. A while later Hyrum asked him to sing it again.

"I replied, 'Brother Hyrum, I do not feel like singing.'"

"Oh, never mind; commence singing, and you will get the spirit of it," Hyrum answered. John did so.

"Soon afterwards," he wrote, "I was sitting at one of the front windows of the jail, when I saw a number of men, with painted faces, coming around the corner of the jail, and aiming towards the stairs."

Hyrum and Willard Richards immediately jumped to the door, pressing against it with their shoulders as pistols and rifles were thrust forward from the other side. A ball sliced through the door panel and into Hyrum's face, another hit him in the back, and he fell dead.

John parried the gun barrels thrust through the door with a large hickory stick. When that no longer worked, he ran to the window for possible escape. A ball from the door hit him in the thigh and he fell to the floor. While attempting to crawl under a bed, he was shot three more times.

Joseph ran to a window and jumped onto the ledge. Instantly he was shot twice in the back from the door and once in the chest from below. He fell to the ground, dead. Hearing that Joseph was outside on the ground, the mobbers rushed downstairs. That gave Richards, who miraculously was not injured, enough time to drag John into another cell and cover him with a dirty mattress. Someone apparently shouted that "the Mormons are coming!" and the mob quickly ran off.

John Taylor later wrote: "Joseph Smith, the Prophet and Seer of the Lord, has done more, save Jesus only, for the salvation of men in this world, than any other man that ever lived in it...He lived great, and he died great, in the eyes of God and his people..."[5]

During the following years and decades, Taylor was associated with nearly every major event in Church history, meanwhile serving four missions. He was a powerful writer, editing several Nauvoo periodicals and *The Mormon*, a New York-based weekly paper. His efforts earned him the titles "Defender of the Faith" and "Champion of Truth."

"...he has one of the strongest intellects of any man that can be found," said Brigham Young. "...He is one of the strongest editors that ever wrote." [6]

As mobs continued to persecute the saints, Taylor and his family left Nauvoo in the first general exodus of February 1846—bound for the Rocky Mountains, which Joseph Smith saw in vision as a place of refuge for the Church.

In August 1877, after leading the Church and directing the colonizing of the West for three decades, Brigham Young died. As the longest-serving member of the Twelve Apostles, leadership of the church fell to Taylor. Three years later, in October 1880, the First Presidency was reorganized, with Taylor as president of the Church and George Q. Cannon and Joseph F. Smith as counselors.

The Mormons attracted enemies from the beginning, often for narrow reasons that now appear legally and morally untenable. One issue, however, that of polygamy, was widely condemned by western culture at that time as well as today.

The "doctrine of plurality of wives" was revealed to Joseph Smith, who said "I hold the keys of the power in the last days;...and I have constantly said no man shall have but one wife at a time, unless the Lord directs otherwise." [7]

Church leaders point to ancient Israel, including Abraham, Isaac, and Jacob, as an example of when God has sanctioned polygamy. The LDS Church otherwise has made relatively little effort to publicly explain polygamy, simply answering that plural marriage was ordained by revelation. Intriguingly, while society as a whole has long since burst the bands of sexual morality, the Church continues to stand firm in its opposition to sexual relations outside the marriage of one man to one woman.

In 1843, ten years after John Taylor wed his first wife, he married a second. Five additional marriages followed, one each in 1844 and 1846, two in 1847, and, finally, a seventh wife, Margaret Young, in 1856. The wives bore thirty-four children—twenty-two boys and twelve girls. An additional daughter was adopted, giving the family thirty-five children.

Responding to public clamor, the federal government in 1862 passed an anti-polygamy law. Two decades later, in 1882, Congress passed a stronger law, the Edmunds Anti-Polygamy Act, sponsored by Senator George Edmunds of Vermont. Its restrictions were aimed at individuals practicing polygamy as well as those simply voicing support for the practice. More than 1,300 men were imprisoned or fined under the act; those fined included two future presidents of the Church: Heber J. Grant and Joseph F. Smith.

Five years later Congress strengthened the law with the Edmunds-Tucker Act, sponsored in the House by Rep. Randolph Tucker of Virginia. Edmunds-Tucker struck at the heart of the Church. It ordered the Church and its emigration fund dissolved, with assets to be used for public schools. Prospective voters, jurors, and public officials were forced to take an anti-polygamy oath, and marriages required civil licenses. It also disenfranchised women in Utah Territory, who in 1870 had won the right to vote in territorial elections.

Polygamy had many ramifications—for the Church, for Utah, and for those practicing it. B.H. Roberts was a towering figure and chronicler of the Church, a member of the First Council of the Seventy. In 1898 the Utah legislature elected him as a Democrat to Congress. The House of Representatives refused to seat Roberts, however, as he acknowledged he had three wives.

In January 1903 the Utah legislature elected Reed Smoot, a member of the Quorum of the Twelve Apostles, to the Senate. He arrived in Washington the following month and was allowed to take his seat under protest by colleagues. Smoot was also accused of polygamy, but in fact was not a polygamist. Four years of hearings followed, in which senators investigated almost every facet of the Church, producing a 3,500-page record. In 1907 most senators voted to oust Smoot. The vote fell short of the necessary two-thirds, however, and Smoot retained his seat.

Among his supporters was Senator Boies Penrose of Pennsylvania. During floor debate, Penrose, reportedly glaring at one or more Senate colleagues with reputations for philandering, said, "As for me, I would rather have seated beside me in this chamber a polygamist who doesn't polyg than a monogamist who doesn't monog." Smoot went on to serve thirty years in the Senate, becoming one of its most powerful and respected figures.

John Taylor, under the difficult circumstances, seemed to have a pleasant relationship with his children, and was known for being good-humored.

Teen-aged Matthias Cowley, a friend to the family, recalled that when he visited their home, "we would sometimes find him playing checkers with one of his boys..." [8]

Members of the Church in Salt Lake met in the tabernacle on Sunday afternoons. "All of us were expected to be there," recalled a Taylor son, "and at a later time be able to report as to who gave the sermon, what it was about, who gave the prayers, and what hymns were sung." One Sunday he and some pals skipped the meeting, asking other friends to let them know those details. He continued:

> Then came the [family] council and sure enough Father asked me about the sermon, and who gave it...my friend said he couldn't remember very well, [so] I repeated his words, "Oh it was some old windbag, and I can't remember his name, but it was surely uninteresting." With a twinkle in his eye, Father said, "That old windbag was your father," and continued with the council meeting. [9]

Missionary assignments kept Taylor from his family for nine of the eighteen years following his baptism in 1836. A warm correspondence developed between him and his oldest two children, George and Mary Ann, to whom he sent notes enclosed with letters to their mother.

President Taylor's last years were spent largely away from his wives and children and Church headquarters, as he eluded the law and guided his family and church by communications from underground.

By letter he approved of a daughter's marriage to a man he had not been able to meet. A son looking for a job wrote for advice. Letters to his grown children sought to know the health and well-being of their mothers. [10]

In 1886 he wrote his large posterity upon learning they gathered to honor him on his seventy-eighth birthday on November 1.

He expressed concern over the illness of two wives, Jane and Sophia, "and my heart has gone out in prayer for them, accompanied by my brethren, that they may be healed..." He was pleased, he wrote, "to be informed that the health of the family is generally good, and that the disposition and feeling of both wives and children is to fear God, to work righteousness, and to yield obedience to His laws."

President Taylor assured them that "we now are, and always have been, during our exile, supplied with everything that is necessary to our comfort and convenience. Go where we will, we have good accommodations, plenty of food and the necessities of life...If there is anything that any of you require and you will inform me, I shall be happy to supply it, if within my power.

"Some of you have written that you 'would like to have a peep at me.' I heartily reciprocate that feeling, and would like to have a 'peep' at you on this occasion; but in my bodily absence my spirit and peace shall be with you."[11]

John Taylor's final public appearance was in February 1885, when he preached his last sermon in the Tabernacle in Salt Lake City. He went into hiding that night and apparently was never seen again in life except by a few trusted friends. He died on July 25, 1887 in Kaysville, Utah. His body and his family at last were reunited during the funeral in the packed Tabernacle.

Taylor was succeeded as Church president by Lorenzo Snow who, in 1890, issued the "Manifesto" to end plural marriage. "The Lord showed me by vision and revelation exactly what would take place if we did not stop this practice," said Snow. He emphasized that, even given all the possible consequences to the Church and its members, he would not have issued the Manifesto "had not the God of heaven commanded me to do what I did." Among other impacts, Utah was admitted into the Union in 1896. [12]

Among John Taylor's thirty-five children, Frank Young Taylor stood out. His mother, Margaret Young Taylor, was President Taylor's seventh and last wife. They had nine children together, all carrying their mother's surname as their middle name. Frank was born in 1861, the second-oldest sibling.

For twenty-eight years Frank was president of Salt Lake City's Granite Stake [a unit of eight to twelve "wards" or congregations], one of the largest if not the largest stake in the LDS Church. His farsighted tenure led to an impressive list of community and church improvements.

"...under his innovative leadership," wrote one historian, "committees of high councilors and other stake members were assessing local needs and recommending action; Granite pioneered the seminary program [daily religious instruction] for high school students, stake missionary work, and systematic stake supervision of temple work." [13]

Frank Taylor is best remembered for inaugurating the Church's Family Home Evening program, which has been a staple in many members' homes for most of the century since then.

Worried about family closeness, "In 1909 he took his concerns about his stake's families to the Lord and felt inspired to set aside one night a week for 'home worship,' a night free from church meetings." President Taylor assigned one of the twelve members of the stake high counsel to head a committee that prepared a resource booklet for families. It suggested prayer, singing, gospel instruction, discussion of family issues, an activity, and refreshments. That was still the suggested format a century later.

"The program was launched that same year at the largest meeting held in the Granite Stake Tabernacle to date, 2,164 enthusiastic people, most of them parents...The president of the Church himself, Joseph F. Smith, addressed the people and heartily endorsed the program: 'The inspiration that has come to President Taylor...is of the greatest importance to the Latter-day Saints.'"

For the remaining nineteen years of his presidency, Frank Y. Taylor continued to stress the importance of home evening, first held in members' homes on Tuesday evenings, later switched to Monday evenings. On the designated evening, no other church meetings are to be held.

Family Home Evening was formally adopted church-wide in 1915. The program lapsed for a time, then was revived by the Primary, the Church's program for children, and the priesthood correlation program of the 1960s.

"Now, of course," wrote a church historian, "it has become a key to the strength of Latter-day Saint families throughout the world, in a very real sense, a legacy of the Taylor family to the rest of the Church."[14]

Frank Y. Taylor was assistant architect for the Manti Temple. He also worked as a mining engineer, railroad surveyor, realtor, and financier. In his later years he directed LDS real estate operations. He had two wives, Elizabeth Campbell Taylor and Alice Neff Taylor, and lived at Seventh East and Twenty-first South in Salt Lake City. One of the sons born to Elizabeth was Frank Campbell Taylor, in 1885. He would grow to be a genial, soft-spoken gentleman.

In 1889 Bessie Eleanor Taylor was born in Salt Lake City to George Hamilton Taylor and Lois Louisa Foote. They were not closely related to the John Taylor family. George was the only member of his New Jersey family to join the church. He crossed the plains as a sturdy pioneer, and became a deeply devoted husband and father and a pillar in the community. In Salt Lake, George owned a lumber yard and was known as an innovative woodworker. Among other church callings, he served a mission to England and was a bishop.

George, who sported a walrus mustache and sometimes round spectacles, took two additional wives and served time in the territorial penitentiary for what he termed "conscience sake," plural marriage. [15]

Frank Campbell Taylor and Bessie Eleanor Taylor were married on September 22, 1911. They had six children, sons Joe and Robert and daughters Virginia, Helen, June, and Beverley. Beverley was the next-to-youngest child, born April 13, 1924. The family caboose was Robert (Bob) C. Taylor, born three years and five days after Beverley. Well removed in age from other siblings, Beverley and Bob became close lifelong friends. [16]

Church president John Taylor's intelligence and strength of character are reflected in his huge posterity, including his son Frank Y. Taylor, Beverley's grandfather. One of Frank Y.'s sons was Frank Campbell Taylor, her father. On the birthday of the younger Frank in 1943, his father sent him a letter which included these lines.

> For fifty eight years you have been a constant joy and pleasure to me; in all these years of your life, I cannot recall anything about you but was good and uplifting and I have always pointed to you and your god-like life with great pleasure. You have fulfilled every claim of my heart, and added honor to my name. Your family is one to be proud of, the peer of any in the church.

The children's mother, Bessie, was remarkable in her own right. At the age of 20 she rode horseback from Salt Lake City to Oakley, Utah—a distance of nearly fifty miles in one day—to visit her future husband. Bessie had a directness that often startled and amused. Asked by her son Bob Taylor why she was born in Kaysville, Bessie explained, "because that was where my mother was." How did they do laundry in the old days? Bessie: "By washing it." Other family anecdotes include Bessie chasing off burglars; Bessie righting an overturned buggy and riding on; Bessie gliding to the head of the line at the Altman Department Store in New York City when Frank studied there.

Apparently such spunk was healthful. Bessie would live—virtually independent except for the last little while—to just shy of 106 years.

Frank Campbell Taylor was a sales manager for the Taylor Motor Car Company, a Chrysler dealership, and during his life was also involved in ranching and real estate.

They lived in a large, square brick home in a quiet Sugar House neighborhood between Seventh and Eighth East. Upstairs were four bedrooms, one shared by the two boys, two by the four girls, and a master bedroom. Their home was alive with music. A Steinway upright graced the living room, and most of the children learned to play. Beverley's sister Virginia gave piano lessons, and Bev was her first student.

Beyond the piano a set of French doors opened to the outside. The main floor also had a sun room and a wood-burning fireplace. The family gathered around it in the evening as Frank or Bessie read to them. Beverley's favorite books included Black Beauty, A.A. Milne's Christopher Robin series, and, especially, Little Lord Fauntroy. Eighty years later, Beverley recalled with nostalgia how kind the protagonist was to his mother, calling her "dearest."

Their home was a magnet for neighborhood children, and games often were underway inside or out, including checkers, Rook, and jacks. Among outside activities were run sheepy run and jump the rope, including a superfast version, red-hot pepper, at which Beverley excelled. She and Bob also played a more risky game, mumblety-peg, in which two players face each other and throw knives into the ground near their feet.

One day when Bev was four, her father came home with a black and white puppy. She delightedly named the fluffy puppy "Pal," and they became inseparable.

The Taylors were happy and healthy but not wealthy. The large house on a large lot was deceptive. The lot once belonged to John Taylor and was passed down to them at no cost. About $8,000 of the money to build the house was their share of an inheritance upon the death of Beverley's maternal grandfather, George Hamilton Taylor, in 1907.

The Taylors' idyllic world was rocked in the fall of 1929. Frank Taylor came home from work early one day to announce, "They closed the doors." Numbly he kept repeating, "They closed the doors, they closed the doors."

Beverley, a child of five, pictured two gigantic doors clanging shut. "I knew it was bad, but I didn't know what it really meant."

The Taylor Motor Car Company joined tens of thousands of businesses swamped by the wave of the Great Depression, which was touched off the last week of October. Frank would be largely unemployed for the next six months.

### CHAPTER SIX

# FIRST LOVE

The 1920s were an exuberant, optimistic time in America. In 1918 the nation emerged from World War I far less scathed than its European allies or enemies. Over there, one in every five combatants from all countries was killed. France suffered most, with 1.4 million combat deaths, 27 percent of men aged eighteen to twenty-seven. The U.S. had 117,000 killed.

Its potential just starting to be realized, the United States was on its way to becoming the dominant world power through the rest of the twentieth century.

In 1920 women voted for the first time and Prohibition began, outlawing alcohol production and consumption. Later that decade came the first Olympic winter games and the first talking movie, "The Jazz Singer." Charles Lindbergh flew solo across the Atlantic and a woman swam the English Channel.

Life for many women would never be the same again. Millions left their homes and entered the work force to replace men who were fighting overseas. It was widely accepted in the United States that men should earn the bread and women should return to their homes. The feminist genie had escaped the lamp, however, and was not about to return without a fight.

Before the war, the Gibson Girl style was the rage: a woman wore her long hair loosely atop her head, along with a straight skirt and high-collared shirt. After the war the Gibson Girl was pushed aside by the flapper, who cut her hair short, wore make-up, donned shorter and lighter clothing, and, at least outside Utah, often smoked and drank.

It all came crashing down with the Great Depression, whose causes are still debated. There were, in fact, multiple causes, high consumer debt, poorly regulated markets that enabled citizens to push stock prices unsustainably high, and major bank failures. While the Depression hit almost every country, it began in the United States with the stock market crash on Black Tuesday, October 29, 1929.

Virtually every country, rich and poor alike, was devastated. Personal income, tax revenue, profits, and prices all fell. Unemployment in the U.S. between 1929 and 1933 rose from 4 percent to 25 percent. By March 1933, more than 800,000 nonfarm mortgages were foreclosed, and gross farm income fell nearly 60 percent.

The Taylor family, through its own exertions, was better off than most. Their large yard hosted a large vegetable garden and fruit trees, and they seldom went hungry. Bessie was an excellent cook. The children routinely came home from school to the smell of something tasty in the oven, baked potatoes, pies, cakes, breads, and other foods.

Beverley helped her father plant vegetables. "He dug the holes and I put in the seeds." Frank and the boys hoed furrows between rows of corn, tomatoes, beans, and other produce. A ditch ran near their property, and each week in the growing season they diverted water to irrigate the precious plants.

Fall harvest kept the family busy. Bessie and the girls put up hundreds of bottles of cherries, apples, peaches, pears, and tomatoes. Decades later, Beverley would do the same thing with her children. A cold-storage cellar under the house provided space to store the produce to feed them throughout the year.

Other chores around the house likewise called for group effort, and the children pitched in. With no electric washer, dishes were cleaned by hand. Downstairs was a clothes washer; a hand-cranked wringer was the closest thing to a dryer.

Their house was heated with coal. Periodically a dump truck showed up, lumbered behind the house, and emptied its load through a chute into a basement coal room. During cold months family members fed the coal into a furnace and, once burned, retrieved the clinkers which went out with the trash.

Coal was not as clean-burning as other forms of heat would be in the future, and a thin layer of soot clung to the walls. In spring the Taylors went to a paint store and bought a sizable box of wallpaper dough. Each family member would take a fistful, roll it into a ball, and roll the ball back and forth across a wall covering. As the ball darkened from the dust and soot sticking to it, the worker kneaded the dirt into the center of the ball to produce a clean surface, and continued rolling. Also in the spring, beds were hauled out to the front lawn, their springs scrubbed and mattresses aired and beaten.

Bessie was a model homemaker; no doubt some would say she went overboard. The Taylor home was kept nearly spotless. She stripped the beds and washed the sheets each week, ironing them until dry. Bessie was kind and nurturing, but also a stern disciplinarian.

Beverley was close to her soft-spoken father. "He was very loving and kind to me always, and never, ever spanked me." Frank Taylor played quarterback in college and was an avid fan of the University of Utah. He took Beverley to Saturday games and organized touch football on their front lawn. "It was playing with him on the lawn that made me love football the way I do," said Beverley.

Frank baptized Beverley into the LDS faith when she turned eight, and was the spiritual leader in their home. "I would sneak around the door to the room where he was," she said, "and he would be in there praying on his knees." As a young man he served a mission in England, and now led his family in morning and evening prayer.

After the car dealership where he was a sales manager closed at the start of the Depression, Frank for a time tried to sell an egg-based salve for muscle ache. He was like millions of others, hawking most anything that could potentially earn a little money. But he was unemployed for six months and it took a federal program to put him back to work.

Utah was one of the hardest-hit states in the Depression. Its unemployment rate in 1933 was about 36 percent, fourth highest in the nation. Annual per capita income fell 50 percent by 1932. By spring of the following year, 32 percent of Utahns received all or part of their basic necessities, including food, clothing, and shelter, from government relief funds, and 32 of Utah's 105 banks failed.

Churches, Chambers of Commerce, and numerous other groups organized to provide relief. In Salt Lake City, a free school lunch program was set up and vegetable seeds were distributed free, with city land for gardens also offered at no charge. Such resources soon were exhausted, however, and Utah, like the rest of the nation, turned to Washington for help.

Washington's response ushered in a historic era of government activism. Newly elected President Franklin D. Roosevelt, a Democrat, took the oath of office replacing Republican President Herbert Hoover in March 1933.

His first 100 days in office provided a benchmark against which every president since then has been judged. The two dozen or so relief programs announced or rolled out then and over the next several years did not end the Depression; it took another world war to do so, but provided considerable relief to individual citizens.

The New Deal was a good deal for Utah. Because the Depression hit Utah so hard, federal employment and other programs were extensive in the state. Federal spending per capita in Utah during the 1930s was ninth highest among the forty-eight states. For every dollar Utahns sent to Washington, the federal government, through various programs, returned seven.

In April 1936 the LDS Church inaugurated its own welfare program, telling federal agencies that no more Mormons would be added to public relief rolls. That small acorn, planted for the Church by Harold B. Lee, one of its youngest stake presidents and later an apostle and Church president, would grow into a worldwide system offering necessities to needy church members and assistance to others throughout the world.

In the early years, however, the LDS program supplemented but did not come close to supplanting New Deal programs. "Federal non-repayable expenditures in Utah for the period 1936-1940 were ten times as great as the accountable value of church-wide Welfare Plan transactions," wrote a Utah historian. "The Works Progress Administration (WPA) alone employed an average of 12,000 [Utahns] annually between 1935 and 1942." [1]

Frank Taylor finally found employment in a New Deal agency, the Homeowners Loan Corporation (HOLC), which began in 1933 to help citizens keep their homes. The government bought mortgages that were in default from banks, and lowered installment payments by stretching out the amortization period. HOLC saved the homes of more than a million people.

Frank appraised homes to help prepare the paperwork of new mortgages. He later started his own real estate company.

Music and art, considered luxuries by many families, were necessities to the Taylors. Their culture encouraged the performing arts. Mormon pioneers brought many instruments with them to Salt Lake Valley, and theater was a favorite pastime. Social Hall—called the first Little Theatre in America—its stage measured twenty by forty feet, was the principal place of amusement from 1852 to 1857, and local amateur dramatic groups flourished throughout the state. Many orchestras started up, though they typically struggled for finances to remain viable.

Within a century however, Utah boasted several world-class arts organizations, including the Utah Symphony, Ballet West, and the Mormon Tabernacle Choir.

The Taylors did not own a record player, but live music often filled their home. Most of the children took music and dance lessons, and the older Taylor girls entertained their mother's friends, who met once a month in each other's homes. Teenage friends often visited and, recalled Bessie, "Our living room carpet was worn to threads with all the dancing up and down."

Their investment paid big dividends in a practical as well as esthetic way. The Taylor children of necessity earned their own money while attending school, and music often provided the means. Virginia was an excellent pianist, and Beverley was the first of her many piano students.

At the age of fourteen Beverley went to Irving Junior High and held down an after-school job playing piano at the Jean Renae dance school, across the street from Irving. She played for two to three hours each day and up to six hours on Saturdays, making an enviable fifty cents an hour. In high school she earned seventy-five cents an hour playing for dancing school.

She took ballet lessons from Pete Christensen, an uncle to William Christensen, founder of Ballet West, Salt Lake City's professional dance company. Several times a week Beverley caught the streetcar to Christensen's downtown studio. She became especially adept at adagio, a slow ballet with a male partner that requires great skill and strength in lifting, balancing, and turning.

Beverley had a beautiful figure and became a graceful, enchanting dancer. She and her sisters performed both as instrumentalists and dancers in local LDS wards, in hotels, and in movie theaters, entertaining audiences before the film began.

Beverley was shy, and dancing boosted her confidence. "I wasn't one of those real pretty, popular girls; I was just a plain Jane."

One school experience early on influenced Beverley the rest of her life. Her sensitive kindergarten teacher chose her to be queen of a May Day celebration. In the schoolyard she sat on a throne in her elegant dress as other children danced around the maypole with colorful streamers.

"This memorable event, however small, proved to be something of a turning point in Beverley's life," reads her biography. "Within it she found a measure of confidence and a feeling of importance. Playing a role offered a safe vehicle in which she could interact in public and transcend her shy nature...that early thrill of feeling special gave her a love for all things theatrical and a desire to instill in all children that same excitement she felt." [2]

Beverley developed into a good writer and excellent penman. At the age of fourteen in May 1938, she turned in an eighteen-page school report on "My Early Childhood." A person she admired was Abraham Lincoln: "Of all the good traits Abraham Lincoln possessed there is one which I admire most." It was his uncompromising honesty.

Beverley told about a time that Lincoln borrowed a book on "The Life of George Washington" from a neighbor. He read until bedtime, then placed the book on a high shelf. That night a rainstorm sent water through their leaky roof, ruining the book. Lincoln did not have money to replace it, but labored on the neighbor's farm equal to the cost of the book. "I have read or heard of many good traits which Abraham Lincoln possessed, but this to me is outstanding," wrote Beverley.

Readers of the essay learned how her first name came to be spelled

"Beverley" instead of the more common "Beverly." It was brought home from England by her father who, as a Mormon missionary years earlier, bicycled through a bewitching, pastoral place called Beverley Woods.

The philosophy in a favorite quotation in the essay would serve Beverley well, especially throughout her adult life. It was by nineteenth-century Christian writer J.R. Miller: "A thankful heart finds roses amid its thorns and rejoices, where the unthankful heart finds thorns amid the roses and complains."

Time spent earning money left less time for homework. In junior high and high school, Beverley was an average student, earning As and Bs in subjects she liked—music, art, and language—with an occasional C or D in math and science. Her report card for 1937-38 showed all As, except in algebra, for which she got a D.

The algebra teacher, a Mrs. Heiges, apparently resented the time Beverley spent at the dancing school, as she had resented Helen before her. "You'll never amount to anything," the teacher told Beverley. "You're just like your sister Helen."

By then, in fact, Helen, a gifted pianist and promising composer, had started to soar. Nine years older than Beverley, she studied piano at the McCune School of Music in Utah, then earned a master's degree at Columbia University in New York City.

In 1941-42 Helen was on the faculty at Columbia Teachers College, and accompanying famed dancer and choreographer Martha Graham as she prepared to dance the lead in Aaron Copland's "Appalachian Spring." Copland won the Pulitzer Prize for the ballet.

Helen won a fellowship and studied composition at the prestigious Juliard School, while playing for Graham. She earned a doctorate at Julliard and was becoming a nationally known composer, her family back in Utah occasionally hearing her works on the radio.

"She practically starved there," recalled Beverley of her vivacious sister, "but when she came home we were all excited. She was just the life of the family."

A brother, Bob Taylor, strikingly handsome, became a professional actor and singer in his adult years and a member of the Mormon Tabernacle Choir. He went to Hollywood as a staff assistant for Howard Hughes Productions. Bob was president of Deseret Theatrical Artists in Hollywood, and married a model and actress, Katherine Cook.

One of the pre-eminent concert pianists of the era was Grant Johannesen, also born in Salt Lake City.

He would play an important role in the Taylor familiy's future. A neighbor who taught piano discovered him, when he was five years old and already could play by ear. "...one day she came knocking at my mother's door and said, 'Look, someone in this house is making fun of my practicing,'" he said. "I think I was five at the time, and my mother pointed to me, I was sitting at the piano, and I apparently tried to imitate her playing, whatever it was she was playing. [His mother] said 'He just loves to sit there, and he hears you across the street, and he does what he can.' So that is how I was taken up by a teacher, it was an irate teacher, at the door." [3]

Early in his career Johannesen performed Gershwin's Concerto in F, broadcast on radio. Duke Ellington sent him a telegram saying the performance was the best Gershwin he had heard. [4]

Johannesen emphasized the importance of courage and taking risks to achieve something great. Not content with performing more standard works, he specialized in interpreting French composers. His New York concert debut came in 1944 when he was twenty-three. His first tour of Europe was five years later as a soloist with the New York Philharmonic. That same year he won first prize at the Queen Elisabeth of Belgium International Music Competition.

Johannesen's performance at Moscow's Tchaikovsky Conservatory in 1963 is legendary. A correspondent for the *New York Herald Tribune* was there:

A wildly cheering audience refused to let American pianist Grant Johannesen leave the stage...Wednesday night in one of the greatest triumphs ever scored by a visiting artist. Johannesen, a 40-year-old native of Salt Lake City, played encores lasting 45 minutes before the houselights were ordered turned off and workmen rolled the piano from the stage. [5]

For his final encore he improvised a classical version of "Come, Come, Ye Saints," a favorite hymn of Mormon pioneers. Later he wrote it down and called it "Improvisations on a Mormon Hymn."

Beverley graduated from East High School in the spring of 1940 and entered the University of Utah that fall. A highly regarded public university, the "U" prided itself on not being the "Y," LDS Church-owned Brigham Young University, forty miles to the south in Provo. The U is a broad-based academic institution with both a law and medical school. The oldest state university west of the Missouri River, its doors first opened in 1850.

Beverley still needed to put herself through school but had long since tired of doing so on the piano. She took a job tossing mail at the downtown post office. The pay was good but the hours, six each night, were daunting while going to college. A mailman who befriended her was Orlando Anderson, father of Jack Anderson, later a crusading, Pulitzer-prize winning columnist in Washington. Bev regretted her years of casualness toward academics and found college classes difficult. During her first term she got Cs in every course but physical education, in which she got an A.

As she thought about the future, one thing close to her heart was working with children. Teaching kindergarten became her goal.

Beverley hoped to have a family as large as hers, with six children. In the meantime she joyfully interacted with children in Junior Sunday School. She began teaching them at about the age of twelve and by nineteen was directing her congregation's entire LDS children's program, called Primary.

As a senior at East High, Beverley began dating her first serious boyfriend. He was suave, extremely handsome Lloyd Rumph. He had dark hair and was a good dancer. He was also patient: Beverley was shy about kissing and vowed never to kiss on a first date. Lloyd not only honored her vow, but waited six months before surprising her with a goodnight kiss.

"There was a lot of kissing after that!" she said. Lloyd called her his "lovely little lady," and spent a lot of time at the Taylor home. They fell in love and began to talk of marriage.

Everything changed on December 7, 1941. Beverley was walking home from church that day when a neighbor boy called to her: "They just bombed Pearl Harbor!"

"Where's Pearl Harbor?" Beverley wondered.

"Little did I know the trauma and changes that would take place as a result of that event," said Beverley. "All the men were gone. The student body president of East High had to go to war and he was killed. We'd see these boys that we knew, in the paper, having been killed." Unless you lived in wartime, she believed, "you cannot know what it felt like to have these men that you knew, and some of them you dated, die."

Her boyfriend immediately joined the Navy and left Utah. At the end of that school year she left for San Francisco, where Lloyd was stationed.

Beverley found a job as a secretary, and they had a romantic summer. They took in movies and good restaurants, spent time at Fisherman's Wharf and in Chinatown, and visited the redwood forests.

"It was one of the happiest times in my life," said Beverley.

But the war stole their dreams, as it did with endless other couples. In 1944, shortly before Christmas, Lloyd wrote Beverley that he needed to concentrate on his work and she was too much of a distraction. He hoped they could connect again after the war. Beverley believed that Lloyd, whose humble home was headed by a widowed mother, resented Beverley's opportunity to go to college.

Beverley was crestfallen. "I was really hurting and thought I would never be happy again." Leaning on her faith and her family, however, time healed, and other aspects of life improved. Beverley's goal of teaching kindergarten was clearer in view. Her grades improved dramatically during her junior and senior years at the U, when she got mostly As. In the spring of 1945 she graduated with a bachelor's degree in elementary education.

Her warm, loving father helped Beverley through her challenges. Frank was always at her side when needed. Through the years Beverley often daydreamed, of graduating from college, becoming a kindergarten teacher, and saving $1,000. Those goals were all close to reality.

She also daydreamed of what her husband would look and be like. He would be kind and self-effacing, like her father, and would be a muscular, California-type, with wavy blond hair.

Half her dream would come true: He would be a strong, blond Californian.

# War Bond Sales Expected to Exceed $100,000 Mark by Saturday Night

## At 95, Mr. Sorenson Still Buys Bonds

Jim's great-grandfather, Hans O. Sorenson, emigrated from Norway to the U.S. in 1871. With 12 great-grandchildren in the service in 1944, he buys a bond to support the Allied war effort.

Robert and Emma Blaser family in Langnau, Switzerland. The family emigrated to the U.S. in 1900 and eventually numbered thirteen children, including Jim's mother, Emma.

The Hans Sorenson family in 1898, including Jim's grandfather, Joseph Leonard Sorenson (*top row, second from left*).

Emma Blaser as a bright, spirited teenager. Her free-thinking views, including women's liberation, were far ahead of her time in conservative Rexburg, Idaho.

Joseph and Emma were callow teenagers when Jimmy was born. Neither of their families fully accepted their respective young new in-law.

Jimmy in Rexburg, Idaho.

Jimmy as a babe in Emma's arms. The profusion of wavy hair followed him through life.

In Yuba City, California, impoverished for lack of money but not for
love, which filled their tar paper-
shack home.

Emma with Eileen and Jimmy, who
was especially close to his mother.
She refused to accept a teacher's labeling of Jim as "retarded," and unfailingly encouraged his ambitions.

Jimmy *(second from top right)* in second grade in hardscrabble Yuba City.

Jimmy at 13.

Teenage Jim meditating above a cool current in Lincoln. Over his lifetime he will acquire many thousands of acres of land intersected by such streams.

Starting a dozen years after Eileen, Emma had four daughters in a row, beginning with (*left to right*) Carol, Lois, and Emma Jean. Joy is yet to be born. At age 11 Carol was tragically killed in a car-pedestrian accident in 1946.

Practicing the violin in the yard of their home on "Bandy Track Alley."

Jim's innovative genius was evidenced after he shrewdly began working at the Lincoln peach cannery at 14—four years before the allowed age. He made a dangerous job far safer for himself and others who followed. Jim is circled in photo.

Quick and strong, Jim was a standout athlete. Nicknamed "Silver Streak" when he played for the Lincoln High Zebras, he attended Placer Junior College on a basketball scholarship in 1940.

The family moved to more up-scale Lincoln in 1935 when Jim was 13. He helped deliver ice and beverages for a distributorship managed by his father.

Joseph and Emma Sorenson with five of their six children *(left to right)*: Lois, Jim, Joy, Eileen, Emma Jean. Another daughter, Carol, died in a car-pedestrian accident, ca 1948.

The Sorensons' home in Lincoln, California.

Joseph Sorenson came far from when he dug ditches to feed his family. He helped launch this major livestock auction house in Roseville, California.

Missionary companions, Elders Hollman and Sorenson, proselyting in New England.

When piloting a small plane, clouds obscured the airport and Jim nearly bailed out. Later inspection indicated his parachute would not have opened.

Elder Sorenson, giving volunteer service chopping kindling during his two-year mission.

Basic training with the Merchant Marine on Catalina Island.

As an officer candidate at the Maritime Training Station, Sheepshead Bay, New York. He resented being treated better in an officer's uniform than in a recruit's.

Medical training at the U.S. Marine Hospital in San Francisco. Years later he invented the paper surgical mask to replace cloth masks such as this one.

Beverley Taylor and Jim met at church and courted in Manhattan.

Beverley in her Manhattan apartment, a place of respite for Jim.

Their courtship
was intense if
not long—strolls,
movies, dances, and
swimming.

They married in the Logan, Utah LDS Temple on July 23, 1946. Her great-grandfather John Taylor, third president of the Church, had dedicated the temple in 1884.

Newlyweds off on a brief honeymoon between Utah and San Francisco Bay, where he was assigned to the U.S. Public Health Service.

The bridal party at a Salt Lake reception included Bev's parents, Frank and Bessie Taylor (*far left*), next to Jim's parents, Joseph and Emma Sorenson.

At their first home, in Rose Park.

With Carol, the first of eight children.

Their first home, in Rose Park, Salt Lake City. For an extra $150 the builder roughed in a second story and extra bathroom.

In an unsolved mystery, an assailant fired a bullet through the kitchen, barely missing Bev and Carol and lodging in the refrigerator.

The entire family, ca 1964, including six daughters and two sons. *(Left to right, back)* Jimmy, Shauna, Carol, Ann, Joan, *(front)* Joe, Jim, Chris, Beverley, Gail.

Jim was athletic all his life, running and doing pushups daily, playing squash, and here coaching son Jimmy's *(front, second from left)* baseball team.

The Sorenson children as young adults, ca 1975. *(Left to right)* Chris, Gail, Joe, Joan, Ann, Jim, Shauna, Carol.

A favorite photo on Jim's wall, with grandson James Luke Sorenson. The caption: "Give me the reins, Grandpa. Now get off!"

The three Sorenson men, James Lee, Joseph Taylor, and Jim.

A grown-up Luke with his dad, James Lee, and grandpa.

### CHAPTER SEVEN

# MISSION

## Trumps Medical School

By standard yardsticks Jim was a mediocre student at best during his first years of high school. His report cards were filled with Cs and Ds, and friends seemed unanimous on one point: Nothing about Jim suggested he would ever achieve anything remarkable.

Three classmates who were interviewed sixty years later gave strikingly similar responses. William (Willy) Gamboa, who owned a chain of nursing homes. "I was really surprised at the things Jim accomplished." Ken Bayless, a CPA: "There was no indication at all back then that he was destined for great things." James Ragsdale, who also played for the Lincoln Zebras and became a dentist: "Nothing at all stood out to suggest he'd do great."[1]

Beneath Jim's tanned good looks, striking blue eyes, and shock of wavy blond hair, however, burned a deep desire to do something important with his life. Perhaps it started when his confidence on the basketball court and baseball diamond started to be reflected in the classroom. He still remembered the time a teacher named Brown gave him a B-minus in science. Jim went to Brown, afraid there was a mistake. "Do you realize you gave me a B-minus?" Jim asked. "Yeah, and you deserve it!" answered Brown. It was a turning point in his academics.

With few close friends, Joseph and Emma were his main influences. From them he learned a principle that would be at the core of his personal philosophy: the importance of balance. His parents were opposites in many ways, yet complemented each other beautifully and created a harmonious synergy. Joseph was quiet, methodical and careful; Emma was verbal, passionate and daring. Joseph was inventive, tough-minded and conservative; Emma held to traditional family values at home and a progressive world view outside it.

As Jim sought direction, another person became important in his life. He was Arthur McArthur, the town doctor. Dr. McArthur, in Jim's view, "had the best job in town." His life was spent in critically important service, and he was well-respected and well-paid for it. Jim, who often seemed more at ease with adults than with those his own age, met McArthur soon after the Sorensons relocated to Lincoln. McArthur was impressed with Jim and became a friend and mentor. "He had a beautiful and spacious house," said Jim. "We'd sit in his parlor and play chess."

Dr. McArthur stressed to Jim that this was an ideal time to enter the field of medicine. The most important medical advancements in history were in just the last few decades: X-rays that "see" inside the human body; radium, a powerful weapon against cancer; sulfa drugs and vaccines to fight diseases; and—especially—penicillin, the first antibiotic that would revolutionize the treatment of disease.

Jim thought of his baby brother Donald who died in a flu epidemic in 1926. He also considered the rash of five early deaths in his father's family during the 1920s. Joseph's mother, Annie, 46, died of cancer. Two brothers, Leonard, 18, and Wendell, 13, died of complications from typhoid fever and a ruptured appendix, respectively; and two sisters, Zola, 3, and Gazelle, 21, died of diphtheria and rheumatic fever. Jim could not help but believe that some of them could have been saved with better medical care.

The good news, said Dr. McArthur, was that after centuries of relatively few major breakthroughs in fighting such diseases, they were now yielding to medical advances. The twentieth century, in fact, ushered in the greatest scientific and technological achievements the world had seen. "If you don't believe me about our progress, just ask George Washington," said McArthur.

Jim looked blank. "George Washington? He's dead."

"Exactly!" said McArthur. "The point is how he died."

McArthur took a book from the shelf and read of the events leading to the death of America's first President on December 14, 1799. Two days earlier Washington rode his horse in rain, snow, and hail for five hours on his Virginia plantation, Mount Vernon. The next morning Washington complained of a sore throat, and was hoarse by that evening. Twenty-four hours later Washington was dead. This is part of the account written by two physicians who treated him:

> ...General Washington was attacked with an inflammatory infection of the upper part of the windpipe, called in technical language, cynanche trachealis [laryngitis or croup]...[he] procured a bleeder in the neighborhood, who took from his arm, in the night, twelve or fourteen ounces of blood...[An attending physician and two consulting physicians arrived between 11 a.m. and 4 p.m. the next day.] In the interim were employed two copious bleedings [and other remedies, including a laxative]...but all without any perceptible advantage, the respiration becoming still more difficult and distressing. Upon the arrival of the first of the consulting physicians, it was agreed...to try the result of another bleeding, when about thirty-two ounces were drawn, without the smallest apparent alleviation of the disease. The powers of life now manifestly yielding to the force of the disorder...till half after eleven o'clock on Saturday night, when retaining the full possession of his intellect, he expired without a struggle.
>
> (Signed) James Craik, Attending Physician
> Elisha C. Dick, Consulting Physician[2]

Little wonder that Washington "expired without a struggle." He was bled to death. A large man for his time, weighing about 175 pounds, he started with a total of between five and six quarts of blood. Presuming the above account is accurate, his doctors removed more than half, taking the volume needed to feed his body's cells with food and oxygen, remove waste products, and fight the disease, which present-day doctors believe was a streptococcal infection of the throat.

Washington's doctors were some of the best-trained in America, and their methods represented the state of medical care at that time. There is no indication that they did more to diagnose the problem than to stand by and watch Washington deteriorate, occasionally feeling his skin to estimate the degree of fever. No mention is made of examining his chest or throat; they lacked both the tools and training to do so effectively.

Jim resolved to become a doctor. He shared his ambition with his mother Emma. Her response was typical: "Jim, I think you can do it."

Such high hopes were tempered by Jim's prudent side. Eileen remembered that her brother wanted to go to a particular school dance but felt inadequate on the floor, "so Mom arranged for both of us to take private ballroom dancing. It was important to Jim to keep it a secret." He took Eileen to that dance and others. "While we weren't exactly Fred Astaire and Ginger Rogers out there, by Lincoln standards we were smooth and darn good!" she recalled.

Jim put the lessons to good use, dating popular girls, including a dark-haired beauty named Betty Grey. His growing confidence was not always rewarded, however. In his senior year of high school he ran for student body vice president and lost. The following year Eileen ran for student body vice president and won—then used her charm to run student affairs from behind the scene by inducing the student president to do her bidding.

Eileen later became a wife and mother of six, and taught in the LDS seminary system—formal religious instruction for members of high school-age—for four decades.

Jim's life lessons formed into a personal resolve not to take chances "unless the odds are in my favor." His cautious nature was reinforced at the age of eighteen by a near brush with death during a three-hour solo flight to qualify for his private pilot's license.

He had a visual contact flight plan and a map, but no navigational instruments. The weather turned bad, rain and snow pelted the little plane, and fierce winds blew it off course and threatened to tear off the tail section.

Unable to see any landmarks through the cloud cover, Jim fingered the rip cord on his parachute repeatedly, preparing to bail out. Finally he spotted the airport and fought a ferocious cross-wind to a crash landing from which he walked away unscathed. Days later, in checking his chute, other pilots discovered a defect. Had Jim bailed out, it would not have opened and he almost certainly would have plunged to his death.

Each summer season, Jim continued to work at the Lincoln cannery. He also helped deliver ice for his father's business, which included a beer and soft drink distributorship.

"As a member of the Church of Jesus Christ of Latter-day Saints, I was expected to abstain from alcohol," he explained. "Young people in the Mormon Church are frequently tested by peer pressure regarding this principle. In my case, in my early teens in a town with very few other Mormon young people for support, the pressure became intense."

One Saturday his friends chipped in and gave Jim money to purchase beer from his father's company. They got drunk and Jim got very ill. "I was too ashamed to go inside when I was finally brought home," he recalled. "That night was spent sick and miserable under a bush near my house. When my father found me early Sunday morning, he took me to his company beer warehouse for a cold shower, a change into my Sunday clothes, and some breakfast. Then Dad marched off to church with me, for the first time in years."

Since moving to Lincoln, church attendance had dropped off for Joseph, who was busy managing businesses—including a livestock auction yard he helped launch—and whose family continued to grow with the births of four more daughters. They were Carol in 1935, Lois in 1936, Emma Jean in 1938, and Joy in 1946. Finding their son under a bush that Sunday morning shook LeVoy and Emma with new resolve to attend church faithfully.

"After that, Dad rarely missed a church meeting of any kind with me," said Jim. "He didn't show me the door of the church. He went in with me and the rest of the family to meetings. That event changed the lives of both me and my father. Dad went on to hold local leadership positions in the Mormon Church. And when Dad was called to serve in the local bishopric, he sold his profitable beer distributorship the next month."

Joseph and Emma also journeyed to Salt Lake City and repeated their wedding vows in the LDS Temple, in a ceremony Mormons believe can, under proper priesthood authority, "seal" faithful couples and families to live together for eternity.

Jim's educational progress flowered fully his senior year, when he received almost all As on his report card. By then he had learned to discount limits and labels others placed on him, from the start of his schooling when educators called him retarded to upper classes in high school when they said his IQ was not high enough to recommend him to a top university.

Already Jim was living better than most of his peers, thanks to his initiative and ingenuity. He bought a Model A Ford with a rumble seat for $37. In springtime he'd gather up his mother Emma, Eileen, and his little sisters and take them for a drive through the intoxicating California countryside. Jim grew to have a great love for nature.

On June 7, 1940 he graduated from Lincoln Union High School. That fall he entered Placer Junior College on a basketball scholarship, and also played on the tennis team. The small two-year school was twelve miles down the road in Auburn. It was reestablished in 1936 by Placer County voters after being closed in the wake of World War I because of dwindling enrollment.

Years later Placer would become Sierra College and offer courses at various locations in the region. Typically, Jim figured out how to make money even while commuting from Lincoln to Auburn during his freshman year. He drove the school bus to and from campus, filled with other college-bound students, earning $62.50 a month. During Jim's second year he lived in Auburn in a nice apartment and traded in the Model A for a snazzy gunmetal-green 1936 Chevrolet coup. It was paid for and he had money in the bank.

Planning to attend medical school at U.C. Berkeley, he studied premed at Placer—chemistry, anatomy, physiology, math—and did well. At the end of his second year Placer awarded Jim an associate's degree on May 21, 1942. Five months earlier Japan attacked Pearl Harbor, drawing the U.S. into World War II. Along with most young men his age, Jim weighed his options.

He took a battery of tests and was accepted into two coveted naval programs—V5 pilot training and V7 medical school. The opportunity he dreamed of—becoming a doctor—was at Jim's door. And Uncle Sam would pick up the tab. He would enroll at Berkeley and be a practicing doctor at age 23 while serving his country honorably.

It was perfect. Too perfect, as it turned out. Others had other plans for his life.

Worthy male Mormons are encouraged to serve two-year proselyting missions for the Church, starting at the age of 19 at that time and dropping to 18 in 2013. LeVoy, who forfeited a mission by marrying young, always hoped his son would do so. Now at a crossroads, Jim mentioned the alternate possibility of a mission to naval recruiters. "That's impossible; this is war!" they told him. "You'll never go on a mission. Certainly not now!" When his draft card arrived, they instructed, come back that same day and they would finish the paperwork putting him in the V7 medical program.

Meanwhile, unbeknown to Jim, LDS Church leaders agreed with Washington that no able-bodied men of draft age would be sent on missions after July 1, 1942. This was already the early part of June, so it appeared almost certain he would not serve a mission. Joseph, however, was persistent. "Let's pray about it," he would say. Out of respect for his parents, Jim agreed to accept whichever came first—his draft notice or mission call.

"I thought a mission call could not possibly be processed before a draft notice," wrote Jim, "since in those days a high-ranking church leader in Salt Lake City—seven-hundred miles away—had to conduct a personal interview to determine mission eligibility."

However, Jim's bishop and stake president—the latter is the ecclesiastical leader of a group of local congregations—swung into action. The stake president, I. Homer Smith, was related to Joseph Fielding Smith, a long-time member of the Council of the Twelve Apostles, a leading doctrinal authority, and a future president of the Church. The very next day Sunday Apostle Smith arrived in Lincoln to conduct a personal interview with Jim.

They retired to a small room and the questions began. "Young man, are you worthy? Are you morally clean for this calling? Is there anything amiss in your life?" The directness of the questions surprised Jim. Finally he answered. "Elder Smith, I think I'm just as clean and qualified as anyone in this little room."

The apostle, taken aback, choked a little and cleared his throat—twice. Then he asked several other questions. "I didn't know whether I was going on a mission or not," said Jim.

He fervently hoped not. He struck the bargain to possibly go on a mission because of LeVoy. "It was strictly a matter of my word, honor and loyalty in respecting my father," wrote Jim. "My father had earned my respect. He had been honest and right with me and always had good thoughts and principles. I was not really excited about going on a mission. I was more let down by not going to medical school."[3]

Years later, however, in retrospect, Jim saw his missionary service as a major turning point in his life—an opportunity he wouldn't trade for any other.

"When I left for [my mission], my father promised me I would be blessed. He would quote the Old Testament scripture found in Malachi that states, 'Bring ye all the tithes into the storehouse, that there may be meat in mine house, and prove me now herewith...if I will not open you the windows of heaven, and pour you out a blessing, that there shall not be room enough to receive it.' [Malachi 3:10] It took years before I could appreciate its true meaning."

### CHAPTER EIGHT

# CHAMPION BAPTIZER

Several days after his interview with Joseph Fielding Smith, Jim's mission call arrived in the mail, signed by LDS Church President Heber J. Grant. Jim would be in the last group of missionaries of draft age called until after the war, and would spend the next two years preaching the gospel in New England.

Jim and about sixty other missionaries first reported to a mission training center in Salt Lake City for ten days of orientation. They were taught practical lessons—how to iron shirts, cook a meal, and stay healthy—as well as gospel principles, suggested readings in church books and tracts, and methods of proselytizing.

In a group photo of the departing missionaries—six sisters and about fifty-five elders—Jim with his mountain of hair is easy to spot at the right end of the third row. On June 25, 1942 they departed for their respective fields of labor. Traveling by rail, Jim arrived at mission headquarters in Cambridge, Massachusetts, on June 28. For the next two years he would be known as "Elder Sorenson" and rarely hear his first name.

Four days after arriving in the mission, Jim sent the first of what would be a very faithful weekly stream of letters home. Jim told his parents that, passing through the Rocky Mountain region, "This time I have fallen in love with the Utah, Idaho, Salt Lake country. I like the climate, atmosphere, people etc. much better...I have traveled across the continent and it is easy... for anyone to see there is something a little different there." His attraction to Utah presaged a later life lived in the Beehive State.

A letter from mission headquarters, dated the 29th, was sent to LeVoy and Emma by New England mission president William H. Reeder Jr. It assured them that Jim "arrived safely" and after resting up was "sent to labor in Providence, Rhode Island, a place which I feel he will like very much... You are to be congratulated on having such a son in the mission field and I am sure he will do you honor, as well as honoring the great work of the Lord."

President Reeder, a no-nonsense retired judge from Ogden, Utah, had his hands full. The New England Mission was geographically huge, local priesthood leadership thin, and convert baptisms rare. And not much help was on the way. With war now raging in Europe and Asia, the arrival of able-bodied young priesthood-holding missionaries ended. The Church called 1,257 new full-time missionaries to serve across the world in 1941 but two years later only 261 were called—mostly women, who do not hold the LDS priesthood, and older males.

While Jim's body was in New England, during the early months his mind often was back home. He worried greatly over how his parents could afford to send the $40 or so each month to keep him in the field, and how to buy a couple of suits of clothing and a few other items he saw as essential. He agonized over how to obtain a portable typewriter, mentioned repeatedly in early letters, until finally purchasing one for $35. [1]

Jim broke a mission rule to pay for the typewriter: He and his companion worked for money, picking cranberries for seventy-five cents an hour. Otherwise he seemed to take most mission rules seriously. Another exception was a requirement that missionaries wear hats, something Jim firmly resisted. He and his companions also went to the beach on occasion, at least once scorching Jim's light skin.

Correspondence to his family, already prolific when hand-written, became more so after he purchased the typewriter.

Once Jim made up his mind to acquire something, he was tenacious in finding ways to do so, always at a bargain. But he struggled to explain any extra spending to his parents. "It is another day and I have some news to report," began one letter. "I know it is going to be hard to take." No doubt his parents held their breath as they read on. "...Well I guess I just as well tell you. I bought a suit today. It is a regular $45 suit that I bought at the factory for $26.75. It is certainly a nice looking one."

He kept careful track of spending, sometimes down to the last penny, as in this month: "...$18.50 went for room rent, $10 for food, $11 for books...$2.45 for postage, $4.80 for traveling expenses, $2.85 Sundries etc., $2.03 car fare, $2.25 laundry." Rent was high that month; at other times he paid as little as $4. Jim also reported from New London, Connecticut that "Eggs today were 63 cents a dozen, butter 52 cents a pound, milk 17 cents a quart."

By October Jim obtained all the items he considered necessary to be effective. "I have three suits now, a typewriter, a radio, a camera, a rain coat, a new pair of shoes," he wrote from Washington, Rhode Island. "What more could a missionary ask for. I also have a good alarm clock and some nice church books. I surely do enjoy them and my mission also."

His natural charm paid dividends. Among photos sent home was one he explained this way: "This is the little French girl in an ice cream store a couple of blocks from here. We get a nice big dish of free ice cream whenever we go in and she is there alone." There was also a Mrs. Fist, "a rather wealthy lady that has some fine riding horses. We shall go riding one of these first days."

After being transferred from Washington, Rhode Island, Jim's landlady there wrote him a letter. "Dear Friend," it began, "Since you went to New London, I miss the <u>sunshine</u>, the good talks, and the ennobling thoughts you brought into my household...Your interesting background combined with your mother's careful training have made you an outstanding character among men."[2]

Jim had less reason than he knew for worry over his family's finances. Emma and LeVoy took the same concern to their bishop prior to his mission call. The bishop's advice was for the Sorensons to tighten their family budget. He also told them, LeVoy recalled, that "If we were faithful in keeping within the budget, we would be able to keep Jim on a mission, and if that didn't work, something would change in our lives...that the Lord would help us." LeVoy, in a testimony for his family, explained:

> The second month things happened in such a nice way, at first it
> seemed like a dream. I worked for the National Ice and Cold Storage
> managing their plant...getting $150 a month. The Vice President of
> the company came to Lincoln and asked me if I would care to pur-
> chase the company. My answer was yes, I would if I thought that I was
> getting a good buy. He came back in about two weeks and told me the
> price. I could hardly believe it. I also would be taking it over the first
> of June [when demand for ice was high], which pleased me very much
> I didn't even have to make a downpayment until the 11th of July. I had
> an extra good month in June and it netted me enough money to pay
> them the entire purchase price. From then on there was no problem
> keeping James on his mission. [3]

While Jim and his companions were far from the war, they faced daily
reminders of it, in the faces of families whose sons, husbands, and brothers
were overseas fighting, and on the windows of homes bearing a solemn gold
star—a sign that someone who left from there made the ultimate sacrifice.

"Missionary work is certainly getting harder," Jim wrote. "People's
minds seem to be on the war and everything but religion." He added that
"In a period when men's hearts are full of chance and anxiety and mind
is on war, we try to present a Gospel message to them. We have much to
contend with because of the times and the conditions of the world. Nev-
ertheless the Lord has said: 'And the voice of warning shall be unto all people, by the mouths of my disciples, whom I have chosen in these last days.
And they shall go forth and none shall stay them, for I the Lord have commanded them.'" [4]

Five months into his mission, at his request, Elder Sorenson's parents
sent him a copy of his patriarchal blessing. Such blessings are given by venerable, seasoned priesthood holders in the Church who are specially called
to that office. A patriarch places his hands on a worthy member's head and
pronounces a blessing—not a prophecy but admonition and a promise of
potential if the member continues to faithfully follow God's commandments.

Jim's blessing had been given that spring by Patriarch Herbert C.

Prince in Sacramento. As you go through life, said the Patriarch, "there shall arise many disturbing things" and you will need the inspiration from God to help you over the rough places..." Do nothing without first placing yourself in His hands." He added, in part:

> Teach the Gospel wherever you are... and you shall have the power to know what men and women think of you. The actions of those who would lead you astray shall be revealed unto you...keep yourself circumspect in life and God will bless you. In His own good time will you meet that one whom you will take into the House of God, and she shall be your helpmate, and all others will not matter in your life.[5]

Jim was results-oriented and not comfortable with the prevailing laissez-faire approach to missionary work. "The general attitude [has] been mainly to break the ice and make friends," he reported to his parents. The New England Mission reflected that attitude, with one of the lowest missionary-to-convert ratios in the church. It was not unusual for a missionary to serve his entire two years without baptizing someone. Jim set higher goals and went about accomplishing them with the same zeal and creativity as when growing up in Yuba City.

His self-described salesman's approach to preaching the gospel, honed through years of hawking newspapers and magazines back on "King's Row," produced rapid and surprising results. Jim said he told one longtime investigator of the Church, a Sister Burnham, that "we're going to have a baptism Thursday. Do you have your white clothes ready?

"No, but I can get some," she replied. With that, Jim telephoned President Reeder and told him someone wanted to be baptized. Could he come and interview her?

"We haven't had a baptism in months," said the mission president.

"Well," answered Jim, "she's a lovely white-haired lady who is ready to join the Church." Reeder met with Burnham to determine her worthiness and understanding of the commitment she was about to make. Afterward he met with Jim and said "You're right, she is ready. She is a beautiful person."

"She just needed someone to help her make the final decision," Jim wrote. On other occasions, Jim used this approach: "Look, we're leaving now. The war is on and we're going to need more members and leadership here when we leave. We've come 2,000 miles just to help get you ready for this great and important work."

Jim was ahead of his time. A decade later, in 1952, the Church published its first official proselytizing plan—six missionary discussions taking an "investigator" logically through gospel principles and, along the way, committing him or her to baptism.

Missionaries teach but, as Jim noted, only the Spirit converts. He seemed to have the Spirit with him most of the time. Jim often expressed his strong belief in the restored gospel, but also kept his feelings in check. "I am developing more and more to be a missionary," he wrote in a stream of consciousness, "But never I don't think...will I become fanatic...I shall always look at things as a whole and be rather broad minded."

On the first Sunday of most months, LDS congregations participate in a "fast and testimony meeting," where members are invited to stand and express their feelings. On one such month in Providence, Jim shared his testimony. The Sunday School lesson preceding fast and testimony meeting was on scientific vs. spiritual knowledge. He explained to his parents:

> I summed it all up for them and said we must look at life as a whole. That the Gospel of Jesus Christ imbrassed [sic] all truth. That we as Latter day Saints should see life through all possible channels of light, lest we become fanatic. A fanatic is one that doubles his speed when he has lost his direction...Great is the man who can see that spiritual is stronger than material force, that thoughts rule the world."

Tracting—going door-to-door seeking interested individuals—is the bane of most LDS missionaries, who often are treated rudely. Jim not only tolerated tracting, he thrived on it, finding the challenge bracing. "The more I [tract] the more I like it," he wrote home. In another letter he said that "Today I put in about 6 hours of tracting. I have had doors slammed in my face, but nothing worse." To celebrate his twenty-first birthday on July 30, 1942, Jim and his companion tracted for ten hours.

A key to Jim's singular success in New England was sheer hard work. It is interesting to note that, both before and after his mission, he often lacked physical stamina. But during his mission, stamina did not seem to be a big issue. More than once his energy and enthusiasm on a doorstep led the occupant to invite him to speak to another church's congregation, notably to Baptists.

Studying hard for such occasions yielded a nice byproduct, as reported in one letter: "I have done much reading out here...I am certainly thankful though that I have overcome that slowness of reading. I am sure I could do much better college work now."

Jim's compassion also touched lives. Mormon missionaries live and travel in pairs, and each one typically serves with a half-dozen or more "companions" during his mission. One of Jim's first companions had a widowed mother back home and "has to get by on as little as possible," wrote Jim, "so I adjust my needs to his and get along on the same amount, not because I feel poor but it's the only decent thing to do."

He liked milk but wrote that he did not buy it often because "I couldn't sit at the table and drink milk while my companion drank water, when I know he likes milk as well as I do." Jim sometimes bought groceries without adding their cost to an expense ledger they shared.

When a single woman in the small town of Fall River, Rhode Island grieved over her lost dog, Jim and a different companion went to the local animal rescue league and bought a replacement. He reported that "It cost us $3 but I think it was worth it. She likes this dog better than the other one she had."

Success crowned his faithful service. In March 1943 Jim and his companion brought into the Church five converts in a baptismal service held in the rented Second Baptist Church in Newport. Some forty church members throughout the region attended the event, the Church's first convert baptisms there in several years.

In a private interview afterward, President Reeder told Jim that "I have liked you ever since the first time I saw you when you arrived in the mission field. You have an alert look and sharp eyes. I expect to see you become one of the leading missionaries in the New England Mission." He appointed Jim district president for southern Maine, responsible for other missionaries laboring in that area.

Along with success came a touch of pride. Jim generally was a good speller, but one word eluded him—that of "owe," which he used often and consistently spelled as "ough." Midway through his mission, Jim's mother gingerly corrected him. He shot back a defensive letter, saying "...and mother note how you spell etc. I got it back on you for ough? Or owe?"

Jim's personal views matured. "In this as in all works the line between failure and success is so fine that we scarcely know when we pass it; so fine that we are often on the line and do not know it," he wrote. "A little more persistence, a little more effort, and what seemed hopeless failure may turn to glorious success." Jim wrote to his parents that "Self-reliance is my aim, but the most lonesome one is he who cannot call upon the Lord in prayer."

Given the exigencies of wartime, Jim was asked to extend his mission beyond the customary two years. He did so, and was released some twenty-six months after being called to New England. In a letter dated August 29, 1944, President Reeder wrote to Jim's bishop back home:

> The excellence of his service prompts us to commend you for sending such a splendid young man into the mission field. Elder Sorenson was humble, prayerful and earnest in his missionary efforts. He made many friends for the Church wherever he labored. He was dignified and circumspect in his conduct so as to reflect credit on our people. We say in all sincerity that Elder Sorenson fulfilled a good mission for which we are very grateful.

Jim and his companions baptized nineteen converts—more than the entire mission had baptized the year before he arrived in New England.

After he returned to California, Jim overheard his mother tell someone that "Jim was the best missionary in his mission." Immediately he corrected her. "No, I was not the best missionary. There were other missionaries more spiritual, more obedient, more diligent. They were the best missionaries. I just baptized more. It was a challenge I enjoyed and I worked hard at it."

"Years later," said Jim, "I came to see that my missionary service was a major turning point in my life. It gave me a chance to solidify my values. I look back on my missionary experience with tremendous thankfulness and satisfaction."

His mission also guided Jim in starting to assemble the building blocks of his life philosophy—a philosophy that would help propel him to phenomenal success as an inventor and entrepreneur. He explained:

> Through my missionary service, I began to see that everything in life is three-dimensional. God made us three dimensionally and we must balance three dimensionally as we live.

> There are many ways to view the three-dimensional nature of life... Prior to my mission, I knew that I needed to "think" about problems and then "do" something about them. I applied that principle in my studies, in working at the cannery and in many other places. But missionary work showed me that a third dimension can add balance to that formula. [It] showed me that if I add "tell" to the equation, I can draw on the strengths of many others to accomplish any goal.

> Think. Then tell. Then do...A successful life is one that is three dimensionally balanced. Life is not an event. It's a journey. And the key to making things work is maintaining that balance as you are moving along. That's what makes balancing so hard, keeping it up while everything is moving and changing inside you and in the environment all around you...[6]

"I returned from New England," he wrote, "to begin my life as an adult with a new sense of what it takes to remain three-dimensionally balanced amid change."

### CHAPTER NINE

# WHIRLWIND COURTSHIP

War still raged in Europe and Asia as Jim returned home from his mission in the summer of 1944. But the tide was turning.

On D-Day, June 6, Allied forces under General Dwight Eisenhower stormed across the English Channel to the beaches of Normandy, France, in history's largest military invasion. In the Pacific, B-29 Superfortresses were pounding Japan, and in October the U.S. Pacific Fleet crushed Japan's navy in the Battle for Leyte Gulf.

Germany and Japan, however, were far from finished. Adolph Hitler was preparing a counter offensive in the Ardennes Forest, a last-stand on-slaught to break the tightening Allied vice. The attack would become known as the Battle of the Bulge. On the other side of the world, Japanese generals were forcing U.S. troops to retake Pacific islands one by one at great cost.

Jim's draft board, still smarting from his decision to serve a mission, was waiting with open arms when he returned home to Lincoln. Opting for some control over his destiny, he quickly enlisted in the Maritime Service before the board could act.

The Maritime Service, or Merchant Marine, is the fleet of ships that carries imports and exports in peacetime and becomes a military arm in wartime. In 1938, with war on the horizon, President Roosevelt created the Maritime Service as a naval auxiliary, prepared to deliver the men and materiel that would carry war to the enemy throughout the world. From seven to fifteen tons of supplies were needed to support one soldier for a year, and the Normandy invasion alone would involve almost 3 million men and 16 million tons of supplies.

Merchant ships were lightly armed and usually not provided escorts or air cover. One result was the highest casualty rate in the armed services. One in 32 mariners was killed in the war, compared to one in 34 serving in the marines, one in 48 in the army, and one in 114 in the navy.

President Roosevelt called the Merchant Marine's effort "the biggest, the most difficult and dangerous job ever undertaken." General Eisenhower said "When final victory is ours there is no organization that will share its credit more deservedly than the Merchant Marine."

At the outset of war, the Merchant Marine numbered fifty-five thousand. The U.S. launched a massive recruiting effort, multiplying that number five fold. In the process it cast normal military standards to the wind. Recruits ranged from seventy-six-year-old James A. Logan who served as cook on the SS *Joshua Hendy*, to boys as young as sixteen. There were even recruits with one leg, one eye, or heart problems.

In the fall of 1944 Jim Sorenson was thrown into this chaotic cauldron. Eight maritime training centers were established across the U.S., and Jim was sent for basic training at Avalon, located on Catalina Island off the California coast. He had fallen from mission heaven and landed in boot camp hell.

Recruits began training within twenty-four hours of arrival, supervised by an "indoctrination officer." Jim was assigned to a barracks and began physical training on an obstacle course. The men learned emergency procedures including how to swim under burning oil and survive a poison gas attack. After orientation, trainees began four weeks of instruction in twenty subjects, mostly seamanship, that were taught in eight-hour classes, five days a week.

"Boot camp was a shock, especially right after my mission," Jim recalled. "The worst thing was the swearing and the stinking bodies, the low level of human thought, and the snoring. I couldn't believe what came out of people's mouths, or that they could smell that bad. I had been exposed to rough language in Yuba City, but never that rough. I had never even heard my dad swear."

Jim vowed to do something about it. Three thousand new trainees arrived at Avalon every two weeks and about thirty—one in a hundred—were selected for Officers Candidate School (OCS). Jim desperately wanted to be among the thirty. Encouraging him was another Avalon trainee and soul mate, Joe Henroid, also a former Mormon missionary. Henroid had just been selected for OCS in New York. Jim passed the written exam used to screen applicants and was then subjected to a series of oral interviews, including a last, brutal one that tested his composure to the limit.

"So you're a Mormon," began the psychiatrist, blowing a cloud of cigarette smoke Jim's way. "Do you believe all that crap about Joseph Smith and all those gold plates and all that polygamy junk? How can you be normal and believe in that fraud?"

Taking a deep breath, Jim answered calmly. "Well, you find me something better and I'll be glad to carefully consider and discuss the merits of it with you."

Failing to rattle Jim, the interrogator got vulgar, asking him leeringly about his sexual history. By now Jim's pulse was beating wildly. "I wanted to tear him apart." But he stayed calm. Finally the interviewer visibly relaxed and sat back in his chair.

"I've sent a lot of you good young Mormon missionaries to OCS," he said. "I'm recommending you too, so don't disappoint me. I want you to graduate and not waste the taxpayers' money."

Jim survived boot camp and was on his way to becoming a commissioned officer.

He was assigned to the U.S. Maritime Training Station at Sheepshead Bay, New York. Jim would be part of the Hospital Corps School, training to become a purser pharmacist, to handle records and dispense medication aboard ship.

The coast-to-coast trip by rail was exhilarating but vaguely disquieting. "The trip gave me my first glimpse of something that both troubled and motivated me for many years to come," he reflected. "I was sent to New York first class. The train went from Los Angeles to New York and I had a Pullman sleeper berth that was made up with fresh white sheets every day. I had three fine meals a day and excellent service in a dining car with napkins and flowers. It was so new to me, all of a sudden being on a train and enjoying these accommodations.

"I compared it to the train ride to boot camp a few months earlier in which I was packed into a crowded car with no air conditioning and lots of foul-mouthed, stinking recruits. The difference disturbed me. I was the same guy who was in boot camp one week before where we were treated like cattle. Suddenly, overnight, I was treated very differently." [1]

Sheepshead Bay was a seventy-five-acre training center on the eastern tip of Brooklyn. It graduated its first OCS class two years earlier. The center was a city within a city, with ten thousand trainees at a time and an annual output of about thirty-five thousand men. The basic regimen was similar to the one at Avalon, plus advanced, specialized courses for officers.

Of particular interest to Jim and other athletes were the physical training facilities. During warm months the men trained on an outdoor obstacle course, 560 yards long—nearly the length of six football fields—with thirty-eight obstacles including log piles, hurdles, cargo nets, smooth and knotted lines, and a fifteen-foot wall. Training during winter months was in Bowditch Hall, with pommel horses, vault boxes, parallel bars, lines, and ladders.

Naval Reserve Captain John L. Beebe was base superintendent. "This is Sheepshead Bay," he wrote in a cheery greeting to new arrivals. The center's wartime record, he said, "is one that the nation may view with pride. It is well to remember too that the men who have trained and will train at this and other Maritime Service stations are among the heroes of the war... thousands have come, learned and shipped from this station to action on the seven seas."

Jim's fellow Mormon and Avalon escapee, Joe Henroid, met him at Grand Central Station in New York City. "Let's go get your clothes pressed. I've got a double date for us tonight and yours is a beautiful blonde," said Henroid, who was handsome and had a little black book filled with telephone numbers and biographical information on virtually every eligible LDS woman in Manhattan. In the following months, between classes at Officers Candidate School, the two young men drank in the New York social scene, with a procession of young women on their arms.

Beverley Taylor, 21, also was in New York. She and a friend of her sister Helen's named Lois Lisez traveled there by rail in July 1945—after the end of the war in Europe and days before Japan's surrender in the Pacific. Beverley's aim? A new, yet-to-be-defined adventure in the Big Apple—which loomed large in her family's imagination, sparked by Helen's rapturous descriptions of the city where she was making a name for herself as a pianist and composer.

There was much to do in the wake of history's most destructive war, but after years of crisis most of the world breathed easier. New York was a teeming mass of humanity as servicemen and women returned from war across the globe. Refugees who fled their homelands helped make the city a veritable Babel of tongues and customs. For many newcomers, housing was almost impossible to find, and inconveniences of all sort were the order of the day.

Still, the iconic picture that would outlast all others was a joyous one: a sailor planting a passionate kiss on a nurse in Times Square, celebrating Japan's surrender. Beverley was in the city right at that time and, indeed, may have been in Times Square the very moment of The Kiss.

Beverley was more fortunate than most of those crowding into New York. Another friend of Helen's named Elsie Cook was looking for a flatmate. Beverley moved into the apartment at 380 Riverside Drive, a highrise overlooking the Hudson River, and Helen's piano was moved into her room. For nearly three months Helen herself had been at the Taylor family's home out in Utah, where she was uncharacteristically quiet and ill with some type of stomach disorder.

In October Helen returned to New York, feeling better, and moved in with Beverley. One afternoon Beverley returned to their apartment as Helen was penning a long letter.

"Who are you writing to?" asked Beverley.

Helen took a deep breath. She answered that she was writing their parents to break some news: In June she secretly married Grant Johannesen, their fellow Utahn who was rising fast as a concert pianist. They met and fell in love at the Julliard School. Why she had not told her family was unclear, although she knew her parents had another young man in mind for her. When this news arrived they were indeed crushed. Helen's "stomach flu" was in fact morning sickness. Months later she would return to Utah to have the baby boy, David.

Prospects for her own future pleased Beverley. She was hired as an assistant kindergarten teacher at a private Quaker academy called the Brooklyn Friends School, and was taking piano lessons from a good instructor. Beverley also felt anchored by worshipping and taking part in social activities at the LDS Manhattan Ward.

Jim also attended church services at the ward. In a Sunday School class late that fall, wearing his Navy bellbottoms, he stood out for two things in Beverley's memory: his "great mountain of curly hair" topped by a sailor hat, and strong opinions. "He was very thin and young-looking," she added "He was really verbal and didn't mind making his opinions known. I got the impression he was a bit of a maverick."

Beverley danced in a talent show sponsored by the ward. In the audience was Jim, spellbound. "Her silhouette immediately caught my eye," he wrote. "She was beautiful and she danced beautifully. She was extremely well put together." Afterward Joe Henroid introduced the two and a warm friendship followed. "Beverley and I soon began to discover what we had in common," said Jim. "She also had a quality that might be called 'drive.'"

Early in December, now wearing an officer's uniform, Jim saw Beverley at church and asked to escort her home. She accepted. They rode the subway to her apartment near Columbia University. Jim led Beverley through nearby shops, stopping to buy what she considered "weird" foods, including head-cheese—jellied loaf made from edible parts of a pig or calf head. "He was adventurous and exciting," she recalled. "I felt like I'd always known him, like he was someone who could have been my brother."

Beverley, Helen, and several strangers rented separate rooms in a large apartment, sharing the kitchen and bath. Jim accompanied Beverley there for some pleasant chitchat. Preparing to leave, he tried to kiss her. She resisted.

"Aren't you going to let me kiss you goodnight?" Jim asked.

"No, never on the first date."

Jim was insulted. "He was a moving force, and he was used to getting his way," said Beverley. "That first evening was typical; he gets right to the point." They parted amiably, both intrigued.

On their third date Jim asked Beverley to marry him. "I can't marry you," answered Bev. "I don't know you well enough." But he landed his first kiss that evening. He was very direct, telling Bev that "I don't have time to romance you. I have to leave soon, and I don't have time for some girly romance."[2]

Beverley helped organize the ward Christmas party, and Jim assisted. As she carefully made finger sandwiches, one by one in her kitchen, he set up an assembly line and quickly mass produced the rest of them. Then it was on to the Christmas tree. Beverley artfully placed silvery icicles on it. Jim took a large handful and threw them on the tree in clumps. "He didn't want to be decorating; he wanted to have me in his arms!"

Her apartment was a refuge for Jim, away from quarters at Sheepshead Bay, where he was a group leader handling discipline problems as well as his own training. He still tired easily and often took the subway across town to Beverley's place to nap.

On December 29, 1945, Jim was commissioned an officer in the Maritime Service, with the rank of Pharmacist's Mate Third Class. "Again I found it interesting that when I was in my Navy bellbottoms, people generally ignored me. I was just another in a sea of sailors. Then one day I got my officer's commission and uniform and I was in gold braid. What a difference when I walked down the street or went to the USO."

Jim believed Beverley was among those who didn't take him seriously until he was in gold braid. She insisted otherwise. "He made an impression the first time I saw him."


Jim explained that "I had been raised in the Church and was looking for certain qualities in the person who would be my wife and partner. When I was young I went with a lot of beautiful girls. But there were many I wouldn't have married. As I matured, I began to look for certain qualities I sought in the person I was going to have children with and spend my life with. And Beverley had those qualities. I saw her holding a baby one time and it made such an impression on me. The way she held that child told me there was something special about her."

Jim waved all kinds of red flags. He was possessive and extremely jealous, even of Bev's memory of her first love, Lloyd Rumph.

(Later, after they were married, Jim found a bundle of old photographs and letters from Rumph among Bev's possessions. He was furious and left their apartment until the next day. Jim returned, without explanation, saying "Let's just you and I get along." Bev said "Jim was never very good at apologizing...He would just explode, chew me out and tell me everything I was doing wrong, and then wonder why I was upset.")

Jim hurt people's feelings with small cruelties—he mocked Beverley's roommate Elsie, who had a lovely singing voice, for "singing out the side of her mouth"—and occasional bursts of anger. His moods changed in an instant, with no forewarning.

Another trait was essential to numerous future triumphs: Jim quickly assessed and found flaws in any system or design, and figured out ways to improve it. The problem came when he turned a critical eye on fellow humans, insulting them needlessly.

Jim made Beverley's family nervous, especially her sister Helen, who considered him too strong-minded. But Beverley saw deeper She admired his fearlessness. "Jim was like a force, like what I was supposed to do. I knew if I married him he would be difficult to live with. I also knew he would make things happen—big, world-shaking things."

Their whirlwind courtship was interrupted when an epidemic of scarlet fever swept Sheepshead Bay. Many mariners were struck down, including Jim who had a temperature of 104 and skin rated at four-plus flush—as red as you can get. Penicillin, a new wonder drug being mass produced to cure a wide range of diseases, was being tested on the sick sailors, along with gamma globulin. One mariner in sick bay would get penicillin, the next gamma globulin, the next a combination of the two, and the next man neither of the medications.

"Fortunately, I got both penicillin and gamma globulin," said Jim, "but the sailor next to me got neither. He didn't even look red. He was young, probably eighteen or nineteen. Instead of taking care of himself, he ran around looking out the windows at the ice and snow. Not me, I dove under the covers, took my shots, and enjoyed the rest. Within five days, that young sailor was dead."

Jim saw the difference medicine can make, further stoking his desire to become a doctor. He was enervated by the scarlet fever but "ate like a horse." Within ten days he gained four pounds and was cured. Doctors warned him to take it easy over the following weekend. Instead, not having seen Beverley since going into quarantine, he hopped the subway to her apartment and they went swimming at the YMCA. "I thought at the time it was pretty dangerous because of possible after effects," she said, "but Jim had a way of knowing when he could take risks and come out okay."

In February 1946 Jim completed OCS and was transferred for medical training to the U.S. Marine Hospital in San Francisco. As he was about to leave, Beverley told him she would marry him that summer. They sent her parents a telegram, asking them to meet Jim at the rail station in Salt Lake City when he stopped there on his way to San Francisco. However, they inadvertently said he'd arrive at 9 p.m. instead of the correct time of 9 a.m.

When his train pulled in to Salt Lake, no one was there to meet him, so Jim found his way to their home at 2020 Lake Street. His future mother-in-law answered the door, hair in curlers. "You can't be here! The telegram said 9 p.m.," sputtered Bessie Taylor, who made a quick exit up the stairs to remove the curlers and retrieve the incriminating telegram.

Jim stayed overnight with the Taylors, laughing and playing board games, and went on to San Francisco the next day. He served a pharmacy internship at the hospital, giving shots and dispensing medication to men wounded in the war. By April he finished his internship and was promoted to Junior Assistant Purser-Pharmacist Mate, now qualified, said a certificate, "to serve as a staff officer on vessels of the U.S. Merchant Marine."

Jim was assigned to teach first aid at an officers' training school across the bay in Alameda, ninety miles from Lincoln. His family was thrilled that Jim was close enough to visit easily. The proximity gave him a chance to get better acquainted with his four young sisters who were like an entirely new family for his parents. The newest was 1-year-old Joy. The others were Emma Jean, 8; Lois Marie, 9; and Carol, 11—a beautiful girl with long golden hair and a perpetual smile.

Beverley stayed in New York until May when her year of teaching was complete, then returned home to Salt Lake. In June Jim took a two-day leave and joined her there, bringing an engagement ring.

They attended an "endowment" session in the Salt Lake Temple, Beverley going through for the first time. In such sessions Mormons make their most sacred promises to the Lord regarding the conduct of their lives— during the first session for themselves and, in subsequent sessions, vicariously for their deceased ancestors or others. Mormons believe that those for whom the temple work is done have the choice on the other side of the veil to accept or reject the ordinances.

The next exciting days were filled with visiting friends and making wedding plans, and the evenings with dancing at Saltair, a dance hall on the Great Salt Lake, and Pinecrest. Jim and Beverley also drove to Rexburg, Idaho to see his mother's family, the Blasers, staying overnight with Emma's brother, Ernest. Jim returned to California and Beverley to Utah to prepare for the wedding.

Days later a telegram from California arrived at the Taylors'. Beverley eagerly tore it open, certain it was about the wedding. Instead it bore tragedy. Carol, Jim's little sister, was hit and killed by a car. Details would come later: Carol was walking to a movie theater with Lois and Emma Jean when struck down. The Sorensons were loved in Lincoln, and the entire town shared their grief. In a rare gesture, Lincoln's stores and banks closed for the funeral.

Beverley telephoned Jim to suggest they postpone the wedding, just three weeks away. Jim got angry, saying "I don't have time to grieve," and that he needed to get on with his life. He believed the best thing for his parents and himself would be to occupy their time with wedding preparations; Beverley later agreed that that seemed to be the case.

The Salt Lake Temple was temporarily closed for renovations, so the wedding took place ninety miles north at the Logan Temple. That edifice had special significance for the Taylors. Beverley's great-grandfather, John Taylor, dedicated it on May 17, 1884. Two of President Taylor's sons and their sweethearts were in the congregation that day, including Frank Y. Taylor and his fiancée Elizabeth Stewart Campbell.

President Taylor, apparently on the spot, asked the two young couples if they would like him to perform their marriages immediately. They agreed; thus Frank and Elizabeth—Beverley's grandparents—were the first couple to be married in the Logan Temple.

On July 23, 1946, Jim and Beverley followed in those footsteps. Both of their families gathered as the handsome young couple, dressed all in white and kneeling across a sacred altar, repeated their wedding vows in a ceremony intended to "seal" them and their righteous posterity together for eternity. Conducting the wedding was temple president El Ray L. Christiansen.

Then it was back to Salt Lake for a wedding breakfast at the home of Beverley's uncle, Staynor Richards. As guests mulled around, Uncle Staynor took Jim aside and grilled him on how he intended to support Beverley, reminding Jim that she had grown up in relative affluence.

Her parents hosted a wedding reception at their home that evening, the *Salt Lake Tribune* reporting that "the bride wore a gown of white jersey with rounded neck and capped sleeves. Her draped finger-tip-length veil was caught to flower clusters to each side of her head. She carried a white bouquet..."[3]

Rice rained down on the newlyweds as they left the Taylor residence. And then the chase was on—literally. In an old tradition, Beverley's brother Bob and several friends piled into a car and were right behind, intent on disrupting first-night wedding plans as Jim and Beverley were chauffeured away toward a secret destination.

At the wheel of Jim's dad's Chevrolet was an experienced race-car driver, Willard Smith, Jim's brother-in-law and best man at the wedding. Next to him was Jim's sister Eileen, egging on her husband as they roared through the valley, trying to shake Robert and his friends. "We must have been going ninety miles an hour," recalled Beverley. "I was scared to death and screaming to stop, but we kept careening through back streets."

Willard lurched into a yard, breaking a water spigot which shot a stream of water into the night air. A man rushed out of his house with a shotgun. "Stop or I'll shoot!" Eileen, neither cowed nor at a loss for words, jumped out of the car, turned off the faucet, and yelled back, musically, "Oh mister—you forgot and left your water on! I'll just turn it off for ya!"

She jumped back in and they sped away. The chase unnerved Beverley, now in hysterics. Willard stopped the car and asked Bob to go home. He complied, and Willard and Eileen delivered the newlyweds to their hotel. The next day they headed for California, in the Chevrolet and with $60, both borrowed from Jim's father.

It was a harbinger of a half-century of wild rides to come. As Beverley predicted, Jim would make things happen. And Uncle Staynor needn't have worried.

### CHAPTER TEN

# UPJOHN

The newlyweds returned to the Bay area via Donner Lake, where a business associate of Jim's father offered his "rustic" cabin for a brief honeymoon. They drove 500 miles non-stop in Jim's father's dilapidated 1940 Chevy, arriving at dawn

The cabin, it turned out, had not been used in months. Mice scampered across the floor and it was filled with cobwebs, grime, and a thick blanket of dust. Jim and Beverley nonetheless were exhausted. With no other option, they fell onto a dirty mattress and were soon asleep. The next day they drove to Lincoln, where Beverley began to get better acquainted with her in-laws.

As a married officer, Jim could live off base. They rented a room on the third floor of a small house. Their room had a hot plate but no running water or bathroom. Those luxuries were shared with the second-floor renters. "When we'd take a bath, we had to repeatedly turn the hot water on and off so the tank wouldn't explode," recalled Beverley. Occasionally Jim's mother gave or sent them relief packages of bacon, butter, and other items still being rationed.

Beverley took a job as a secretary, and on weekends they went to Lincoln to be with his family. Without a car initially, they sometimes hitchhiked the ninety miles, Beverley staying in the shadows as Jim thumbed down a passing car, then both hopping in for a free ride.

Millions of servicemen were being demobilized, but as a latecomer to the military, Jim was still on active duty. He was assigned to the U.S. Public Health Service at a base facility in Alameda, assisting a medical doctor who was about to have a life-altering influence on his future. He was Sigfried Zoffer, an ambitious young Jewish doctor from the Bronx, New York.

Restless to practice his craft, Zoffer busied himself circumcising the sailors. Jim had the unenviable job of inspecting and choosing the reluctant servicemen to be circumcised. He also worked in sick bay, dispensing drugs.

One day a salesman from Abbott Laboratories, a leading pharmaceutical firm, came by, raving to Jim and Zoffer about vitamin supplements, then on the frontier of medicine. Abbott was a broad-based medical company and one of five firms enlisted by the U.S. government to mass-produce the antibiotic penicillin. The salesman left a bundle of literature explaining how vitamins work, including a brochure on the "Krebs cycle." It describes the complex series of chemical reactions that occur within a cell and break down food molecules to produce energy.

Jim, fascinated, devoured the brochure. Casually he mentioned to Zoffer that he planned to attend medical school on the GI Bill after his impending discharge from the Merchant Marine. "Sorenson, you don't want to be a doctor," said Zoffer emphatically. "Pharmaceutical salesmen make more and have a better life than doctors do. Look at this Abbott man. He has a brand new car. I can't even afford one."

Zoffer added that "The Upjohn Company's regional headquarters is right where we get off the bus in San Francisco at 199 First Street. We're going in there and you are going to interview for a job. You can work there until you go to medical school if you'd like, but don't tell them that's your plan." Days later, Lieutenant Zoffer and Ensign Sorenson walked in the front office of Upjohn. "For me, it was mostly a lark," said Jim. "I really wasn't interested in pharmacy."

Manager Richard Sellman greeted them. "I'd like to apply for a job," said Jim. Sellman was  recently discharged as a naval lieutenant commander and ran Upjohn's operations in eleven western states. He was a wealthy son of one of Upjohn's founders. Eyeing the familiar uniform, he immediately took a liking to Jim. After a few perfunctory questions, he wanted to hire Jim on the spot.

But another supervisor, Deb Young, a balding older man, started asking tougher questions, recalled Jim. "Do you have a degree in pharmacy?"

"No."

"Do you have any four-year degree?"

"No."

Young was extremely dubious. But Sellman persisted. As a military recruiting officer he had spent time in Salt Lake City, married a former reporter for the *Salt Lake Tribune*, and knew about Mormons.

"How did you do as a Mormon missionary?" asked Sellman..

"Oh, fine," said Jim.

"Did you make any converts?"

"Yes, quite a few."[1]

Sellman turned to Young. "Did you hear that, Deb? If he can sell that, he can sell almost anything!" Young dug in his heels, arguing that all their salesmen were pharmacists. But maybe they don't all need to be, said Sellman, who told Young to find out what Jim knew about pharmaceuticals.

The older man obviously relished the chance to trip up Jim. They moved to Young's small office, where he stood behind his desk. Turning randomly to a page in a book, he asked Jim what he knew about vitamins. "What about this Krebs cycle?" German-born British physician Hans Krebs recently discovered the process, and in 1953 would win the Nobel Prize for that and other work.

The Abbott company brochure still fresh in mind, Jim deadpanned, "Well, this looks like the slow oxidation and reduction whereby energy is released from the glucose molecule, probably at the pyruvate stage."

Young was stunned. Apparently he didn't understand the Krebs cycle himself. After a few minutes, Young closed the book and they returned to Sellman's office. "Dick, this guy is absolutely academically qualified," reported Young. "I don't know what his real background is, but he can handle being a vitamin salesman." That's all Sellman needed. Jim was hired, effective upon his release from active duty a few weeks later.

An alternative course threatened—that Jim would be assigned to a ship and sent to sea for a lengthy tour. He did not relish that prospect, especially since he and Beverley were expecting their first child. To eliminate the possibility, Jim gained access to his personnel file and "lost" it. Without that record the Maritime Service did not know what to do with him. Finally they simply issued Jim an honorable release, dated November 25, 1946, less than two years after he enlisted.

Jim dove into his civilian job with gusto. Upjohn was founded in 1886 in Kalamazoo, Michigan, by William E. Upjohn, inventor of the "friable pill"—the first dissolvable pill. During the sixty years since then it became one of the nation's most respected pharmaceutical houses. Upjohn's contribution to the recent war effort was substantial.

It produced, for example, nearly half of the U.S. Army's sterilized sulfanilamide powder, used to dust medication on open wounds. In 1944 Upjohn received the Army-Navy Production Award for "high achievement" in making materiel for the military.

Upjohn was led by a forward-thinking chief executive as it prepared for the postwar world. Donald Gilmore was a son-in-law of the founder and, since 1943, Upjohn's president and general manager. Like Jim, Gilmore was not formally trained in medicine, technology, or the nuts and bolts of production. But, writes an Upjohn historian, since joining the company in 1930, the thin, shy businessman "had put himself through a vigorous self-training, learning not only the technical details but learning to gauge the men who made things work at Upjohn."

As Jim joined Upjohn on the West Coast, an enormous steel skeleton of the company's new factory—Don Gilmore's brainchild—was rising in a cornfield outside Kalamazoo. It would replace fifteen old wooden buildings downtown with a state-of-the-art manufacturing plant—thirty-three acres under one roof.

Medicines had been made in a vertical process. Raw materials were taken to the top of a building, mixed and shaped into product form on lower floors, then packaged and shipped out at the bottom. The new one-story plant would enable Upjohn for the first time to accomplish everything more efficiently in one continuous motion.

A new era in medicine was at hand, and Upjohn was in its forefront. Earlier research led to antibiotics, sulfas, endocrine hormones, and the start of drug synthesis. No one could predict all that the new era would bring, but for those involved in pharmaceuticals, the times were heady and the opportunity exciting.

Upjohn's sights were set on becoming a worldwide institution, and it needed a fresh infusion of bright, equally ambitious salesmen. While Upjohn's employee ranks grew during the war from 2,164 in 1942 to 2,668 in 1946, technical personnel accounted for most of the increase, while the sales force decreased by 136 men.

Between Jim and opportunity, however, lay intensive study. Deb Young's initial hunch was right, Jim's practical experience in the Merchant Marine did little to prepare him for the cutting edge of pharmaceuticals. Upjohn instructors at first were dismayed by his lack of knowledge. Through a crack in a door, Jim overheard an exasperated Young say to Sellman, "Sorenson doesn't know anything. His knowledge about pharmaceuticals is zero."

"Is he learning?" asked Sellman.[2]

"Yes, he seems to learn fast," answered Young.

"All right then, don't quit; keep teaching him."

Sellman also fended off Young and the instructors by arguing that Jim "has other natural talent," and, besides, "I like his smile." Jim soaked up the arcane and fast-changing world of pharmaceuticals like a sponge, greatly shortening the usual learning curve. As their gamble on him began paying off, Sellman and Young hired another non-pharmacist salesman a few weeks later—Larry Hoff, a new business graduate of Stanford University. That gamble paid off as well. Decades later, Hoff became president of Upjohn.

After a few weeks of training in San Francisco, Sellman offered Jim the sales territory in Santa Cruz or Sacramento, California, or Salt Lake City. Immediately he chose Sacramento because "it was full of opportunities. It was considered a much richer territory, a faster growing area, and closer to home—my home." Jim returned to their apartment in Alameda and told Beverley the good news. She burst out crying. "I was both homesick and really ill with morning sickness," she recalled. "I had lost about fifteen pounds, and had fainted a couple of times. I would have given anything to return to Salt Lake City."

The next day Jim phoned Sellman to see if the Salt Lake territory was still available. Sellman, also married to a former Utahn, laughed. "You've talked to your wife, right?" Jim said yes. "Well," said Sellman, "I'd rather have you in Salt Lake anyway. I don't know when another Mormon may come in here."

Beverley's insistence probably was pivotal to their future. If they had gone to Sacramento, she believed, Jim inevitably would have become involved in his father's businesses while selling Upjohn products. Given Jim's need to lead, that could have been difficult on the father-son relationship. In addition, such a diversion may have kept Jim from the land-purchase and development opportunities he found in Utah, which provided the financial foundation for a series of world-class businesses created over the next half-century.

Just before Christmas Jim and Beverley loaded their belongings in the ailing '40 Chevy they bought from Jim's dad. Pulling a one-wheeled Sears trailer, they headed for Utah, 700 miles away. Jim was sound asleep late at night with Beverley at the wheel as their car bumped and rattled across the Great Basin Desert.

"I was so anxious to get home that I wasn't watching the speed," she recalled. Jim woke with a start, saw that they were going seventy-five miles an hour, reached over, and turned off the ignition key. The car rolled slowly to a stop. Jim sleepily chided her, and they were back on their way.

"What I remember most about entering the Salt Lake Valley in 1946 is simply the Christmas lights," said Jim. "I had never seen such a profusion of Christmas lights in my life. Little did I know I'd be seeing those lights every year for decades to come...I had no idea that we were moving to Utah permanently." Upjohn, like most large national companies, moved its people from place to place, and Jim assumed they would fall into that pattern.

Utah had changed considerably since Jim first visited the state three decades earlier. From the arrival of the Mormon pioneers in 1847 until the First World War, Utah largely succeeded in isolating itself culturally and economically from the American mainstream. That changed forever as three global cataclysms—the two world wars and the Great Depression—threw Utah's destiny to the same fate as the rest of the nation.

The federal government, which owned two-thirds of Utah's land mass, now had far greater say in state affairs. Utah's isolation came at a price: Utahns suffered more from the Depression than residents of most states, and personal income lagged the national average. On the eve of World War II, Utah still struggled to loosen the Depression's stranglehold.

Political and church leaders saw the gathering storm as a potential way out of the region's economic slumber, as well as a way to demonstrate again the state's patriotism after a history of confrontation with Washington. They encouraged strong support for war efforts. In June 1941, prior to the attack on Pearl Harbor, about 7,000 Utahns were in military service. In June 1945 the number swelled to some 60,000—one of the highest ratios per capita in the country.

On the economic front, writes a historian, "World War II induced a more extensive alteration in the economic activity of Utah than any other event in her entire history."

Utah's relative security from possible foreign attack, and its equidistance to key ports on the West Coast, made it ideal as a military bastion. Among important developments: Fort Douglas became headquarters of army operations for the Rocky Mountain and Pacific Coast states; Hill Field, near Ogden, repaired and maintained aircraft, becoming one of Utah's largest employers; aircraft thundered out of Wendover Air Force Base, unloading on bombing and gunnery ranges in the western desert. Alumni included the crew of the Enola Gay, which dropped the first atomic bomb, on Hiroshima, Japan.

To assure a safe supply of steel, the nation's most modern plant, U.S. Steel's Geneva Works, was constructed in Utah County with $200 million in federal funds—to that time a record federal investment in an industrial plant. Nationally the U.S. Government spent $188 per capita for new plants during the war. In Utah the figure was $534. Defense spending created nearly 50,000 new jobs in the state by 1944, and was critical in pulling Utah out of the Depression. Tens of thousands of outsiders flocked to the state to construct facilities, train for combat, and supply services and materiel to the defense establishment.

The Beehive State, in short, percolated with opportunity for the ambitious young couple who arrived in time to celebrate the year-end holidays with Bev's family in 1946.

Upjohn had three other representatives in Utah, two salesmen and a supervisor. The company paid Jim $275 a month plus expenses for travel and miscellaneous items, and furnished him a car. After turning in his first weekly expense account—all of $4.67—he got a heated call from his supervisor. "You're not dry behind the ears yet young man," he was told. "You've got to change this report or you're going to spoil it for all of us." Genuinely puzzled—even concerned that he was extravagant in buying gas and a couple of Cokes—Jim asked what was wrong.

"You really don't understand, do you?" his boss said brusquely. "What do you make me look like when I write an expense account for fifty dollars a week and yours is only four sixty-seven?"

"Okay," said Jim, "how am I supposed to do it?"

His boss explained the art of creative padding. "From now on, don't think of this as an expense account. You think of it as a 'fudge' sheet. You put down this and this and this. Don't you ever buy whiskey?"

"No, am I supposed to?"

"Sure, you idiot! You can't sell to Dr. Jones without buying him a fifth every so often. But don't put down just any cheap whiskey. Put down something like Cutty Sark Scotch. You've got to make your expense report intelligent."

Jim asked for an example of an "intelligent" expense report and began submitting them as instructed, in the weekly range of $30 to $40—a huge amount to him. It paid for groceries, clothes, and other necessities, leaving his salary to buy furniture and other capital goods to set up a household. The largesse did not change Jim's careful spending habits; he salted away every spare dime.

His frugality put Jim crosswise with the corporate culture in additional ways. While other Upjohn representatives flew to monthly sales conventions in San Francisco, Jim took the overnight bus, buying two pillows at a quarter apiece for sleeping, and pocketing the money not spent on plane fare and lodging. He paid $32 for the round-trip, less than half the $88 typically paid by his Utah colleagues for plane fare alone.

Jim was the butt of jokes and name-calling—"cheapskate" among others—but he remained quietly determined. He also was one of the few salesmen who didn't drink or smoke, further distancing him from most of his colleagues.

Many years later Jim was asked if he felt dishonest in padding his expense accounts.

"Yes, I felt dishonest from a government-accounting point of view," said Jim, "after all, this was tax-free money. But my boss said you do it or else; you're making me look bad. Then I was called a cheapskate. I don't know how to evaluate dishonesty."[3]

If Jim's idiosyncrasies set him apart, they were largely overlooked because of his obvious intelligence, uncanny sales ability, and consistent production. He focused on the best new products with laser-like intensity. One such pharmaceutical was called cyclogesterin, hormonally balanced and ingested by women to help them get pregnant. Sensing a winner in baby-happy Utah, he gathered a mound of technical information, holed up for days, and memorized it. With cyclogesterin down cold, Jim proceeded expertly to pitch it to doctors across the state, becoming Upjohn's top salesman of that product.

In March 1947 Jim joined twenty other rookie salesmen for an intensive two-week training seminar in Kalamazoo. He was the only attendee without a bachelor's degree in pharmacy, yet, in a test given at the end of the session, scored the highest grade in the class. A photo taken on the granite steps outside company headquarters shows the rookie class, all standing stiffly in pale shirts and buttoned-up suits.

It was a gingerbread-men pose that belied the fact that one of them—the guy in the third row with the familiar grin and heap of hair—would break out of the mold and create his own business empire. One day he'd return to those same steps to discuss joint ventures with Upjohn, not as an employee but as an equal.

With Upjohn, Jim again proved to be a natural-born salesman—energetic, resourceful, glib, and gutsy. It seemed he could charm his way through almost any doorway; he had a keen sense of how hard to push and when to back off—though backing off was never his style.

On April 26, 1947 Beverley and Jim's first child was born—nine months and three days after their wedding. They named her Carol, after Jim's beloved late sister. Beverley became dangerously ill during the pregnancy, dropping in weight to ninety pounds. She remained in the hospital five days, shaking so hard she could not even hold a glass of water.

Once at home, her mother Bessie came and stayed for a week to help out—a great comfort to Bev. Jim, however, put a large damper on Bessie's stay by clashing loudly with her. "He didn't like to have anybody else in the house," explained Bev. When their next child was born, Beverley suffered a lot of postpartum pain but "wanted to spare her mother the denigration Jim had heaped upon Bessie during her last visit" and instead hired a girl to assist.[4]

Where others saw roadblocks, Jim saw irresistible challenges. He had an internal compass that separated arbitrary rules written for someone's convenience from rules of genuine importance. The same compass guided him as a boy in Yuba City, trading marbles, hawking magazines, and walking nearby almond groves.

"The wind would blow some of the almonds to the ground, and the orchard owners said it was fine for me to pick up the almonds as long as I didn't shake the trees," he recalled. He could earn fifteen to twenty cents a bucket for them. "I always played fair. I never picked or knocked almonds off the tree—but I did watch for windy days."

As a husband and father the stakes were higher, increasing Jim's penchant for seeing and exploiting opportunity all around him. This time the groves included several large hospitals in Salt Lake Valley and a number of smaller hospitals in the Utah hinterlands. The individual trees were hospital administrators and scores of medical doctors who practiced in those facilities, whose healing touch depended in good part on the array of modern medicines produced by Upjohn and other pharmaceutical houses.

The granddaddy facility was LDS Hospital, a five-story structure in the avenues, the steeply sloping north end of the city. Opened in 1905 as an eighty-bed hospital, by mid-century it boasted five-hundred beds and was the largest medical center between Denver and the West Coast.

Clarence E. Wonnacott, a hotel manager before a recent tour of war duty in the Pacific theater, was tapped by the Church in 1946 to administer the hospital.

Also in 1905, the University of Utah started a Medical Department as a two-and-a-half-year program. It became a full-fledged, four-year medical school in 1942, housed in the county hospital at 21st South and State streets. The hospital was refurbished and renovated into a 250-bed facility.

Jim rose at 6 a.m. on workdays—a habit established in the mission field. Typical salesmen while away long hours in client waiting rooms. Not Jim. As doctors made their morning hospital rounds, he was there to greet them. He kept literature and three-by-five cards in his pocket, filled with notes on the latest medications.

"They enjoyed not being bothered in their offices," he said. "I gave them a reward: Get rid of me now and you won't see me for two months." It worked so well that often before the two months were up, doctors would ask him to come show them the latest medicines.

Doctors and hospital administrators relied on Jim for good reason. Pharmaceuticals were changing at a dizzying pace and no individual practitioner could expect to stay up with them. Half the drugs prescribed in 1953 were unknown ten years earlier, and 90 percent did not exist fifteen years before. Even some drug salesmen—many of whom got their pharmacy degrees before the advent of penicillin—had difficulty keeping up.

With no such degree, Jim used the deficit to his advantage. He had less obsolete information to forget and perhaps more capacity and incentive to master the fresh knowledge pouring out of Upjohn and other laboratories.

Fueling the new medications was a fast, tense research and development race that took off following World War II. The brass rings went to whoever got there first, and Upjohn was determined to grab its share. In May 1950 Upjohn's research team numbered 297; by the end of 1952 it swelled to 421, with director Richard Schreiber, a brilliant organic chemist, announcing that Upjohn research was "the best of any pharmaceutical house in the United States, exclusive of Merck & Company."

Jim had a solid list of doctor-clients and developed a camaraderie with many of them. He found that—contrary to his supervisor's whiskey warning—doctors were motivated by new solutions to patient problems, and required neither fancy lunches nor Cutty Sark to buy from him. Jim always met or exceeded sales goals, receiving a pay raise every three months.

While Jim soon found the value of prospecting in hospitals rather than doctors's offices, it took longer to learn what sales activities were acceptable in those halls of healing, which ones were unacceptable, and which ones might be negotiable. Hospitals routinely erected obstacles to keep unauthorized visitors—especially salesmen—separated from physicians.

Jim became adept at breaching such barriers, flashing that million-dollar smile and winning the collusion of sympathetic personnel such as the Mother Superior at Holy Cross Hospital. On Jim's word that his wares could help cut time and costs for the hospital, she waived the rules and allowed him to set up a twelve-foot display table in an alcove. "First you realize that you have something really good that other people need," Jim explained. "Once you are convinced of that, it gives you courage to do things others may not do."

Jim rarely let a line on a floor or a sign on a door keep him out of an area. Early on he took his visiting sales manager through the maze at one hospital—from one restricted area to another, in and out of several operating rooms. Finally his supervisor threw up his hands: "I've had enough. You go where angels fear to tread!" Jim calculated every step and intuitively knew where and how far he could go without great risk.

On rare occasions when someone in authority actually challenged his presence, Jim relied on humble charm: "Okay...where do you want me to go?"

One day Upjohn's West Coast manager Richard Sellman, who initially hired Jim, came to town. Unlike Jim, he was all spit and polish and would not think of seeing a client without an appointment. Jim was eager to demonstrate his prowess. They went to a doctor's office where he was to explain a new product called calmagen, a multi-vitamin formula to be mixed with milk.

"I had it set up on the doctor's desk in the middle of all his papers," recalled Jim. "Then I accidentally knocked the bottle over and this stuff went everywhere, including in Sellman's lap." Jim was mortified but the doctor was nonplussed. "Tell you what," he said calmly as Jim scrambled for something to sop up the mess, "you clean this all up, and I'll use the product." A lemon became lemonade: When they were alone, Sellman barely mentioned the accident, raving instead about Jim's rapport with the doctor.

Not all doctors warmed to Jim's unorthodox ways, however, and some of the more prominent ones in Salt Lake Valley treated him curtly. "I simply had to plow around them, like a stump in a field," he said. Instead, Jim made common cause with physicians who, like himself, were not afraid to question old ways of doing things. He enjoyed leaving the Wasatch Front—Utah's principal urban corridor—and visiting hospitals in rural areas, where technology often was outdated and his insights and innovative ideas were welcomed. Once a month he made an overnight sales trip to outlying communities.

Jim liked his job—especially the chance to learn something new each day—but still harbored thoughts of going to medical school. He could do so on the GI Bill, he reasoned, as a brother-in-law, Robert Matheson, recently had done. Jim had revered doctors since he was a boy playing chess in Dr. McArthur's parlor, and still had great reverence for the healing arts. However, he came to see individual doctors more objectively.

"When I started calling on them, I thought some of these guys weren't nearly as smart as most people thought they were." He saw the difference between perfunctory medical care and truly concerned care, and vowed that, if given a chance, he would practice the latter.

The contrast between caring and uncaring was starkly brought home to the Sorensons when baby Carol was about six months old. Her temperature shot up alarmingly. A frantic call to a doctor was met with a nonchalance that still angered Beverley a half-century later. "He didn't give me any way to handle it." Carol's temperature climbed to 106.5 degrees and she went into convulsions in Beverley's arms.

They sped to nearby LDS Hospital, where doctors acknowledged the gravity of the baby's condition and took emergency steps to treat it. Early the next morning, Jim and Beverley anxiously went to the hospital.

Peering through the nursery window, they saw that Carol had grabbed the name plate on her crib and twisted it down. "Jim knew she was coming out of it," recalled Beverley. "He was so happy he just stood there and cried."

### CHAPTER ELEVEN

# HIKING GOAT PASTURES

I n January 1947, after spending the holidays with Beverley's family in Salt Lake City, Jim and Bev rented a brand-new three-room basement apartment nearby in the Highland Park area on the upscale east bench.

"For the first time in my life I was ready to put down roots," said Jim. As World War II continued to recede, the city stirred with optimism. It was a good year for milestones and new beginnings. LDS Church membership passed the one-million mark for the first time.

Also arriving in Utah that year was a Swiss-American conductor named Maurice Abravanel, 44, whose lasting contributions to the arts scene were especially applauded by Beverley and the musical Taylor family. Over the next thirty-two years Abravanel molded a community orchestra into the widely respected Utah Symphony Orchestra. Crowning his achievements was construction in 1979 of Abravanel Hall, a splendid home for his beloved orchestra.

Utah was emerging from the backwaters of the nation's economic and cultural activity. It was a dynamic time in the state's history, due in good part to the civilian and uniformed workers drawn to the state to build and operate major defense installations. The state's population swelled from about

550,000 in the 1940 census to 700,000 in 1950—an increase of more than a quarter.

The influx strained housing and other resources, and altered social as well as economic patterns of life. In 1940 one Utah woman in six earned an income—the second lowest ratio in the nation. As their men went off to war, 24,000 Utah women entered the workforce. Many remained after the war, and by 1950 one Utah woman in four was employed outside the home.

The 1950s saw a number of important capital improvement projects in Salt Lake City, including a new airport terminal, construction of the city's first water-treatment plants, upgraded storm sewers, and improved parks and recreational facilities.

Many well-off families were leaving the city proper and relocating to all-American suburbs in the south and east valley, with ranch-style homes, garages, and well-watered lawns. Postwar labor and housing shortages, coupled with the baby boom that followed the war, also led to new inner city developments, including Rose Park in the northwest quadrant.

Rose Park—some streets formed a rose when viewed from the air—was developed by Alan Brockbank, son of a gardener at England's Buckingham Palace. It included shops, parks, and a golf course alongside new tract homes.

About nine months after moving to Utah, Jim and Beverley bought their first home in Rose Park, with a $50 down payment. They paid an extra $150 to have the builder rough in a second story and extra bathroom. It was the nicest house Jim had lived in, with cement curb, gutter, and sidewalk, instead of the dirt streets he grew up on in California.

Their address was 420 North 11th West, two blocks from where Salt Lake County opened the Northwest Multi-Purpose Center to provide recreation and social service programs to a diverse population.

Samuel Clemens aka Mark Twain visited Salt Lake City and wrote about it nearly a century earlier in a celebrated tome called *Roughing It*. One tongue-in-cheek observation: "Salt Lake City was healthy—an extremely healthy city. They declared that there was only one physician in the place and he was arrested every week regularly and held to answer under the vagrant act for having 'no visible means of support.'"[1]

Since Twain's quaint description, however, Salt Lake's crime rate, like other measures of growth, had risen. As in other inner cities, this was especially true of the area near the railroad tracks in the northwest section of Salt Lake, which was a magnet for blue-collar workers and immigrants from many countries. "There were gangs in the area even then," recalled Beverley.

She was in the kitchen one afternoon, with baby Carol on her hip, and had just moved from the refrigerator to the stove. Beverley heard a loud popping noise and then noticed the fridge door was ajar. That evening, returning from work, Jim examined the fridge and was shocked. "That's a bullet hole!" The bullet struck precisely where Beverley was standing with Carol moments before. No suspect was ever found.

The incident no doubt played a part in their later decision to leave the area, but for the moment Jim had opportunity in mind. Stayner Richards, who was married to Beverley's mother's sister, Jane Foote Taylor, was the developer of their neighborhood.

Richards, 61, whose father was Stephen L. Richards, a senior member of the LDS Church's Quorum of the Twelve Apostles, had a number of unsold homes. Jim approached Richards. "What if I were to help you sell your homes?" Richards readily agreed—especially to Jim's proposed commission of $50 a house. Only later did Jim learn that the customary commission was $500 ten times higher. "I sold myself short too soon," noted Jim, "a lesson I would have to learn over and over again."

Jim especially targeted other young salesmen he met on his rounds. He invited them to dinner at his home—already a showcase because of its expanded size—then made a pitch for them to purchase a similar residence from Richards. Quite a few did so, with Jim selling as many as three homes in a single week. The experience convinced him that real estate could be a very profitable business, and whetted his appetite for what would become a lifelong passion.

"I learned from that first experience that the best way to profit from real estate is to own it, not just sell it. And real estate seemed to carry rewards for me that were not just monetary. The rewards were also emotional, because I had never owned any ground. Owning it made me feel more satisfied, more secure."

Jim was ahead of his time. Relatively few other lone individuals were investing in real estate in the valley, leaving the field wide open. Profitable investment required gut-instinct as well as careful planning and cash. His determination was spurred in part by the responsibility of a growing family. In November 1948 their second child, Shauna, a delightfully happy baby, was born.

Jim continued to meet Upjohn's targets, his sales increasing by 15 to 20 percent a year. He did so despite starting early and ending most workdays before noon. With the extra afternoon hours he created other streams of income. Jim got a bonus every few months for productivity, and his expense account exceeded expenses. The extra became capital for investing.

Often Jim went home for lunch or carried one packed by Beverley. While other salesmen were taking clients out for a round of golf or time- and money-consuming meals, Jim hiked undeveloped "goat pastures" in the arid foothills east of the city. Sitting among the sagebrush with a tuna sand- wich, he carefully noted the changing patterns of growth in the valley, and began to buy land in what he believed was the path of the coming develop- ment, at $25 to $50 an acre.

"I was told there was no water there," Jim recalled. "People said the land would never be worth anything, just sagebrush and grazing. I even hopped on the bandwagon and said, 'Do you have any more goat pasture for sale?' When I would approach a prospective seller, I offered him the glitter of money for the drab, dry sagebrush. It was a gamble."

A gamble, yes, but a carefully calculated gamble, like most of Jim's en- trepreneurial ventures. Rather than risk big on one shake of the dice, he took many small gambles, and only when he believed the odds were in his favor.

Jim was keenly aware of Utah's long history of inventing irrigation in the intermountain region—starting within a day of when Brigham Young led the first company of Mormon pioneers into Salt Lake Valley on a scorch- ing July 24, 1847. Some men with shovels dug a narrow irrigation ditch to divert water from City Creek onto the stubborn, sun-baked earth. In the decades since, enterprising Utahns collected snow-melt in mountain reser- voirs, and devised ingenious ways to lift the water higher and higher in Salt Lake Valley.

Jim was confident that one day water would reach his arid acres. "I perceived that there was value in the future," he wrote. "I was young and had lots of future and little money. So what little money I had, rather than put it in the bank I put it in goat pasture, sagebrush ground that I perceived to be in the natural line of development."

That gamble would pay off handsomely.[2]

Often only he could see the potential. Once Jim proudly took Beverley to a barren hillside above the city where he had purchased a parcel of land. With a sweeping gesture, he asked: "Well, what do you see here?"

At first Bev was silent, not wanting to hurt Jim's feelings. But she was honest. "I'm sorry, Jim, but all I see is rocks and sagebrush." Disappointed but not deflated, Jim pressed on. "Beverley, look at that field of wild flowers beyond the rocks and sagebrush. One day this whole hillside will bloom like those flowers—with beautiful houses and yards for hundreds of families."

The area became one of Salt Lake's most exclusive housing developments. And decades later Beverley saluted her husband's foresight in the title of her biography, *Look Beyond the Weeds*.

Jim refused to pamper himself with new clothes, fancy cars, or other trappings of growing affluence. Beverley shared the sacrifices, receiving $10 a week for groceries, later raised to $15—sometimes bought with Jim in tow—and making Christmas gifts by hand.

"There were a lot of things we wanted, but we just did without," she remembered. The vacuum cleaner and refrigerator needed replacing; the clothes washer and dryer didn't match. Frugality was such a watchword that even the purchase of a new piece of clothing was long remembered. Fifty years later Beverley recalled the day Jim surprised her with a gift of a plaid jacket. On another occasion he bought her a black-and-white plaid winter coat. Days later, walking down a city street, they spotted an identical coat approaching, worn by an obese woman. The next day Jim returned Beverley's coat to the store.

Jim paid all the bills, keeping track of everything they owed—including mortgage and utilities—on three-by-five cards. The cards were a lifelong habit. Jim even had Beverley sew pockets on his pajama tops, often out of non-matching fabric, to carry his precious cards when relaxing at home.

Beverley knew vaguely that Jim was starting to buy land, but knew little of the specifics. He purposely did not share financial details with her, following an example set by his father back in California: "My mother [spent] wildly," so his father secretly saved money for the future, said Jim. "He was creating some wealth. If my mother had known about the wealth she would have spent it on creature comforts. He thought wealth should be used to create wealth."

In his own case, said Jim, "I did not dare let my wife have any knowledge of that money." However, with Beverley, he acknowledged, "I probably overreacted." [3]

Beverley worked hard to pay her own way in life from the time she was a teenager and her father lost his job. She was excellent at economizing. Now, as a young mother, with little complaint she went without conveniences most of her peers took for granted. When they belatedly bought a clothes washer, she rhapsodized over no longer having to wash diapers by hand.

In June 1950 their first son, James Lee, was born, joining Carol, now three, and Shauna, one and a half. That same month they bought a corner lot in the Logan View Subdivision on the east bench, and hired a general contractor to build them a house. [4]

On October 5 Beverley's sister, Helen Taylor Johannesen, was a passenger in a car returning from Heber City, Utah after performing in a concert. In Daniels Canyon a cow strayed onto the road. The driver swerved and the car rolled, ejecting all four occupants. The other three were not seriously injured, but Helen, at 34, was crushed and killed instantly.

Thus ended a beautiful life and a promising career as a brilliant musician. At a time when there were few women composers, Helen completed her first symphony a month before her death.

Helen and Grant Johannesen had one child, David, who was four at the time of his mother's death and whose grief was inconsolable. Grant's career and extensive travel schedule as a concert pianist precluded a role as a full-time father. Instead, Beverley and Helen's mother Bessie Taylor lovingly assumed the care of David. He lived with his grandparents until he was ten, when his father sent him to a military academy.

The holidays were somber as the Taylor and Sorenson families adjusted to the loss and Jim and Bev and their children prepared to move into their new home on Logan Circle. The day after Christmas they relocated to the large, lovely house near 17th South and 23rd East. A year later they bought an adjacent lot as well, paying Bev's father to negotiate the transaction through his company, Frank Taylor Realty. In coming years they would repeatedly assist Bev's parents in that and other ways.

In 1953 Jim made his first major real estate development deal—an instructive, high-wire learning experience. For years he steadily saved and Beverley scrimped, finally accumulating $700 for the down payment on a three and a half-acre parcel of land above the Salt Lake Country Club. Its total price was $13,500. The land was purchased over several months from the R.A. Gardiner family, with the first deed recorded on September 25, 1953.[5]

Jim divided the land into fourteen small lots, valued at $3,000 to $4,000 each, and immediately began selling them. However, he neglected an important detail: It was against the law to sell lots without obtaining a bond that guaranteed the property would be improved with water, sewer and roads.

After selling a number of lots, he took the escrow to United States Fidelity and Guarantee Company to apply for the bond. Approaching the insurance company's president, Robert Sonntag, Jim explained he had $9,000 in cash escrow and the improvements would cost $13,000. "May I have a bond?" he asked.

"No!" Sonntag answered sharply. "You can't start selling these lots until you have final approval." Then he handed Jim a balance sheet and asked him to list his assets and liabilities. Looking over the sheet, Sonntag underscored the bad news. "Young man, you have no net worth. I can't give you a bond. In fact, it was illegal for you to take these people's money."

"But I've already got the money," Jim protested, "and I can pay for the improvements out of the receipts."

"No you can't," said Sonntag. "You have to give it all back to them."

Thinking quickly, Jim persisted. "I've just built a new home on Logan Circle. How did the developer get the bond to develop that subdivision?"

"Well, there's no problem there," Sonntag answered. "That developer's name is Richard Hoyt. He's affluent and has an established track record. If you had his signature on this subdivision document, I wouldn't care if your name was on it or not. You'd be granted the bond at once."

Jim paid a quick visit to Hoyt, offering him two of his fourteen lots, valued at $7,000, if Hoyt would co-sign the bond application. Hoyt asked many questions about the property and Jim's plans for it. He promised to think it over that night and invited Jim to come back. "I did not sleep well that night," said Jim.

When he returned the next morning, Hoyt said, "Young man, I've been thinking about this overnight and what is really wrong here is you are definitely under capitalized. You need a partner. Tell you what I'll do. I'll put in $700 to match your $700 and we'll become equal partners."

It was a good deal for Hoyt, who was suffering from Parkinson's disease. Jim would do much of the legwork and all the selling. But it was good for Jim too—Hoyt had a lot of know-how Jim could use—and, besides, he had little choice. "Fine," Jim said. They shook on it and were partners in the Upper Country Club Subdivision.

The development went beautifully. Within months Jim and Beverley's $700 investment became a $10,500 profit. Hoyt then invited Jim to join him in a forty-acre development in Arcadia Heights, high on a mountainside with a spectacular view of Salt Lake Valley. Jim again did the legwork, Hoyt supplied the expertise, and once more they split a healthy profit.

At last equipped with both experience and capital, Jim was ready to go it alone. He bought more land on the east bench, as well as in North and South Ogden, and began to develop his own projects—an involvement in real estate that would be lifelong.

Jim was inspired in part by other local visionary land-developers, including Claude Richards—Stayner's older brother—and Don Carlos Kimball, who in 1908 formed Kimball & Richards. Like Jim, they thought big. They hired a large staff and, between then and 1925, platted more than thirty subdivisions, including Highland Park, where the Sorensons rented a home when first moving to Salt Lake.

Only one other major subdivision of that era arguably eclipsed Highland Park—in quality, definitely not in size. It was Federal Heights, which stretches from Virginia Street to the foothills of the Wasatch Mountains and includes the University of Utah. Federal Heights was developed by Telluride Real Estate Company, starting in 1909, and its name symbolizes the government's previous ownership of the property and neighboring Fort Douglas. Unlike most subdivisions later annexed by Salt Lake City, Federal Heights has maintained its original integrity and identity.

Highland Park was the colossus of all Salt Lake City developments. Like Federal Heights, it too has maintained much of its original character as well as its name. Highland Park was notable for its distance from the central city, beyond that of other suburbs, and as the first subdivision on the south side of the natural boundary of Parley's Creek.

Kimball & Richards bought 246 acres of vacant unincorporated land, including all water rights, from the LDS Church in August 1909. That same day they took out two mortgages totaling $90,000. The company divided the 246 acres into 3,124 lots over six years.

No doubt their LDS blue blood helped smooth their path. Richards was a son of LDS Apostle Stephen L. Richards; Kimball was a grandson of Heber C. Kimball, a colorful early church leader who was a counselor to Brigham Young in the First Presidency.

The first of Kimball & Richards' five plats alone was enormous—about twenty-five times larger than most Salt Lake City subdivisions of that period. In March 1910 that plat became part of the Sugar House annex, the largest in the city's history by thirty times. Annexation was critical, since the county did not furnish services including schools, water, garbage pick-up, mail service, and police and fire protection.

The company aggressively put infrastructure in place—dwarfing efforts in Salt Lake City as a whole. During a three-month period in 1910, more than twenty-two miles of sidewalk were laid in Highland Park; in Salt Lake less than three miles were laid that whole year. In 1914 more than a third of the city's road-paving was done in the subdivision, mostly funded by the developers. In 1912 Kimball & Richards contracted with Utah Light & Railway Company to extend a line from Sugar House through Highland Park. By 1914 the subdivision also had running water, mail service, and new police and fire stations.

In 1913 the subdivision became the first Salt Lake County neighborhood to sell lots having a significant number of fruit trees, peaches in this case, as well as shade trees. A century later the development with its abundant foliage continues to stand out on a gently sloping hillside.

Like clockwork, the Sorenson's fourth child, Ann, was born in February 1952. Now there were four under the age of five at home. Ann was a delicate, whimsical baby, and Jim and Beverley agonized when she developed a severe case of chickenpox a few months after birth.

The four children were unusually energetic. Jimmy, from the start, was especially vocal, curious and active. Bev dubbed him a "force"—the same word she used to describe her husband during their courting days.

"That was the hardest time in my life, when I had four children under five," said Beverley, who kept the home fires burning as Jim's growing range of business interests consumed an increasingly larger share of time. Emma, Jim's mother in California, sensed Beverley was overwhelmed and took two of the children—Jimmy and Shauna—home with her for an extended stay to give Beverley a breather.

Beverley relied on her husband and trusted his judgment. He was firm-er with the children and could turn chaos to order. When he was out of town she missed him greatly. "I hated it when Jim was away on those overnight sales trips; it was really hard on me. The children responded to his discipline, but I'd get nervous when he was gone." One trip especially stood out in memory. It had been an awful day. One child got lost and the police helped find her; the house was upside down; a washing machine had overflowed.

"By the time Jim got home I was a nervous wreck. I got the children into bed and was relating some of this to him. All he said was 'My home is a like a bit of heaven on earth. If you'd go where I have to go, sit in those smoke-filled rooms, and hear the stories I hear, you'd know that coming home to you and these innocent children is so wonderful.'

"If he had brought me a dozen roses it couldn't have been better than hearing him say that."

### CHAPTER TWELVE

# BOY'S DEATH

## Sets Course

As Jim Sorenson pursued outside ventures, his family was fortunate to be financially anchored by the Upjohn Company, one of the largest and most respected drug manufacturers in the United States.

Upjohn developed a broad line of antibiotics during World War II, and was selected by the armed forces to process human serum albumin and penicillin. By 1958 Upjohn was the sixth largest manufacturer of antibiotics in the country.

The company was a world leader in developing medicines to treat central nervous system diseases and injuries, and manufactured a large line of prescription drugs used in the treatment of conditions including cancer, heart disease, and arthritis.

In 1952, during Jim's tenure, Upjohn scored a major breakthrough in the manufacturing of cortisone. The chemical was first identified two years earlier by an American biochemist. Cortisone is used in a variety of important ways—to give short-term pain relief, reduce the swelling from inflammation of a joint, treat a severe sore throat, or deliberately suppress immune response in individuals with autoimmune diseases or after an organ transplant to prevent rejection.

Cortisone is produced naturally in the body as a reaction to stress, elevating blood pressure to prepare the body for a fight or flight. Initially the only way to produce cortisone in a lab was through a lengthy synthesis from cholic acid isolated from bile. In 1952 two Upjohn biochemists, Dury Peterson and Herb Murray, succeeded in introducing a crucial oxygen atom by fermenting the steroid progesterone with a common mold. This made possible large-scale production of cortisone.

Jim was proud to be affiliated with Upjohn, a forward-looking company which treated its employees well. The company personnel manual, updated the same year Jim joined Upjohn, said "there has never been a day of shutdown in operations during sixty plus years except for holidays."

Upjohn paid competitive wages—Jim made $4,563 in 1949—and offered an array of benefits, including vacations, sick pay, retirement and life insurance, the latter for "each employee with a wife or dependent child under 19 years of age...this insurance is also granted to wives with invalid husbands."

The manual said "The standard work week begins at 11 p.m. on Sunday night and consists of five 8-hour days, Monday through Friday, or a total of 40 hours for the week." It also said Upjohn's policy was "to avoid discharging employees for cause until we are certain that we have been fair in corrective efforts."[1]

Jim disregarded Upjohn's hourly schedule, making his sales rounds early each morning. He usually ended his Upjohn duties before noon. This meant Jim put in something less than thirty hours a week instead of the prescribed forty. However, he consistently met goals, increasing his sales by 15 to 20 percent each year, and routinely earning bonuses.

The way Jim sold pills for Upjohn was not unlike the way he sold the LDS gospel during his mission. In New England, Jim disregarded standard, softer proselytizing methods and created his own path. The result was that he and his companions baptized more converts during his two years than the entire mission baptized the year before he arrived.

In the case of Upjohn, however, it seemed inevitable that in the end Jim would be punished rather than rewarded as his interests and efforts increasingly were directed elsewhere.

Uranium was another of those outside interests. To the democracies, enriched uranium—the fuel for atomic bombs—became for a time more important and precious than gold, with the stakes not wealth but survival itself. The Second World War ended in August 1945 only after the world's first two atomic bombs—"Little Boy" and "Fat Man"—were dropped on Hiroshima and Nagasaki, Japan, killing some 150,000 immediately, tens of thousands who later died of wounds, and maiming still thousands more for life.

The war ended three months earlier in Europe. As the impatient western allies left the continent, Russia's Red Army marched into one country after another, setting up puppet regimes. The hot war was over and the Cold War on. In March 1946, Britain's Winston Churchill noted that "an iron curtain" had descended across Europe.

The U.S. monopoly on atomic weapons lasted four years. In September 1949 President Truman announced that the Russians exploded their own nuclear bomb. Washington panicked. Known sources of uranium in significant quantities were all abroad; the need to find domestic sources to build a reliable deterrent against Soviet aggression suddenly became an urgent priority.

The deterrent that developed was called Mutual Assured Destruction, otherwise appropriately known as MAD.

Late in 1949 the U.S. Atomic Energy Commission publicly called for prospectors to locate a domestic supply of uranium. The AEC enlisted eager civilians, offering a guaranteed market and spurring a massive treasure hunt—similar to the California gold rush a century earlier. The chase centered on the Colorado Plateau—where Colorado, Utah, Arizona, and New Mexico meet—whose sedimentary rocks and sandstones occasionally hold veins of commercial-grade uranium.

While the immediate need was for weapons, the heavy radioactive metal would later be required for assorted peaceful uses including power plants and cancer research.

Among those who answered the call was a maverick Texan, Charles Augustus Steen. Broke and unemployed at the time, he became a western legend. Bespectacled, mild-appearing Steen earned a geology degree in 1943. He did field work near Houston for the Standard Oil Company of

Indiana. After two years Steen was fired for insubordination and blacklisted as a geologist across the entire oil industry.

In December 1949 Steen read an article in *The Engineering and Mining Journal*, announcing the federal government's call for uranium. Steen, 30, had three sons, all under the age of four, and his wife, Minnie Lee (M.L.), was expecting their fourth son. With $1,000 borrowed from his mother, they relocated to the Colorado Plateau, living first in a small house trailer in Dove Creek, Colorado, then moving to a tarpaper shack near Cisco, Utah.

Most uranium prospectors used a Geiger counter to detect radiation. Steen was too broke to afford one, so he settled for a broken-down diamond drill rig. He also had a pet theory that uranium could be found in anticlinal structures where oil was found. Other prospectors in the Colorado Plateau with their fancy equipment spoke of "Steen's folly."

Steen spent two fruitless years in the search, meanwhile feeding his young family on cereal and poached wild game. On July 6, 1952, southeast of Moab, Steen struck pay dirt, hitting a uranium-rich vein of ore at 173 feet.

It was the nation's first big uranium strike. Overnight, Steen was to uranium what Sutter's mill was to gold a century earlier. Washington breathed easier: Steen showed there was a lot of uranium on the Colorado Plateau.

Steen called his mine Mi Vida (My Life), and proceeded to stake other claims all around its flanks, each with its own romanticized Spanish name. Two years later Mi Vida was estimated to be worth up to $150 million.

The "Uranium King" built a $250,000 mansion overlooking Moab, with a swimming pool, greenhouse, and servants' quarters. He and M.L. shared their good fortune with the entire population of Moab, inviting them to annual parties in the local airport hangar. He donated $50,000 toward a new local hospital and gave land for schools and churches.

While a great majority of others had about as much chance of finding another Mi Vida as winning a lottery today, Steen's strike ignited the uranium rush.

The *Utah Economic and Business Review,* a monthly publication of the University of Utah, normally was dry and level-headed. But in April 1954 it sounded like a circus barker:

The magic word in Utah and the Intermountain West these days is—Uranium! Prospectors, miners, promoters, speculators, teachers, students, doctors, patients, clerks, lawyers, traders, farmers, truckers, tourists, housewives—people from all walks of life—all are fascinated by the fabulous fantastic possibilities of Uranium...they are interested because they believe uranium is the one single modern word synonymous with heaps of gold and silver and diamonds, or any other form of riches...This chance for rapid monetary gain...has touched off one of the largest mineral hunts in history; surely the most significant in modern times.

The local stock market boomed. During the previous three months alone, reported *Business Review*, fifty-eight new uranium corporations were chartered or registered in Utah. Circulars with offerings of various companies "may be seen in business firms, stores, service stations, [and] barber shops. Executives, laborers, salesmen, clerks, secretaries, and students alike are pouring savings and spare cash (some not so spare) into uranium securities, and fabulous earnings from investments are not uncommon."

This time it was Beverley Sorenson urging Jim to join the fray. She learned that their neighbor bought $1,000 worth of stock at five cents a share; it was now worth $8,000 and still heading up. The neighbor planned to sell when it got to $20,000.

Jim quickly bought $500 worth at ten cents a share. When it reached twenty cents he sold, taking a modest $500 profit and provoking laughter from those who knew of others' huge gains. The stock continued to rise from twenty to thirty-five cents a share, with Jim starting to doubt his conservative approach. But then it started to go down, slowly, ending at less than a penny. Their neighbor—and thousands of others—rode it all the way up and all the way down.

Typically, Jim was not content to make money from uranium like most others—by simply purchasing stock from promoters. Following the adage that luck favors the prepared mind, he got into uranium the same way he got into land: with intuition backed by every scrap of information he could lay hands on. Jim frequently made sales calls for Upjohn at the University of Utah Medical Center. Afterward he began to visit the U's mining and geology departments.

"By chatting with the professors, I learned more about uranium. And by hanging around the assay offices and the geology lab, I often saw 'hot' rocks and was able to find where they came from. So I looked at the big picture and took to staking claims on public lands."

Jim's target area was public land in parts of Utah, Wyoming, New Mexico, and Colorado. Since he could not personally stake claims across such a vast territory, he hired salesmen traveling to the hot areas to do it for him, during their time off on weekends. Jim watched others stake claims—literally pound stakes into the ground—and taught fellow salesmen how to do it in the field. He paid colleagues $50 to stake the claims and register them in his name at the local county courthouses.

In addition to deputizing fellow Upjohn salesmen to stake claims for him, he enlisted the help of other pharmaceutical salesmen as well, at $50 a pop, from Merck, Lilly, and Squibb. [2]

Jim sold his $50 claims to penny stock promoters for $3,000 to $6,000 each—netting a profit of between 600 and 1200 percent. "During the workday, I would finish seeing the doctors by 11 a.m. The rest of the day, I took the certificates in my briefcase to the stock brokerage houses" and exchanged them for cash.

Promoters usually gathered between twelve and thirty such claims and opened for business, writing a brochure or prospectus with the help of geologists and lawyers and selling penny-stock offerings. Greed primed the pump and, when uranium was riding high, the offerings usually sold out immediately.

The stock typically went to a high and stayed there a few months, then dropped to zero. Most buyers, tantalized by promoter claims that twenty times the asking price—if not the sky itself—was the limit, rode it clear to the top and then clear to the bottom.

Meanwhile Jim stuck with his conservative formula, selling shares when they reached double the asking price, at the same time making far more money from his own claims. As the dreams of others disappeared down worthless mine shafts, Jim was building a fortune on numerous $10,000 deals—at a time when $20,000 was the price of a nice house.

Not content with two streams of uranium income, Jim created a third, requiring options on the stock sold from his claims. If it sold for a penny, for example, he wanted the right to buy ten shares for a penny.

"I carried stock certificates in my drug sample bag, and would show them to doctors and some of the other salesmen. As soon as the stock doubled in value from the offering price, I sold. That way I always hedged against a loss. I also sold the options without having to use money to buy the stock. So I was making money rapidly, both from the sale of claims and options on stock."

He preferred profits to status. Many friends became officers or directors of uranium companies, restricting them from selling stock. As a major stockholder, Jim could have done the same, but declined, leaving him free to trade stock with impunity.

He never promoted the stock and didn't trust those who did. "If a promoter told me to hold, I would probably sell at the very first opportunity. I had studied the oil business and knew that a lot more money was going into the ground in prospecting than ever came out. I played the 'uranium fever,' not the true market. I didn't know if my claims adjacent to where they had found hot ore were going to show or not. But either way I made money."

"Uranium King" Charlie Steen unfortunately did not have such a happy ending. Steen did some commendable things with his new-found wealth—donating money for a hospital in Moab and for land to build schools and churches. Each year he and his wife M.L. treated local citizens to a giant party in an airplane hangar. He formed a number of companies to continue his uranium work.

Steen spent as if there was no tomorrow, and eventually there was none. He had his prospecting boots bronzed, and flew in his private plane to Salt Lake City each week for rhumba lessons. In 1961 the Steens moved to a ranch near Reno, Nevada, building a 27,000-square-foot mansion.

He diversified into other businesses—a pickle plant, Arabian horse breeding, a prop-airplane factory, a marble quarry, real estate. Losses mounted and the IRS came after him for back taxes. In 1968 Steen declared bankruptcy.

Three years later he suffered a severe head injury while operating a coring drill. He was afflicted with Alzheimer's the last years of his life and died in 2006. Minnie Lee had died in 1997.

The uranium boom fizzled out in the late 1950s, when Washington had all the ore it needed and stopped supporting high prices. By then Jim had made a killing.

Upjohn leaders liked Jim and encouraged him to climb the corporate ladder, offering promotions in Denver or Albuquerque. However, he was earning far more from uranium and real estate than from selling pharmaceuticals, and made excuses not to leave Salt Lake. He had the best of two worlds—a monthly paycheck and rich rewards from private ventures. But his reluctance to accept upward mobility or otherwise adapt to Upjohn's corporate culture inevitably put him on a collision course with management.

The collision itself came after Jim started to become a sideshow at Upjohn that detracted from the company's main event. Other salesmen learned about his ventures in land and uranium as Jim strutted his stuff. At a sales convention, a boss dressed him down, saying Jim's colleagues were more interested in his latest uranium deal than they were in the company's new products.

"What I was doing was more exciting to those salesmen than the latest prenatal capsule or a new cure for athlete's foot," Jim deadpanned.

For Upjohn, the final straw came during a supervisor's visit to Salt Lake City. As he and Jim drove along Foothill Boulevard, near Arcadia Heights, the visitor bragged about his family wheat farm out in Kansas. A 220-acre crop had just been harvested and he received $4,000 as his share.

Jim couldn't resist. "You're driving through my farm now, and we grow houses." Later, Jim ruefully recalled that "That was dynamite, and they began to tail me." His days with Upjohn were numbered. The company learned how much outside business Jim was involved in, and decided it was too much.

In a subsequent visit, in 1955, his boss dropped the bomb. "Jim," he said, "you're not a company man. You'd be happier if you were no longer with us." Jim started to protest, noting he always met or exceeded sales quotas. But it was no use; the decision was made. "It would be to your benefit to terminate with Upjohn," said his boss.

After an eight-year career with Upjohn, Jim's pride was grievously wounded. "In retrospect he was right—it was to my benefit to be completely on my own," said Jim. "But at the time it did not go down so smoothly. Beverley and I had five children by this time [daughter Joan was born in March 1954] and the security of a regular paycheck was reassuring.

"The process of being fired also was unpleasant. It was a real ego crunch because I thought I was doing so well." Only years later would Jim fully realize that a marriage with a large, mature corporation simply would not work for such an aggressive, independent-minded entrepreneur.

Reluctantly, Jim also gave up hope of becoming a doctor. There were too many mouths at home to feed and too many other interests beckoning. He was now well on his way to becoming rich. But he was still powerfully attracted to the healing arts and longed for a life mission that would answer an urge to make a difference.

Fleetingly, Jim sensed such a mission over the years in making his rounds of hospitals, where doctors' tools seemed somehow primitive. Then, shortly before leaving Upjohn, he witnessed a dramatic life-and-death struggle of a young boy that would confirm the direction his own life would take.

It was a quiet spring day and he was making a routine call on Holy Cross Hospital, then a red brick building on a tree-lined street downtown. While there, the emergency room doors flew open and a young accident victim was trundled in. As doctors and nurses rushed to the treatment room, Jim was drawn closer. This is what he saw:

The victim was a blond eleven-year-old boy. He was bleeding profusely. Working frantically, a team of several doctors and nurses divided responsibilities. Some tried to find and stem the sources of the bleeding. Others inserted an intravenous line and began to pump in blood expanders and replacement fluids as quickly as possible.

It was a life-and-death struggle. The boy needed the replacement fluids and blood to stay alive. But as the blood replacements circulated to the damaged arteries, the bleeding became even more profuse. Finding and repairing those damaged arteries was the top priority.

But in concentrating on that task, a tragic complication occurred. A glass bottle of replacement fluid ran dry. Before it could be replaced, an air bubble entered the boy's body and moved to his heart. The heart spasmed. He died almost instantly. [3]

Jim left the hospital emotionally drained. "As I drove my car from the parking lot and down South Temple Street, I began asking myself, 'Isn't there a better way? There's got to be a better way!'"

It would not be the last time Jim would ask himself that question.

Jim's first job in medicine, with other rookie salesmen on the steps of the Upjohn Company in Michigan, 1947 *(third row, second from right)*.

Forty years after Jim began with Upjohn he returned to the same steps with his own team, including Jim, Jr. *(far right)*, to discuss possible joint ventures.

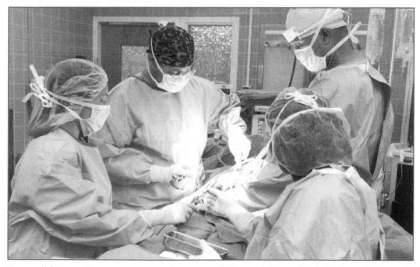

Jim and his co-inventors created scores of disposable medical devices that made patient care safer and less traumatic. Their inventions continue to be used globally.

Jim watched an 11-year-old boy die in Holy Cross Hospital *(top)*, when better equipment might have saved him. He also studied doctors at LDS *(middle)* and Salt Lake County Hospitals, learning what they lacked. *Used by permission, Utah State Historical Society, all rights reserved.*

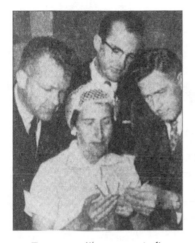

Deseret Pharmaceutical's first blockbuster product, the flexible catheter, being examined in 1959 by company founders *(left to right)* Jim Sorenson, Victor Cartwright, and Dale Ballard.

Jim oversees as workers assemble parts of a disposable medical instrument at Sorenson Research.

Jim recruited Gordon Reynolds *(left)*, a sewing-machine repairman, and K. Pannier, a metal-stamp fabricator, to launch Sorenson Research. Starting from ground zero, in fifteen years their inventions built the firm into a $100 million company. Photos by *Salt Lake Tribune*.

Checking garments at LeVoy's, Inc. The sleep wear firm included creations by a Hollywood designer.

Jim founded a clothing company, LeVoy's, which funded the development of medical products invented by Sorenson Research. Beverley played a major role in the 25-year-plus success of LeVoy's, a direct-marketing company with hundreds of representatives. Family members lent a hand, including daughter, Joan *(bottom right)*.

Drs. Homer Warner (*inset and left*), the father of medical informatics, with Alan Pryor (*center*) and Reed Gardner, at LDS Hospital in about 1975. The three helped invent and field test some of Sorenson Research's most important systems, including real-time monitoring of the heart. *Courtesy Special Collections Department, J. Willard Marriott Library, University of Utah.*

The Sorenson Research team. Fourth from the left in front is LeVoy Sorenson, Jim's father. Continuing to the right are K. Pannier, engineering vice president; Jim, chairman and president; and Perry Lane, CEO.

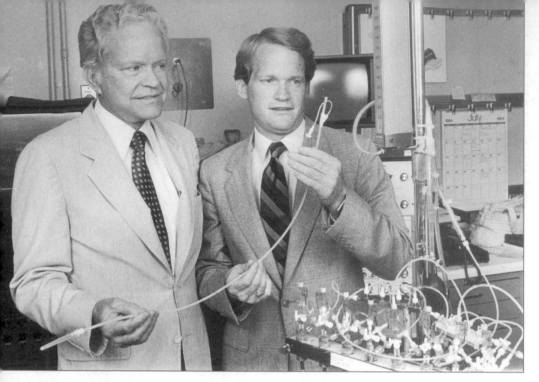

Jim inspects catheters with his son, James Lee. Courtesy *Deseret News Publishing Company*

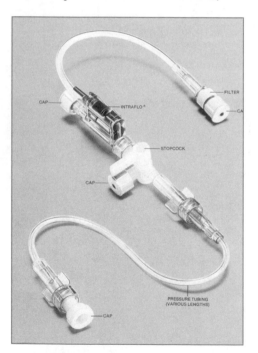

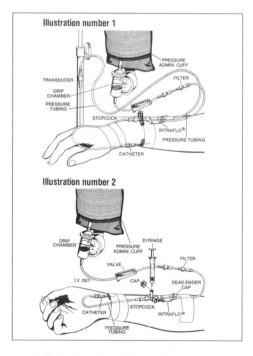

Sorenson Intraflo monitoring kits continuously flush the tip of the catheter to prevent clotting. The system, diagrammed above, invades the radial artery only once, lessening vessel trauma and danger of infection. Intraflo in turn led to Dialaflo to regulate the infusion rate. *[See Appendix for more Sorenson patents.]*

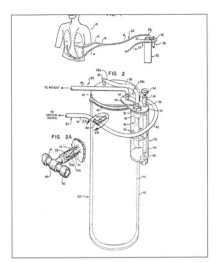

Suction Drainage Apparatus: A suction drainage system for body cavities includes a suction collection container and a disposable suction control chamber through which an essentially constant level of suction is applied to a body cavity. *[See Appendix for more Sorenson patents.]*

Jim was a remarkable entrepreneur as well as inventor. Here he inspects products being shipped to hospitals throughout the world.

Sorenson Research moved to new quarters in 1975. Jim is on the roof, seemingly, in his words, "contemplating how to fund the next expansion!" Annual growth of 40% required more new buildings soon afterward. Photo by *Salt Lake Tribune*.

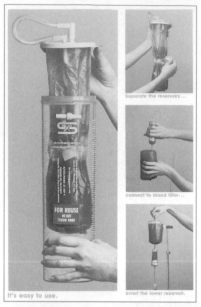

It's easy to use.

Separate the reservoirs...

connect to blood filter...

Invert the lower reservoir.

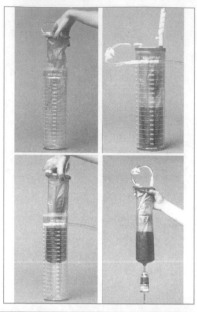

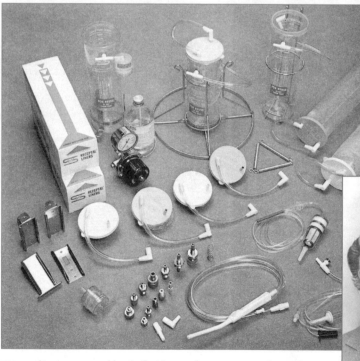

Discarding unwanted body fluids——often messy, stinky, and even dangerous——was always a serious problem. Sorenson Research's Receptal solved it. A sterile, disposable liner collects fluids that are never exposed to the atmosphere. Jim demonstrates one of his inventions.

# "Something new and wonderful"

Jim sold Sorenson Research to Abbott Laboratories for $100 million, *Forbes* magazine ran this article in May 1982, noting that his business interests were more diversified than ever.

Sorenson Vision, headed by James Lee Sorenson, had a hand in Apple's recovery from near-bankruptcy. Apple's Quick Time 3.0, unveiled by Steve Jobs at this 1998 MacWorld Expo, was powered by Sorenson's video code software.

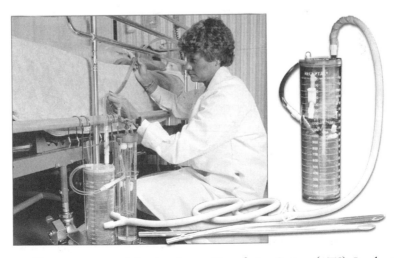

Jim and his team invented the Autologous Transfusion System (ATS). It salvages blood lost during trauma or surgical procedures, filters the blood, and re-infuses it into the same patient. *[See Appendix for more Sorenson patents.]*

### CHAPTER THIRTEEN

# DESERET PHARMACEUTICAL

The fourteen years living on Logan Circle were some of the happiest in the Sorenson family's life. Jim and Bev planned carefully to make it that way.

Their cul-de-sac saw little auto traffic, leaving it open for roller-skating, bike-riding, and games of every sort. "A couple of the houses had long drive-ways, and we would skate or slide down," recalled Joan.

"We had a huge double lot, and Dad built a big playground for the children that had two levels," said Carol. In back was a large swing set and a concrete pad that seemed the size of a tennis court. [1]

Family mattered to Jim. He and Eileen were adolescents when Emma had the first of four little sisters to join their family in quick succession. As a teenager, Jim helped ease the financial strain by giving his parents money as well as time, and purchasing items for their home—including a $60 radio that represented a month's wages.

"We would all go to a movie once a week, but in the spring Jim would want to go for a ride," recalled Eileen. "He'd gather up Mom, Dad, me, and all the new little sisters and we'd climb into his Model A. We'd go out and enjoy the beautiful wildflowers."[2]

As a father himself, Jim demonstrated his love for his children in many ways. "I remember that Carol was scared one night by a tree rubbing against her bedroom window," recalled Gloria Sorenson Backman, Joseph Levoy Sorenson's youngest sister. She thought it was Captain Hook. "The next day Jim went out and cut the tree down."[3]

"He went to an effort to make us feel safe at home," added Carol Sorenson Smith, Jim and Bev's oldest child. "When I cried at night and was afraid of something, he had a deadbolt put on the door downstairs to make me feel safe." [4]

Shauna fell and hurt her knee while running a race in junior high school. "Jim rushed over to the school and was very tender with her," said Backman. "When I was over at their house, Jim showed me the bulletin board in Joe's room. It was filled with quotes from the scriptures and other uplifting things. Jim was thrilled."

Family photo albums include pictures of Jim as coach of a Little League team that included their first son Jim Jr. Recognizing something of himself in his son, Jim occasionally took him on business trips. In addition to the educational value to Jimmy, Jim believed his son's presence sometimes gave him an edge with family-oriented individuals and companies.

The earliest of the eight children born to Jim and Beverley got the best from their father. Years later, when he was a renowned inventor and entrepreneur, Jim expressed regret that he did not take the time to bond with the younger children as well as he had with the older ones. The younger ones included Joseph (Joe), the second and last of the two boys in the family, born in December 1956, followed by Gail in February 1959 and Christine (Chris) in April 1962.

As business commitments increasingly took him away from home, one heartfelt letter indicated how deeply he felt about his children, and how much he appreciated others who helped them. The letter, written in 1964, was to an elderly woman who dedicated her life to assisting special-needs children. Eight years earlier she had helped a Sorenson daughter catch up with her age group. Now Jim was writing again seeking help for another child:

[After driving to her home to seek help again] I watched you teach a boy for about 20 minutes before we were able to discuss the possibility of you teaching [my child]. It was during that 20 minutes that I believe I caught a glimpse of a "little bit of heaven on earth" and the true meaning of the words of our Savior when he spoke, "Inasmuch as ye have done it unto the least of these, ye have done it unto me…" I am writing this letter to express my appreciation for what you have done for my children, something that I could not have done myself—nor anyone else I know could or would have done…I especially want to thank you for one of the closest examples I have observed here on earth of what heaven might be.[5]

Jim was devastated by being fired by Upjohn. While acknowledging a lot of outside interests and that he did not follow its prescribed daily schedule, he believed the fact that he always made or exceeded his sales quota insulated him against being terminated.

His reputation saved him. Just two days after leaving Upjohn in 1955, he was hired by the LDS Church Hospital System as administrative assistant to its director, Clarence Wonnacott. (In 1974 the church divested itself of its fifteen hospitals, turning them over to a private nonprofit group called Intermountain Health Care.)

Wonnacott offered to send him to the University of Minnesota to earn a master's degree in hospital administration. "I could have done well in that environment," Jim wrote years later, "but I would have gotten ulcers…It was too restrictive for me. You had to worry about politics, doctors, and the intricacies of church ownership. I was so stifled; I could not run free."

The stately downtown Boston Building was constructed in 1908 as Salt Lake's first skyscraper. In its basement was the Prescription Pharmacy, *the* hangout for doctors and pharmaceutical salesmen. For nearly a decade Jim congregated there to swap tales, eat lunch, and make uranium deals.

Two of Jim's chums at the pharmacy hideout were Dale H. Ballard and Victor I. Cartwright, both salesmen for Parke-Davis, the nation's oldest and largest drug maker. For some time the two men had talked of leaving Parke-Davis and forming their own Utah-based pharmaceutical firm to sell drugs to doctors and hospitals in the intermountain region. Ballard and Cartwright invited Jim to join them as an equal partner.

After a series of conversations, Jim bit—launching his professional life on a dizzying trajectory no one could have predicted.

Their partnership looked promising from the outset. Each man was in his thirties and each was among the top pharmaceutical salesmen in the region. Ballard and Cartwright held degrees in pharmacology—Ballard from the University of Utah and Cartwright from the St. Louis College of Pharmacy, where he was valedictorian. Perhaps most important in the area's unique culture, each was a member of The Church of Jesus Christ of Latter-day Saints.

The other two men tentatively had decided to call their company DalVic. With Jim in the mix, that name obviously wouldn't work. He suggested a name that stuck and would pay dividends: Deseret Pharmaceutical. "Deseret," in Mormon jargon, means "honey bee," and Utah's state seal features a beehive, symbolizing a cooperative, hard-working citizenry.

LDS doctors across the U.S. were especially responsive to the new name. One doctor in New York called Jim, saying "Tears came to my eyes when I saw the name 'Deseret.' I haven't seen it since I was a boy. I am at Bellevue Hospital and can determine what they buy."

Ballard and Cartwright severed ties with Parke-Davis, and Jim with LDS Hospitals, to devote full energies to launching the new company. Their partnership was sealed at a Kentucky Fried Chicken restaurant at 3900 South State Street in Salt Lake City—the site, appropriately, of the first KFC outlet.

"We flipped a coin to see who would be president," said Jim. "I lost the coin toss and was named vice president." Ballard became president, Jim first vice president, and Cartwright second vice president.

Their initial idea was to purchase large quantities of new hormone drugs, vitamins, and antibiotics from a small manufacturer in St. Louis, and sell them to the intermountain medical community at prices significantly lower than those of large national pharmaceutical firms.

Until that time, the St. Louis company, Keith-Victor Pharmacal, made drugs only for private labeling by large retail chains. Both sides stood to benefit: KVP would have additional capital to develop new product lines, and Deseret Pharmaceutical would have products to sell.

The president of the St. Louis company was a man after Jim's own heart. He was Victor M. Hermelin, 42, the inventor of time-release capsules. Hermelin graduated from Washington University in chemical engineering. Shortly afterward Hermelin invented the skinless frankfurter, which reportedly saved his employer, Swift & Co., millions of dollars. His reward was a weekly raise of seventy-five cents. [6]

No doubt that paltry reward helped convince Hermelin of what similar circumstances long ago convinced Jim—that ownership alone returned the rewards equal to his contributions.

"Most drugs had a tremendous mark-up," explained Jim. "A bottle of hormone pills might actually cost sixty cents to make and would bring $13 from the customer. Our new corporation would sell them for $8, making a good profit while lowering the cost to the patient."

A number of drug patents were expiring at about that time, opening the market to produce a generic variety of drugs already widely used.

To raise capital, the partners formed a public corporation, formally registered with the state on July 27, 1956. It received permission from the Utah securities commission to sell $300,000 in stock. The men priced the shares at $1 each and agreed that each of them personally would retain up to 45,000 shares—15 percent of the company—and sell the rest in amounts not to exceed 500 shares. To begin, each of the three purchased 15,000 shares.

Deseret would be the only large pharmaceutical distributing firm in the Intermountain West. Its stock-offering circular said it was "the intent of the Corporation to supply every possible type of drug, pharmaceutical supply, as well as drug store, hospital and other related items through drug stores, hospitals and other outlets." [7]

They especially targeted doctors as potential investors, figuring physicians would have a dual incentive to purchase Deseret Pharmaceutical products—secure cheaper medicines for their patients while benefitting individually from the company's growth. The partners divided the sales territory into thirds, stretching from Boise on the north to Las Vegas on the south and San Bernardino, California on the west. They set about pitching the stock to doctors, about 600 of whom wrote most of the prescriptions in that corridor.

Jim wrote to Keith-Victor, explaining that "a number of druggists, doctors and salesmen" were forming a stock company to distribute pharmaceuticals in the Rocky Mountain region." He expressed special interest in vitamins and hematics—the latter tend to stimulate blood cell formation and increase hemoglobin. Jim also wrote:

> We are interested in all suggestions you may have. We would like all quantity quotations on prepared therapeutic vitamins and mineral tablets packaged with our label in quantities such as 5000 - 100's, or 5000

- 60's, or 5000 - 30's. In like manner we would like such quotations on hematics and supplemental vitamin formulas packaged as above and bulk quotations as well...Along with your quotation we would like to know how soon delivery could be made after you have our order. [8]

Victor Hermelin telephoned Jim in response, and followed up with a two-and-a-half-page letter. He wrote that his company could provide any service needed in launching Deseret Pharmaceutical, and invited Jim and his associates to visit their plant in St. Louis, where "we will get you started in business, design your lines for you, take care of all your requirements of labels, literature, and promotional material, and leave you with only the problem of going out and doing a good selling job..." [9]

Deseret Pharmaceutical was an overnight success. Doctors and other medical practitioners bought stock so fast that it led to contention between Jim and his partners. The three had agreed that each would buy 45,000 shares, starting with initially purchasing 15,000. After the flurry of selling, however, Jim discovered that his partners sold more than their allotted amounts and only 6,000 total shares were left unsold.

Each partner bought 2,000 of the additional shares, ending up with 17,000 shares each—6 percent of the company instead of the 45,000 shares—15 percent—they agreed to. Jim was deeply disappointed, believing the $300,000 in capital they raised was more than the company needed. And, in fact, a year later a significant portion of that amount was still in the bank.

On August 31, 1957—the end of the company's first fiscal year—President Dale Ballard told stockholders that Deseret had $137,331 in net sales during the year and a net profit, before taxes, of $28,202. The company sold seventeen different items and forty-five package sizes and potencies.

Deseret's quick success alarmed competitors. Another pharmaceutical firm complained to the state securities commission that for doctors to own stock in Deseret was a conflict of interest, and the practice was "unethical, unprofessional and possibly illegal." Commission director Milton Love turned to the state attorney general for a ruling.

Assistant Attorney General Maurice Jones, in an informal opinion, said Deseret Pharmaceutical supplied drugs to wholesale distributors on a competitive basis, and the drugs were available to anyone.

"Although a doctor's stock interest in a pharmaceutical company may at times cause him to give preference to the products of that company," wrote Jones, "there is no law that would prevent a doctor from owning stock in a pharmaceutical company."[10]

In August 1958 Ballard reported that net sales for the year were $243,329, and net profit was $50,021. Both figures were about 44 percent higher than the previous year.

Deseret's meteoric rise continued to alarm competitors. The following January a Salt Lake drug-distribution firm called Brain, Kay, McQuarrie, Inc. filed a $225,000 damage suit in Third District Court against Deseret. The suit named 200 John Does as co-defendants, reserving the right to later substitute the names of doctors and pharmacists who were company stockholders.

Brain, Kay alleged that Deseret was organized "principally, if not entirely" from among medical and pharmaceutical practitioners and their immediate families, "with the express purpose" of monopolizing part of the distribution of drugs and vitamins in Utah. Individual defendants, the suit argued, prescribed certain pharmaceutical products prior to becoming stockholders in Deseret. Since then, individual defendants "began prescribing competing pharmaceutical products manufactured, distributed or sold by the said defendant corporation in which they and each of them had a direct pecuniary interest."

The plaintiff said that, as a direct result of Deseret's practices, it suffered a loss of $75,000, and was suing for $225,000, treble damages as provided under the Utah law on trusts and monopolies.[11]

The 1959 Utah Legislature, which meets during the early weeks of each calendar year, also got in on the act. A member introduced House bill 37, which stated that ownership by any person engaged in the practice of medicine "of an interest in any sole proprietorship, partnership or corporation engaged in the manufacture, sale or distribution of drugs, vitamins or pharmaceutical products is guilty of unprofessional conduct."

A similar bill was introduced in the U.S. Congress. Both were obviously aimed at Deseret Pharmaceutical.

In addition, the Salt Lake County Medical Society in February passed a resolution that said: "...a physician should not profit financially from the care of his patients apart from fees for professional services rendered. In particular, we would discourage profit sharing in any pharmaceutical enterprise or medical supply organization."

Deseret hired a lobbyist to help defeat the proposed law in the Utah Legislature. Jim assumed the role of public affairs manager for the company, spending numerous hours with the lobbyist meeting one-on-one with members of the legislature. "We argued that the legislation would be intrusive," he recalled. "We also argued that it would be a regulatory nightmare, that many doctors would simply shelter their holdings under family members' names."

Jim and the lobbyist succeeded—defeating the proposed legislation by a single vote.

While his partners continued to focus on medications, Jim grew disenchanted with pushing pills at doctors. "Chasing doctors with halos was demeaning to me," he explained. "Some of the doctors we dealt with were very inconsiderate...it's inexcusable to frequently stand people up when they have an appointment."

Jim had often observed and profited by what others couldn't see, whether gathering walnuts after a California windstorm, watching miners take chunks of uranium ore to the assayer's office, or studying residential growth patterns on the city's east bench. That unique ability was about to pay off in a big way.

"As I became increasingly less enamored with the selling process, I became increasingly more interested in watching how doctors worked. It was then that my creative sparks truly began to fire." Jim's uncanny insights were about to lead him in another healing direction: disposable medical devices.

One day Jim sat in the doctors' lounge at Holy Cross Hospital. "I noticed how each doctor put his surgical mask in a laundry bin when he came in. When each one returned to work, he would pick up several clean masks and smell them until he found one that was free of tobacco smoke and halitosis."

To Jim, it appeared the gauze masks were ineffective and probably disease-ridden.

Decades of research indicated the value of masks to inhibit the spread of air-borne droplets from the mouth or nose of a diseased individual. Dr. Carl Flugge, a German bacteriologist and hygienist, in the 1890s performed extensive research on the transmission of such diseases as tuberculosis, malaria, and cholera. His work led to the development of surgical gauze masks, starting in 1897.

In 1914 two doctors in Texas modified masks to avoid the frosting of eye-glasses by the wearer's breath and to move the upper edge of masks out of the field of vision. Their technique was to slip a piece of lead-foil, one-half inch by four inches in size, into the upper hem of the mask, so it could be form-fitted over the bridge of the nose and down onto the cheeks.[12]

The need to stop the spread of disease assumed a new urgency in 1918. As World War I wound down, a vicious new enemy emerged: influenza. The pandemic began in January of that year and lasted until December 1920. Before it was eradicated, an estimated 20 million to 40 million people died, more than those killed in four years of war.

Medical researchers estimate that up to a fifth of the world's population was infected. An estimated 675,000 Americans died of the flu, six times more than were killed in combat. Half of the American soldiers killed in Europe were slain by Spanish flu rather than by enemy bombs and bullets.

In the U.S. the disease was first reported in January 1918 by a doctor in Haskell County, Kansas. Three hundred miles away, on March 4, Army cook Albert Gitchell reported sick at Fort Riley, Kansas. By midday on March 11 more than 100 soldiers were in the hospital. Days later, more than 500 men at the camp were sick, and the virus had reached Queens, New York.

The benefits of using face masks to protect hospitalized servicemen and women, as well as those attending them, were outlined by an Army doctor at Camp Grant in Rockford, Illinois. His report appeared in the *Journal of the American Medical Association* (JAMA) in March 1918—as flu was exploding across the globe.

"One of the most troublesome problems confronting the medical staff of the base hospitals in camps is the prevention of cross infections," wrote Dr. Joseph Capps. He noted that the cubicle system—sheets suspended on wire between beds—restricts the spread of mouth and nose droplets as long as patients remain in bed. How to keep active, convalescing young men in their beds, however, had not been solved.

Tested over a five-month period, face masks were "remarkably" effective in protecting medical personnel, said Dr. Capps. "...not one nurse or physician contracted the disease of the patients with whom he or she was working." He added:

It seems reasonable that patients by wearing the mask should receive similar protection from either primary contagion, or if already ill with one infection, from a second contagion. The experiment of masking the patients was first tried in a measles ward in which six successive cases of scarlet fever developed at intervals of several days. After introduction of [mask-wearing], one more case of scarlet fever broke out in five days, but none subsequently. The system has since been tried in other wards with excellent results...The essential principle of the method is that patients out of bed and out of the cubicle must never be unmasked, except when alone in the wash room. [13]

Capps and his colleagues posted a set of "Rules for Contagious Wards," that included: all patients wear masks when out of cubicles; wash basins and bathtubs are not to be used (use running water over sink); only one patient at a time in the wash room—outside of which a guard is to be on duty; masks may be removed only when in bed; all eating utensils are to be sterilized after each meal.

Researchers hoped that, in addition to stopping the spread of disease, masks worn by surgeons would reduce surgical wound infections. Research, however, has failed to prove that benefit. A medical researcher concluded that there is "proof that a costly device commonly used in the operating room [a mask] may be another 'sacred cow' and could be eliminated.

"Its elimination would help surgical team members by giving them more energy and, if some form of 'splash shield' is made available, would offer comfort and greater protection for the surgical team." [14]

Guidelines from the Centers for Disease Control and Prevention indicate that surgical face masks are of doubtful value in reducing the risk of surgical site infections. However, the guidelines support the use of masks for personal protection.

Gauze masks have been faulted through the years for a number of reasons, including shrinkage after washing. In one nine-year study, "The practice of surgical masks was hindered by surgeons' dissatisfaction with the poor quality and discomfort of two-ply gauze masks," reported one medical scientist.

"Gauze masks have ineffective filters," she wrote. "Wetting lowered [their] efficiency," and "improper fitting allowed leakage around the sides." Many studies have shown surgical mask filter efficiency to be "extremely variable," ranging between 20 percent and 80 percent. In a 2009 study of a surgical mask worn by twenty-five subjects, 5 to 8 percent of leakage was from the filter and 25 to 38 percent was from failure of the mask to seal properly.[15]

Jim probably did not know much if any of that history, but he was confident he could do better. Sitting in the doctors' lounge at Holy Cross, where physicians discarded their surgical masks, "I began to think," said Jim. "I asked doctors if they would pay ten cents, the price of a cup of coffee, for a disposable surgical mask that worked."

Their answer was always yes.

Jim drove to the University of Utah and sparked the interest of Dr. Paul Nichols, a microbiologist. "We dyed billions of bacteria and blew them through different filters until we found one that was 99.9 percent effective," explained Jim.

The question now was how to mass-produce masks with the filter. For the answer, Jim visited a factory where he bought his underwear. He arranged with the owner to have the factory's best seamstress sew some mask designs Jim sketched on paper. "It was a useful exercise, but the sewing heads were too cumbersome and slow," said Jim.

Finally he contacted a boyhood friend named Alan Schlisler, who had an engineering degree from UC Berkeley and designed machinery for mass production. One of his successes was a machine that made the cardboard carrier for a six-pack of beer.

Jim asked Schlisler to design a machine for making sterile surgical masks out of paper, by gluing instead of sewing them together. The price tag to develop and produce the machine was $65,000—a princely sum for the young Deseret. With Jim's arm-twisting, his partners agreed to toss the dice and invest the money.

It was exactly the right decision. Deseret was soon producing the world's first successful disposable surgical masks—over 3,000 of them an hour, initially selling for seventeen cents each ($510 an hour). The masks became standard equipment in hospitals across the globe.

(The paper surgical mask is one of his few inventions that does not carry Jim's name on a patent. "But there is no question we did it," he told Forbes magazine. "If anyone has questions, have them come to me and we'll have a little talk.") [16]

### CHAPTER FOURTEEN

# FIRST DISPOSABLE

## Surgical Mask, Catheter

Deseret's next breakthrough after the first paper surgical mask was a disposable plastic catheter. Suddenly the little company tucked out of sight in sleepy Utah was turning heads across the country.

Jim was spending almost all his time developing new devices, as his partners Dale Ballard and Vic Cartwright continued to push what they knew best from their educations and training in pharmaceuticals.

One attempt to create a wholly new medicine to help asthmatics required juice from the cocklebur, a pesky weed found along fence lines and roadsides throughout the West. They spent $50,000 gathering a barn full of cockleburs and extracting the juice.

"A parade of asthmatics was shuffled through the company's office to sample the new concoction," said Jim, but "nothing ever came of the experiment."

Deseret's ingenious catheters advanced modern medicine after decades of attempts that sought but failed to accomplish the same thing.

"One of the outstanding problems in the treatment of the seriously ill patient is intravenous therapy," wrote Dr. Lawrence Meyers in 1945. "The advent of penicillin brought doctor, nurse, and patient face to face with the necessity of intravenous and intramuscular injections around the clock.

"The mental anguish, pain, and loss of sleep to the patient, in some measure, always counterbalanced the good effect of any medication that has to be administered parenterally [by a process other than swallowing] several times a day."[1]

Three methods were used back then to give multiple intravenous injections: first, the typical puncture of a different vein each time medication was given. Common problems were running out of usable veins or jarring the needle into surrounding flesh, flooding it with blood.

In a second method, a pump infused medication through a tube. The patient, however, could tolerate only a given amount of fluid intravenously. The third method, called the "cut-down," seems macabre. An incision is made in the skin and muscle to locate a vein. A needle is then inserted. After medication is administered, the vein is closed off, destroying it permanently.

Jim's interest in catheters came after years of seeing patients suffer with black and blue marks all over their bodies from being injected repeatedly. "When a patient moved, the steel needle would puncture a vein and cause inner tissue bleeding," said Jim. "There was a lot of trauma and suffering."

A solution, Jim and his colleagues believed, would be to thread and leave in place a flexible plastic catheter instead of the rigid steel needle. They decided to try to develop a plastic tube small enough to fit inside a hollow needle. Jim found a small company in Connecticut with the required needle technology.

"We were able to get them to make a thin-walled needle and match it up with a little plastic tube," Jim explained. "We could make the puncture with the needle, advance the tube, and then pull the needle out of the patient."

The first clinical trials were at Salt Lake County Hospital. An elderly man named Oscar, in pain from multiple injections, was one of the first to test the new system. "We put a plastic tube in Oscar's arm and taped it," said Jim. "Then the nurses didn't have to strap him to an arm board, eliminating multiple vinipunctures several times a day. Oscar, with no restraining arm board and repeated punctures, was relieved of pain, did well, and began healing immediately."

Deseret Pharmaceutical was the first company in the world to produce and market the disposable catheter system, which sold for about $1 each.

On March 10, 1958, the system, first called the "Deseret Intracath," was registered with the U.S. Patent and Trademark Office, under "intravenous catheters," "intravenous catheter placement instruments," and "devices for the administration of anesthetics." It was sold in a sterile packet.

Deseret lacked the marketing power to sell its new invention nationally and internationally. It enlisted the help of a respected, well-known medical-products company called C.R. Bard. The company, headquartered in Summit, New Jersey, had been in business for more than three decades. Deseret continued to manufacture the system and Bard marketed and sold what came to be known as the Bardic Deseret Intracath.

The catheter system was a huge success. "A Salt Lake firm founded just three years ago is winning national recognition in manufacture of a new medical item," reported the *Salt Lake Tribune*. "It expects to gross 2 ½ million dollars in 1960 and no doubt will win an eternal 'thanks' from patients forced to undergo the nerve-wracking ritual of intravenous feedings over a long period...The company has a dozen white-clad women assembling 6,000 of the catheters daily at its Stratford Avenue location." [2]

That same month in 1959, after the catheter was used on more than 500,000 patients in the U.S., Canada, and abroad, three Utah doctors explained the Intracath to their colleagues.

"During recent months an inexpensive, disposable catheter and needle unit called the Deseret Intracath, which offers the advantages of a catheter without the disadvantages for the hospital-prepared catheter-passing set or the plastic needle...has come to our attention," they wrote. [3]

Advantages of the Intracath over other catheter types, they said, include (1) it comes sterile and ready to use; (2) the tubing slips easily into the thin-walled needle, yet is so close to the size of the puncturing needle that usually there is no leakage at the puncture site, and (3) because of the close fit, there is no need for insertion of a smaller needle inside the catheter that would impede the fluid flow.

In addition, they wrote, the advantages of the Intracath over a plastic needle (then in use) are "easier insertion of the needle and catheter, greater choices of sizes to fit varying needs...the catheter is long enough to be threaded so far into the vein that it will not become dislodged with movement of the patient's extremity," and the Intracath costs so little that it can be used on almost all patients who need it.

The Utah doctors said they tested the Deseret Intracath on more than 1,000 patients in local hospitals and carefully studied 127 patients—many of them emergency cases. "Few complications of a technical nature were encountered." In five patients it was "impossible to advance the catheter in a vein," in two patients it was difficult to make the puncture, and in one there was leakage at the puncture site. However, no catheter dislodged prematurely from a patient.

"The low cost, ease of insertion, and widespread applicability of the Intracath recommend its routine use in all intravenous therapeutic procedures," they concluded.

The Deseret Intracath was only the beginning of the types and uses of catheters Jim would help invent in coming years. There were critical needs in other parts of the body. One of them was to safely place a catheter in the inferior vena cava. It is one of the two main veins bringing de-oxygenated blood from the body to the heart, emptying into the right atrium of the heart.

At the same time as the Intercath hit the market, insertion of a catheter into the inferior vena cava was considered a life-saving measure, but one with considerable risk. In one study of twenty-four patients, the catheter usually was inserted through a needle into a femoral vein and guided into the vena cava.

"Thirteen patients tolerated the indwelling catheter for from 3 to 14 days with no complications," reported three physicians. "The remaining 11 patients suffered various complications." Autopsies showed that four of the patients died from problems associated with use of the catheter.

"The employment of this therapeutic tool is recognized as important in many instances," wrote the doctors, "but attention is directed to contraindications and hazards which may arise." [4]

Jim and other medical detectives and inventors had their work cut out for them.

Deseret Pharmaceutical continued to soar. In August 1959 Ballard reported net sales of $461,770 and net profit of $77,558—90 and 55 percent higher, respectively, than in the previous year. In 1960 net sales were

$662,703 and net profit $104,442—44 percent and 35 percent higher.

Deseret's fast growth was demonstrated in other ways. Initially the three owners sold its products. During the first few years they added up to ten more experienced salesmen and expanded into new territories in Idaho and the San Bernardino areas.

In the beginning the three partners rented an office on the fifth floor of the Boston Building. In 1957 they moved to a 1,000-square-foot facility in an old building at 2300 South State Street. After five years of operation, Deseret built a modern 50,000-square-foot structure at 9400 South State Street in Sandy.

While Deseret was doing well, Jim was not. His ownership of 6 percent of the company, rather than the 15 percent originally agreed to by the partners, continued to grate. He believed he was contributing more than his share to Deseret—especially as he reoriented the company away from simply pushing pills to inventing and producing medical devices.

Jim considered his best contribution to Deseret was courage and a can-do attitude. He credited Ballard and Cartwright with being perhaps smarter as businessmen.

Finally Jim laid it on the line for Dale and Vic. He still wanted the 15 percent of the company originally envisioned by the three. His two partners, not surprisingly, resisted. "Instead, they wanted raises, good expense accounts and new cars. I burned inside for want of the 15 percent equity. The friction between the partners grew more intense, and I frequently found myself on the short side of two-to-one votes."

Another issue dividing them was Jim's reluctance to pay royalties to physicians who had tested and proved the value of Deseret inventions. Finally Jim decided to sell out to his partners, and did so in 1960, less than three years after Deseret was founded. They gave him $137,000 for his 6 percent, a sum he considered a fortune at the time. A key part of the settlement was that he would not compete with Deseret for two years.

Cartwright eventually retired in Palm Springs, California. Ballard, like Jim, felt driven to stay in business, and remained on the local scene. He founded his own highly successful medical products company, Ballard Medical, constructing its headquarters in his home town of Draper, Utah.

Jim continued to be on friendly terms with the other two, especially

Ballard, whom he considered one of the most enthusiastic people he knew. They got together once or twice a month at some out-of-the-way café to chat. Their friendly rivalry became something of a legend in the medical device industry.

In 1992 Jim and Dale both attended a meeting held by Utah Senator Orrin Hatch, concerning the Food and Drug Administration. Jim commented about the increasingly tough stands being taken by the FDA. Hatch responded: "Well, nobody here would want to punch Jim Sorenson in the nose."

After a perfectly timed pause, Dale Ballard deadpanned from the back of the room: "Speak for yourself, Orrin."

Jim was a rainmaker at Deseret who defined its future. By 1967 the company, created a decade earlier to sell pharmaceuticals, would abandon medications altogether and develop, manufacture, and sell only disposable surgical instruments and other medical products.

When Jim left the company in December 1960, Ballard and Cartwright did their best to curb his ability to compete against them. The two-year non-compete clause their lawyer drafted and Jim signed specified that, among other limitations, he would not use or disclose "any procedural, operating, management, compounding, trade, customer relation or other secrets which he has learned" at Deseret.

They could not, however, control his mind. Jim was scarcely out the door when he began scribbling ideas for other inventions and stuffing them into a desk drawer. His greatest creations in fact waited over the horizon.

### CHAPTER FIFTEEN

# SORENSON RESEARCH

## Soars

Before leaving Deseret Pharmaceutical, Jim acquired the small sewing company in downtown Salt Lake whose seamstress had tried to create surgical masks. The company, named Kelly's, was a business compatible with Jim's agreement not to compete against Deseret for two years.

The sewing company previously made the special underwear(called "garments")worn by many adult members of the LDS Church to signify sacred covenants made in a temple. It also produced lingerie, which represented about 20 percent of the business, and other sleepwear that covered LDS women's garments and was attractive for other modest women.

Around the time Jim was experimenting to make surgical masks, the owners of the company lost their franchise from the Church to continue making garments. Kelly's sold all of its equipment to the Church. Jim picked up the non-garment portion of the business from the Church, apparently at no cost except to lease the manufacturing machinery.

He and partner J.W. Kelly adopted the motto "The elegance of modesty" and soon produced about forty underclothing and sleepwear items in sizes to fit infants, children, and teenagers, as well as women. Then Jim had second thoughts. His former business associates ribbed him for "being big in ladies' underwear." He also had self-doubts about entering an industry of which he knew nothing.

In June 1961, a half-year after acquiring controlling interest in the company, Jim sent a two-page letter to Harold B. Lee, a senior member of the Quorum of the Twelve Apostles. Jim explained that they had put on many successful fashion shows and that stores likewise showed strong interest in their products.

He stressed the unique approach of Kelly's to produce modest but stylish clothing that LDS women would be proud to wear. "I feel that there is such a great need of a program of this type where we show the youth what to wear instead of telling them what not to wear, that there is no compromise, apologies or bashful defensiveness and that the only true elegance in dress is modesty."

Then Jim got to the point, explaining that since the previous November he put almost $32,000 into the company and others had added another $26,000, for a total new investment of $58,000. "I will be glad to offer my controlling interest to the Church for a tithing receipt covering the number of dollars I have put into the company."

Jim sent along several samples of clothing items with the letter. Elder Lee answered Jim two weeks later. He explained that he gave the samples to leaders of the Relief Society [the LDS women's auxiliary]. "They were asked to look over these items and to express frankly, their opinions and observations..." The Relief Society, led by a woman named Belle S. Spafford, inspected the lingerie and had some members model it. This was their memo in response, said Elder Lee:

There are reservations on the part of the Board members as to the ready salabilty of these items. It was the feeling that they were somewhat homemade looking, also rather impractical even for the average bride. It was the opinion that both design and fit could be improved... we would hesitate to endorse the program of Brother Sorenson, if the articles which we saw represent the general styles and fit of the articles they produce. [1]

Jim did a slow burn. "I can't even *give* this company away."

With the writing on the wall, he dug in and got down to business. Jim changed the name of the company to LeVoy's, his middle name, and moved it to a small, 1,500-square-foot building at 2235 South West Temple Street. Jim inherited six seamstresses from Kelly, and bought Kelly's share of the business the following year.

LeVoy's was a multi-level marketing company, a popular approach in the sixties and seventies, when many women who needed or wanted to work chose to do so from home. LeVoy's bypassed middle-level distributors and reached potential customers through a network of several hundred women located mostly in western states. The sales representatives typically held neighborhood fashion shows. The close control enabled Jim to keep overhead low while increasing sales and profit margins.

"I had to learn to deal with an entirely new type of people," Jim said. "Instead of trying to charm doctors and nurses, I was leading sales rallies in rooms full of homemakers."

He also had to learn how to manage his own employees. One of his most valuable production managers was a woman named Dale. She was talented at keeping the operation running smoothly, but seemed slow to respond to Jim's directions. At first he talked tough with her, which led nowhere. Then he gave Dale a raise, which only helped marginally.

Finally a business associate suggested he use a spoonful of honey instead of vinegar. "I returned to the office and called Dale in. I told her how important she was to the operation and how much I needed and appreciated the work that she did."

Tears rolled down Dale's cheeks. As Jim scrambled for tissues, she said "If you had talked like that last week, you wouldn't have had to give me that raise." Jim later said the lesson he learned was that when leading people, "you can't force them to follow, you need to invite them along." Jim gave Dale increasing responsibility as well as stock in the company.

Years later Dale sent Jim an undated hand-written note: "You will never know how grateful I am to you for all the wonderful blessings you have given me. Thank you for being a friend as well as a good boss...You have given me love and wisdom...Beverley and you shall always have a very special place in our thoughts and prayers."

While successful by most standards, Jim's enthusiasm was tempered by regret as he watched the explosive growth of Deseret Pharmaceutical.

He and two other men, with a part-time bookkeeper, founded Deseret in 1956 in a portion of a small building. Three years later he sold his share of Deseret to his partners for $137,000. By 1976, a few miles south of Salt Lake City,  Deseret had its own plant of 300,000 square feet, another 82,000 under construction, and 1,700 employees.

New Jersey-based Warner-Lambert purchased Deseret in 1976 for $138 million. If Jim had retained his 15,000 shares of stock until then, he would have made nearly $6 million on the sale, 44 times more than he sold out for a decade and a half earlier.

Jim vowed he would never sell himself short again. But he needn't have worried. His gray matter was working overtime, churning out ideas for more medical innovations. He bided his time at LeVoy's, waiting for his non-compete agreement with Deseret to expire in 1963.

Jim had many ideas, but who could turn them into reality?

K. Pannier could.

Jim relocated LeVoy's to a larger, 6,000-square-foot concrete-block building three blocks south, at 2511 South West Temple. The move was extremely fortuitous. Just across a narrow alleyway was Panniers Instaco, also known as Intermountain Stamp Company. The small firm had six workers, led by brothers Karl and Clyde Pannier who owned it, and made a variety of rubber and metal items, including commemorative plaques for historic sites. Working with them as vice president was Karl's son of the same name, known by just the letter "K."

Jim, always a friendly sort, got acquainted with his neighbors, especially K., who he soon discovered also had a genius for inventing.

A local bank note company asked the Panniers to build a one-ton off-set press. K. took the challenge and designed and built it in a little more than a year. The frame was made of hot-rolled steel cut to K.'s specifications. The press worked so well, according to a Salt Lake newspaper, that at least eight more companies from New York to California ordered presses.

"K. had this amazing ability to look at something and say 'I can make it better or improve it,' noted Todd Hyer, who is married to one of K.'s three daughters. "He could see a first step to solving or making something, and could also see what had to be done three or four steps into the future."

K. was tall and slender, with some resemblance to the late actor Gary

Cooper. He had dark combed-back hair and a cigarette perpetually dangling from a corner of his mouth. [2]

The variety of what K. built or improved was amazing. When his only son Scott was six or seven, K. built him a steel race car, powered not by gravity but by a six-horse-power Briggs and Stratton engine, and with independent front suspension. None of the parts were bought new. While his father worked inside the stamp building, Scott raced his red-and-white roadster in the parking lot. When Scott got older, K. cut the car in half and made it two feet longer.

K. was a Depression-era kid and learned from his parents that, if he wanted something, he had to make it. The family basement in Sugar House, a Salt Lake suburb, had every tool imaginable and a variety of machines all powered by one generator. A shaft the length of their house turned a series of wide belts.

Among numerous other things K. created were a rock waterfall in their front yard, a clay-pigeon thrower, ski bindings, and a boat. When it was awkward for his wife Georgene to move from the captain's chair to the bow, K. cut the windshield in two and hinged it for Georgene to step through.

He was confident and proud to the point of arrogance, yet remarkably good with people, perhaps a reflection in part of the fact that his college degree was in psychology. Commanding in demeanor, K. did not waste words. When he spoke others listened.

On May 24, 1962 Jim signaled clearly where he was heading. He and five other individuals, including Bev, met at the Walker Bank Building and organized Sorenson Research Corporation. Officers of the new company were Jim as president, Christian Ronnow, vice president; Beverley T. Sorenson, secretary, and Alice R. Ring, treasurer.

Before Sorenson Research started making money, Jim set up an irrevocable trust for estate planning purposes. He established and kept about 10 percent of the Sorenson Development stock, which owned Sorenson Research, for himself and gave the other 90 percent in the trust to his wife and children. There were eight voting shares of Sorenson Development stock––one per child––that he owned and controlled during his lifetime.

Jim's bid to return to inventing medical devices had an inauspicious beginning. He was still in non-compete limbo, and could not bring any new invention to public notice for many months to come. Sorenson Research was a small subsidiary of LeVoy's, and when the two formally merged four and a half years later, LeVoy's was the parent company.

But not designing new products and not making or marketing them were two different things. Realizing K. Pannier's talent and burning interest undoubtedly further stoked Jim's desire to follow his heart and reenter the medical-products industry.

"Jim knew the two of them could make miracles together," said K.'s son, Scott Pannier. From the moment Jim met K. there was a strong synergy. K. already was anxious to tackle something bigger. In the small family company, headed by his father and uncle, he saw no room for moving upward. Jim was his ticket to an exciting new professional life.

Jim and K. began sitting down in LeVoy's upstairs break room and tossing around ideas. Occasionally the two couples or their families got together socially. "We had a boat and took Jim to Lake Powell a couple of times," recalled Scott Pannier. "Jim was gung ho to go, but once we were there his mind was going every which way and he couldn't relax much. After a couple of days he had us come home early."

The two men got along well, feeding off each other's ideas, said Scott. "I never heard any bad things said between them."

Several years after they began collaborating, Jim discovered a third inventive wizard, Gordon Reynolds. Shorter than Jim and K., and often with a full beard, Gordon kept LeVoy's sewing machines humming, a job previously performed for another clothing manufacturer, Mode O'Day. Gordon focused on ways to speed up LeVoy's production.

"Reynolds was a repairman who was hired to keep the sewing machines running," explained Jim, "but I soon discovered that he had a talent for translating new ideas into prototypes and finished products."

"K. and Gordon both appreciated each other's abilities," said the latter's son, Val Reynolds. "My dad had the ability to take parts from something old and use them for something new. K. worked on the engineering side of things. Gordon would noodle what ideas were worth pursuing, what needed to be built." [4]

Children of his employees often worked for Jim's companies as well.

They too were expected to put the job first.

"One time I was working on a project that Jim had just given me the day before," recalled Val. "The next morning Jim said 'How is it coming?' I said 'I have worked sixteen hours on it.' And he said 'What did you do with the other eight hours?'"

Another man who played a role in the early days of Sorenson Research was Ott Hamman, who lived next door to the Panniers and became a human guinea pig. Potential new products, including needles and catheters, were taken home by K. and poked into Ott, who later was hired by Jim.

Jim's associates were expected to move out of their comfort zones at a moment's notice. "One day Jim called K. and asked 'Are you going to wear a tie today?' said son-in-law Todd Hyer. "K. asked why and Jim said 'We've got to go see a bank.' K. couldn't see how they could get money out of a bank, but that was Jim's skill and he did it well."

Regrettably, K. and Gordon had something else in common: a deep addiction to cigarettes, which would cost each man his life many years prematurely.

In 1965 Jim added a $70,000, 11,500-square-foot addition to the building. Sorenson Research began taking products to market the following year, soon accounting for a quarter of Levoy's sales. Jim bought the Pannier company. A construction crew built a walkway between the Sorenson and Pannier buildings, and the two businesses became one.

"Where did my creativity come from?" Jim once pondered. "I used to think it was a quality all my own. Then I remember the last of the many lessons that my father taught me." He had traveled from Salt Lake City to his parents' ranch in California. His 89-year-old father Joseph immediately bundled Jim into a golf cart and headed for the vegetable fields.

Stopping at a row of peas, Joseph handed him a curious hoe he had jury-rigged, with a sharp, serrated cutting edge on all sides. The angle of the handle enabled the blade to rest comfortably parallel to the ground.

"Hoe!" said Joseph, handing Jim the tool. Jim did so in the usual way, clipping off several pea plants. His father took the hoe and "silently and proudly demonstrated its proper use to me." Joseph ran the blade about an inch below ground, cutting on both forward and backward strokes. "The wedged shape of the blade allowed him to reach around the stems of the peas to clip close-growing weeds without harming the plants," far faster than could be done with a conventional hoe, said Jim. He added:

> This was the last opportunity he had to teach his son a most valuable lesson in innovation. I realized then that my creativity in medical devices may be a mirror of my father's creativity!  This event called to mind a thought that now comes back to me again and again: "There's a man up there ahead of you. It's someone you ought to get to  know. It's you grown older."[5]

### CHAPTER SIXTEEN

# LEVOY'S,

## Religion, Music

Byron Russell is an African American who helps raise funds for non-profit organizations, including the Utah Symphony.

As they accumulated wealth, the Sorensons hosted fundraising events for various groups, including the symphony. One such evening brought Russell and members of the symphony together with potential fat-cat donors at the Sorensons' home.

"Jim and Beverley were standing together across the foyer as I came in," recalled Russell. "Immediately Jim rushed over to me. He asked: 'Do you know any black people?'"

Russell could have answered "my mother" or "my father." Instead he swallowed a chuckle and sounded Jim out. Jim explained that he had written a song that needed "soul" to sing it properly. He wanted to find a black group to sing it.[1]

Russell put Jim in touch with France Davis, a prominent African American and pastor of Salt Lake's Calvary Baptist Church, who had such a choir. Reverend Davis's choir subsequently performed one of Jim's songs. Among other groups that have sung lyrics written by Jim is the Mormon Tabernacle Choir.

Jim's wide-eyed innocence in such everyday matters was endearing to friends.

Jim had an innate need to be considered the best at whatever he attempted. Music was no exception, though the portents were not promising.
Some of his children were excellent soloists, but family members agree that
Jim "could not sing a note." During one church hymn when the children
were young, 4-year-old Jim Jr. set the congregation to laughing by blurting
out, "Stop Dad, you hurt my ears!" [2]

Jim's forte was writing poetry for others to put to music. "I collaborated with Jim on a dozen or so songs," said Barlow Bradford, a prominent
Utah choir director and songwriter based at the University of Utah. Many
of Jim's songs were spiritual in nature. [3]

Jim also took credit for both the text and music of a song he called
"Share the Warmth." When a songwriter in Mesa, Arizona saw Jim's version, she complained that he had appropriated her song of a different name.
In May 1998 the two settled their differences, agreeing that each was en-
titled to claim ownership of his or her version of the song. The agreement
cost Jim $5,000. [4] Lyrics to "Share the Warmth" include:

> Like a drop of rain becomes a raging storm,
> Like a tiny spark becomes a fire that's warm,
> Like the grains of sand surround the deep blue sea,
> Like a tiny seed becomes a mighty tree.
>
> Share the warmth, Share the love,
> To see more clearly, follow more nearly, our dearest Lord,
> day by day...Giving to others, making the difference.
> Share the warmth, share the love,
> To see more clearly, loving more dearly,
> We'll follow thee day by day.

Jim could claim bragging rights for accomplishing what most would-
be songwriters only aspire to: actually selling their music, albeit for small
sums in Jim's case. Three months after settling with the Arizona woman,
he signed a royalty agreement with Jackman Music Corporation in Orem,
Utah. Jim sold Jackman the written compositions for "Share the Warmth"

and three other arrangements: "We Do Believe" for voice and another version for flute, and "Unity and Love."

He was to receive a royalty of 20 percent of the wholesale selling price. Two years later, in 2001, Jim received a royalty check from Jackman for $3.42. Six years after that, in 2007, he got a second Jackman check for $4.43. Jim was so proud of his accomplishment that he saved the checks rather than cashing them. [5]

Jim's real genius was reflected in the gusher of new ideas continually flowing from him, as well as in his uncanny ability to uncover people able to turn them into reality.

Jim knew nothing about running a clothing factory when he bought LeVoy's in 1961. But he knew enough to hire talented people who helped make the company hum. One of them was Klis Hale Volkening, a Hollywood designer with grace and eloquence who created Jim's own line.

Klis had a degree in costume design and was uniquely prepared for the position. She was a devout member of the LDS Church, joining a company that would come to specialize in white attire worn by Church members in temples. Klis held a succession of impressive jobs in Hollywood—costume designer at MGM studios, editor of a national cosmetics magazine, assistant publicity director for Max Factor.

"Klis worked for us from Los Angeles at the start, then moved to LeVoy's in Utah," recalled Ben Smith, who joined the company as an accountant in 1966 and became general manager a decade later. "Klis was a very good designer. She was a key reason our products were so popular." [6]

Klis's contribution to LeVoy's was reflected in the respect and love Bev and Jim had for her. After she died in her ninetieth year in the summer of 1997, the Sorensons threw a "Klis-mas" party at their home honoring her memory that December. [7]

Another irreplaceable individual who entered into the Sorenson world through LeVoy's was Gloria Yamada Smith. Her Horatio-Alger life saga was a counterpoint to Jim's, and perhaps figured in his hiring and/or steadily promoting of Gloria, who eventually became his most trusted aide.

Gloria was born near Tokyo in occupied Japan at the end of World War II to an American serviceman and Japanese mother. Soon after her birth, the American deserted his young Japanese family. Gloria's mother, suffering the shame and prejudice of having a mixed-race child in post-war Japanese society, abandoned her new baby.

Gloria was rescued by Miki Sawada, a granddaughter of the founder of the Mitsubishi Corporation, who took her in at the Elizabeth Saunders Home, a home Ms. Sawada established to care for mixed-race Japanese-American orphans. Ms. Sawada, knowing what a difficult life Gloria faced if she remained in Japan, found an American couple to adopt Gloria and take her home to the United States.

The Air Force family adopted Gloria at about the age of two. For the next decade the family traveled across the world from one air base to another. They finally settled in Draper, Utah, not far from her new mother's hometown of Springville.

In 1970 Gloria began working at LeVoy's on a piece-rate basis, operating a straight-needle sewing machine and assembling the countless clothing items in the company's product line. Over the next twenty-three years she worked her way up in the company—floor supervisor, satellite plant manager, and several other steps to head designer. In the last role, she was responsible for creating and producing clothing designs for each new season as well as for designing and producing the company's sales catalogues.

Gail Williamsen, the Sorensons' second-youngest daughter, worked at LeVoy's for a decade, starting in high school, and also designed clothes and the company catalogue.

In the early 1990s LeVoy's business would begin to slow down, largely due to increased competition from manufacturers who produced clothing with cheap labor in foreign sweatshops. Though the closing of LeVoy's became inevitable, Jim did not want to lose Gloria's loyalty, talents, and worth ethic. Among Gloria's abilities that impressed Jim was her remarkable memory and ability to recall names and their associated telephone numbers, even years later.

During the LeVoy's transition, Jim appointed Gloria to assist one of his key managers. Shortly thereafter Jim's assistant left the company and he tapped Gloria to be his new executive assistant. She would serve in that role for the last fifteen years of Jim's life. Two years later Gloria retired, having served Jim and the Sorenson empire for forty years.

While clothing was not an industry that made Jim's heart beat faster, he typically threw his energies into it and was richly rewarded. Jim educated himself on what was required to succeed in a homemaker-centered clothing company, and expertly built LeVoy's. He communicated encouragement to saleswomen, and instituted national sales conventions, where top saleswomen, mostly from western states, were awarded prizes, including new cars.

"That was a highlight of our year when we attended LeVoy conventions," said Carolyn Muir of Twin Falls, Idaho, a tall, trim, dark-haired LeVoy's saleswoman for twenty-five years. "Jim and Beverley were great hosts. We liked them a lot. And the clothes were so well made they almost never wore out." A case in point was pajamas and a handsome robe worn by her husband, Leland J. Muir Jr., in the summer of 2012. Although three decades old, the black robe trimmed with a white stripe looked new. [8]

LeVoy's grew fast, grossing $75,000 its first year, at the end of 1961. Sales approximately doubled each year thereafter until the company —by then including Sorenson Research —had sales in the range of $9 million. By 1967 LeVoy's offered a line of nearly 790 items, ranging in price from $3 to $35.

In the fall of 1968 LeVoy's, including Sorenson Research, was called the biggest employer in South Salt Lake City, with about 200 workers and an annual payroll of $1 million. [9]

"[Jim] reasoned that frocks, housecoats and lingerie that could meet the requirements of both fashion and modesty would find a ready market in the Mormon community," wrote Robert Woody, business editor of the *Salt Lake Tribune*. "But amazingly and happily for LeVoy's the requirement for fashionable modesty extended far beyond Zion.

"Over the nation, women in their 30s and over were seeking the fashionable but subtle concealment of upper arms and shoulders that were beginning to show the encroachments of maturity. Now 600 saleswomen distribute and direct-sell LeVoy's fashion items in neighborhoods over the U.S. and Canada. And LeVoy's is a name that is found in the advertising of such [magazines] as *Mademoiselle, Harper's Bazaar, Seventeen* and *Vogue*." [10]

Although the company initially was best known as a source of modest lingerie, its best-selling clothing items came to be panties for toddlers and temple-worthy white dresses for women and white one-piece suits for men.

Much of the cloth came from a Jewish supplier in New York City. When he asked why LeVoy's needed so much white cloth, Jim explained that "White is 'kosher' in our temples." The man understood.

As noted earlier, Jim relocated the company into a building across an alleyway from the Pannier stamp company. It was in a nondescript industrial neighborhood. Jim purchased the site for $40,000, and moved his personal office into the first floor of the two-story building.

LeVoy's time came and, after several decades, went, as cheap labor abroad flooded the U.S. market with less-expensive clothing. Some homemakers who sold LeVoy's clothing to their neighbors as a part-time business instead joined the full-time workforce. Convenient shopping malls were springing up. A generation of younger women was not keen to buy styles their mothers wore. In addition, "Women were buying lingerie that was more risqué than what we sold," said general manager Ben Smith. The cumulative weight would finally sink LeVoy's.

Jim learned through LeVoy's that he could build a business almost anywhere he found an opportunity and an interesting challenge. More important, LeVoy's profits provided the capital to launch Sorenson Research, which became the cornerstone of Jim's fortune and his future.

In 1967 it was a quarter-century since Jim served an LDS mission to New England. Since then, alongside his professional prowess had grown a unique philosophy of life—an outlook he traced to experiences during his mission.

Jim's philosophy centered on "balance," as achieved by what he saw as the law of threes. "God made us three dimensionally [mind, body, spirit], and we must balance three dimensionally as we live," he wrote. He noted that the most complete thoughts usually are expressed in threes: Peter, James, and John; red, white, and blue; tall, dark, and handsome; life, liberty, and the pursuit of happiness.

"Everywhere in nature, from the smallest objects to the largest," he wrote, "existence is expressed in three dimensions. The atom, the cell, the human body, the Earth, the universe. All have height, width, and depth...all are constantly moving, growing, adapting."

Humans, Jim explained, must constantly adapt to change and re-balance their lives to survive. "Think. Then tell. Then do...a successful life is one that is three dimensionally balanced. Life is not an event. It's a journey. And the key to making things work is maintaining that balance as you are moving along."

A favorite biblical personality was Paul, who Jim called "a prophet of action and accomplishment." In [I Corinthians 13], "he referred to the virtues of faith, hope, and charity. There is a formula for successful life...Faith, which is the entry portal to the spirit. Hope, which is the wellspring of life itself. And charity, which represents the *doing* of good work on the Earth."

Jim's approach to life meshed with his approach to religion. During most of 1967 he taught classes in their congregation, first for male priesthood meetings and later for Sunday School, attended by both sexes. He prepared by neatly hand-writing an outline of his lessons on legal-size sheets of paper.

In a lesson on repentance, Jim cited a standard biblical list of sins and shortcomings, including adultery, hate, fear, envy, deceit and false pride. For good measure, he added some secular sins to repent of: "inefficient ways," "outmoded methods," "careless thinking," "letting others do our thinking."[11]

The following week he taught that it is as easy for the "weak and poor" to enter heaven as it is for the "rich and powerful." God's spirit has inspired men and women to develop industries, create art, and make scientific discoveries as surely as it has taught them to obey God's laws, said Jim. Scriptural examples: Adam practiced agriculture and tailoring, Noah and Lehi [a figure in the *Book of Mormon*] learned ship-building, and Moses learned architecture.

There is order in the universe and in God's kingdom, said Jim. "All things require delegation and distribution of authority." He asked class members, "Has anyone in the class ever tried to arrest a man for speeding?... There is not one instance in holy writ for anyone taking to himself the authority to officiate in sacred ordinances, and be accepted of the Lord."

"The holy priesthood descended from Adam to Noah under the hands of the fathers," said Jim. Mormons, he noted, believe the same priesthood—the authority and responsibility to act for God—was restored in 1829, the early years of this era (dispensation) of the gospel. Members believe that John the Baptist himself returned to the earth and conferred one form of priesthood directly upon the heads of Joseph Smith and his scribe, Oliver Cowdery. Later, Peter, James, and John also appeared and conferred a higher priesthood upon the two men.[12]

Jim liked a talk given by Don Lind, a nuclear physicist, astronaut, and fellow Mormon. Jim carefully underlined sentences that especially struck him, in a newspaper report of the sermon. The underlined portion:

I wasn't in the Sacred Grove with Joseph Smith but I have just as strong a conviction of the fact that he saw God and talked with him face to face as I have the conviction of something I got my doctoral dissertation on, and that is the existence of pi-mesons [three subatomic particles], because I haven't seen pi-mesons either, but I accept their existence on secondary evidence. And on secondary evidence I believe that Joseph Smith saw God in the Sacred Grove,... [13]

Jim's religion was practical. "Many people spend their lives watching and waiting for signs and miracles," he told one class. "...We talk about speaking in tongues, when we have not studied well enough to express ourselves in English. We seek the gift of prophecy, when sometimes a greater miracle would be to obey the commandments we already have."

Miracles are all around us, Jim taught, if only we have the eyes to see them. He was in Montreal the previous Sunday and home by Tuesday—a time warp impossible before the twentieth century. Man had been to the bottom of the ocean, under the North Pole, and the U.S. was on track to land a man on the moon, something accomplished two years later, in the summer of 1969.

Life expectancy in Jerusalem at the time of Christ, said Jim, was 21 years; in George Washington's time in America, 35 years; in 1953, 70 years; and in 1967, 74 years.

The greatest miracle, said Jim, was suggested by the Savior when he said "Stir up the gift of God that is within thee" [2 Timothy 1:6] and promised that "If you keep my commandments and endure to the end you shall have eternal life [dwell with God], which gift is the greatest of all the gifts of God." [Doctrine and Covenants, 14:7 (an LDS book of scripture)] [14]

Jim defined hell in two ways: (1) "When the man I am meets face to face with the man I might have been," and (2) "Truth seen too late."

In years to come, Jim would be known for his appreciation of other religious creeds. His attitude was reflected in the lessons he taught in the fall and winter of 1967, in which he explored world religions, including Islam, Buddhism, Confucianism, and Shintoism.

"You are what you are for what you have been," he taught, "you are fast becoming what you will be." [15]

Jim had a strong humanitarian instinct and was often generous to men and women down on their luck. He and Bev paid tithing to their Church—10 percent of their gross income—and in later years contributed large sums to major LDS projects. They donated to numerous other institutions, including other religions.

The Sorensons took the children to Sunday services and taught them Christian principles at home. The LDS Church encourages families to set aside time each Monday evening for Family Home Evening, a practice intended to bring families closer together by sharing a religious lesson and/or recreation, and refreshments.

It was not a favorite time for Jim when the children were young, squirming, and sometimes screaming, but Bev insisted, and was generally successful in pulling off some kind of family togetherness on Monday evenings. No doubt she felt especially obligated given the fact that her grandfather, Frank Taylor, introduced the program in the Church early in the twentieth century.

LDS families usually have two "home teachers" from their congregations, who represent the bishop in visiting assigned homes each month to help with spiritual and temporal needs. On one occasion the Sorensons' two home teachers were about to leave when Jim had a parting word for them. "Bring a lesson next time you come," he told them. "Otherwise you're just wasting my time."

Given Jim's executive ability, normally he would have been called to serve in a variety of church leadership roles. However, he did not take kindly to following someone else's directions, and his reputation as a maverick precluded his serving in leadership.

The Church has no paid local ministry, so lay members take turns giving inspirational talks in Sunday services. The meetings are usually solemn and reverent. When a grandchild gave a talk in church, however, Jim was known to walk to the front of the congregation and stand in front of the pulpit with a camera to capture the moment.

Jim and Beverley tithed, paying ten percent of their gross income to the Church, and gave far more than that in later years. But he did not like Beverley serving in church positions and leaving the children at home with him.

On one occasion she was called to serve in the presidency of their ward's Relief Society—the women's auxiliary. During a weeknight Bev was in a church building, meeting with other Relief Society leaders, when the door opened suddenly. In marched Jim, followed by all the children, clad in pajamas. He deposited them at her feet and left just as suddenly. "It was very embarrassing," recalled Bev, "...He wanted me out of that position, and that was the way he did it. I decided I couldn't accept the job."

Jim's reluctance to be home alone with the eight children did not reflect his genuine love for them. He simply was not a nurturing parent when the children were toddlers. But he was proud of their six daughters and two sons and the large posterity they gave him and Bev. On the slightest pretext Jim would open his wallet and let accordion-style photos of them cascade downward.

Asked two decades later who he most liked being with—his family, himself, or others—Jim answered that "I enjoy all three, but family does come first...I think the reason I do enjoy my family so much is because I do enjoy being by myself. Enjoying your own company enables you to enjoy being with others."

Jim's priorities—in his heart if not always on his schedule—were visible in his office at LeVoy's. Only three photos hung on the walls. One was of himself as a small boy in front of his family's ramshackle house in Yuba City, California. A huge one, taken on a staircase inside the Utah State Capitol, showed the dozens of Sorenson grandchildren. When a visitor asked about his accomplishments, Jim routinely began by stepping to that photo and bragging about the thirty-nine boys and girls in it. (Sorenson grandchildren presently number forty-seven.)

The third picture was Jim astride a horse with his oldest grandson, J.L.

Sorenson the fifth, then three years old. The caption says, "Give me the reins, Grandpa. Now get off!" Jim is smiling broadly.

Beverley was the epitome of nurturing, and is greatly beloved by the Sorenson children and grandchildren. Jim was the family disciplinarian. "Dad was pretty impatient," recalled James Lee. "He would tell us 'You do this, and you do it now!'" When a child failed to respond promptly, Jim sometimes spanked.

The children banded together to lessen the likelihood of facing their father's ire. Often when he returned home in the afternoon he made a quick check of the activities they were engaged in, and forcefully told them if he thought they were wasting their time. The children sometimes took turns watching out for their father returning from work. When his car was in sight, the lookout sounded the alarm. "We'd really scatter," recalled one daughter.

Their second-youngest daughter, Gail, believed her parents' opposite attributes "made for great kids." She explained that "I saw my dad get results from using blunt, frank language; if there was something wrong, he laid it all out on the table...[My mother] was more long-suffering. There's a balance to be struck. They are such beautiful people in their own right..." [16]

LeVoy's represented a type of Sorenson enterprise that lent itself to family involvement. As each child matured, he or she worked in a family business—early preparation for assuming major roles in Sorenson entities as adults. "I worked with Dad on and off," said Jim Jr. "He didn't believe in child labor laws." Encouraged especially by his father, Jim learned to work hard, in a withering array of businesses, family-owned as well as independent.

Joan Sorenson Fenton added that, "With all that material being cut and sewn throughout the day, by the time we got there after the workers had gone, the scraps on the floor were about three to four inches deep. Our job was to clean it all up."

After selling his share of Deseret Pharmaceutical to his two partners in 1960, Jim bought a downtown property, the Miles Hotel (today the Peery Hotel) with the proceeds. A year later he sold the hotel for a nifty profit of $100,000. That windfall financed the Sorensons' next home. It was in Arcadia Heights, about a mile from their home on Logan Circle.

The last of the Sorenson children, Christine (Chris), was born in April 1962.

In 1965 the family moved into their new home at 2857 East 2100 South. It was lovely but fairly modest, on a steep hillside with a panoramic view of the valley. Otherwise, the Sorensons continued to live frugally. Jim continued to carry three-by-five cards in his pocket, listing money spent, bills owed, and daily priorities. Beverley ran things at home.

Jim continued to pour every spare nickel into real estate. By the mid-sixties he had acquired about 4,000 acres in Salt Lake County and another 1,600 acres in North Ogden, Weber County.

Although the Sorensons were now wealthy, Jim and Bev were determined not to spoil their children. They also lived frugally themselves.

"I continued to reinvest gains rather than purchase the trappings of wealth," explained Jim years later. "Looking back, I probably should have been more liberal with family expenditures." Although they had five children during the first decade of their marriage, they made do with one car all that time.

Jim could not abide what he saw as waste at home or at the office. A former employee said he reported for work one day in a new silver-colored car. Jim asked what happened to his previous car of the same color. "I told him I traded it in for this one," said the man. "I could tell Jim did not approve. At the end of that year I didn't get a bonus."

Jim personally set an example of frugality. Most obvious was his unpretentious ground-floor office in LeVoy's cement-block building at 2511 South West Temple—a space he kept for decades, despite the urging of family and friends to buy or build something more befitting a budding billionaire. It had no lavish furnishings, no objects of art, no desirable views. One magazine writer called its wood paneling "early insurance agent" before it was covered by wallpaper in 1989.

There were no pictures of his inventions on the walls, only family photos. "It's not because I'm shy...But my business style has never accommodated showiness...It is a style that has worked well for me...Many people picture entrepreneurs as brilliant creative thinkers, with little sense for day-to-day management," Jim wrote. In contrast, he called his style "highly methodical."

"I believe genius is, in large part, simply a product of tenacity and intensity. Genius is the ability to burn deeper and more intensely than others might. It is being tenacious when searching every part of a problem. Then, after examining all parts of the problem, it is the ability to draw back, to relax and listen, to get in touch with yourself. You have to listen for sounds both inside and outside of yourself. That is when new ways of seeing and solving the problem emerge."

Jim also believed inspiration plays a role. He likely agreed with one university philosopher, who, after carefully studying important breakthroughs, said "every great scientific discovery came as an intuition to the mind of the discoverer."

Despite saturating his mind with a problem, the scientist invariably found progress blocked by an impenetrable wall. Then, "as if out of nowhere," the answer came in a flash of light. He was positive that "no great discovery had been made by pure reasoning. Reason would lead to the borderland of the unknown, but could not tell what was within." [17]

Jim said "I hope I'm not just a man with good ideas. I like to think that I'm a man with the vision to see that good ideas are directed toward useful ends, and a 'do it' kind of guy who makes things happen."

LeVoy's showed conclusively that Jim could make money. However, he wondered, could he also make a difference?

### CHAPTER SEVENTEEN

# THE GREATEST MIND

An elderly Scottish woman we'll call Elizabeth was one of hundreds of thousands of individuals felled by cholera in a pandemic that spread across Europe in 1829-1830. Victims suffered profuse, watery diarrhea and vomiting after being infected by drinking water or eating food contaminated by the feces of an infected person, including one with no obvious symptoms.

Dr. Thomas Latta, Elizabeth's physician, had treated other victims by injecting warm salt water directly into their large intestines, and having patients take the same solution by mouth. These approaches had no benefit and, in some cases, increased vomiting and purging.

Elizabeth was near death when Dr. Latta took a radical approach to save her. He mixed a solution and prepared to "throw the fluid immediately into the circulation." Latta inserted a tube into the basilic vein, which passes along the back of the forearm, and began injecting the solution. Initially there was no visible effect. Then Elizabeth began to breathe easier, her sunken eye and fallen jaw "began to glow with returning animation."

After six pints of fluid were injected over a half-hour period, she announced in a strong voice that she was now "free from all uneasiness." Dr. Latta, sure she was well, left Elizabeth in the care of another doctor. Unfortunately she again began vomiting and purging, and died within five hours.

Latta, in his report, emphasized that to have lasting effects, such injections needed to continue, and failures were caused by giving a patient too little fluid too late.

Unfortunately Latta's innovative approach and Latta himself—who died in 1833—were soon forgotten. A report on Edinburgh cholera victims in the epidemic of 1848-1849 indicated that out of 739 patients, only 19 were given IV saline.

Several more decades passed before intravenous saline became standard practice for hypovolemic shock—when severe blood and fluid loss leads to multiple organ failure.[1]

Periodically since then, doctors, scientists, and engineers have invented new ways to use catheters and related devices to enter and heal the bodies of patients. Jim Sorenson and his co-inventors belong high on this list.

"Jim was beyond genius," said one former collaborator, Robert Hitchcock, a professor of bioengineering at the University of Utah. "A 'genius' is someone who does well on an IQ test. Jim's abilities went far beyond thinking and reasoning." Notably, Jim sold an idea to others, breathed life into it, and pursued its practical possibilities to the nth degree.[2]

James Larson, who joined Jim's enterprises as chief financial officer and, over thirty years, rose to chief operating officer, said "Jim had the greatest mind I've ever been around in terms of ideas. He would bury us with ideas...his mind just raced. He would call somebody, then forget why he called them. Some of his ideas didn't work out, but those that did were tremendous successes and far outweighed the losers."[3]

Ross Workman, a former partner at a prestigious Utah law firm that specializes in protecting intellectual property, was chief outside counsel in asserting and defending early Sorenson inventions.

"Ross said that, better than anybody he had ever encountered, Mr. Sorenson could take a gizmo, turn it over in his hand, and decide if it would succeed in the market," said Reed Winterton, an in-house Sorenson attorney for a quarter-century, who specializes in patents. "He said that Mr. Sorenson did this with an extraordinarily high degree of success."[4]

Jim operated near the edge of his contract not to compete with his former company, Deseret Pharmaceutical, for two years. The agreement was signed in December 1960. The following year, while running LeVoy's, he applied for patents on at least three disposable medical products. Apparently his efforts did not violate the contract. All three patents were granted by the federal government, an average of three years after application.

His first patent—No. 3,095,972—from the U.S. Patent Office (today called the Patent and Trademark Office) was granted on July 2, 1963. It was for a "self-sealing sterile packaging method." Two other 1961 inventions likewise were awarded patents: one for "sterile packaging" and a second one for an "intravenous catheter placement unit."

To be patentable, a proposal must be novel, non-obvious, and useful. It also is to be more than a minor refinement of an existing product. Researchers at the patent office—experts in a variety of fields—pore over previous patents to ensure that a proposal has not already been invented and patented. All inventors of an item must be listed on the application.

The patent office's function is "to exclude others from making, using, offering for sale, or selling the invention throughout the United States or importing the invention into the United States" for a period of limited time. In exchange, inventors agree to public disclosure of their inventions once a patent is granted.

After the three patents noted above, which carry only Jim's name, collaborators worked with him on almost all the rest of his forty-plus patents. How many additional Sorenson applications were turned down by the patent office is unknown.

What can be said with near certainty is that Jim's success rate was remarkably high. The rule of thumb is that from 80 to 90 percent of all inventions will not become patented. This is either because someone does not pursue a patent—farmers, for example, routinely invent something practical—or are discouraged by the cost and bureaucratic hoops they must jump through.

In 2012 a first application for a patent in the U.S. cost between $5,000 and $10,000. If the patent office reaction is encouraging, the applicant gets a second chance to clarify and strengthen the application. After that, additional bites of the apple cost more money.

The cost of defending a patent in the courts is much greater, often more than $1 million. Many individuals and small businesses drop out at that point. Wealthier businesses that can afford to fight a challenge to a key product often pursue it, to protect the millions of dollars worth of market they have built.

Of the patents that are issued, 10 to 20 percent go to market, and of those items, 10 to 20 percent succeed commercially. Jim's success rate was much higher, both in the number of products approved for marketing and the dollar return on the products.

Although other inventors collaborated with Jim in later years, during the pivotal period under Sorenson Research, K. Pannier and Gordon Reynolds were his key collaborators.

"Our working styles were different but complementary," said Jim. "I would identify a need and a basic concept to address the need, some aspect of medical care that left patients or their doctors wanting something better. I was there in the [viewing area outside] the hospital operating room...I saw the hurts and all the ways medicine could clobber people.

"I would visualize a possible solution to the problem. Once that vision formed, I would call Pannier and talk to him about it. Pannier would take the concept, question it, commit it to paper and help refine it. Then Pannier and Reynolds would build it." Explained Jim:

> In the quiet morning hours I often came up with my best ideas. I'd often stay up nights thinking about solutions. Sometimes in the middle of the night I'd phone Kay and explain my latest version of a solution to some problem. When Kay said "OK, go back to sleep," I knew he had the gist of it. The next day the drawings would be done beautifully, and we would go over them. That's how we invented many things. With my medical background I could conceptualize, and my associates had the engineering instincts that I didn't have. They would take my ideas and suggestions and make them better. [5]

One trick that sometimes spurred his creativity was soaking in a bathtub with a wet wash cloth over his face.

Jim prided his three-man team on results, not resumes. "There were no marketing committees, no memos, no fancy R&D department, no consultants or big research budgets. There was just a former drug salesman, a master machinist, and an innovative sewing machine repairman. None of us had any kind of scientific college degrees or honors. One high school diploma was lacking." [6]

During the first few years a man named Wallace Ring was another member of the team. In about 1970 Ring's place was taken by Reynolds, who remained with Sorenson and Pannier for the long haul.

The three men had something else in common. Each was a workaholic. K. often took a project home and settled into a chaise lounge while he fiddled with it. "He'd bring these catheter things home," recalled his son Scott. "Sometimes he would turn the stove burner on and stretch them over the flame to make them fit."

Jim, K. and Gordy turned LeVoy's' upstairs employee lunchroom into a skunkworks where they created a variety of disposable medical devices. Initially they focused on new versions of the catheter designs Jim had introduced at Deseret Pharmaceutical.

"I thought if we can place a catheter into the body successfully, why can't we start using the catheter to handle more jobs?" said Jim. "Why can't we thread catheters deeper into the body? Why can't we insert catheters into arteries as well as veins? Why can't we add measuring devices to gather information that is important during therapies and surgeries?"

One widely felt need was for a better catheter for children in a crisis. "There is no more exasperating situation than the inability to establish intravenous (IV) access in a critically ill child," wrote one pediatrician. "It is not uncommon for a child to come to an emergency room in severe shock, with no visible or palpable veins, or for the only venous access to a child to be lost in an emergency...Surgical exposure of a vein is a time-consuming process that exhausts valuable lifesaving minutes in an emergency." [7]

Jim and his colleagues invented several catheter placement units to address this and other needs. They were marketed as MiniCath and E-Z Cath. One used a smaller than normal needle and short catheter especially suited to infants and adult surface veins such as those on the back of the hand.

Similar units then in use could not be withdrawn after the catheter was positioned. In addition, those units did not prevent rotation between the needle and catheter. The danger, Jim and Pannier explained in their patent application, was that, while withdrawing the needle, it could cut the catheter, with a piece of it "remaining in the vein of the patient." In their system, the needle could be readily withdrawn after placing the catheter.

In a crisis, their system also enabled medical personnel to begin infusion of liquids before the needle was withdrawn. [8]

Jim hired two salesmen and in 1966 Sorenson Research began taking products to market. The items included the new catheter placement units as well as the sterile packaging Jim invented several years earlier. One type of packaging protected a variety of surgical instruments. Another type, for catheters, enabled a doctor or nurse to press the needle into the patient while the tubing remained sterile inside the package, ready to be inserted through the hollow needle.

Sorenson Research, which burst suddenly onto the medical scene, had to fight for respect. Jim and K. had been working on ways of introducing soft plastic catheters through veins deeply into the body—not for infusions of liquids but for computer-based monitoring of cardiovascular dynamics. They were close to discovering how to thread a catheter through the subclaven jugular nearly to the heart.

Jim, ever the salesman, attended various medical conventions and seminars to demonstrate his wares. At one event he was showing the system for threading a catheter close to the heart to about fifty doctors. A Dr. Moss from the Mayo Clinic challenged Jim, suggesting his system was unsafe.

"He grabbed my catheter in front of all those doctors, held it in the air, and sheared it on the end of the needle, saying 'This is what can happen.' It was absurd. What he did would never happen in a patient. It was irritating, humiliating, and so outlandish."

Jim was so troubled by the incident that he could not sleep that night. As he tossed he thought of a way to improve their system and make it even more foolproof against possible shearing. Around 3:30 a.m. he phoned K., who answered sleepily, heard Jim out, and said "Go back to sleep." Jim slept well the rest of the night, with "a warm feeling inside."

By morning K. had beautiful drawings of the idea spread out on the table. Jim forgot many of the elements, but could see that the drawings were different from what he suggested.

"Well, this isn't exactly what I told you over the phone last night," said Jim.

"It's better!" answered K. curtly.

Upon reflection, Jim acknowledged it was indeed better:

It was a thrilling experience, not only to see what I had told him, but even more thrilling to see how he had made it better. And literally he had made it much better. That kind of synergy continued in waves of ideas and pulsations. As we developed ideas, we dialogued with each other. I would bring others into the circle, saying, 'Give us your ideas, your thoughts.'...Every man had a different thought process, a different footprint in his sands of thought. We solved problems, we came up with medical devices and ideas that became milestones in the operating room and intensive care areas, and are the basis of many things that are done today. [9]

Jim was resourceful and an unusually astute observer. Many ideas for inventions came from talking to doctors as well as watching their operations and other healing work. He also credited communing with nature and with God. "I think the kernel starts where there is some basic need that you would like to see fulfilled," said Jim. "If you are a compassionate person, you find it most rewarding to deal with medical needs, whether it be drugs, diagnostic devices, or nutrition."

Given his great number of creative ideas, Jim had a few tricks to keep the most promising ones on the front burner. Since the early years of his marriage Jim carried three-by-five cards listing bills coming in and money going out. Later he added three-by-five cards listing things he hoped to accomplish each day, in priority order. If he got the most important one or two tasks done during the day, he gave himself an A for effort. He also carried a pencil with an eraser to facilitate changes on a card, and slide rule for quick calculations.

He used the same system with co-workers, directing and, when necessary, re-directing their efforts on his top priorities. "This is where you put yourself and your attitude in other people's minds," explained Jim. "Getting your team to continue, to be as persistent as you want them to be, courageous where they weren't courageous, persistent where they weren't persistent, or to delve deeper when they tended to think only on surface or veneer issues."

Jim's enthusiasm and tenacity unnerved some employees, while others thrived on it. "A lot of people were afraid of Mr. Sorenson," said a manager named John Brophy. "He could be very short with people, and sometimes lost his temper and got very upset. But it was a great creative environment."

Many of Jim's associates have favorite stories of his frugality. One of Brophy's is the time he and Jim went to Denny's restaurant on 45th South. After talking business over lunch, the multi-millionaire and Brophy got up to leave. Brophy had to pick up the tab. [10]

### CHAPTER EIGHTEEN

# JIM, DR. HOMER WARNER

## Team to Mend Hearts

Following heart surgery at LDS Hospital, Charles was in the ICU as a nurse nervously checked on him. A yellow light on the panel indicated something was wrong.

The nurse was pumping up a blood pressure cuff on Charles' left arm when she spotted Dr. Homer Warner observing. Embarrassed, she said she didn't know what to do next. Warner motioned toward a computer terminal and both sat down.

A computer-connected catheter was in Charles' left side, from the radial artery in his wrist, all the way to his heart. Quickly checking the computer screen and the patient's chart, they determined he likely was suffering a cardiac tamponade—potentially fatal pressure on his heart from a swift buildup of blood or other fluid in the sac (pericardium) surrounding the heart.

They alerted the surgeon, who wheeled the patient back to the operating room. Charles was lucky. Prompt diagnosis and treatment are critical to survive tamponade.

Although Charles probably did not know it, the man most responsible for the computer system that saved his life was none other than Dr. Warner, considered one of the fathers of medical informatics—using computers in medicine.

Jim and his colleagues invented the catheter that was a critical part of Warner's diagnostic system.

Dr. Warner and Jim are in a long line of outstanding medical practitioners, researchers, and inventors who were reared in or attracted to the Beehive State. Altogether they helped turn Salt Lake City into one of the nation's leading medical centers.

During the previous century, medical education in the U.S. was unregulated and often haphazard. In 1880 Dr. Frederick Kohler established Utah's first medical school, in Morgan, about forty miles northeast of Salt Lake City. Two years later the institution graduated six students—its first and only class—and shut its doors.

The University of Utah was founded in 1850. A half-century later, in 1905, two medical milestones were taken in Salt Lake City—the start of LDS Hospital (formerly Deseret Hospital) and the Medical Department at the University of Utah (the "U"). The latter was a two-year program, whose name was changed to the University of Utah Medical School in 1912.

The Army in 1920 turned over to the medical school a new building it constructed on campus as a dormitory for military officers. The red-brick facility became the medical school's basic science building, the first facility in which the school was housed separately.

When Japan attacked Pearl Harbor in December 1941, drawing the nation into war, there was a shortage of doctors in the American West. With no medical school between Denver and San Francisco, Washington pressured Utah to expand its medical school to a four-year institution, which it did the following year.

The school's teaching facility was Utah's only public hospital, aging Salt Lake General at 21st South and State Street. A practicing physician, Dr. A.C. Callister, was named part-time dean, and helped attract a small but superb group of medical teachers and researchers to the fledgling program.

Henry P. Plenk, who completed his residency in radiology at Northwestern University in Chicago, was one of the new recruits. "My wife and I left Evanston [Wyoming] April 30, in a snowstorm, and three days later drove into Salt Lake Valley, seeing green grass, lilacs, flowers in bloom, and fresh, glistening snow on the awe-inspiring Wasatch Range," he wrote.

Despite a low budget and austere facilities—Salt Lake General already was fifty years old, with several departments housed in Army-like barracks—Plenk and his wife were won over by the warmth of the medical group of about sixteen individuals. They "impressed us with the close relationships among the high-quality faculty not found in any other medical school in the country." Another plus was "skiing in Alta." They arrived to stay in June 1947. [1]

Nationally noted faculty who helped get the U's medical school off the ground included Louis Goodman, a discoverer of the first effective anti-cancer chemotherapy and author, along with Alfred Gilman, of a book considered the bible of pharmacology, and Maxwell (Max) Wintrobe, author of the leading textbook on hematology, who left Johns Hopkins University in Baltimore to become head of the new medical school in 1943. [2]

The four-year school's first class—thirty-one men and four women—graduated on September 10, 1944. The following year the school won the first grant awarded to any medical school by the U.S. Public Health Service; it was renewed annually for thirty-three years, for a total of nearly $10 million.

Utah's growing status was affirmed in 1948 when it was one of four laboratories chosen to help develop an effective polio vaccine. Later the vaccine was successfully produced by Dr. Jonas Salk at the University of Pittsburgh.

Health-care giants who later chose to make Salt Lake City their home included Mario Capecchi, an Italian-born molecular geneticist and Harvard professor who joined the U faculty in 1973. In 2007 he was co-winner of the Nobel Prize in Physiology or Medicine for discovering a way to create mice in which a specific gene is turned off. Today a street on campus carries his name.

The world's attention was riveted on the University of Utah Hospital on December 2, 1982 as Barney Clark, 61, became the first human recipient of a permanent artificial heart. Cardiothoracic surgeon William DeVries, whose team performed the landmark operation, was one of several individuals who made it possible.

DeVries, the only person authorized by the Food and Drug Administration to perform the operation, was the son of a U.S. Navy surgeon.

The younger DeVries was born at the Brooklyn Navy Yard and earned his bachelor's and M.D. degrees at the U. He was a resident at Duke University Medical Center before returning to Salt Lake City.

Willem Johan Kolff, considered the father of artificial organs, in 1967 became head of the university's Division of Artificial Organs and Institute for Biomedical Engineering. Kolff was born in the Netherlands and, during World War II, made major discoveries in the field of dialysis for kidney failure. In 1945 he first saved a patient's life with hemodialysis treatment which has since rescued millions of individuals with renal failure.

In 1971 Robert Jarvik joined Kolff's staff. Jarvik, born in Michigan and reared in Stamford, Connecticut, had completed two years of study at the U's medical school when he joined Kolff. Jarvik received his M.D. degree from the U five years later. He and Kolff together invented the grapefruit-size artificial heart, the Jarvik-7, which kept Barney Clark alive for 112 days.

Through the years other nationally prominent physicians likewise made their way to the U. What attracted such talent?

Not the size of the faculty, in the early years, however eminent its members. By 1949 the clinical departments had expanded to only twenty faculty—even after a recruiting push that followed World War II.

Neither was the attraction to the U the relatively modest salaries or, in the early years, the facilities. The County Hospital was not a pleasant place to practice. Patient facilities were primitive and unsanitary. There was scarcely any laboratory space, and no blood bank. Not until the opening of the University Hospital and Basic Science Building at adjacent Fort Douglas in 1965 did the U's medical team finally get facilities worthy of their abilities.

One attraction to Utah was the quality of life, especially skiing, fishing, and hiking among breathtaking scenery. Some faculty routinely took Thursday or Friday afternoons off and left together to enjoy "the greatest snow on earth." Another attraction, judging from what a number of them wrote, was the especially friendly Utahns and medical colleagues who welcomed them.

No doubt another attraction, especially to a cohort of individuals acutely aware of public health issues, was Utah's reputation as a place where most citizens grow up and grow old in better health than in almost all other states. One obvious reason is Utah's majority population of Mormons, whose scriptural health code (the "Word of Wisdom") forbids the use of tobacco and alcohol. Consider these differences, represented by a national population of 100,000 vs. Utah population of 100,000:

In 2007 there were 126 deaths from coronary heart disease in the U.S. In Utah the figure was 84 deaths. In 2009 there were 173 deaths from cancer in the U.S., and 121 in Utah.

In 2010 life expectancy in the U.S. was 75.7 years for males and 80.8 years for females. In Utah the corresponding figures were 78.1 and 82.2 years. [3]

Samuel Clements aka Mark Twain loved to lampoon the Mormons. Yet, during a storied two-day visit to Salt Lake City, even Twain acknowledged it was highly agreeable.

> Next day we strolled about everywhere through the broad, straight, level streets, and enjoyed the pleasant strangeness of a city of fifteen thousand inhabitants with no loafers perceptible in it; and no visible drunkards or noisy people; a limpid stream rippling and dancing through every street in place of a filthy gutter; block after block of trim dwellings, a great thriving orchard and garden behind every one of them, apparently...and a grand general air of neatness, repair, thrift, and comfort, around and about and over the whole. And everywhere were workshops, factories, and all manner of industries; and intent faces and busy hands were to be seen wherever one looked; and in one's ears was the ceaseless clink of hammers, the buzz of trade and the contented hum of drums and fly-wheels. [4]

University Hospital is one of twenty-nine hospitals in the greater Salt Lake City-Ogden area. Another is LDS Hospital, a venerable urban institution nestled in the northern section of Salt Lake City between Temple Square and the state Capitol. It was at LDS where Homer Warner performed the pioneering research and clinical activities that made him a legend in combining computers and catheters to monitor cardiovascular functions and save the lives of heart patients.

Warner would become Jim Sorenson's most important doctor-ally.

They had some traits in common. Both were high-energy and enthusiastic, with enormous willpower. They both encouraged colleagues with variations of "We can find a better way. Let's do it!" Also like Jim, Warner was indefatigable when pursuing a goal, choosing work over sleep.

On one occasion Warner and a colleague had worked for months on a joint-venture imaging project with the Mayo Clinic. They developed a modest prototype and applied for a grant. The day before the grant-review team arrived in Utah, Warner went to the lab for a last look—and decided what they had was not good enough. He suggested modifications.

"I had worked hard to make sure the program would not explode during the demo and I was very reticent to do a 'quick and dirty,' but Homer was so enthusiastic that he couldn't wait to try two or three new variations," said his colleague. "Finally we left for home about 4 a.m. The algorithm worked noticeably better and we had a chance to shower and change our clothes before meeting the site visitors." They won the grant for a fruitful five-year project. [5]

Warner was home-grown, born in 1922 in Salt Lake City and reared there. He received bachelor and medical degrees at the University of Utah. Tall, athletic, and genial, he played football at the U and served in the Navy two years. Several decades later Warner took up serious sailing—purchasing a forty-foot ocean racer and living on it for six months during a sabbatical while writing a book, then racing in the TransPacific from Vancouver to Hawaii.

He spent a year as a resident in medicine at the University of Minnesota, then continued his residency at the Mayo Clinic in Rochester, Minnesota, about seventy-five miles southeast of the university. Mentored by physiologist Earl Wood, Warner was fascinated by the groundbreaking work of Mayo researchers to find new ways to diagnose heart problems.

Wood interested Warner in developing a method for estimating stroke volume—the volume of blood pumped from the left ventricle of the heart with each beat—from the shape of aortic pressure waves. Warner's work was promising enough that it became the basis for his doctoral dissertation when he returned to the University of Minnesota and completed the requirements for a PhD in physiology in 1953.

Warner, his wife Kay and children, who eventually numbered six, returned to Salt Lake City with a one-year fellowship to work in cardiology at County Hospital. While there, Clarence Wonnacott, head of LDS Hospital and Jim Sorenson's one-time boss, invited Warner to move to LDS Hospital and set up a cardiovascular laboratory. Homer jumped at the chance. He thought he would be at LDS a few years; he was there thirty-five.

Warner was with other Mayo Clinic researchers as they conducted some of the very first experiments using catheters to measure heart functions. He set about to improve on those relatively crude experiments.

"We essentially built a lab like the one at the Mayo Clinic," explained Warner. "We bought a big old door and put it on a couple of sawhorses." On one end they mounted a bank of galvanometers—instruments for detecting and measuring electric current. Then they threaded a catheter into a cardiac patient's arteries and to his heart. Electric current from pressure waves was reflected by a small mirror into a camera whose eleven-inch-wide film was then studied by physicians.

Two others who worked closely with him were Reed M. Gardner, an electrical engineer and Warner's second graduate student, and Dr. Alan Toronto, an intern.

Later, with the help of Dr. Robert Stepheson, an electrical engineer at the U, Warner built a tunable circuit with a resistor, a capacitor, and a coil, with knobs on the panel to adjust each component. Warner used the crude analog computer to measure a pressure wave as recorded through one catheter at the aorta and another catheter down at the radial artery. As he suspected, the shape of the pressure wave changed from one location to the other.

Warner and Toronto studied eighty patients with this technique and published their findings. It was the first time that type of measurement was made on living patients. On the strength of that work, the National Institutes of Health gave Warner funding to purchase components for an analog computer.

Within a few years the department had a roomful of amplifiers that were used to model complex equations that would have been impossible to solve without a computer.

In June 1955 LDS Hospital received a $220,000 grant from the Ford

Foundation. Warner convinced hospital administrator Wonnacott to use it to establish a cardiac research foundation. One-third of the funds were used to build a two-story animal research facility on the hospital's roof, right over the cath lab. Dogs were kept in cages on the top level, and the lab was immediately below.

These were the early years of heart surgery. "Not many people knew we had dogs coming into the hospital," said Warner, "but without them we could not have done the open heart surgery or other procedures. We had to develop our own bypass machine and develop the whole field." [6]

LDS Hospital's commitment to cardiac care attracted a number of other heart surgeons to the hospital. One of them was Russell M. Nelson, later the president of Gardner's LDS stake (a group of congregations) and still later a member of the Church's Quorum of the Twelve Apostles.

The hospital had a large backlog of patients with congenital heart disease who could not be operated on until diagnosed by Warner's team. There was a problem, however. The catheters available to them for diagnostic procedures were not ideal. They were made of polyethylene, the most common form of plastic at the time, and they tended to clot at the tip when in the body. In addition, much care had to be taken to ensure that the needle as well as the tubing to pass through it were kept strictly sterilized. Both concerns cost precious time that could make a difference in the outcome for a patient.

At the same time that demand for cardiac diagnostics at LDS Hospital was increasing, Jim Sorenson and his colleagues at Sorenson Research were experimenting with ways to thread a catheter all the way to the heart.

"I was designing devices that could get into the heart while remaining sterile," said Jim, who tried, at first in vain, to interest Warner in his work. "Homer was so involved in computers that he didn't realize I had things that would help his projects."

Sorenson Research had largely solved the dual catheter problems of clotting and sterile insertion. The company replaced the polyethylene plastic with the tongue-twister polytetrafluoroethylene, better known by the brand name DuPont gave it: Teflon. Popularly used as the plastic non-stick coating on frying pans, Teflon is hydrophobic—neither water nor water-containing substances wet it. Therefore by using Teflon, catheter clotting is sharply reduced.

Jim's company likewise had long since solved the issue of sterilization. Their cardiac catheters and catheter-packaging was sterilized and ready for instant use. A physician or nurse could quickly open the package and insert the needle and Teflon catheter into the patient, through either the radial artery in the wrist or femoral artery in the thigh.

Since doctors and nurses threaded the device directly from the germ-free packaging into the patient, the possibility of contamination was all but eliminated. The system was intended for one-time use, then discarded.

Failing to get Warner's attention, Jim approached his associate Alan Toronto, who later replaced Warner as director of the catheterization lab.

"I showed Dr. Toronto my wares," said Jim. "Toronto was overwhelmed. He said 'You've got it! You've got it!' When Dr. Toronto showed my products to Dr. Warner, he too became one of my greatest supporters."

Dr. Warner said, "I gave Jim the specs that we needed and he developed a new catheter that could go through this thin-walled eighteen-gauge needle. It was stiff enough that it had the physical properties to accurately transmit the pressure waves from its tip to the pressure gauge.

"We already had catheters for the veins, which were commercially available. Jim's contribution was giving us catheters that made it possible to record central aortic pressure."

This was huge. Central aortic pressure is the blood pressure measured at the root of the aorta, the largest artery in the body. It originates from the left ventricle of the heart and distributes oxygenated blood to all parts of the body. Measuring blood pressure at the aorta itself is a stronger indicator of cardiovascular disease than traditional measurement through a stethoscope and a pressure cuff on the brachial artery in the arm.

Blood pressure varies throughout the body, as Dr. Warner's experiments proved. With Jim's ingenious catheter it was now possible to do the measurement that counts the most in day-to-day clinical work.[7]

Jim was extremely grateful to Dr. Warner and even offered him stock in Le Voy's, the parent company of Sorenson Research. Warner declined, concerned that it would be unethical. "But I'll be your best salesman," he told Jim.

True to his word, Warner sang the praises of the new catheter system. The two men went to a medical convention in San Francisco. Jim set up a small booth to display his wares, as Homer gave a speech to surgeons at one of the meetings. As they left the meeting, doctors rushed to Jim's booth to ask questions and place orders.

"Jim did a lot," said Warner. "They were sure successful."

Chase Peterson *(center)*, president of the University of Utah, and Jim served together on the First Security Bank board of directors. Also serving was David B. Haight, a member of the LDS Church's Quorum of the Twelve Apostles.

**The Salt Lake Tribune**

Section A      Wednesday, September 6, 1989      Page 10

In 1998 Peterson proposed naming the U's medical center for Jim in exchange for a \$15.2 million gift—largest in school history. Jim made the stock gift, but the U reneged on its proposal and eventually returned the gift.

Jim pioneered the use of DNA to link families together, starting a billion-dollar industry. His goal: Promote world peace by showing people how closely they are related. The Sorenson Molecular Genealogy Foundation collected 100,000 DNA samples from across the globe. **Courtesy** *Deseret News Publishing Company.*

A villager in Mata Ortiz, Mexico, gives a mouthwash DNA sample to a Sorenson field worker. Courtesy *Deseret News Publishing Company*

Noted genetic scientist Scott Woodward *(left)* left Brigham Young University to establish and direct the Sorenson Molecular Genealogy Foundation. With him is Doug Fogg, head of Sorenson Genomics. Courtesy *Deseret News Publishing Company*

A Sorenson DNA collection team in Mongolia. Other Sorenson efforts abroad included identifying human victims of the 2004 tsunami that killed a quarter-million people in Thailand and neighboring countries.

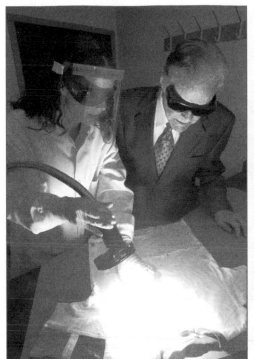
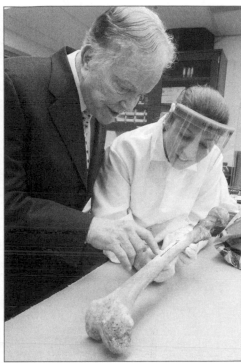

Sorenson Forensics has solved many crimes, including cold cases. Jim watches one lab technician search for DNA evidence on a T-shirt, and another on a human femur bone. Courtesy *Deseret News Publishing Company*

Looking over the shoulder of Sorenson Genomics' chief scientist Lars Mouritsen. Courtesy *Deseret News Publishing Company*

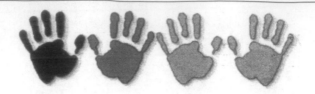

## "All mankind are my brothers and sisters. And the world is my country."

J.L.S.

Inside the brochure at the grand opening of the Sorenson Multicultural Center in June 1996. Jim often cited the mission statement and motto.

Utah Youth Village helps troubled youngsters learn from good role models how to live productive lives. Sorenson has also given to numerous other youth efforts such as $1 million to the YMCA's Camp Roger in the Uintah Mountains.

The 2006 Utah Legislature cut Medicaid, including dental care for 65,000 low-income residents. Jim donated $1 million anonymously to help cover the gap. He was thanked by Governor Jon Huntsman (*center*) and House Speaker Greg Curtis. Photo by *Salt Lake Tribune*.

The inner west section of Salt Lake City lacked facilities to keep youth off the streets. The Sorensons gave major gifts to develop the Sorenson Multicultural and Unity Fitness Center there. Jim hands off the basketball to a teammate as Beverley raps with other children. Courtesy *Deseret News Publishing Company*

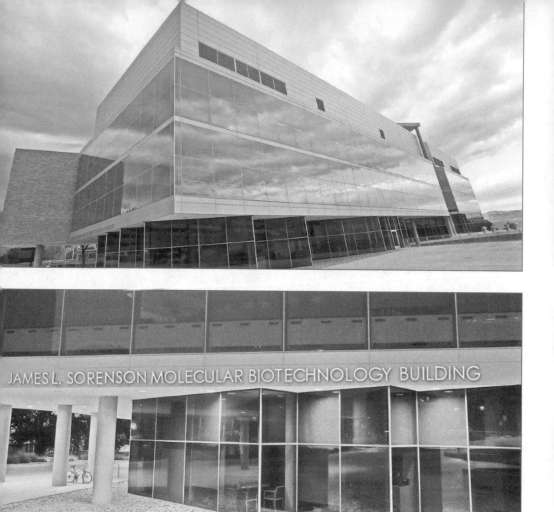

The James L. Sorenson Molecular Biotechnology Building opened in 2012 at the University of Utah. It is part of the Utah Science Technology and Research Initiative (USTAR), state-funded collaboration between the U and Utah State University. The Sorenson Legacy Foundation contributed $15 million of its $130 million cost. *Photos by Eric Roderick*

A researcher uses a high-tech electron microscope in the building. Courtesy *Deseret News Publishing Company*

### CHAPTER NINETEEN

# CARDIAC CATHETER

## Opens New Era

I t was an exhilarating time for Jim Sorenson, K. Pannier, and Gordon Reynolds, and for Homer Warner's team at LDS Hospital. Together they were discovering secrets to critical health care and innovating ways to treat patients throughout the world.

Jim, whose lifelong interest was medicine, worked primarily with Dr. Warner himself. K. and Gordon worked primarily with Dr. Reed Gardner, a biophysicist and electrical engineer. He was Warner's second graduate student and became his right arm in the budding science of applying computers in medicine—medical informatics.

Gardner, a pleasant man who had high praise for Jim's team, was born in 1937 in St. George, southern Utah. He attended school there, including Dixie College—a two-year community college, where a superb math and science teacher convinced him to become an engineer. He won a scholarship to the University of Utah, where he got a bachelor's degree in electrical engineering in 1959.

Gardner showed Homer Warner's power of persuasion. Gardner worked at Hewlett-Packard in California before graduation and considered making his career there. Then a University of Utah professor suggested he go visit Warner, who was "doing interesting things." Gardner drove up into the avenues to LDS Hospital to see for himself.

"That changed my entire career," said Gardner. "Homer probably had as good a computing facility at LDS as there was anywhere in the country at that time." He passed on the Hewlett Packard offer and enrolled in the U's graduate school, earning a PhD in medical biophysics and computing. Gardner joined Warner as a pioneer in medical informatics.[1]

He recalled when Henry Eyring, an eminent scientist and dean of the U's graduate school, called Homer into his office, along with the deans of the university's engineering and medical schools.

The medical school dean didn't think it would fit with their curriculum at the time, which was to train medical students. The engineering dean, on the other hand, was delighted at the offer, and proceeded in 1964 to organize the Department of Medical Biophysics and Computing. It was the first department of its kind in the world. Although Warner was physically at LDS Hospital, he chaired the new department at the U.

Gardner began a close collaboration with K. and Gordon. "Both of them were brilliant men and fantastic to work with," said Gardner. "Gordon could build anything from anything. K. was more of a conceptual idea guy. "Sometimes they'd come up here, sometimes I'd go down there [to 2511 South West Temple]. We did that many times."

"Their disposable catheter system made the insertion of the Teflon catheter through a needle much easier and faster," explained Gardner. "We just sterilized a little bit of skin, usually on the wrist, where we inserted the needle. You can do this in five to ten minutes. Before that you'd have to take much more time preparing the patient with a sterile field, gloves, mask, the whole works."

Although Sorenson's central arterial catheters were made of Teflon and did not clot as easily as those made of other plastics, clotting was still an issue. The clotting problem occurred within hours of insertion, at the tip of the catheter near the heart. Since the catheter was connected to a pressure transducer, the sensing diaphragm of the transducer moved very slightly with each arterial pulsation. As the diaphragm moved, a tiny amount of blood went into the tip of the catheter which eventually led to a clot formation at the catheter tip.

The team's original response was to have a nurse inject a small amount of saline solution into the catheter every hour or so to keep the catheter from clotting. However, this was prone to forgetfulness or other human error and was not a satisfactory long-term solution.

Jim's team and Gardner came up with a continuous-flush system marketed as "Intraflo" to eliminate clotting. A pressurized plastic bag with a saline solution was positioned above the patient. A capillary tube was connected from the bag to the catheter, to allow a small amount of saline fluid to flow through the catheter and out the tip at the other end to prevent clotting.

Another plus for Intraflo was that it largely solved a problem of air bubbles in the system. Previously, when an air bubble entered a catheter, it distorted the pressure waveform, so the clinician could not get an accurate reading to determine cardiac output.

Intraflo revolutionized critical-care pressure monitoring. With this one device, physicians could now insert catheters not only into veins but into arteries. Overnight they had new tools to accurately gather more useful cardiac information than ever before.

Sorenson Research's cardiac catheter system helped open a new era of improved, computerized care for patients, before, during, and—new to medicine—after surgery.

Other uses of computers had led members of the medical profession to wonder if computers likewise could be used to monitor acutely ill patients. "A system directed toward this ultimate end has been in operation in the Latter-day Saints Hospital in Salt Lake City, Utah, since March, 1966," wrote Dr. Warner and two colleagues.

"To date, 215 patients have been monitored with this system. Many of these patients developed complications which were detected by the computer system earlier than would have been the case by the usual methods of monitoring." Information gathered by the system often led doctors to change postoperative patients' therapy, they reported. [2]

Starting in the early 1900s, the standard way to check blood pressure—a most important vital sign—was with a stethoscope and arm cuff. Although it is generally conceded that this is not the most accurate way to measure central arterial pressure, the method remains standard a century later.

Dr. Warner and his colleagues invented a better way. "The system, operating 24 hours a day, seven days a week, has now established itself as an integral part of the postoperative care of open-heart surgery patients in this hospital and is well received by the patient, nurse, and physician alike," they wrote.[3]

The first goal of their system was to find ways to obtain important physiological information by the computer online and in real-time. Data had to be easily and continuously gathered from sensors without impeding patient mobility and comfort. A second goal was to help the doctor and nurse sort through all the computerized data to spot what indicated a serious change in the patient's status. A third goal was to provide a clinical diagnosis based on the information.

On the afternoon before surgery, a portable arm board unit on wheels is pushed to the patient's bedside. Sorenson's catheter system enters the picture. It is encased in a solid plastic shield, from which it is threaded directly into the patient, eliminating the need for sterile drapes or gloves.

A thin-walled eighteen-gauge needle is pushed into the patient's radial artery while pressure is monitored at a remote computer station. The Teflon catheter is advanced through the needle up the artery to the subclavian artery, which is about the size of a man's small finger and one of two major arteries between the upper chest and collarbone. When the catheter tip is inserted to the central location, the lower end is taped to the patient's forearm.

A measure of how widespread their breakthroughs became was an editorial in the American Medical Association's journal in 2005. The subject was how to treat acute coronary syndromes. It was titled "To Cath or Not to Cath: That is No Longer the Question." The only question was *when* to catheterize.

The editorial synthesized a debate that raged throughout the 1990s between cardiologists who supported an "invasive" approach to heart monitoring—routinely catheterizing patients prior to surgery—and a "conservative" approach, doing so only in response to a restriction in blood flow that caused a shortage of oxygen and glucose needed to keep tissue alive.

Based on careful analysis of clinical experience with more than 9,000 patients, the article reported that "routine use of an invasive strategy substantially reduced risk of subsequent myocardial infarction, severe angina, and rehospitalization. There was a trend toward mortality reduction during the follow-up period with an invasive approach,..."[4]

Warner, Gardner, and Sorenson Research were far ahead of the AMA. Three decades before the editorial, they had shown clearly the advantages of early catheterization.

By mid-1970 Warner's team had used the system on thousands of patients at LDS Hospital—in the major cardiovascular surgical unit, in general surgical intensive care wards, and in the coronary care unit. They announced results, based on "extensive work over the last 4 years by our research group and Sorenson Research Company."

"The catheter and its introduction system has greatly simplified and facilitated introduction of catheters into human patients, while the flush system has permitted long-term (greater than 2 weeks) measurement of central arterial pressure without the usual complications," they wrote.

"Experience with over 2,500 patients has shown the scheme to be reliable and the complication rate to be negligible."[5]

The Sorenson continuous-flush catheter system gives the clinician a broad quantitative look at a patient's condition, including eight measurements: volume of blood pumped with each beat, heart rate, cardiac output, systole, systolic pressure [the top number in a blood-pressure reading, the force of blood in the arteries as the heart beats], diastolic pressure [the bottom number in a blood pressure reading, when the heart is at rest], mean pressure, and peripheral resistance.

They summarized: "Our experience...has shown that catheters are easily inserted and can be kept in place for long periods of time with a minimum of discomfort and demobilization of the patient. Complications have been few and minor. Catheters have been left in patients for more than 4 weeks and continuous flush systems have been kept on patients for more than 2 weeks to keep the catheters [open]."

Intraflo was a godsend to patients and critical-care-givers. It was also a blockbuster product for Sorenson Research, and came to account for some 40 percent of company sales.

The concept eventually expanded to dozens of other devices. One of them was Dialaflo, an infusion-rate regulator. It controlled even more precisely the rate of solution flowing across the catheter tip. Other Intraflo spinoffs included Myocath, which monitors pressure within muscle compartments; hemodialysis catheters, and the dual lumen needle used in kidney dialysis monitoring.

Reed Gardner not only helped invent Intraflo, he helped sell it. "When Jim and his sales force went out to sell the catheter and flush system, people didn't understand them," said Gardner. "So a nurse and I went out a lot, and did training demonstrations, mainly at hospitals and universities."

They also produced films, including an eighteen-minute sound movie called "Arterial Pressure. Its Relevance to Clinical Medicine." It was written by Gardner and a nurse named Rosanne Schwartz at LDS Hospital, and K. Pannier at Sorenson Research.

Direct catheterization, said the script, "allows beat-by-beat observation of pulse pressure without disturbing the patient. Accurate indirect methods require inflation of a cuff, which does disturb the patient." They noted that there are major differences between pressure measured in the central aorta and pressure measured at peripheral arteries:

"Mean pressure obtained from the arterial wave form is the best indicator of patient status...Experience with flush systems has proven flow rates of 1 to 3 cc per hour can maintain the [effectiveness] of the catheter."

Gardner, in an interview, said "Intraflo revolutionized the whole field of continuous blood pressure monitoring. You could now reliably monitor every beat."

Gardner's travels took him to England and Europe, where he saw Intraflo being employed in hospitals. "The system is still being used around the world today," he said in 2012. The catheter part has changed, with practitioners generally using shorter catheters. Widespread use had driven down costs. The blood-pressure transducers first used at LDS Hospital cost $400 to $500 each. Today a $15 silicon chip accomplishes the same purpose.

He called Jim "an unbelievable marketer. He was genuine. The product he had was a real product...He sold what he had, but didn't oversell it..."

By embracing and collaborating with Jim and his colleagues, Homer Warner had given Sorenson Research increased credibility in the mainstream medical community. Sorenson's quid pro quo was innovative catheter systems that enabled Warner's team to accomplish in reality what they had discussed and dreamed of doing.

Real-time monitoring of central aortic pressure was a huge step for medical science. Arguably, however, Warner's most important contribution—aided by Gardner, T. Alan Pryor, Paul D. Clayton, and others—was creation of a system called HELP (Health Evaluation through Logical Processing). It gave physicians more timely and quantitative information than ever before to optimize patient care. HELP, created in the 1970s, was the result of considerable, computer-aided work.[6]

Warner and colleagues years earlier were intrigued by the difficulty of diagnosing congenital heart disease, primarily in children. They determined that there were thirty-five distinct congenital heart defects.[7]

Warner set out to identify how often fifty different findings occurred in each defect, such as murmurs of different kinds and cyanosis   a bluish or purplish tint to the skin or mucous membranes caused by lack of oxygen in the blood.

The team collected data from referring doctors on several hundred of Warner's patients. Then they built a matrix, with the diseases on one axis and findings on the other axis. At each intersection of the disease and symptom they added a number corresponding with the frequency of that finding in patients with that disease. This was the basis for diagnosing a patient.

"They compared the computer diagnosis against the diagnosis of the referring physician," wrote one observer, "and were pleased to find that the computer was right...more often than any of the referring physicians. This was due to the fact that the average practitioner may only see 2 or 3 cases of congenital heart disease in a year and thus doesn't have much experience in diagnosing it."[8]

This marked the first time that heart diseases could be automatically diagnosed, based on computer-driven results of symptoms and proper interpretation. Four decades later, heart doctors and their patients across the globe continue to rely on HELP to diagnose and properly treat cardiac disease.

In 1985, after thirty years at LDS Hospital, Dr. Warner relocated to the University of Utah Medical Center. He had done double duty since

1964, working at LDS while chairing the U's informatics program. After starting in the engineering college, informatics a decade later was split in two—half remaining in engineering as Bioengineering and the remainder relocating to the School of Medicine as the Department of Medical Informatics.

After several name changes, the program in the school of medicine received its current name in 2006, the Department of Biomedical Informatics.

Thanks to Warner's leadership—and that of Reed Gardner, who succeeded him as department chair from 1996 to 2005—the U has a distinguished record of harnessing the power of computers in the service of medicine. It became the world's first biomedical informatics department and has graduated more informatics PhDs than any other program in the world. Nine high-tech companies have been built on research conducted by the informatics department.

Meanwhile Dr. Alan Toronto took over as head of LDS Hospital's cardiac diagnostic lab.

Decades later, Jim Sorenson and Homer Warner are still collaborating posthumously—at Intermountain Medical Center, one of the nation's most technologically advanced hospitals. Located in Murray, a Salt Lake suburb, it is also the largest hospital in the Rocky Mountain region, opening its doors in 2007.

Its parent company, Intermountain Healthcare—a nonprofit group of twenty-two hospitals in Utah and southeastern Idaho—transferred LDS's informatics diagnostic lab and other specialty services to the new medical center, leaving LDS as a general patient-care facility.

The Sorensons have given the medical center major philanthropic gifts. Two of its five buildings carry the family name: the J.L. Sorenson Heart & Lung Center and the J.L. Sorenson Patient Tower. In one corridor is a heroic-size bronze statue of Jim, with the slogan "Finding a Better Way."

The center's programs include the Homer Warner Center for Informatics Research, which carries on the work of Warner, Jim, and their colleagues. In recent years the hospital performed about 12,000 catheter lab procedures and twenty heart transplants annually.

Two hearts were implanted in Eric Skousen, who received the first one in 2000. A severe infection followed, and he received the second heart in 2008, along with a transplanted kidney. Today Eric lives a normal life. "Surely, the legacy of the James LeVoy Sorenson family is to bless people like me, and by blessing me, to bless my family and friends," said Eric. "Thank you to Beverley and her family—and to our friend Jim—from the bottom of my heart(s)."[9]

As for Dr. Warner, he "identified the [informatics] field and then defined that field," noted Intermountain's chief quality officer, Brent James. "It's hard to describe that contribution not just to the medical profession but to the patients we serve...building on Homer's foundation, we're now on the cusp of a massive transformation of care delivery."[10]

### CHAPTER TWENTY

# INVENTION SAVES,

## Recirculates Patient's Own Blood

The most promising moment for peace in the Middle East during the last half of the twentieth century was on March 26, 1979 when the Egypt-Israel Peace Treaty was signed at the Jimmy Carter White House. Egypt was the first Arab state to officially recognize Israel.

Israeli Prime Minister Menachem Begin was hailed as a hero throughout the western world. The other signer, Prime Minister Anwar El Sadat of Egypt, was denounced as a traitor throughout the Arab world, and later assassinated.

A critical question was how Saudi Arabia, the most strategically important Arab country to the West, would respond. The answer, as President Carter wrote in his memoirs, was that King Khalid and Crown Prince Fahd of Saudi Arabia assured him of their quiet but "unequivocal support for Sadat."

Sorenson Research played a small role in King Khalid's personal commitment to the United States. A tall, genial man, he had long suffered from heart ailment, and in 1970 had a massive heart attack. Two years later the King had heart surgery at Cleveland Clinic Hospital.

In the fall of 1978 Khalid bin Abdulaziz again faced surgery, and once more made plans to face the scalpel at Cleveland Hospital. His entourage arrived in spectacular fashion: in two Boeing 707 jetliners—his with a complete operating room in case of emergency—which flew nonstop from Arabia.

The 65-year-old king's wife and thirteen children, and dozens of others, were whisked to the clinic in a large motorcade, taking up residence for a month in a thirty-room compound on the eighth floor. Security was tight, supplied by Khalid's own detail and additional guards furnished by Washington.

Preparing for the October 3 operation, the King's personal physician was anxious that the blood transfused into him would be absolutely safe. Cleveland's crack surgical team hoped to avoid the question altogether by using the safest blood possible: the King's own blood. About 200 cubic centimeters—twelve cubic inches—of his blood were lost during surgery. Surgeons returned all the rest of the King's blood to his circulatory system.

Sorenson Research invented and supplied the unique autologous blood technique and equipment used by surgeons to pump the King's own blood back into him. No other transfusion was necessary.

The Sorenson Auto-Transfusion System (ATS) grew out of an earlier Sorenson invention called Receptal. Both use a transparent, hard-plastic canister that is thirteen inches tall, three and a half inches in diameter, and is fitted with valves and tubes. The other major part is a removable liner.

Prior to Receptal, an onerous duty in a surgical room was getting rid of the blood, pus, and other body fluids that accumulate during a procedure. This was typically accomplished through a vacuum tube leading from the patient to a glass or plastic container. The container had to be removed, cleansed, and reused—an unsanitary chore often accompanied by unpleasant odors.

"The cleansing of such a receptor is a most laborious and messy operation," the company explained in its patent application. "The changing and cleansing of the receptor places an extreme burden upon the nurses, other hospital workers, and the sterilization facilities in the hospital." Potential spreading of infection is another constant hazard.[1]

Some patients require the use of up to fifteen containers during a single hospital stay. The cumulative time, labor, and care of the old approach was costly.

"My team developed a bag, a sort of plastic garbage can liner, to fit inside the hard-plastic container," explained Jim. The trick was building a system that did not make the bag collapse during suction. Jim's team devised a unique valving system that caused the liner to inflate first, then fill with the suctioned material. Once full, the liner could be closed and lifted from the container for disposal, with the material never being touched or exposed to the atmosphere.

Once the technical bugs were ironed out, the only problem was producing Receptal fast enough to meet demand. Soon it accounted for 30 percent of Sorenson Research sales.

Jim, K., and Gordon, who invented Receptal, instinctively believed they could transform it into something even more medically significant. After five years of development, assisted by a surgery professor at Baylor College of Medicine in Houston, they unveiled the Auto-Transfusion System used in the cardiac surgery on King Khalid.

The history of blood transfusion is long and colorful. Successful transfusions between animals dates to the seventeenth century. Attempts on humans, however, were usually fatal. The first fully documented transfusion into a human was administered by a French doctor in 1667, injecting sheep's blood into a 15-year-old boy. He survived, almost certainly because it was a very small amount of blood that did not cause an allergic reaction.

Dr. Jean-Baptiste Denys, who did the human transfusion, did others as well, using calf's as well as sheep's blood. After patients died, France outlawed the procedure in 1670, followed in kind by the British Parliament and even the Pope. Human blood transfusions remained in disuse for the next 150 years.

Since then, of course, many scientific and technological advances made human blood transfusions commonplace. A British obstetrician named James Blondell in 1818 or 1829—the year is in dispute—performed the first known successful transfusion of human blood. He saw many patients die in childbirth, and was determined to save a woman suffering from postpartum hemorrhage. Using a syringe, Dr. Blondell extracted four ounces of blood from the woman's husband and transfused it successfully into her.

Between then and 1830, Dr. Blondell performed another ten transfusions, five of which apparently were beneficial. He also invented various instruments for the transfusion of blood, and died wealthy, through a combination of selling instruments and serving a large clientele.

The next milestone came in the first decade of the twentieth century. In 1900 Austrian Karl Landsteiner identified the main blood groups and how to tell them apart. He taught correctly that types should not be mixed. Transfusions became much safer. Landsteiner was awarded the Nobel Prize in Physiology and Medicine in 1930.

Sorenson Research's Autologous Transfusion System, unveiled in 1975, marked another major milestone in the development of transfusion. Long before then, of course, homogolous blood transfusion—from one human to another—was standard throughout most of the world. With the ATS, it became possible to save and reuse a patient's own blood, and for the first time the matching of blood types did not need to be an issue.

Sorenson CEO Perry Lane announced the breakthrough at a sales meeting in Park City, Utah. By then the system had been used on more than 60 surgical patients, usually handled by an operating room nurse. After five years of development the ATS was ready to be marketed, he said, and "there is nothing on the market to compete with it." [2]

"This system," explained Jim Sorenson, "salvages blood lost during trauma or surgical procedures, filters the blood, and allows it to be reused by the same patient...[it] provides an invaluable tool in battlefield settings and other areas where donated blood may not be readily available. The system saves money. No blood typing is required. There are no rejection complications, no hepatitis risk and no AIDS."

Homologous blood from someone else presents other serious complications. Elective surgery sometimes must be postponed for lack of compatible blood. In smaller towns and cities, there is often a lack of qualified donors with the needed blood types. Homologous blood must be crossmatched to determine compatibility, taking precious time that may prove fatal to an accident victim or other person in critical condition.

Another valuable use of the system is for Jehovah's Witnesses, who are commanded not to use another person's blood. Autologous blood transfusions apparently are specifically sanctioned by the religion. [3]

Sorenson's autologous system comprises at least two interconnected

blood receptacles. The first receptacle is evacuated and connected to a suction device for aspirating [drawing in] blood. The second receptacle takes
blood from the first by overcoming the vacuum in the first with a stronger
vacuum in the second. The system retrieves blood from the hemothorax
[the space between the chest wall and lung] and makes it immediately
available to the patient, without delays from typing, cross-matching, trans-
ferring or washing.

"Blood is aspirated from the chest cavity and collected in a sterile au-
totransfusion liner," explains the ATS instructions. "When reinfusion is
desired or when 1900 [milliliters] of blood is collected, the liner is removed
from the canister, a...filter is attached to the liner and reinfusion is begun."

The value of autologous transfusions was acknowledged well before
the Sorenson system. "Until this present invention, however," reads the
patent application, "no structure and method has been known which would
accommodate reinfusion of a patient's blood without interrupting the ability to simultaneously collect the blood... [4]

The medical community enthusiastically welcomed Sorenson's invention. "...when you give a patient a unit of his own blood, you not only save
a unit for someone who can't be autotransfused, you also save the considerable cost of drawing, banking and administering a unit of blood," noted
one medical publication. "...the Sorenson apparatus was simple, efficacious,
inexpensive and particularly good for emergencies." [5]

Johns Hopkins Hospital reported in 1979 that during the previous
two years, it used the Sorenson system on more than 2,000 postoperative patients, and it was now "used routinely in all cardiac surgery cases at
Hopkins."

It added that "Cardiac surgeons at Hopkins say the system is safe as
well as simple and has saved the lives of a number of patients with rare
blood types when banked blood was not available." [6]

During the 1970s Jim brought aboard a highly competent chief executive officer named Perry Lane, and continued to rely on the creative wiz-
ardry of Gordon Reynolds as director of research and development and K.
Pannier as the company's engineering vice president. K. also played an important if unofficial role as a sympathetic friend to employees who needed
to get something off their chests.

K.'s slender physique, slicked-back hair, and piercing eyes belied the man behind them. Though he often seemed stern and reserved, K. was in fact quick to break into a grin and offer solace or help wherever it was needed. He was well liked by employees as well as among outsiders to whom he represented the company.

K. was a heavy smoker until felled by a heart attack at the age of forty. That apparently scared him into breaking the deadly habit. Twelve years later, however, in 1977, he suffered cardiac arrest while sleeping and died, at a far-too-young age, fifty-two.

Condolences poured in from across the U.S. and around the globe, including Hong Kong, Italy, Iran [two years before the Islamic revolution], Japan, and France.

"We are all deeply touched by this unexpected and sad occurrance [sic], and my Staff is joining me in expressing our sincere sympathy for the loss of such a fine Collaborator," wrote the administrator of a hospital in Trieste, Italy.

"I am extremely distressed to learn of the death of Mr. K. Pannier...I am particularly sorry that Sorenson should have sustained this loss," wrote the sales manager for a hospital supply department in Hong Kong. [7]

Company CEO Perry Lane, in a general staff meeting on June 1, said "Some people are more interested in the bottom line than in the fun of getting there...not so with K. He enjoyed the 'getting there.'...[he showed that] too much work is *not* bad if one enjoys it...Success comes more often to those who get a thrill in doing things well...I am sure it is obvious to all of us that K. was a success." [8]

Jim delivered a eulogy at K.'s funeral, saying he personally lost "a dear and true friend," and the company lost "a faithful, creative, and innovative leader."

Jim rehearsed the early days of Sorenson Research and K.'s pivotal role in moving ideas from Jim's desk drawer all the way to saleable products. "K. was a major contributor in helping to set up [Sorenson Research] and to get it going...Not only did he conceive many of the ideas for the products and make them work, but he built the work force that produced them." He added:

He was a craftsman who constantly sought to make things in this life

better. He was a man of high integrity and never compromised his
principles. He never boasted of his achievements or was caught over-
reaching, but humbly sought to build the other guy...In our common
workshop, together we were able to work on projects that would relieve the suffering and improve the quality of life. K. believed no one
can harm us but ourselves, that sin is misdirected energy, that there is
no devil but fear, the universe is planned for good, and perhaps death
is a manifestation of life and just as good. [9]

By now, thanks to shrewd real estate investments as well as inventions,
Jim was a millionaire many times over. He kept a close watch on the bottom
line, but not so close that he turned a blind eye to genuine human need he
saw around him.

One such need was that of kindly Dr. Stanley Marcus, professor emeritus of microbiology and immunology at the U's School of Medicine. Marcus, who played squash with Jim, also was a giver. Balding, with white side-
burns and a thick white mustache, he had been a devoted teacher at the U
and mentored thirty-two graduate students before retiring in 1981.

Like many retired academics, Dr. Marcus found it hard to tear himself
away from the friendly, stimulating setting where he labored for more than
three decades. At the age of about eighty he still was a presence in the U's
microbiology lab. There he experimented on laboratory animals, searching
for a canker medication to treat herpes.

Finally university officials apparently told Dr. Marcus that they needed his space. When Jim learned of Marcus's plight, he set up a small area at
the LeVoy's building and invited him to occupy it to continue his testing.
Jim also paid him $1,000 a month, bought a shed and the rabbits and mice
to occupy it, and instructed a couple of employees to assist Dr. Marcus with
his experiments. Dr. Marcus's efforts led to the development of a new and
effective product for the treatment of canker sores, called ViNox, subsequently sold through local pharmacies.

After about a half-dozen years, when Sorenson Development was
tightening its belt, Jim told Marcus that he no longer could pay him a
monthly stipend.

"Can I still come in every day?" asked Marcus.

Jim said yes, and Dr. Marcus continued his research, until the day came when macular degeneration robbed him of the necessary eyesight. [10]

Jim always loved a bargain. On one trip to visit his parents in California, he found a pile of jeans on sale for just $5 in a Longs Drug Store. Jim, who exercised religiously, was trim almost his entire life, wearing pants with about a 32-inch waist and 29-inch inseam.

He dug through the stack of jeans and bought a pair. Jim took them home to Utah and gave them to his executive assistant Gloria Smith, previously a seamstress at LeVoy's, instructing her to make them fit him. They were size 36 x 36.

Jim was quick to share such news whenever he got a great deal. After Gloria cut the jeans down to size, he wore them to work. "He called me into his office," recalled one of his company presidents, Doug Fogg. "Jim stood up and said, 'How do you like these pants?' I told him they were very nice."

"How much do you think they cost?" asked Jim.

"They look pretty expensive," answered Fogg, "probably cost a lot."

Jim, grinning broadly, said "Five dollars!"

On another occasion Jim told his co-workers that a man was going around his neighborhood trying to get people to sign up for a service. If they did, he gave them a T-shirt. Jim proudly recounted that he talked the man out of a free T-shirt without signing up for the service. [11]

### CHAPTER TWENTY-ONE

# SELLING SORENSON RESEARCH

Jim Sorenson's worldwide impact is pervasive.

Not all of his inventions were patented; the paper surgical mask an obvious example. At any rate, the U.S. Patent and Trademark Office credits him and his collaborators with forty-seven registered patents, almost all in the medical field. The patent office said Jim probably has the same number of foreign patents, bringing the total to 94.

Commenting on Jim's first 40 patents, the agency said "Each of his U.S. patents has been cited as relevant prior art in an average of 16 subsequent patents." Assuming his last seven patents had the same ratio, Jim's work contributed to more than 750 other inventions.

K. Pannier is credited with Jim on 21 patents, Gordy Reynolds on 17 of the same 21. After 1980, when Jim began to purchase or create a series of new companies, another 21 co-inventors are listed with him on patents.

The largest number of patented inventions involved catheters, including continuous catheter flushing systems; followed by Receptal and other disposable systems for body fluids; autologous blood transfusion systems; apparatuses for aspirating and ventilating [removing fluid from the body and breathing]; and portable pumps for peritoneal dialysis.

A cross-section of other inventions: a light-emitting surgical laser probe; a laser surgical instrument; a system for the diffusion and dispersion of medication directly into an injured or pathologic body part; implantable sensors within the peritoneum [the abdominal cavity], for determining levels of glucose; surgical probe and smoke eliminators, and the list goes on.

Jim was the lone inventor of two types of sterile surgical instrument containers and—in a category all its own—a high-tech brassiere. His bra, patented in 1970, no doubt was inspired by Jim's clothing company, LeVoy's, most of whose products were for women. Jim's abstract said each of the bra's breast cups was separately and quickly adjustable through "the cleavage of the brassiere without the necessity of removing any outer garments." The benefit to the wearer is to "present uniformity in appearance between the breasts..." He named the bra "Tru-lē-urs."

Jim was a peerless salesman with a unique ability to read people and understand what truly moved them—from the time he was a child on a doorstep selling magazines in Yuba City, California, to when he was an adult, selling medical items or companies, or sensing talent in individuals and harnessing them to his purposes.

Some of the best talent was in his own family.

Jim and Beverley's oldest child, Carol, born in 1947, earned a degree at the University of Utah, then taught high school for two years. When she returned to the U for some post-graduate classes she met Douglas Smith, a tall, intelligent-looking doctoral candidate. They were married in the Salt Lake Temple and headed off to Tallahassee, where he was a professor at Florida State University, teaching anatomy, physiology, and exercise science.

His son-in-law's scientific bent got Jim to thinking. "Dad said to Doug, 'Since you're out there in Florida, why don't you take this product to a hospital and introduce it to the doctors and nurses," said Carol. Doug found that, indeed, medical personnel were eager to purchase Sorenson items. "Doug could see that he'd make a lot more money selling these products than just by teaching," said Carol.[1]

In 1978, convinced that representing Sorenson Research was their future, the couple moved to California, living in Ventura, with Doug driving to Los Angeles. The value of the products came forcefully to Carol one day when she got a call from the Los Angeles Police Department looking for Doug. There was a medical emergency for one of the devices and the LAPD was looking for Doug to get it.

Another son-in-law, Gary Crocker, married the third oldest Sorenson child, Ann, a lovely red-head, and played a pivotal role for Sorenson Research. Gary's father was a fireman, and the families lived next door to each other.

Years earlier, when Ann was a teenager, Jim wrote a tribute to her and, by implication, to his other five daughters. "There is no experience in life greater than raising a girl," wrote Jim. "Memories of their growing years fill my heart with tears of joy and gladness...I look back and I realize now more fully each day the speed at which we travel through this life...All too soon material beauty perishes, intellectual beauty is limited to times and seasons, but moral beauty as exemplified in a [chaste]...daughter, is lovely, beautiful, everlasting, perfect." [2]

Gary had a thick crop of dark hair and wore oversize horn-rimmed glasses that made him look nerdish. He acknowledges that was accurate. "I was a fairly studious fellow," he said, "perhaps excessively so." Among academic achievements: representing Highland High School's state-champion debate team and beating future Republican guru Karl Rove, who attended Olympus High.

All the studying paid off, and Gary and Ann went east to Harvard, where he earned a bachelor's degree in economics, graduating magna cum laude, and then an MBA. Jim Sorenson coveted those credentials, especially after Gary, with Jim's blessing, prepared a case study based on Sorenson Research and its challenges in the mid-seventies.

The paper, twenty-six single-spaced-pages long, was used for class discussion at the Harvard Business School and distributed by HBS Case Services to other business schools.

Some of the questions facing Sorenson included how well they were serving customers and controlling costs, how to improve the distribution system, how to properly compensate the sales force, and how to handle inventories. A continuous issue was how to position inventories so that a lack of product in one geographical area could quickly be filled by another. [3]

Prior to 1969 Sorenson products were distributed through independent dealers, supplied by independent sales representatives. Dealers received a 40 percent margin on retail hospital sales, and sales representatives 12 percent. Most dealers supplied existing markets with popular items, and did little to open new markets or introduce new products.

In 1970 Sorenson began to develop an in-house sales force and cut ties with outside dealers. Company sales representatives had a greater incentive to work hard, as they were paid on a straight commission equal to 20 percent of sales revenue.

The company had a system of twenty-three regional and "garage" warehouses, the latter often literally in a salesman's garage or car. Hospitals typically were not designed to store large inventories; they expected suppliers to do so, and most did. Sorenson instead promoted a service program that promised delivery within twenty-four hours to most major hospitals.

Sorenson headquarters in Salt Lake monitored all movement of inventory from a central warehouse to field warehouses. However, for various reasons, the home office's field-inventory records often did not track with actual movement of inventory.

A related issue was back orders—caused largely by serious production delays in the firm's most popular items. Jim worried that back orders caused ill-will at hospitals. Especially maddening was that a warehouse in one region often had an ample supply of back-ordered items urgently needed in another region that did not know where to find them.

Such were the real Sorenson Research issues in Crocker's case study put before some of the nation's brightest business-minded academics.

During his last three years at Harvard, Gary sold his father-in-law's products to twenty hospitals in the Boston region, earning more on commissions than many of his peers did after graduation. Crocker credited that experience with his decision to work in the medical field. As he was finishing his MBA, Jim asked Gary to be a sales manager. He declined, much to Jim's annoyance, believing he was ready to "conquer the world."

Crocker joined a large, well-established pharmaceutical firm in Chicago, Baxter International, where he soon began to climb the corporate ladder.

Sorenson Research's biggest problems, ironically, were a result of its remarkable success. The company hit one home run after another—with Receptal, ATS, Intraflo, Dialaflo, innovative catheters, and other disposable medical devices.

Some of the nation's leading medical centers purchased Sorenson products, including the Mayo Clinic, St. Vincent's Hospital in Los Angeles, Boston Hospital, and the Cleveland Clinic.

With those seals of approval, other medical centers followed. "Before a surgeon treats a heart attack, he has to monitor vital signs," noted Jim. "Some hospitals performed three to four thousand heart operations a year, using our products in every case."

With more than 500 separate items—most of them small variations within about two dozen product lines—hospitals purchased large quantities of company products. Sorenson Research prospered and grew, and its need for additional space became urgent. Jim delayed a decision on whether to build a new facility, expanding the company's quarters at 2511 South West Temple more than a half-dozen times.

When hiring enough workers proved difficult, Jim found a way to do good while doing well. He hired disabled individuals in work shelters, employing up to fifty at a time, who were carefully supervised and paid at the same rate as regular production employees.

He also hired almost the entire female population in the Utah state prison system, who also were paid at the regular rate. Both groups helped ease the workload while satisfying Jim's innate sympathy for those down on their luck or born and reared in difficult circumstances.

"The benefit to the handicapped person or woman prisoner," said Jim, "was personal satisfaction, self-esteem, gainful employment, and better preparation to return to society." When female inmates began out-producing regular employees, Jim asked one of their foremen why. "Maybe one reason is that we don't have as high a turnover rate as on the outside," was his logical answer.

Those commending the prison program included the warden and Utah Governor Scott Matheson, who called it "the greatest morale booster that was ever implemented for the women at the prison." [4]

The company was still bursting at the seams. Jim purchased a parcel of land at 4500 South, west of Interstate Highway 15. In 1975 he began relocating operations to the site, which would be developed into Sorenson Research Park by Jim Jr. and son-in-law Ralph Johnson, later joined by son Joe and son-in-law Tim Fenton. The company first built a 55,000-square-foot facility at 4500 South and 900 West. In two years the building was too small, and a second one was constructed nearby. Then, in 1980, a third facility was added, bringing the complex to 360,000 square feet.

The three original leaders—Jim, K. Pannier and Gordon Reynolds—expanded to a workforce of more than 1,700. They included executive vice president Perry Lane, who was highly disciplined and well organized. Lane gave the company operational stability, and was a good counterpoint to Jim's visionary leadership.

Sorenson Research began with two salesmen, and now had 180. In 1979 the company had about $40 million in sales, an increase approaching 50 percent over the previous year, and expected to continue growing at an annual rate of more than 40 percent.

The company required around $60 million in 1980 simply to meet demand. It also was in hock for new buildings and furnishing them, and the legal costs of defending its products. Large corporations often copy products, especially those of smaller companies, who they figure might not have the resources to fight them in court.

Ironically, despite its remarkable success, bankruptcy of Sorenson Research was not out of the question.

Jim considered several options, including taking the company public and letting shareholders supply the needed capital. That, however, would cost him the control his psyche required. Another possibility was selling off part or even all the company—also distasteful, though not as much so.

As a stopgap measure, Jim had borrowed money. By mid-1979 he owed $15 million to First Security Bank, at a murderous interest rate of 21 percent during the fiscal malaise under President Jimmy Carter. First Security Corporation had more than 100 affiliates and was the largest banking system in the Intermountain West by 1990.

George Eccles, the bank's longtime chairman and CEO, did not rise to command a banking empire by soft-headed judgments. One can only wonder how Jim persuaded the 80-year-old chairman that investing in badly undercapitalized Sorenson Research was a sound financial decision. Eccles apparently was haunted with recurring second thoughts. Not long after signing off on the loan, he began to phone Jim often to inquire about his physical health and Sorenson Research's fiscal health.

One night in the spring of 1979 Jim called Gary. "George Eccles is really putting the screws on me," Jim told him. Sorenson Research had hit a $15 million credit limit, and could not get its credit line extended (although subsequently the bank extended it to about $21 million to keep the company viable while Jim searched for a solution).

The only solution, Jim decided, was to sell Sorenson Research. Jim told Gary he had talked to a number of investment bankers, each of whom wanted between 5-6 percent of the sale price as a commission. "I'm not going to pay that, that's ridiculous," Jim said. He noted that Gary was an MBA and knew what the investment bankers knew. "Why don't you come back and help me sell the company?"

Gary said Jim offered him a commission of 1 percent of the sale price. With that, Gary and Ann left Baxter and Chicago and returned to Salt Lake City in May. That began an extraordinary adventure in the high-stakes world of corporate wheeling and dealing. Making it especially tricky was Jim's insistence that only he and Gary, and presumably Ann, were to know of Gary's true mission. "Absolutely no one else was to know the company was going to be sold," said Gary. [5]

Officially he returned to Sorenson headquarters in 1979 as international sales manager. Although he would in fact set up new distributorships in Europe and Asia, that was a cover for Gary's primary mission of finding a buyer. He estimated that nearly 80 percent of his trips were sale-related.

"Usually these things are done with a lot of organizational support—a five- or six-member team including people from manufacturing, marketing, and finance, who spill their guts and tell the investment bankers everything they want to know," explained Gary. "I had to gather all that information clandestinely, making up various reasons why I needed the data."

Gary collected every scrap of information he felt would help justify a princely price for Sorenson Research, and assembled it all neatly in binders. He added a five-year financial forecast, based on formulas learned at

Harvard. Finally, he stressed the value to any company of owning the fertile brain of Jim Sorenson, which no doubt would continue to spin off marketable innovations.

Over the next year Gary talked to about eight large medical supply companies. Three showed enough interest to come to Salt Lake, under the guise of being international distributors, to "kick the tires" at Sorenson Research. Two of the three companies entered into serious negotiations: The Kendall Company in Massachusetts, a subsidiary of Colgate-Palmolive; and Abbott Laboratories in Chicago, one of the best-managed companies in the United States. Abbott manufactured health-care products worldwide, with sales of $1.7 billion in 1979.

Gary learned of Abbott's potential interest from a fellow Mormon in Chicago, where Gary's former employer, Baxter, also was located. His friend, a business development executive at Abbott, told Gary that the company's chairman, Robert Schoellhorn, was looking for a cardiovascular strategic alliance. Schoellhorn had been at Abbott for seven years and was appointed president and CEO the previous year.

The question of price loomed large. Jim coveted the round number of $100 million, and told Gary to justify it on paper. Using conventional modeling, the most Gary could credibly justify was a price of $75 million to $85 million. Pressed by Jim, Gary added a couple of new prospective product lines to his calculations, and bumped up the projected profit margins, ending up at about $102 million.

On the face of it, $100 million was a preposterous asking price — thirty-three times earnings, when a normal business purchase is ten to twelve times. Nonetheless, Jim dug in his heels at that number, banking on Gary's ability to sell it. Kendall offered $70 million for the company and wouldn't budge, believing it would already be overpaying. Schoellhorn's offer was in the low eighties.

Jim was very upset and sent Gary back to Chicago to negotiate with Abbott's Schoellhorn and its executive vice president Charles Aschauer. A fallback position was to sell one product line to Abbott, Dialaflo, for $21 million, giving Jim what he needed to get First Security Bank off his back. Schoellhorn and Aschauer didn't want a product line, however, they wanted all of Sorenson Research.

"What do we have to do to make this work?" the two executives asked Gary.

"You've got to hit that $100 million number," answered Gary. "If you guys can do that, you've got a deal. If not, Jim will probably work with one of the other guys."

Gary's response was a huge bluff. The two executives didn't know that there were no other guys in sight whose offer was close to what Abbott already had put on the table. Jim, always crafty, guessed correctly that, for whatever reason, Schoellhorn wanted to end his career as chairman in a few years with a large, sexy acquisition.

Gary returned to Salt Lake as Schoellhorn and Aschauer pondered their options.

In May 1980, with First Security pressing hard, Jim phoned Schoellhorn to offer Dialaflo to Abbott for $21 million—the full amount he owed the bank. Desperate by now, he was ready to go as low as $12 million, the amount the bank insisted on immediately. Their conversation went like this, according to Jim:

"I think Dialaflo would fit beautifully into your I V business," said Jim.

"Let's talk it over," Schoellhorn answered. "I'll be out there at eight o'clock tomorrow morning."

"How can you make plane reservations that fast?" asked Jim.

"Don't worry," said Schoellhorn, "We'll take the corporate jet."

Schoellhorn landed in Salt Lake the next morning, accompanied by a team of experts, for a tour of Sorenson's facilities, including its brand-new, largest building still being completed. They licked their lips.

Finally Schoellhorn said, "We're not really interested in Dialaflo alone. We're more interested in your whole company. How much do you want for it?

"Well, I'm building a $100 million company here," said Jim.

Schoellhorn: "We'll take it." [6]

### CHAPTER TWENTY-TWO

# JIM TURNS HIS BACK

## on Family

On June 13, 1980 Bob Schoellhorn and Jim, in a joint news release, announced they agreed in principle that Sorenson Research would become a wholly owned subsidiary of Abbott Laboratories. Details were to be worked out.

The announcement startled the 1,700 Sorenson employees, from CEO Perry Lane all the way down to the maintenance crew.

"The transaction will involve the issuance of Abbott shares and the assumption of certain debt obligations in the aggregate amount of about $100 million," read the news release. "Completion of the merger is subject to the execution of the definitive agreement and approval by both companies' directors and Sorenson shareholders."

Sorenson Research would retain its name and still be led by Jim as president, with a salary of $100,000 and, among other perks, a company car. As the single largest shareholder of Abbott stock, he would sit on its board of directors. That was one prospect that Jim dreaded.

As the two sides negotiated the final deal, it was clear that Abbott banked on buying not only Sorenson Research but Jim himself. They wanted him for two obvious reasons—to own his future brilliant ideas, and so he would not be able to leave Abbott and compete against them anytime soon.

No doubt Abbott executives were well aware that, in a similar situation years earlier, Jim left Deseret Pharmaceutical with an agreement not to compete for two years. The minute the two years were up, he proceeded to launch Sorenson Research, now well on its way to parity with Deseret.

Schoellhorn tried to bind Jim to a ten-year no-compete agreement, but Jim balked. "Why restrict me for ten years when you're restricted for no more than one year?"

"Because I could never start a company from scratch like you've done," answered Schoellhorn. "...I have learned how to run a large corporation when it's already there, but I could not create it. Abbott has to be protected against what you might do again." [1]

They compromised, Jim agreeing not to compete for five years from the time his Abbott employment ended.

On August 22 Abbott's corporate jet landed again at Salt Lake International. Both sides had prepared carefully to ensure a smooth signing. Jim and Gary dressed to the nines in suits and ties to meet the Abbott team at the airport—while Schoellhorn and his colleagues stepped off their plane dressed like cowboys.

Schoellhorn and Jim signed the four-page agreement. Its longest clause, 29 lines, said, in part: "All discoveries, inventions, improvements and innovations, in the Health Care Field whether patentable or not... which you may invent, discover, originate or conceive during your employment by Sorenson [now owned by Abbott] shall be the sole and exclusive property of Sorenson."

Abbott assumed Sorenson's debts, and Jim took the balance of the $100 million in Abbott stock, then trading on the New York Stock Exchange in the $50 range. He had always regretted selling his share of Deseret Pharmaceutical to his partners for cash, leaving him unable to benefit from future sales of products he had invented. He was not going to make the same mistake again.

The *Salt Lake Tribune* noted that the sale echoed that of Deseret in 1976 for $138 million. "[Jim] recalled retrospectively had he retained his interest to the time of the sale of Deseret to Warner-Lambert, his take could have been nearly $6 million. However, he pursued his own star at Sorenson Research, a journey which reached a $100 million way station this week." [2]

Gary Crocker and Jim drove Schoellhorn to the airport after the final papers were signed. Heading home, Jim asked, "What do you really think, Gary?" "Dad," he answered, "we creamed 'em!" [4]

Abbott was rewarded serendipitously almost before the ink was dry on the sale documents. That same day in Washington, D.C. the U.S. Patent office granted Sorenson—now owned by Abbott—a patent for a "cannula [a tube inserted into the body] and method for bidirectional blood flow." [3]

Gary and Ann, with a growing family, had decided to build a new home with his 1 percent commission from the sale—a cool $1 million. Now that the deal was finalized, Gary asked Jim for his fee.

"You know, Gary," responded Jim, "I think we ought to look forward to the future, and not look backwards." Jim declined specifically to address the fee—then or anytime later. [4]

Gary confronted his father-in-law several more times about the fee, with the same result. "Each time," said Gary, "Jim said something like 'We need to look to the future, let's not dwell on the past. We have to move forward together. We have capital now. I want to build new companies and I want you to work with me.'"

Asked if Jim ever did compensate him for finding and landing Abbott, Gary, smiling wanly, said "Yes. I got a nice lapel pin."

(Knowledgeable family members say Beverley was not aware of this or similar business differences between Jim and their children or spouses.)

Gary was not the only one Jim left at the altar. A number of other executives at Sorenson Research apparently were led to believe they would see a fat payday if the company was ever sold. They not only failed to receive bonuses, most of them were soon fired by Abbott. "Dad would create an expectation, sometimes an outright promise, and then not live up to it," said Jim Jr. "This bait-and-switch was central to his failures with the family." [5]

Even more difficult to understand were Jim's activities during the period between the start of secret negotiations with Abbott and the sale. Jim systematically approached the half-dozen or so who held minority shares of stock in Sorenson Research, pressuring them to sell him their shares at a tiny fraction of what he alone knew they would soon be worth.

The largest minority share apparently was held by Georgene Pannier,

K.'s widow, estimated at about 15 percent by her children. Jim and K. together founded Sorenson Research in 1963, and K. is listed with Jim on more than twenty patents. He continued to play a major role in the company until his untimely death in the spring of 1977.

Three years later Jim called on Georgene and talked her into selling him the shares of stock earned by her late husband. "Mom got just a teeny-weeny fraction of what it was actually worth," said their son Scott Pannier. "She was so worried after that, and kept saying 'What am I going to do?'" Georgene Pannier died in December 1989.[6]

Smaller shares had been parceled out to a handful of other individuals, including Gordon Reynolds, the other major inventor of Sorenson medical devices; Sorenson CEO Perry Lane; Karl Pannier Sr., K.'s father; and Ott Hamman, another early hire. Also: Dr. Robert Matheson, who was married to Bev's sister June and furnished early seed money to Sorenson Research and LeVoy's; and Jim's own father, Joseph LeVoy Sorenson. Apparently all of them sold their stock to Jim except Reynolds, who refused to knuckle under.

"Early on Dad chose to take company stock options," said Val Reynolds, Gordon's son. "Jim tried to buy the stock but Dad refused to sell it. When he later exercised his options with the stock, he made quite a large sum of money."[7]

No one has been able to explain satisfactorily how Jim, innately kind and generous to many down on their luck, could square these actions with his conscience. Some observers believe his rationale dated to when Jim sold his share of Deseret Pharmaceutical to his two partners for a price about forty times less than he would have reaped had he held on until Deseret itself was sold.

Jim seems to have taken the wrong lessons from forfeiting that windfall. If he had been more collegial with his partners, and willing—as they were—to reward fairly others who also contributed to their success, he would have had no need to leave Deseret. Instead, he took the opposite view: future success required his total control.

Jim exhibited growing narcissism during his lifetime. He cut others off emotionally and seemed threatened by the success even of family members if they acted independently of him. He mocked Beverley's public accomplishments. His outlook may have dated to his early childhood and his family's humble circumstances in Yuba City, California, or to other mental health issues that were never addressed.

With few exceptions, Jim required that each business he launched or acquired carry "Sorenson" or a derivation of his name on it.

Later that year he belatedly offered former rank-and-file workers a bonus based on a formula that included the length of their tenure. He took out ads in Utah newspapers telling former employees where to show up and what evidence of their employment to present. The effort reportedly cost him several hundred thousand dollars—a pittance of what more senior staff members felt they should have received.

Abbott wasted no time squeezing blood out of its Sorenson division. Most senior managers lost their jobs, along with the sales force and about 40 percent of production workers.

Gary himself remained at Sorenson as vice president of sales and marketing for the next two years. Then he left, taking the vice president of manufacturing and a key research and development employee with him. After a stint at a pharmaceutical firm, Gary started his own highly successful medical-device company.

Today, despite differences, Gary says he is genuinely grateful to his late father-in-law. "I owe Jim a lot," he said. "He introduced me to the field and gave me a real opportunity in it. He gave me a career path that worked out really well for me." Gary made a large fortune and was named Utah Entrepreneur of the Year by both Ernst & Young and the MountainWest Capital Network.

George Eccles, head of First Security Bank, breathed a sigh of relief when the Abbott-Sorenson deal closed. The bank recouped its $21 million from Jim. Overnight he went from being one of the bank's largest and "riskiest" creditors to a member of its board. At his first board meeting, Jim was introduced to other bank directors.

"We are just getting started and this is just the beginning," Jim told them. "Our bud is just beginning to open." Other board members gave him a standing ovation.

If Abbott leaders really knew Jim, they would have known that their arrangement with him personally was doomed to fail. He could never be content working within a well-oiled corporate structure or, for that matter, any structure where he was required to obey orders. It simply was not in his nature to take directions from anyone.

Jim was 59 and vigorous of mind and body, thanks in part to a daily regimen of pushups and running. Immediately he felt constrained as an Abbott employee. Like most major corporations, Abbott's approach to business was strictly by the numbers, as reflected in a daily blizzard of memos and position papers generated by company managers and committees.

Less than a year after the merger, Jim resigned as president of Sorenson Research. Abbott was not pleased. CEO Bob Schoellhorn, in a sharply worded letter, said Jim expressed a desire to form one or more new ventures, possibly including the medical and surgical application of laser technology.

"...I want you to have a clear understanding of our position on your agreement not to compete contained in the letter agreement of August 22, 1980," wrote Schoellhorn. Ventures in laser technology "would be clearly in violation of the August 22 agreement."

"Your covenant not to compete is a vital and valuable part of what we paid for in our acquisition of Sorenson Research Company. We will be satisfied with nothing less than scrupulous observance of the letter and spirit of your covenant, and will not hesitate to seek legal redress in the event that the covenant is breached."[8]

By wooing and winning Abbott Laboratories—and it them—Sorenson Research hitched its wagon to a fast-rising star. Abbott had $1.7 billion in revenue [income before expenses] in 1979. By 2010 it had $35 billion and was ranked seventy-fifth on the Fortune 500 list of largest U.S.-based corporations.

The company had 90,000 employees and operated in more than 130 countries. It invested $90 million a year to train and develop workers, pairing them with mentors in their respective divisions. Such practices won accolades, including a ranking by *The Scientist* as the fourth-best place in the U.S. to work.[9]

Most important from the Sorensons' viewpoint was that their timing could not have been better. After Jimmy Carter was out of the White

House and Ronald Reagan was in, as of January 1981, the nation's economy started to rebound. Jim's stock in Abbott Labs increased by about thirty times in the coming years, the bulk of his estate.

Jim also involved his two sons, James Lee and Joseph, and four sons-in-law in businesses he purchased or created and real estate he bought and/or developed. They included Carol's husband Doug Smith, Shauna's husband Ralph Johnson, Joan's husband Tim Fenton, and Gail's husband, Thom Williamsen. Chris, the youngest of the eight children, was the last to marry. Her husband, Dale Harris, had his own profession as a medical doctor and radiologist.

Some of these family business relationships also were in for a bumpy ride.

James Lee, the Sorensons' third child and first son, from an early age showed an aptitude for business and crunching numbers. His father tutored Jim, including him occasionally when making business transactions, and encouraging his entrepreneurial spirit.

One such time was years earlier when the Sorensons took a rare vacation in 1967. The ten-member family flew to Buffalo, New York, then rented a Mercury station wagon, stacked thirteen suitcases on top, and drove north to the World's Fair in Montreal. They returned through New England to New York City, where the others went exploring while Jim Sr took young Jim, then 17, to a business appointment.

Beverley recorded in a journal that Jim Sr. did all the cross-country driving, while Jim Jr. navigated by map. "Jimmy has been a fine guide reading the maps," she wrote. "Had Jim heeded his directions we would not have gotten lost."

That was a fitting metaphor for future father-son business ventures.[10]

In 1973 Jim Sr. bought a cosmetics company at auction for $35,000 and presented it as a "gift" to his son. ExCelCis Cosmetics was hemorrhaging money and not far from bankruptcy. More than fifty years old, the Utah-based company was stale. No new products or marketing had been introduced in many years.

Jim told his son that if he could turn ExCelCis around, it was his to own. Jim Jr. had two years of college to finish at the University of Utah and was about to marry when he accepted his father's challenge.

ExCelCis was a direct-marketing operation whose sales representatives, a great majority women, averaged seventy years of age. "These were great people, and loyal," Jim Jr. told a reporter. "But our sales system had reverted to sort of a mail order-type thing where most of the volume was consumed by our sales force and their close relatives."[11]

Jim Jr. and the handful of managers he inherited began to create new training materials. He started a company newsletter, "Cosmetic Career News." In the first issue, March 1974, Jim promised that "big things are in the making" and encouraged sales representatives to increase their profits by recruiting and training new people. He also enlisted some college friends.

During the first year, ExCelCis grossed about $36,000 and went in the hole about the same amount. As Jim gamely plowed on, his father issued a challenge to Beverley: "Quit making quilts in Relief Society [the LDS women's auxiliary] and come down here and help your son."

It was not easy for Bev to accept. She had been a full-time wife and mother at home for nearly thirty years. That was her domain and her refuge from Jim Sr., who was unpredictable and often brusque and difficult to live with. Bev's self-esteem came instead from their eight accomplished and well-adjusted children, their daughters- and sons-in-law, and an adoring cadre of grandchildren.

By moving into the world of business and finance—Jim Sr.'s world— she risked challenge and condescension from her husband on an entirely new range of issues. There was also an up side, however. "It was a way for her to feel more connected to my father and my brother," explained youngest child Chris Harris.

Bev also knew that Jim Jr. was the most likely of all the children to one day stand at the helm of the Sorenson empire. She was determined to help prepare her son for that day. In 1975 Bev went to work, at first part-time, for ExCelCis, with her son as her boss.

Jim Jr. was grateful. "She had good ideas, energy, and a positive influence," he said, noting his mother's strength was not in accounting. "She is a people person,...her skills were oriented toward making connections and motivating people."[12]

They developed a new ExCelCis cosmetic line and created a system of "face design," using colors customized for an individual woman and contouring to de-emphasize facial flaws and accentuate the positive. Sorenco, the ExCelCis plant, was equipped only to manufacture skin creams and lotions, so Jim Jr. ordered related items from other manufacturers, including eye shadow, eye pencils, and lipstick.

They set up a new multi-level marketing system with this theme: "You can get anything in this life you want by helping enough other people to get the things they want." Sales associates were offered substantial rewards for not just selling but for enlisting others to sell.

By 1979 ExCelCis began to show a handsome profit. In December of that year, the company had nearly 500 "beauty consultants" representing every state, and Jim's goal was to expand the force to 2,500.

"We have our eyes on being the No. 1 cosmetic company in the nation," said Jim. "We have a long way to go, but our growth rate is surpassing the leaders. We have developed tremendous pride, competitive spirit and esprit d' corps among our beauty consultants." He added that "I have learned to respect the [cosmetic] industry. It is very competitive, but if you crack it, it can also be very lucrative."[13]

Company revenues topped $1 million. Jim asked his father to make good on his promise to give him the revived company. Jim Sr. responded similarly to how he responded to Gary Crocker. He refused to answer his son directly, instead describing the wonderful things they would do together in the future and suggesting that his son not be too concerned about the present.

"This caused a big rift between us," said Jim Jr. "I knew that whatever he asked me to do from then on, I had to be careful. I needed to have it in writing."[14]

Early in the 1980s ExCelCis continued to grow and was profitable, but the LeVoy's clothing company had been in decline for some time. Jim Sr. decided the best way to strengthen LeVoy's was to merge it with ExCelCis—selling products of both companies in retail stores. Jim Jr. and Beverley heatedly disagreed, but Jim Sr. overruled them.

"They were two different cultures," said Jim Jr. "Combining them killed the momentum of ExCelCis." Both companies limped along after the merger, until 1986 when Jim Sr. closed ExCelCis.

Beverley ached for the cosmetic company employees, and refused to be utterly defeated. She packaged the remaining ExCelCis inventory and a unique system she had developed to match individual women with colors that flattered their features, and began marketing them to retail outlets as Beverley Taylor Cosmetics. This did not sit well with Jim. "He hated the fact that his name wasn't on it," said Beverley. The effort ultimately failed.

LeVoy's continued to operate for another decade, in the latter years apparently not making much, until it too was shuttered in 1997.

Several years earlier, when the picture was still bright for ExCelCis, Jim Jr. said "Besides gaining some self-respect and self-confidence, I have had a business lesson I could not have received in any other way. It has been an individual triumph to know I was able to take a sick business and do something with it."[15]

Jim Jr. also became an entrepreneurial superstar and, echoing his brother-in-law Gary Crocker, credited Jim Sr. with jump-starting his career. Jim Jr. has founded a number of highly successful companies and social-service-oriented ventures, and is independently wealthy. Among many other awards for business and humanitarian leadership, he was named *Utah Business* magazine's CEO of the year in 2007.

He credited his parents with being the largest influences in his life. "My mother was always a nurturer, and both of them instilled within me self-confidence...the idea that I could do whatever I wanted to do. The sky was the limit.

"...with my father it was really observing his business skills and judgments...my dad was very tenacious, as well. When others would have fear or fail, he'd continue on...[His success] was decades in the making...[he] cobbled together the right people and built on the ideas, and all those things that come together in making a business."[16]

Another son-in-law, Thomas (Thom) Williamsen, also experienced Jim Sr.'s dark side. Thom, like most Sorensons, graduated from the University of Utah, then earned a master's degree at Northwestern University.

He and his wife Gail Sorenson Williamsen were living in Dallas,

Texas, where he worked for the Trammell Crow Company, developing industrial space. "Jim threw out a lot of carrots to get his daughter back to Utah," explained Thom. "He really liked Gail—he said she had her mother's looks and his brains. "He had a way of making it appear that there were some really good opportunities here."

In 1984 Thom and Gail and their children returned to Salt Lake City. Jim had partnered with attorney/developer Walter Plumb to develop space at several Utah sites, including Arrowpress Square and Snowbird ski resort, and foster energy development from tar sands in the far northeastern corner of the state near Vernal. Thom assisted both men.

Then something went wrong—Thom declined to be specific, not wanting to open old wounds. "Jim fired me," he said. "Walt was a lot more fair to me." Thom continued to work with Plumb for another four or five years, then started his own company, called Chasebrook, which specializes in retail real estate.

Jim also was hard on his younger son, Joseph, whose strengths did not include the natural leadership abilities of his older brother and some brothers-in-law. "Dad was cruel to Joe," said Jim Jr. "He would belittle him in front of others. Once when Jim Jr. expressed this to his father, Jim Sr. took a three-by-five card out of his pocket and wrote a note to himself to be kinder to Joe. It failed to change his behavior.

Beverley herself was not infrequently embarrassed and humiliated by her husband. On at least one occasion she wept as she shared her frustration with a neighbor couple. The man gently asked if she had considered leaving Jim. "Everyone would understand," he said.

"I can't," said Beverley. "I'm a Taylor."[17]

Bev loved her husband despite the difficulty of living with him; she forgave freely and often. She once told her son Joe, "If there's one chance in a million that he can change, I want to be there for him."[18]

As some sons-in-law became reluctant to attend Sorenson family events, Jim complained that they were shunning him.

Jim formed Sorenson Development Inc. (SDI) to hold old businesses not sold to Abbott, and many other businesses to come. Beverley and their children owned the same stock equity in Sorenson Development as they had in Sorenson Research, with Jim continuing to control the eight voting shares.

In 1983 the youngest Sorenson child, Christine, married Dale Harris. Jim and Bev were now empty-nesters. They moved into a large luxury condominium in the Avenues, northern Salt Lake City between the LDS temple and the state Capitol, also keeping the house on 21$^{st}$ South to entertain guests and provide a place for Jim to have a quiet place to think.

Most people with a fortune like Jim's kick back and take life easier. But that was not for him. He had a full quarter-century of productivity left in him, and would burn it right to the end.

### CHAPTER TWENTY-THREE

# LURE OF THE LAND

The young Sorenson family often went riding on weekends, but not to enjoy the scenery.

"Dad's form of recreation was to hunt for land," remembered Carol Sorenson Smith. "We'd all pile in the car and off we'd go, to Vernal or Flaming Gorge. He's looking out the window for land—'I wonder who owns this mountain?—' and I'm getting car sick. He'd say 'Think what you can do with land,' and told us over and over about water rights."[1]

Don Wallace, who handled several thousand real estate deals for Jim, said "He'd call me on a Sunday afternoon and say 'I just drove past such and such…Go take a look at it.' Don and Jim went on hundreds of land-hunting trips. "We went through a lot of gates we probably shouldn't have gone through," quipped Don.

"He sent me on a trip one time down through the entire state on I-15, from Idaho on the north to Nevada on the south. He said 'I want you to look at every off-ramp, in every corner of Utah. Come back and tell me what land is available and what looks valuable. Then we'll go from there.'" Wallace found a few promising tracts around Cedar City; several of which were later acquired. [2]

Jim's fortune became enormous. It rested on two pillars: his stock in

Abbott Labs, which skyrocketed in value in coming years, and real estate, whose total value was perhaps one-half that of the stock. Jim loved to own land, from when he and Bev first relocated from California to Utah at Christmas time in 1946 until his death six decades later. By then he was reputed to be Utah's largest private landowner.

After his impoverished early years growing up in a rented shack in Yuba City, real estate's rewards were emotional as well as financial. "I had never owned any ground. Owning it made me feel more satisfied, more secure."

Jim first dabbled in real estate when buying a home in Salt Lake City's Rose Park. The developer, Beverley's uncle, paid Jim a $50 commission for every home he sold in the development. Later Jim learned the customary commission was $500. The lesson, he said, was that the best way to profit from real estate was to own it.

Early on he bought several parcels of land in Salt Lake and Weber Counties, subdivided them into building lots, and sold them. For decades afterward, however, he purchased undeveloped land and left it that way as a long-term investment.

While representing the Upjohn Company, he also wandered Salt Lake City's sagebrush-covered east bench, surmising where new housing developments were likely to blossom. He approached owners of some of the "goat pastures," buying land for as little as $25 an acre.

Jim even put his eight-year career with Upjohn on the line—and lost it—primarily because of what the company saw as excessive extracurricular real estate activities.

As his financial picture improved, with ownership of Deseret Pharmaceutical and later LeVoy's and Sorenson Research, Jim's real estate purchases also quickened.

Jim routinely sought sole control of whatever he owned. An important exception was a purchase in about 1975. He spotted and immediately fell in love with an idyllic 600-acre river-front ranch property in Weber Canyon. Stretched for cash at the time with the rapid growth of Sorenson Research, Jim approached two men he trusted and formed a consortium to tie up the property in the Smith-Morehouse Ranch area.

The two were Perry Lane, executive vice president and day-to-day manager of Sorenson Research, and LaMar Crocker, the Sorensons' next-door neighbor and father of their son-in-law Gary Crocker. Jim called his neighbor "Crock," and they got along well. The three men formed a holding company, SCL Inc., for the "SCL Ranch." Each bought one-third of the $230,000 property.

The SCL Ranch had one main house that was used mostly by the Crockers. Other cabins nearby were rented out to third parties, providing a return to the owners. Years later, after Jim acquired substantial wealth, he asked the other two men to sell him their lots. Lane sold out to Jim but Crocker did not—which, according to a Crocker family member, hurt their friendship.

The Sorensons also looked elsewhere for pristine canyon property worthy of their imprint. One they found was in the Timberline area in Parley's Canyon—named for prominent early Mormon Parley P. Pratt, who in 1848 surveyed the area to find an easier route through the Wasatch Mountains than the one used by the first pioneers the previous year.

The Timberline cabin was enlarged and remodeled several times through the years, giving it a master bedroom and a loft with three additional bed spaces, plus two bathrooms, a kitchen, and dining and living rooms. Harsh winters required annual repairs of the roof and deck. Over the years Jim acquired several hundred additional acres surrounding the cabin. Jim enjoyed going there to hike and relax in the afternoons and enjoy the flora and fauna, rarely staying overnight.

Roads were constructed from the cabin to remote areas of the property, giving access to the entire property by driving or hiking. Later Jim reconstructed two historical fish ponds on Timberline Creek, washed out by a spring thaw a generation earlier.

The Timberline cabin was quaint and not very functional for large family gatherings, so the Sorensons soon looked for more accommodating cabin property. They found an area they liked in Weber Canyon near Smith-Morehouse called The Pines. Over time they bought a cabin at the east end of the development, which became commonly known as "Beverley's cabin." Assisted by their son Joe, Beverley had the cabin enlarged and remodeled several times as the family grew and prospered.

Jim later acquired another large lot on the west end of The Pines abutting the Weber River. He constructed a large family structure commonly known as the Sorenson Lodge. Again assisted by Bev and Joe, Jim had the lodge remodeled in about 1997. It was the scene of many reunions of the huge extended Sorenson/Taylor family.

As Jim and Bev's grandchildren began to come of age and marry, Jim acquired a large twenty-seven-acre parcel abutting the Weber River just west of the Sorenson Lodge. Again assisted by Bev and Joe, Jim spared no effort or expense to build a 4,000-square-foot log "cabin," complete with its own culinary water system and direct access to the river. Jim called it the "honeymoon" cabin, intending it as a getaway for his many grandchildren as each got married. All three of these latter cabins continue to host family gatherings at this writing.

Joe, a genial dark-haired man—most of his siblings had light hair—was well liked by those who worked with him. He was a dutiful son and assisted his mother and father with many other projects as well over the years, including construction of the Sorenson Vision building and research campus in Logan, in the north end of Utah.

Electrical engineers at Utah State University (USU), a major research institution in Logan, invented a video-compression technology with a number of potential communication applications, including satellite and cable set-top-box integration, videophones, online multimedia, and help-ing the deaf and hard-of-hearing communicate.

Jim Sorenson Jr. was a volunteer on a panel for the State of Utah Centers of Excellence program, which was charged with finding promising research, development, and technologies in the state's higher-education in-stitutions and awarding grants to assist in their ultimate commercialization and economic impact. The intent of the assistance was to facilitate private companies to license the technology or start new companies commercial-izing technologies developed at the state's universities.

Jim Jr. was impressed enough with the USU compression technology that he recommended it to his father. Jim Sr. then negotiated an exclu-sive license agreement for Sorenson Development Inc. (SDI)—the overall company name following the sale of Sorenson Research to Abbott—to in-vestigate it further and, if feasible, produce marketable products.

Don Wallace purchased a fifteen-acre site on the west side of Logan and subdivided it into eight lots as Sorenson Industrial Park. In 1998 Wallace, along with Joe, oversaw construction of a building on one of the lots for the new company which emerged from the Utah State license, called Sorenson Vision. It housed research and product development, and was Sorenson Vision's headquarters.

The Sorensons hired a number of USU engineering professors and others to exploit the technology. However, company leaders had difficulty defining exactly what they hoped to achieve. In making the transition from an academic to a for-profit focus and operation, the enterprise struck out in different directions and the fledgling company hemorrhaged cash.

Three years after launching Sorenson Vision, the global dot-com bubble burst. The historic speculative bubble began in 1997 and saw huge fortunes made almost overnight. By the end of 2000 many pioneering dot-coms went belly-up or were barely surviving. Jim Jr. was asked by his father to rescue Sorenson Vision. He had to let two-thirds of its employees go and move the operation to Salt Lake City. After traveling a rocky road, Sorenson Vision was consolidated into Sorenson Media. Under Jim Jr.'s direction, Sorenson Media ultimately was destined for a fabulous outcome.

Don Wallace is another good example of Jim Sr.'s ability to spot potential in someone. Wallace, a pleasant man with sandy-colored hair, was born and reared in Missoula, Montana. After high school he worked for a number of mortgage companies before beginning college at the age of 28.

Once started, Wallace didn't stop until he had three degrees, all from the University of Utah, graduating summa cum laude with a bachelor's in finance, a law degree, and an MBA. While still in law school, Wallace began working part-time for Sorenson Development as a law clerk. Wallace asked two of his bosses for a full-time job. In 1993, when both superiors were unwilling to commit to a full-time position, Wallace took his request directly to Jim.

Jim often saw Wallace around the office but didn't know his name. When Jim learned in the interview that Wallace hailed from Missoula, with a population then of about 40,000, he immediately asked if he knew a certain medical doctor there. Wallace quickly said yes. Jim tested him.

"How many kids does he have?" asked Jim.

"Twelve," answered Wallace.

"What religion is he?"

"Catholic."

"What's his wife's name?"

"Millie."

Jim sat back, satisfied. "You *do* know him." After a long pause, Jim added "I hated that guy." He explained that, back when he co-owned Deseret Pharmaceutical, the Missoula doctor worked with Jim and his two partners, Dale Ballard and Victor Cartwright, to prove out some of their early technology. When Deseret began selling the product, Jim opposed sharing profits with the doctor, but his two partners repeatedly outvoted Jim two-to-one and continued sending him royalty checks.[3]

Wallace's family, to his good fortune, had lived next door to the Missoula doctor, who treated all of their family members, usually by house call.

The job interview continued and Jim asked Don what he thought he could do for the company. "I don't need any more lawyers, I have enough lawyers," emphasized Jim. "What I need is someone who can get things done." Don answered that his goal in fact was "to get into operations management in one of the Sorenson companies. I know how to get things done." Don passed the strange interview and a few months later Jim hired him to direct his real estate operations.

Most of Jim's property was held in his name personally. Prior to tapping Wallace to manage it, Sorenson real estate was managed by Jim's legal department. Wallace created limited-liability holding companies for all of Jim's major holdings and for all the development projects to come, relieving Jim from extensive personal liability. Jim understood virtually every property he owned and had an innate ability to separate valuable real estate from the worthless. While he knew every piece, he cared little for daily management details, disparaging the many small ones—such as rental houses and vacant city lots—as "cats and dogs."

While a great majority of the properties were in Utah, some interesting ones were not. Late in life, based on a recommendation from an acquaintance, Jim acquired three estate lots for investment in a gated community in the remote town of Dominical, Costa Rica. To further expand his investment opportunity he acquired three subsistence farms in the mountains of Costa Rica. The property included several tico houses—an informal word for a native Costa Rican—and one North American-style home.

At Jim's direction, Don improved roads leading to the farms and the electrical system, and rebuilt the culinary water system. They intended to divide the properties into many estate lots and sell them to expatriates. Jim, however, died before the development could be accomplished, and the work was suspended.

Jim made several land deals in Wyoming. In the mid-'90s he secured approval of a commercial land plan on thirty acres in Rock Springs, installed public improvements, and sold the parcels to local developers. He did the same thing on fifty-five acres nearby. Jim also acquired substantial acreage in picturesque Teton County, Wyoming, near sensitive wilderness areas, later selling it to conservation groups for preservation.

Jim often studied communities and analyzed where their path of progress was leading, then bought undeveloped land in that path. "Buy land, they're not making any more of it," was his motto, along with "Water is king" in Utah's high-desert country. "Get the water and never, never sell it."

His longtime approach to investing in real estate was to purchase raw land. He sold off enough to cover his "taw," patiently sitting on the rest as an investment. No one ever lost money in land by not selling it, he said. The word taw was from Jim's youth, when he excelled at marbles. A taw is a favorite marble, used to knock other marbles out of a circular area.

Among Jim's other real estate maxims: Don't borrow money to invest in real estate or development; work only off internally generated funds. Usually you can "trade up" easier than you can "buy up." The greatest profits in a deal are made not when you sell but when you buy. Ponder carefully before you purchase.

Although Jim made public improvements as required by local officials, he did not otherwise develop land as an investment. That final step, in his mind, held too many risks, including fluctuating interest rates, strength of the local economy, and other factors he could not control. Jim held onto some undeveloped land for decades, waiting for its value to rise until developers purchased it at a price substantially higher than the price Jim paid.

Jim sometimes included special personal provisions in real estate deals. In the 1970s, for example, he purchased and remodeled an old diner down the street from the Sorenson headquarters building on South West Temple. In leasing Chuck "N" Fred's to two colorful partners who decorated its walls with trophy fish and fishing gear, Jim included a clause giving him the right to a dozen free meals each month.

"He collected on those meals," recalled Brent Mathews, who owned a store in the neighborhood that sold kitchen equipment. "I saw him in there quite often, and he always ordered the same meal—pot roast and mashed potatoes and gravy, with corn on the side." [4]

In 1975 Jim helped his parents purchase and rebuild a home on a farm in Loomis, California. It was about a ten-minute ride north of the home they left in Roseville, a suburb of Sacramento.

"No matter where I go and what I see I just become more appreciative of our dream house up here in the Sierra foothills—I wouldn't trade it for anything I see," wrote his mother Emma. "Every morning when I draw the drapes or step out on our porch or deck I experience the same thrill and sense of wonder as when we first came here. It can't help but lift your spirits to live in such a natural scenic place...

"I want you to know too, Jim...[that] I feel a sense of gratefulness to you for making this all possible. Dad and I both appreciate what you have contributed and are continuing to contribute to make this place such a pleasant, beautiful and hopefully a happy place for all who live here or come to visit us." [5]

Years later Jim bought the property again from his parents' estate, and, with the help of his son-in-law Tim Fenton, turned it into Emma's Bed & Breakfast. Jim had the home and nearby buildings remodeled into guest suites, built a reception center called the Gathering Place, and installed a commercial kitchen. A handsome brochure explained it was located on forty acres "filled with views of horses and llamas running playfully on the hills, a pond...a petting zoo, winding trails...and a horse named Clyde ready to take you on a carriage ride to remember."

Jim and Bev also deeded a finished residential lot to each grandchild—who eventually numbered forty-seven—in an upscale residential development in Riverton City, called Deer Mountain Estates. Jim's grandson Luke Sorenson managed the development of the lots. In a poetic letter on colorful stationery, dated October 1999, they expressed to each grandchild their hopes for the property:

Here's a building block for your future—a new lot!

Do with it what will work best for you—build on it, sell it, trade it or hold it.

Hopefully whatever you do, you'll use it wisely and join in to make a beautiful community out in this Deer Mountain area. If you build, you'll make the area beautiful, if you sell you'll sell to someone reputable, if you trade it you'll find a way to upgrade it, and if you hold onto it you'll join in building the area in the future. We're proud of you. We love you and wish you the very best in life.

Love,

Grandpa Jim and Grandma Bev

Back in the mid-1970s, when Sorenson Research was bursting at the seams, Jim bought fifty or so acres near 45th South and 9th West, constructed three buildings, and moved most company operations there. Typically, he sat on the rest of the land.

The site was ideally located, with quick access to I-15 and I-215 highways, two golf courses nearby, and close to retail shops and hotels.

Jim Jr. envisaged something much greater at the site—a state-of-the-art research park. He planted the idea in his father and persisted until Jim gave him the green light. Jim Jr. and a brother-in-law, Ralph Johnson, married to Shauna, formed a general partnership called Sorenson Associates, with Sorenson Development—the family group of companies—as the limited partner.

They steadily bought adjacent land. By the end of 1985 roads were completed for phase one of the 100-acre Sorenson Research Park—a multi-use research, business, and residential complex. A ribbon-cutting in June 1988 officially opened the park as well as its third major tenant, DataChem, a $10 million chemical analytical laboratory. DataChem at the outset created 133 new jobs.

By the end of 2013 the park's blue-ribbon tenants also included GE, Wells Fargo, ITT, and Convergys. Of the park's 100 acres, about thirty were yet to be developed.

The success of Sorenson Research Park helped lower Jim's resistance to developing his land holdings. Jim Jr. then proposed creation of a technology park.

In about 1988 Jim purchased 220 acres of land at auction from the Union Pacific Railroad, paying $6,500 an acre. It was in the western part of Salt Lake City, at the northwest corner of Bangerter Highway and California Avenue. Between 1992 and 1997 he acquired 160 more adjacent acres through a series of purchases.

Some developers offered Jim $13,000 an acre for the land—double his purchase price. Two of Jim's advisors urged him to sell the land, but Don Wallace opposed a sale and instead suggested they develop the land themselves. By then the key real estate players were Jim Jr. and Don.

Jim Jr. and Ralph Johnson had other pressing business matters. After several meetings with Don, they told him he would have to carry the ball. Jim Sr. asked Don if he could direct the development. Don had not developed real estate before, but swallowed hard and said he could.

The project turned out to be especially complicated. Wallace consulted with industrial developers, engineers, and real estate brokers before tackling it. Environmental and wetlands problems had to be overcome, irrigation canals rerouted, and access points across power corridors acquired. Canal shares downstream were selling for $50, but one owner insisted on selling his acreage with his water shares, for a total of $250,000. The Sorenson team was forced to pay it to keep the project moving, but a year later, after rerouting the canal, Don sold the same parcel for twice as much.

Jim's style with such projects was to think big but not get entangled in details. One day, after about $2 million was spent on the project, he had Wallace drive him out to the site to inspect the project. Upon getting a glimpse of the new roads and construction activity, Jim was satisfied and they returned to the office.

Sorenson Technology Park, including water, sewer, gas, power, and phone lines was constructed in four phases between 1996 and 1998. Marketing and selling of the industrial lots was completed in 2000.

Jim Jr. and Don developed two more technology parks—one at 700 South and 5600 West in Salt Lake City and another at 7000 South Airport Road in West Jordan.

Jim Sr. was handsomely rewarded. From initial investments of $5.6 million in the three parks, the company saw $75 million in revenue and $23 million in net cash flow.

Once more Jim had taken a calculated gamble and won big.

### CHAPTER TWENTY-FOUR

# SORENSONS CREATE A CITY

Rerouting canals and roadways for a technology park was child's play compared with creating a city. That is what the Sorenson team did when midwifing the rebirth of Herriman, in the far southwest corner of Salt Lake Valley. Sorenson's leadership led all growth in the area and created a model all-America community.

Herriman's story began much earlier. In 1851, four years after Brigham Young led the first pioneers into the valley, one of the families went searching for a pure stream of water, and found it near the Oquirrh Mountains, nineteen miles from Salt Lake City.

The next spring, three other families joined them, including the Henry Harriman family. The small settlement took its name from this family, though tax collectors and other officials misspelled it, with an "e" instead of an "a."

The settlers were farmers and ranchers who lived in log cabins, rock homes, and crude dugouts built into hillsides. To protect against Indians they also built a fort.

By 1855 there were about ninety residents on the tax lists, including twenty-six men who paid a $10 poll tax. By 1870 Herriman's population was about 150. For more than a century Herriman continued to grow slowly, a small, sleepy bedroom community out of the mainstream that was not significant enough even to be incorporated into its own town.[1]

Jim Sorenson aimed to change all that. With uncanny foresight, and once more against the advice of advisors, in the 1980s he began to acquire land in the vicinity from farmers and sheep ranchers. His son-in-law, Thom Williamsen, led the purchasing effort. By the 1990s most sellers dried up and prices shot up.

Sorenson purchased around 2,400 acres, with about half the land in the city of Bluffdale, half in unincorporated Salt Lake County, and a small piece in Riverton City. Sorenson, through an entity called South Farm LLC, proposed a sweeping project called Rosecrest. The name derived from the fact that it was primarily located above Rose Creek which runs west to east along the northern boundary of the property.

Rosecrest was designed as a comprehensive Planned Unit Development (PUD) community to include single-family and multi-family residential development, schools, retail, office, and other commercial facilities, with an abundance of parks and trails and community services.

A long struggle lay ahead. Sorenson drew up a master plan and for several years worked with Riverton, which indicated it would annex the new development into the city. When annexation plans were announced by Riverton, the abutting city of Bluffdale protested, citing previous unresolved boundary issues with Riverton unrelated to the Rosecrest lands. Riverton asked Sorenson to withdraw the annexation petition until Riverton resolved its differences with Bluffdale. After months passed without progress in the Riverton/Bluffdale dispute, the Sorenson team applied to Salt Lake County to develop adjacent unincorporated lands.

At the same time Sorenson began pressing Bluffdale to approve the Rosecrest development plan on lands located within Bluffdale's boundaries. Many residents of Bluffdale opposed multi-family housing, commercial development, and building lots smaller than one acre. The issue became so contentious that, for one four-hour city council meeting, the Bluffdale mayor posted two sheriff's deputies inside and warned vocal locals that they could be charged with a crime if they turned disorderly.[2]

True to its name, Bluffdale apparently was bluffing. Sorenson real estate president Don Wallace worked with Bluffdale for more than a decade, in more than 300 meetings with city officials to get the Rosecrest plan approved. Officials, under countervailing pressure from many citizens, would not move.

Starting in the mid-1980s developers offered more than fifty different land plans, six to eight of them by Sorenson. In the end the effort with Bluffdale proved fruitless.

"They just would not approve any reasonable development at all," said Wallace. "After working through three mayoral administrations, four city attorneys, and several city managers with no progress and many broken promises by officials, we came to the conclusion that Bluffdale had no intention of ever approving sustainable development plans on our lands."

Apparently Bluffdale's true agenda was to leave the Sorenson land and land belonging to others as open space. It would take nearly fifteen years and a lawsuit to wrest control of the Sorenson lands from Bluffdale's domain.

Meanwhile Riverton City, with a population of 25,000 in the year 2000, sought to swallow up the tiny Herriman community, with a population of less than 750. Descendants of the early Herriman pioneers were alarmed, fearful of losing their historical identity.

One day an enterprising man approached the Herriman Community Council, offering to help the community incorporate as a town to protect it from Riverton's land grab. The catch: It would cost Herriman a half-million dollars. The man told the Sorenson leaders he could also get Rosecrest approved, for another half-million.

Don Wallace attended the late-night meeting in a log cabin in Herriman and heard the man's proposal. Wallace briefed himself on Utah municipal incorporation law and determined that the process was far simpler than the other man suggested. It simply required a survey, a petition signed by a majority of citizens living within the incorporation area, and a study of the fiscal impacts on the proposed town of Herriman. The Sorenson team agreed to provide the survey and funds for the fiscal study, and the Herriman Council agreed to gather the signatures and support the Rosecrest development plan. Total cost: $15,000.

Jim Sorenson Jr., vice chairman of Sorenson Development, played a crucial role in cementing relations with Herriman. He reported directly to his father, while Don executed the strategic real estate decisions handed down from Jim Jr. and Jim Sr. Jim Jr. and Don met extensively with the town council to answer questions and tout the benefits of Rosecrest. Council members agreed. They dug in and soon accomplished their end of the bargain, as Sorenson did its end.

In 1999 Herriman was officially incorporated as a town. Meanwhile, as the Sorenson team assisted Herriman with incorporation, Salt Lake County officials overwhelmingly approved the Rosecrest plan. Sixty days later city fathers in the new town of Herriman added their stamp of approval.

Months later, Sorenson began constructing the Herriman portion of Rosecrest, platting more than 300 single-family lots by the end of 2000. Three years later more than 1,200 single-family lots were platted and hundreds of new families moved to Rosecrest in Herriman.

The portion of Rosecrest lands in Bluffdale remained mired in conflict with Bluffdale city officials. In 2005 Sorenson, joined by sympathetic neighboring land owners, filed a lawsuit in Utah's Third District Court to disconnect their lands from Bluffdale. Sorenson accused the city of taking away its property rights. After a four-day bench trial the judge ruled in Sorenson's favor, ordering the disconnection of 4,000 acres (nearly seven square miles) from Bluffdale—1,250 acres belonging to Sorenson and the rest to more than fifty other land owners.

Bluffdale appealed the decision to the Utah Supreme Court, which in 2007 upheld the lower court ruling. Sorenson promptly annexed the disconnected land into Herriman. A year later, Herriman approved the additional Rosecrest development plan and the Sorenson team could now fully develop Rosecrest in a cohesive and sustainable manner.

Rosecrest and Herriman have both benefitted greatly, the latter becoming an ideal family community. It has been one of Utah's and the nation's fastest-growing cities. In 2000 Herriman had a population of 1,523; by the 2010 census it had grown to 21,785, more than 1,300 percent. It was a town and is now ranked by Utah as a Class 4 city. Bluffdale meanwhile in 2010 had 7,598 residents.

In 2009 the median household income in Utah was $55,000; in Herriman it was $76,500. The median house or condominium value in Utah was $225,000; in Herriman it was $312,000. Twelve percent of Utahns had not graduated from high school, compared with 4 percent in Herriman. Eighteen percent of Utahns had at least a bachelor's degree, compared with 22 percent in Herriman. By all measures Herriman is a model community spurred chiefly by Sorenson's Rosecrest development. [3]

Herriman boasts more than twenty-five parks; at least one park within a quarter-mile of every home. Additions by 2012 included an all-purpose city library and, around the corner on Main Street, a new elementary school next to the J.L. Sorenson Recreation Center, a $30 million facility serving all residents in the southwest area.

Salt Lake County appropriated $24.5 million toward the center, and Rosecrest contributed the land and an additional $5 million. It includes a competition-size indoor swimming pool, racquetball courts, an indoor running and walking track, two full-size indoor basketball courts, exercise and fitness areas, and drop-in child care. Shortly after Herriman's incorporation Sorenson also gave the city $400,000 to complete a 28,600-square-foot outdoor performing arts pavilion at the Butterfield Park and Rodeo Grounds.

Highway transportation critical to the area's growth is also progressing. In October 2012 seven more miles of the Mountain View Corridor, linking southwest Salt Lake County with also-fast-growing Utah County to the south, was dedicated, two months earlier than scheduled. Sorenson spurred this effort with a donation of more than 100 acres of land for the highway corridor through the Rosecrest project.

In 2011 Salt Lake Community College, only thirteen miles away, acquired 90 acres for a new campus in Herriman.

Rosecrest has about 3,000 recently built homes at this writing, with another 5,000 projected to be added over the next twenty years.

Sorenson invested about $6.6 million and developed 2,154 residential lots from 1999 to 2008. That generated $162 million in revenue and $56.7 million in net cash flow.

Something else distinguished Sorenson's Herriman project from similar developments. It was being accomplished with a minimum of staff. At the height of the real estate market in 2007-08, the Kennecott Land Company was developing a similar-size master-planned community in South

Jordan. Kennecott had some 120 personnel working on it, compared with about 20 Sorenson people working on Rosecrest.

In 2007 Sorenson launched the master plan for the $1 billion Herriman Towne Center on 375 acres acquired through an agreement with the LDS Church. It will be the handsome core of the city, with an expansive plaza and retail and office space enabling residents to "live where they work and work where they live," thereby eliminating for some the long commutes common in Utah. Included will be 2,000 residential units—condominiums and town-homes as well as single-family dwellings.

"The Sorenson Group and its Rosecrest community have been great community builders," said Herriman Mayor J. Lynn Crane when the Towne Center plan was unveiled in 2008. He called the project "a tremendous victory for Herriman City and its residents, which will enhance our community's identity and improve the quality of life for families at every income level and stage of life." [4]

Sorenson's Don Wallace paid Herriman the ultimate compliment: He and his wife Gloria now live there.

Two other major development projects with great possibilities but much less progress are in the picturesque Heber Valley, called Utah's Switzerland because of the majestic beauty of the Wasatch Mountains to the west, and the cool climate. The valley is a magnet for marathoners and other outdoors enthusiasts. The two parcels of land, totaling about 9,000 acres, were acquired by Jim Sorenson from Shell Oil in the early 1980s and additional parcels have been added since that time.

Again Jim knew under which tree to place his basket. In 1987 construction began on the Jordanelle Reservoir, and was completed in 1993. The large reservoir is located on the Provo River about six miles north of the small city of Heber. Recreation facilities at Jordanelle State Park were completed on the west side of the reservoir in 1995, offering camping, boating, water skiing, and fish-cleaning stations. Irrigation is another major benefit.

One of the two Sorenson developments is the Jordanelle North Village Project, 3,000 acres north of Heber City. It will be a clustered mixed-use development of about 1,600 homes, intended to span the market demands between the high-end and low-end residential properties. By clustering active development envelopes, nearly 85 percent of the land will be preserved as open space, including abundant trails and other outdoor recreational opportunities.

A benefit already in place in North Village is the Wasatch campus of Utah Valley University, whose main campus is a half-hour-drive away in Orem, Utah County.

The area was essentially dry land used historically for grazing of sheep and cattle. It did not have significant water resources when Jim Sorenson acquired his land. From about 1994 thorough 2010 the Sorenson team aggressively accumulated nearly 5,000 acre feet of water rights for development of this project and its sister project northeast of Heber City. Sorenson, however, ran into problems similar to those it originally faced in developing Herriman City.

For most of its history Wasatch County was staunchly anti-development, a sentiment that stalled North Village Project for many years. Utah Valley University helped break the logjam. The county tried to lure UVU to North Village, but could not provide essential services to the university without assistance from private landowners.

In 2003 the county and landowners formed the North Village Special Services District to bring water, sewer, and storm drainage facilities to the village. Costs would be covered through bonding, with Sorenson providing the largest financial commitment for the bond. This enabled the university to begin construction on its campus and, theoretically, landowners to begin developing their lands.

UVU proceeded with construction, and the first students enrolled in the fall of 2005. The university awarded its first degrees in April 2007. Today it offers associate (two-year) degrees in behavioral science and business management, and four-year bachelor degrees in elementary education.

Despite the essential help from Sorenson and other developers to bring UVU to Heber, Wasatch County officials did not play fair. Between 2003 and 2006 they stalled Sorenson's development through bureaucratic measures including having outside consultants rework the Sorenson plan with little input from the company. In the end, Sorenson rejected the county's blueprint and came up with a modified plan of its own—a development for 1,600 homes which the county finally approved.

As county bureaucrats stepped aside, state bureaucrats stepped up to continue blocking Sorenson. In 2006, when the company moved forward with the first subdivision plat in North Village, the Utah Department of Transportation (UDOT) sent Sorenson a bill for $1,050,000 for the right to access its subdivision from State Route 32 (SR-32). UDOT arrived at that number by appraising the Sorenson property without access rights and than re-appraising it with access rights. UDOT was charging the difference for access.

Based on that logic, over the projected term of the project Sorenson would pay more than $30 million to UDOT to reach its own land!

However, when the Jordanelle Reservoir was built years earlier, it covered old SR-32. The Bureau of Reclamation proposed to relocate old SR-32 to accommodate the new Jordanelle Reservoir. Sorenson donated the right-of-way across its property for a new portion of the highway, at no charge. In exchange, Wasatch County agreed not to charge Sorenson for as many access points as it needed.

Later, Wasatch County transferred SR-32 to UDOT and UDOT refused to be bound by the prior agreement, forcing Sorenson to sue the agency and lobby with state officials to force UDOT's hand. Sorenson prevailed and UDOT withdrew its claims in 2009, guaranteeing Sorenson's access rights to Sorenson property into the future.

Development began in 2007 on the first two subdivision plats in the North Village, and condominium construction began the following year. Delays by the county, coupled with the housing market downturn, brought the project to a halt. A small number of lots were sold prior to the downturn, and since 2008 most of the condominiums have been sold. Otherwise the North Village project was on hold as of the summer of 2013.

The larger Upper Jordanelle Development, about 6,000 acres on the plateaus northeast of Heber, has experienced a similar scenario. Plans call for construction of about 3,200 homes, clustered in what Sorenson calls "spectacular development pockets...affording both seclusion and awe-inspiring views."

The project is designed for lower-density, higher-end second homes, with abundant recreational resources and resort-style services. Planned amenities include golf courses, equestrian barns and trails, cross-country skiing and hiking trails, and snowmobiling.

Sorenson succeeded in getting Wasatch County and the Jordanelle Special Services District to create a bond issue to construct a new sewer plant and bring sewer and water lines online to enable development of this project and other private Upper Jordanelle holdings. Construction began in 2007 and Sorenson finished paying off its share of the bond in 2009.

Over time, the Sorenson team has created more than two dozen plans for the project, each new plan improving on the previous plan, and in the meantime securing entitlement commitments, ample water rights, and design concepts that can be deployed once the markets recover. An alternative is to sell it to other investors seeking a shovel-ready project or simply land-banking for the future.

Over Jim's lifetime, he purchased and sold scores of parcels of raw land; business and industrial sites and buildings; residential developments, individual apartment buildings, and houses. Once he had personally gained substantial capital following the sale of Sorenson Research, Jim had a rule of thumb for such transactions. "He did not allow us to go out and borrow money to do them," said Wallace. "He'd prime the pump a little up front, with his own money to get us going. After that we had to operate off the cash we could generate. He taught us to operate lean and borrow as little as possible.

"Bankers, competitors, and others criticized us right and left for being so conservative. Then the [housing] market crashed, and we looked like geniuses, like heroes."

Another rule of thumb was never tell Jim "we can't do that," said Wallace. "That was the worst thing you could say to him. I learned early on to discern Jim's intent from his words and then go figure out how to make it happen and get it done. He didn't want to study spread sheets and pore over market analyses. He had great intuition about what would work in real estate." Jim's appetite for real estate remained insatiable all his life. In the 1990s he wrote:

> I still sneak away from the office at lunchtime occasionally to look over some vacant property. In the '50s and '60s I would prowl the fields on the East Bench of Salt Lake Valley, fields that have long since been blanketed by neighborhoods. In the '90s I prowled the fields at

the south end of the same valley...And the feeling is the same as before...You can go and look at it and touch it and think about all of the
good things that can and will happen there in the future. So the Jim
Sorenson of the '90s is a lot like the Jim Sorenson of the '60s. I'm still
working hard to find an opportunity to grow. I'm still trying to balance
people and ideas and capital to make a company go forward. I'm still
trying to balance body, mind and spirit to keep it all in perspective.
Though I'm still trying, I'm not always succeeding because the world
changes the recipe a little every day. [5]

Well after the 1990s gave way to the 2000s, Jim, now in his eighties,
still took Don Wallace to hike the few remaining undeveloped land parcels
on Salt Lake's east bench, to strategize on how to acquire them and what
wonderful things they could turn them into.

Decades after leaving Yuba City, Jim revisits the family home on Bandy Track Alley that his father renovated from the original tar paper-covered shack.

Jim and Bev's spacious home was the site for many family gatherings, and where they hosted local, national, and international dignitaries.

An architect's rendering of Jim and Beverley's last home in a Salt Lake City suburb.

Jim had few hobbies, but here tries to raise a trout while fly fishing.

A Sorenson family "cabin"—actually the size of a lodge—has seen many family reunions and workshops for family businesses and such groups as Beverley's Art Works for Kids. Joe Sorenson, on the lawn, helped oversee its construction

After his parents passed away, Jim bought their rural home in Loomis, California, turning it into "Emma's Bed & Breakfast."

Visiting the John Taylor home in Nauvoo, Illinois, once the headquarters of the Church of Jesus Christ of Latter-day Saints. Taylor, third president of the Church, was Bev's great-grandfather.

Jim and a partner built the Jordan Queen as a land-based seafood restaurant in Sorenson Research Park. Opened to the public in 1984, the Queen did not live up to its owners' ambitions, and finally was torn down near the end of the century. Courtesy *Deseret News Publishing Company*

Sorenson Research Park is a multi-use research, business, and residential complex at 4500 South 900 West. The 100-acre park opened in 1988; by the end of 2013 thirty acres were still to be developed.

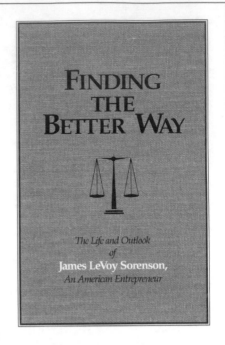

FINDING
THE
BETTER WAY

*The Life and Outlook
of*
**James LeVoy Sorenson,**
*An American Entrepreneur*

Jim's favorite business axiom was reflected in the title of his autobiography, written in 2004: "There has to be a better way!" Courtesy *Deseret News Publishing Company*

Over his lifetime Jim acquired hundreds of thousands of acres. He especially sought land with water on it, such as Coyote Springs in the west desert of Kanosh, where cattle drink. Don Wallace, also in hard hat, headed Jim's real estate division.

Nearly a half-century after launching Deseret Pharmaceutical, the three pals gather for lunch in 2000. Victor Cartwright is on the left, Dale Ballard on the right.

Jim Sr. and Jr. appeared on the cover of *Wasatch Digital IQ* in May 2002. Wrote the publisher: "[Jim Sr.'s] contribution to the evolution of the medical profession has been profound." Courtesy *Wasatch Digital/Utah Business*

Jim stayed physically fit, playing squash into his eighties. In *Finding True Balance,* one of his several books, Jim taught that happiness comes from being balanced physically, intellectually, and spiritually.

Jim acquired White Sage Ranch and farm near Kanosh, Utah, in 1995. In 2013 White Sage owned 71,000 acres and leased another 450,000 from the federal government, placing it among the top 2 percent of U.S. ranches.

White Sage cowboys gather for the semi-annual roundup of about 3,000 cows and their offspring. Ninety percent of the cows drop a calf each year.

Standing by a cattle truck at the ranch are (*left to right*) Jim Larson, a Sorenson executive who oversaw the operation, ranch hand Lane Watts, ranch manager Neuel Chlarson, Jim, and his longtime executive assistant Gloria Smith.

Two Russians at the White Sage ranch. Aleksey Blyumenfeld, a chemist, was sponsored to the U.S. by Jim, and fulfilled a dream by becoming a cowboy for a season. Kody Stott is the youngster above. He was adopted from Russia by ranch hand Kyle Stott (*pictured*) and his wife Stacy. Kody was hearing-impaired and needed cochlear implants, which were arranged by Jim.

Mexican-born farm manager Efren Erreguin and his family. Jim occasionally had dinner at their home. Here he holds Jimmy, named for him as thanks for a financial gift.

Jim loved exploring the ranch, by horse or four-wheeler. Water at White Sage includes a mineral pool (*above*), not quite hot enough to produce hydropower.

### CHAPTER TWENTY-FIVE

# WHITE SAGE RANCH, FARM

Fay, the sassy redhead waitress at the Garden of Eat'n café in Fillmore gave as good as she got. So when bantering with a seventyish new patron with an impish grin, nothing seemed out of the ordinary.

The man was Jim Sorenson and he was pretty full of himself, shortly after winning the bid at the foreclosure sale for the White Sage Ranch in hardscrabble Millard County, central Utah. Jim, his new ranch manager Clyde Smith, and his real estate head Don Wallace had just completed a walking tour of the new acquisition and stopped at the Garden of Eat'n café on their way back to Salt Lake City.

When Fay approached their table, Jim said "Do you know who I am?"

"No."

"Well, you should, I own half of this county!"

"Well," Fay quickly retorted, "you can't be very damn smart if you own half of *this* county!"

For a brief moment Jim looked incensed and in shock, until he glanced over at his dinner companions and saw Clyde and Don snickering. With that, Jim lightened up and continued a friendly banter with Fay. Waitress Fay, far removed from Utah's populous Wasatch Front, where most people live and most of the news is made, didn't know who Jim Sorenson was. Nor did she care.

Until, that is, Jim got up to leave, tipping her with a crisp new $100 bill.

"*That* got all of our attention," said Sandy, a veteran waitress at the Garden of Eat'n. "Mr. Sorenson was always very nice, very polite. He never dressed like he had a lot of money."

Jim liked Fay, who was of similar age and wore oversize round-lens glasses, to wait on him when she was on duty. If Fay—now retired—wasn't there, other waitresses jockeyed to serve him. Whoever did always got a $100 tip.[1]

As a board member at First Security Bank in 1995, Jim learned of a foreclosure auction on a 67,000-acre ranch and farm in Kanosh, down the road a bit from Fillmore in central Utah. He sent two assistants, Craig Larson and Clyde Smith, to Kanosh to acquire it.

Another man also was intent on buying the property, but when the bids were unsealed, Sorenson had won. About two hours later the other man offered Jim a $500,000 profit for the spread, which Jim turned down.

There were times earlier in his life when Jim almost certainly would have taken the half-million-dollars and ran. But the thought of a farm and ranch stirred something inside him—perhaps a combination of his earliest years as a child in rural Idaho and, almost certainly, of the stockyard his father purchased and once ran in northern California.

Whatever influenced him, from the start there was no doubt as to Jim's intent: to develop the biggest and best agricultural holding that anyone in those parts had seen.

Sorenson's arrival in Millard County—named for the thirteenth U.S. President, Millard Fillmore—was a godsend to the region. There is not a lot otherwise to recommend it. Twenty-one percent of county residents in 2000 lived below the federal poverty line, including 27 percent under the age of eighteen. Sorenson ranch and farm property reach into three adjacent counties as well.

Kanosh is named for Chief Kanosh of the local Pahvant band of Piute Indians. He lived more than a century ago and, along with many other Pahvants, was converted to Mormonism and baptized in Corn Creek into the

LDS Church. Kanosh's population in 2000 officially was 485. The entire town is less than one square mile.

Kanosh, just off I-15, has no traffic lights, one service station, and one store, Kanosh Mercantile. The aging Mercantile, known locally as "the mall," has groceries and various paraphernalia on the main floor. Patrons going downstairs have to turn the light on as they descend the stairs, and off as they ascend. Down there in the dark is a modest variety of items useful to local trades, including horse shoes, assorted hardware, fittings to repair irrigation equipment, and the like.

Jim was a different man at the ranch than back at headquarters. He was relaxed, full of fun, and generous with workers and other townspeople alike. He gave several calves to the Pahvant chief, donated to local causes, and often sought out residents to determine their skill sets and how he might employ them.

Each Christmas, accompanied by Beverley and executive assistant Gloria Smith, he donned jeans, cowboy boots, hat and bolo tie and threw a sumptuous dinner party for all of the farm and ranch hands and their families. Cowboys and farmers usually don't mix well, but the party brought all of them together.

After Jim acquired the White Sage Ranch and Farm (white sage is an evergreen shrub that cattle eat) he bought and remodeled several homes in town for use by employees, and an old hotel for seasonal use for family reunions and hunters. A two story, four-bedroom home on White Sage itself was renovated and freshly covered with tan stucco for use by Jim and other Sorensons, though apparently almost no one but Jim actually used it. In about 2001 Jim added a log cabin near the horse barns.

In 2013 the house was the way it was when Jim died in 2008, except for a shotgun over the mantel which was removed by one of the Sorenson children. Jim's bedroom clothes closet included a nice pair of ostrich-skin cowboy boots and a straw hat that he wore cocked to the side of his head.

Clyde Smith, who helped purchase White Sage, oversaw it the first year from Salt Lake City. Afterward the job fell to Jim Larson, a close confidante to Jim and Beverley Sorenson, who grew up on a dairy farm in Garland, Box Elder County. "I could ride a horse, so Mr. Sorenson decided that qualified me to run the operation," deadpanned Larson, a tall, amiable, gray-haired man who subsequently died in October 2013. "All he told me to do was grow it." Larson said he could oversee the operation from Salt Lake only because the on-site ranch and farm managers were exceptionally capable.

Grow it they did, buying everything in sight and carefully assimilating it into the rest of the operation. The average-size farm in Utah in 2010 was 669 acres—almost precisely the size of White Sage when Jim Sorenson bought it in 1995. Sorenson's joint operation now has 71,000 acres owned—5,500 acres in farmland and 65,000 acres in ranch land. It had 700 cows when bought and 3,000 cows in 2011—landing it in the top 280 beef cattle ranches in the U.S., 2.1 percent of all such operations. [2]

White Sage leases another 450,000 acres from the Bureau of Land Management and Forest Service. The ranch's 3,000 cows were down from a high of 3,700 five years earlier. The numbers are subject to a delicate balance between agriculture and nature.

Wildfires in 2006 and 2007—the latter the largest in Utah history—devastated grazing areas on the desert and in the mountains. Lack of feed forced the ranch to reduce the herds to fewer than 3,000 cows. White Sage in 2013 was building the herds back up to the pre-2007 level.

Ninety percent of the cows drop a calf every year—compared with a state average closer to 85 percent. This means that for part of the year there are close to 6,000 cattle at White Sage, including the calves. The ranch also has about 100 bulls that service the cows. Most bulls are kept around for three years, then become hamburger before they can mate with their daughters.

Cows that get pregnant consistently are kept around for up to eleven or twelve years. Older cows and the 350 or so that fail to get pregnant are shipped to market, and the same number of replacement heifers are added to the ranch's two main herds.

Most of the cattle are Angus, which bring a premium price for beef.

"Clyde Smith told me that 'the ranch is like an old cherry wood table,'" explained ranch manager Neuel Chlarson. "He said 'It just needs to be sanded and refinished, and it will be a valuable piece of furniture.' Mr. Sorenson believed the same thing; he had a vision of what he wanted the ranch to be, and drove us to achieve it.

"Mr. Sorenson set these goals and really wanted to reach them. For example, he said 'Let's have 2,000 head by the year 2000.' When December of 1999 rolled around, he'd ask, 'Are we going to have our 2,000? If we're going to be a little short, let's go buy some.' So we bought some and we made it."

Chlarson added that "It's been really fun to work for him. Not only is it a good job and they treat us well, we have really good benefits that you normally don't have when you work on a ranch. Guys like me dream of having our own place, and probably never can. But working for this company is like having your own place, and I treat it like it was my own." [3]

The hiring of Chlarson followed Jim's pattern of trusting his instincts to know who *could* do a big job rather than who *has* done a big job. Chlarson was a 20-year-old ranch hand for the previous owners, Mark and Jay Platt of the Seven Springs Ranch in St. Johns, Arizona. Chlarson and his family moved from St. Johns to Kanosh in 1992.

When Sorenson gave the other Seven Springs cowboys their last paychecks in 1995, they left. Chlarson, however, felt obligated to stay on another month to help with the transition.

Clyde Smith phoned Chlarson and asked him to come up to Salt Lake City. Chlarson, who is medium-built and perhaps five-foot-eight, with a ruddy face and quick smile, looked even younger than he was. When he reached Salt Lake, Smith took him shopping, buying Chlarson a new pair of cowboy boots and ordering a custom-made ten-gallon hat.

"That's when he told me 'You've got to look good,' because they wanted to put me in charge of the ranch." After nearly fainting, Chlarson was taken to meet other Sorenson executives.

Chlarson got to know Jim. "When he first bought the ranch you heard all these rumors about him, how big and rich he was. When I met him he wasn't like that at all. He was really a down-to-earth guy. Made you feel that you were important, that you meant something to him."

Chlarson, who was married and had five children, got the same treatment as Fay the waitress: a crisp $100 bill each time Jim visited. "He'd always tell me to take my wife to dinner." Jim sometimes showed up unannounced at the Chlarson home. "One time he came and found me and said 'Did you know your kids are playing with matches at your house?'"

One price Chlarson paid was his willingness to good-naturedly take phone calls from Jim at all hours of the day and night. "He usually just wanted to visit," recalled Chlarson. "He'd ask how the branding or fall roundup was going, and always wanted to know how our family was doing."

Jim arrived in Kanosh one time as Chlarson was about to leave home. "I told him I was going to see my son play football. Mr. Sorenson said 'I'll go with you.' We went to the game and he kept asking my son's number. He sat there and cheered for him."

One of White Sage's four other full-time cowboys was Kyle Stott. He and his wife could not have children of their own, so they decided to adopt in Russia. They received a picture of a one-year-old boy in an orphanage and decided he would be their son.

When the Stotts reached Russia and the orphanage, however, officials told them to choose another child. The boy in the photo could not hear, and could not speak. He also was severely crippled and could not walk. When the Stotts insisted they wanted the same boy, they were told that if they took him they would be forbidden from adopting other Russian children.

The Stotts returned stateside with their new son, Kody, and pondered what to do next. A cochlear implant seemed to offer Kody the best hope of hearing, but the cost for such surgery in the United States can be $100,000 or more.

A cochlear implant is an electronic device that often can restore partial hearing to individuals who suffer severe to profound hearing loss. It is implanted in the inner ear during a surgery that takes from an hour and a half to five hours. The implant is activated by a device worn outside and behind the ear.

Jim Sorenson heard about Kody and approached the Stotts, quietly telling them he was prepared to help them secure the cochlear implant and arrange for the surgery. Jim used his contacts at the University of Utah Medical Center to find a surgeon to perform the operation, and convinced the cochlear implant manufacturer to donate the device.

The hospital was unable to waive its expenses for Kody's procedure, however, so Jim's assistant Don Wallace, a frequent visitor to the ranch, made a personal donation and organized a funding drive that collected

$10,000 from some thirty companies and individuals to cover Kody's hospital expenses. The effort represented Jim's charitable philosophy of "priming the pump" to encourage others to join in supporting worthy causes.

In 2013 Kody was a healthy 17-year-old who walked, talked, and—after many other surgeries—even ran. "He is a little crooked, and doesn't control his legs really well," explained Chlarson. "But he went on a fifty-mile hike with the Scouts; didn't carry his pack the whole way, but he made the trip."

Jim Larson added that "Kody feels like he's in the mainstream. He likes sports but has some limitations. He's the manager on the football team, and he's pretty bright. He's planning on going on a [Mormon] mission."

A postscript: Russia relented, and the Stotts have since returned there and brought home two baby girls.

Jim Sorenson and the ranch were important in the life of another Russian, Aleksey Blyumenfeld, who was plump and in his fifties when he arrived in Utah. Jim sponsored Aleksey, a chemist, into the U.S., but his visa did not allow him to work at first when he got here. What Aleksey wanted most was to come to America and have a real cowboy experience.

Jim set Aleksey up on the ranch, giving him a place to live and credit to buy groceries at the local store. He did not speak English well. The other cowboys taught him how to ride a horse and do "cowboy work." "Aleksey absolutely loved it down here," said ranch manager Chlarson. He gamely tried to do everything the other cowboys did, coming close to serious accidents a number of times.

On one occasion, when there was a lot of rain, Aleksey returned from the mountains with a basketful of mushrooms. "I said 'Some of those mushrooms are poisonous.'" Chlarson told him, "'If you eat them you'll die.'"

"You worry about cowboy stuff; I'm the chemist," answered Aleksey in a mixture of English and Russian. "There's not a mushroom in the world that you can't eat if you boil it three times. That's the problem with you Americans—you don't appreciate what you have."

After the mini-lecture, Aleksey proceeded to boil some mushrooms three times, then cautiously started to eat them. "He'd take a little bit and wait for awhile to see what happened. But he went ahead and ate them," said Chlarson. The next day he boiled them twice; after that, deciding they were safe, he fried the rest up and ate them.

"He was a nice guy but not a great cowboy," said Chlarson. "He was determined to do his share of work, and he did. He got his cowboy experience. At the end of his stay, after seven or eight months, he had lost all his extra weight and was fit and trim." He had also picked up some cowboy English that couldn't be repeated in polite company.

Later, Aleksey's wife, also a scientist, landed a job in Boston. Aleksey went with her, much in distress for having to leave the ranch, and landed a job in Boston as well. Some of his vacations brought him back to the ranch.

White Sage is an ideal spread, where none of the cattle have to be moved by truck to new feeding ground as the seasons change. During the winter they graze on pasture land on the Sevier Desert, west of I-15. Most cows drop calves there in March and April. In June the ranch hands—and a dozen or so temporary hires—mount their horses and head out on the desert to round up the cows and calves. They herd them through a tunnel under I-15, hoping a trucker won't blow his horn for fun and spook them, and onto the Pahvant Mountains to the east.

Calves grow to between 500 and 600 pounds and are sold in October. They are trucked to feedlots, mainly in Nebraska and other Midwest beef centers where they will be fattened until slaughtered for the table. The ranch also has a second, smaller herd of cows that drop calves in the fall for sale in June.

Beverley Sorenson visited the ranch on occasion. The first time she met Chlarson there she was concerned about the cattle. "She wanted to know if we could build little huts and stuff for them out on the desert to keep them warm," he recalled. She sent the ranch and farm manager families a Christmas card each year.

The original assumption was that the ranch would be more profitable than the farm. The opposite was the case, however, with the farm far more profitable than the ranch. Since purchasing White Sage in 1995, Sorenson invested millions more to make it a state-of-the art operation. The crops and cattle bring in several million a year in profit.

White Sage Farm is a model of efficiency and profitability. Jim gave the farm every tool necessary to succeed, including seven or eight John Deere tractors that sell for about $200,000 each. Alfalfa is the main crop on the

5,500 acres under cultivation. It is usually too valuable to be consumed on the ranch; instead it is bundled into 1,800-pound bales and trucked away, much of it to California. Other crops include corn and grains, mostly fall wheat.

Water is a critical component. In addition to well rights, White Sage is served by a large canal company. As winter snows melt, streams run heavily off the mountains into June. The operation has a large pond to capture the stream flow, which, along with wells, usually tides it over. They use pivot irrigation, in which water is dispersed through a long arm that revolves around the water source and covers a large circular area.

The on-site farm manager was Efren Erreguin, a burly man you would want on your side in a tag-team wrestling match. He had a thick black-and-white goatee and dry sense of humor. Erreguin had been on the farm since 1994, the year before Sorenson acquired it. Born and reared in Mexico, he called Jim Sorenson "the most amazing guy I ever met...he always tried to get things better. When he got the farm it was kind of broken down. We grew 500 or 600 percent; if he was alive we'd probably be bigger."

Erreguin also benefitted personally from Jim's $100 bills, receiving one most of the times when Jim visited. "When I was twenty-six or twenty-eight, [Jim] said 'I wish I had your age,'" recalled Erreguin. "I said 'I wish I had your money!'"

Jim came to dinner at their home several times—they fed him beef fajitas—and loved to swing their three sons in the yard. The boys at this writing are fifteen, ten, and eight. When each boy was born Jim brought him a gift. He happened to arrive at the farm right after the eight-year-old was born and before he was named.

"He told my wife he'd pay her $1,000 to name my youngest boy Jim," said Erreguin. "She did it and he gave her the $1,000." With a wink, he added that "He told me he was going to put me in his will."

Among other challenges for farm and ranch managers are wild animals. Coyotes are the worst predators, and will kill a calf as its mother is birthing it. There are also abundant deer, pronghorn antelope, and elk. The latter present a problem as well as an opportunity.

If elk stray onto desert feeding ground they can be killed by owners. However, the adjacent Pahvant Mountains boast some of the largest deer and elk in the United States—as measured by the spread of their antlers. The Boone and Crockett Club, a hunting organization that records kills of the biggest animals of many species, lists Millard County as the nineteenth best area in the U.S. for trophy elk. Nineteen bull elk taken in the county have made the club's roster.

Hunters come from throughout the western states to hunt elk on land leased by the forest service to White Sage. The ranch sells permits to out-fitters who resell them to hunters. A hunter's price tag to bag a bull elk: $19,000.

Jim Sorenson of course loved the extra cash generated by hunters. He experimented with other creative ways to make his ranch and farm more profitable. Jim had several anemometers installed—tall, slender devices that measure wind velocity—to see if the wind whipping across his spread was strong enough to support a power-generating wind farm. It was just below what would be commercially viable using today's technology.

In another location Jim investigated the exploitation of the geo-thermal resources beneath his land. While the property had substantial geo-thermal activity, the water was not hot enough for commercial power generation.

"What Jim enjoyed most of all down here was just watching how hard these men work," said Jim Larson. The easy chair in his house was turned toward a large window, through which Jim could see some of the ranch and farm operations. He liked watching as the hay was cut, raked, and machine-tied into 1,800-pound bales—vocally adding up, to the amusement of farm hands, how much money each additional bale would bring at market.

"He loved it down here," said farm manager Erreguin. "He was like a little kid having fun. Mostly I saw him riding four-wheelers. Occasionally Jim, who gave major donations to the LDS Church, brought an LDS general authority with him. Two who Erreguin remembered were L. Tom Perry, a member of the Church's Quorum of the Twelve Apostles, and H. David Burton, the Church's presiding bishop.

Ranch manager Chlarson once took Jim to a bull auction in Delta. "They asked him if he wanted to bid and he said yes, so they gave him a card with a number on it. He got so excited that he kept bidding against himself!" They bought a number of bulls and probably paid a little too much in the process.

Jim spoke of bringing his grandchildren to White Sage and built a cabin for them. Except for one occasion when he took a number of boys and girls up a mountain on ATVs, their visits were rare. One grandson who arrived on another day with Jim got more of an adventure than he bargained for. Jim, driving a Ford Explorer, took him deep into the mountains and was on a dry wash when the car high-centered at about dusk—its furiously spinning wheels gripping nothing but air.

Unable to budge the car, Jim and his grandson began walking out—in the wrong direction. They walked all night over the rugged terrain, finally reaching I-15 near dawn. Then they headed south, although the ranch was north, finally flagging down a passing motorist. The motorist took them back to their Ford Explorer and pulled them loose.

"I got home really late that night," recalled Chlarson. "When I went into the house, there was Jim, sound asleep on the couch. He just came in and went plunk, too tired to even go to bed."

Jim Larson said, "Next time I saw him, he was driving a Lexus 4x4, at the suggestion of his son James Lee. I was so glad to see that, 'cause I was sure he'd never drive it into the mountains."

Larson told the true story of another Jim Sorenson tale. For years Sorenson regaled others with how he got bucked off a horse the last time he was at the ranch. "The story got better and better and better with each telling," laughed Larson.

What actually happened was on a spring day when Larson was helping the cowboys brand calves. They all took a break at about one o'clock, including the horses who were tired and almost asleep standing up after dragging calves to the fire all morning. They were tied to a fence.

"Jim decided he'd get on one of the horses, but he didn't tell anyone, including the horse," said Larson. "He put one foot in a stirrup and really spooked the horse. It jumped and knocked him down." Jim rolled into a ball under the horse—which spooked it even more as it pranced around him.

"Pretty frightening to see a multi-billionaire in that situation, said Larson, who grabbed the bridle and guided the horse away from Jim, who was bruised and could have been badly injured but was not.

### CHAPTER TWENTY-SIX

# UNIVERSITY OF UTAH

## Gift Fiasco

W hen Duane Toney became an assistant to Jim Soren-son in 1987, one of the first things that caught his eye was a handsome new leather binder on Jim's desk. Embossed on it were the words "The Sorenson Medical Center and School of Medicine—A Proposal."

Inside were mocked-up examples of medical center letterhead, bearing the Sorenson name. It was delivered by Chase Peterson, president of the University of Utah. He was among numerous supplicants seeking a share of Jim's well-publicized fortune.

Jim had been on Peterson's radar screen a long time. In 1979 Peterson and Ken Garff, a prominent local businessman and university advisor, met with Jim to encourage his financial support. Jim at that time apparently indicated he would endow a professorship in the U's medical school.

Late the following year, months after the sale of Sorenson Research to Abbott Laboratories, Peterson again approached Jim. "...I hope that the philanthropy that you had espoused last year can come about without unwarranted distractions," wrote Peterson. That began a multi-year Peterson campaign of correspondence, meetings, and other contacts with Jim.[1]

Peterson was the U's vice president for health sciences when he began to solicit Jim. After becoming university president in 1983, Peterson's contacts became more frequent and his request far more ambitious.

Peterson had good credentials and was generally well regarded. Born in Logan, Utah where his father, E.G. Peterson, was president of Utah State University, Chase earned bachelor and MD degrees from Harvard. He began a private medical practice in Salt Lake City before returning to Harvard where he was dean of admissions and then a vice president. He was also bishop of an LDS ward in Boston. In 1978 Peterson became vice president for health services at the U, rising to president in 1983.

By 1987, after years of coming up dry, Peterson ratcheted up the pressure on Jim. In March he wrote that the "powerful idea" they had discussed "continues to be at the top of my consciousness." [2]

In a remarkably candid letter to Jim, delivered around the time of the leather gift, an obviously frustrated Peterson wrote: "Jim, now is the time for you to take a deep breath and simply assign $25 million of assets to the endowment of the University for the good of the Medical School and the Health Sciences Center."

"By assigning a new name to the Medical School—The James L. Sorenson School of Medicine—we will have achieved an appropriate focus for your role in this region and nation. Without it, you are another 'rich man' among a couple of hundred others." With the gift, wrote Peterson, Jim would take his place among many other noted American philanthropists affiliated with universities, including "the Pritzkers in Chicago, the Whartons in Philadelphia, the Dukes in Durham, North Carolina, and the Vanderbilts in Tennessee."

"Time is running out for you and me," added Peterson. He was 57 and Jim 66. "Fate could take either one of us out of the picture at any time...I have never been this blunt before in telling another man what he should do with his assets. I do so out of affection for you personally and for fear that a great opportunity for you and the University will be lost by procrastination." [3]

Peterson's request came during a university campaign to raise $150 million in private contributions between May 15, 1987 and July 1990.

The president's persistence finally piqued Jim's interest. Three weeks later he sent a copy of the letter to each of his children and their spouses, asking for "any ideas you may have as to how I should respond to his request."

One son-in-law suggested he make a gift of $15 million, spread over five years, to endow specific chairs at the medical school and fund "particularly promising research proposals." Another son-in-law suggested Jim offer the U enough to endow the "James L. Sorenson Chair in Cardiovascular Medicine." That would require a donation of about $1 million to $2 million.

A Sorenson child advised Jim that $25 million in one lump sum "far exceeds what I feel appropriate for such an honor," suggesting instead that he give $10 to $12 million spread over ten years to hire and retain outstanding faculty and fund promising basic and applied research.

Meanwhile Toney and other professional staff were leery. "They were playing him, and we didn't like it," said Toney. "We saw this a lot. They were appealing to his vanity and his ego...Jim was approached by everybody. Their message was always: 'With your money and my ideas it's going to be fantastic.'" [4]

There were, however, legitimate reasons beyond ego for Jim to consider a major gift. Loyalty was one of them. Beverley attended the U, along with fourteen of their children and/or spouses. In addition, the Utah Legislature—like those in many states—allotted far too few funds to its higher education system. The need for private donors to fill the gaps was real. University presidents like Peterson were judged in good part on how successfully they attracted such gifts.

Jim answered Peterson on November 25. "My concern at this point in my life is not so much to be another rich man, and not so much to have my name bronzed and put on a building, but it is to help my family whom I feel my first responsibility to...Not to give them sums of wealth but to help them create an environment where they can become successful."

While turning Peterson down, however, Jim left the door cracked open: "Possibly at sometime in the future an opportunity will prevail upon us where I might be able to make such a contribution...if I do you need to understand that I do not do it for the generations to see my name bronzed on a building, but I do it that my contribution would be able to help make the world a better place to live in."

That was enough of an opening for Chase Peterson to continue to drive his proposal through. Supported behind the scenes by leaders of the U's Institutional Council, its governing board, Peterson and health sciences vice president Cecil Samuelson continued to meet and correspond with Jim. Gradually Jim warmed to the idea of making a major gift.

In October 1988, south of Salt Lake City in Provo, the Marriott family donated $15 million to Brigham Young University. BYU, in turn, named its business school the J. Willard and Alice S. Marriott School of Management.

That dollar figure may have helped guide Jim's own plans. On May 22, 1989 Jim, Peterson, and Samuelson signed the "J.L. Sorenson Endowment Fund Gift Agreement." The ten-page document called for a gift of 250,000 shares of Abbott stock, then worth around $15 million. The university could divest itself of the stock over a number of years, though it had been rising in value more than 15 percent annually, and Jim made a strong case for the U to retain it as given.

General objectives of the gift were to attract and retain the finest available teachers and researchers, sponsor worthy creative research projects, promote humanitarian care, and "stimulate product innovation and the transfer of technology to the private sector."

"In recognition of the magnitude and importance of this gift," read the agreement, "the University shall rename its School of Medicine the 'J.L. Sorenson School of Medicine,' and shall rename the medical school-University Hospital complex the 'J.L. Sorenson Medical Center,'..."

Naming a medical school for a generous benefactor has been done repeatedly—including the Pritzker School of Medicine at the University of Chicago, J. Hillis Miller Health Center, University of Florida; Albert B. Chandler Medical Center, University of Kentucky; Bowman Gray School of Medicine, Wake Forest University; and John A. Burns School of Medicine, University of Hawaii.

On June 8 the university held a joyous news conference, attended by Jim and Beverley and all their children. President Peterson announced "the largest gift from a single individual in the institution's history." In recognition of the approximately $15 million endowment, said Peterson, the university's medical center and school of medicine both would be named for J.L. Sorenson.

Jim thanked the university and its medical wing, noting that he began his career in the medical field more than forty years earlier. "I found many people [at the U] who were willing to help me form and develop ideas and move them from vision to reality," said Jim. "This contribution is to return part of that favor by helping to create the medical teachers and innovators of tomorrow."

Accolades for Jim poured in, including a note from J.W. Marriott, Jr., who chaired the U's giving campaign. "We're so pleased and grateful that indeed your wonderful gift has become a reality," he wrote. "It will touch—and heal—hearts and so much more." Jon Huntsman Sr. penned a hand-written note on July 1, saying "You will be revered for years to come, Jim, for your thoughtfulness."

There were darker rumblings, however, including some letters to Utah newspapers. "The University of Utah School of Medicine has my emotional and academic dedication," wrote Dona Harris, an associate professor in the department of family and preventive medicine. "I do not want to see the name changed to the J.L. Sorenson School of Medicine."[5]

Within about a month of the gift announcement, campus protest petitions with nearly 300 names—about 100 of them faculty—were delivered to school officials. Dona Harris said many petitioners were unhappy because they were not included in the decision-making process leading to the name change. [6]

A week later the Institutional Council voted 7-to-2 in favor of the name change. Council member Emanuel Floor said "We won't change our decision; we can't. We'll do all we can to allay fears. But it should be understood that we're honoring a man, not advertising him." Such agreements "can't be placed in the public eye when negotiations are taking place," said Floor. [7]

The power of the protests increased substantially toward the end of July. State Senator Chuck Peterson, a Provo Republican, said "The thought of one of our medical students having a diploma hanging on his wall saying he graduated from the James L. Sorenson Medical School is a crock of malarkey." Peterson vowed to enlist other members of the legislature and vote to remove Jim's name from the hospital and medical school. [8]

Senator Peterson's hometown included Brigham Young University, which was fueled by the tithing of LDS Church members and did not have to rely on taxpayer funds for support.

More disturbing was the heated opposition of an influential long-time donor, Joseph Rosenblatt. The wealthy industrialist had given to the university since the 1940s. Among recent gifts was the university president's home. Through the years, said Rosenblatt, supporters have given the university hundreds of millions of dollars. He called Jim's $15 million gift "a drop in the bucket." Chase Peterson reminded Rosenblatt that Jim's gift was more than twice as large as the U's next biggest gift. In addition, the Abbott stock already was rising swiftly in value. [9]

Robert Woody of the *Salt Lake Tribune* chronicled the rise of Jim and his companies since becoming the paper's business editor in 1966. He made it clear in a column that the idea of naming the hospital and medical school for Jim in exchange for his gift originated with the U, not with Jim.

"The sad thing about the brouhaha," wrote Woody, "is the donor didn't ask for his name to be appended as a condition of the gift, U. Development vice president J. Michael Mattsson told the *Tribune* Friday. It was the U administration that asked Mr. Sorenson if it could use his name!" Woody continued:

> Same with Jon Huntsman when he gave $5 million, at that time largest single gift in U history. The giving was not conditioned on having the Special Events Center bear his name, said Mr. Mattsson...but the U. likes the use of the donors' names because of the ripple effect. "It encourages them to give." The Sorenson gift "should be a time of joy and celebration. Just ask any fund raiser about [how] tough it is to get $15,000, much less $15 million." The U is in the fifth and final year of a $150-million campaign. In some areas of need, it has more than met its goal; in others—like faculty support and student scholarship and loans—it is still behind...Mr. Sorenson's gift was

aimed at beefing up medical faculty salaries...Mr. Sorenson [Matts-son] added, is no alien to medicine and science. He not only has been a successful entrepreneur, but has made major contributions to medical equipment innovation and science. [10]

Among many others supporting Jim was his friend and former col-laborator Dr. Homer Warner. He wrote a letter to Jim, saying "those who have expressed these negative sentiments certainly are not representa-tive of the institution," and "the silent majority indeed appreciate your gift and the spirit in which it was given,..." [11]

Some letters to the editor also backed Jim. "Let's forget the gift," wrote one man. "Let's hammer the donor. Let's embarrass James Soren-son so that he will never consider degrading us by giving some of his great achievements to help our great university. Let's show him and all the other would-be donors that they can't mess around with us.

"...We don't want his name to remind us of what it is to have one of Utah's most successful sons share some of his success with his com-munity. Regardless of the ending to this story, the butt-inskis have won. They've sorely embarrassed Sorenson beyond repair,...and embarrassed all of us." [12]

While much of the gift saga was glaringly in the public eye, behind the scenes it also caused problems. Jim and his close colleagues were get-ting irate phone calls, even death threats.

"We were concerned about them," said Duane Toney. "Here we were in an office at ground level on Southwest Temple, with only a cin-der block wall between Jim and the street, and his car parked up against the wall. He was very vulnerable."

One morning Toney arrived at the office early, before anyone else, he thought. As he got to the front door he froze. "There is this device lying on the doorstep that looked like two sticks of dynamite wrapped in a coil. I carefully went in, and found that a woman employee was inside staring at the same thing."

They decided to call police and were about to head for a phone when a Sorenson attorney appeared. He walked to the doorstep, bent over, and picked up the package. Toney and the woman took off running as fast as they could to the other end of the building.

Minutes later, with no explosion, they sought out the attorney, finding that the "dynamite" was simply a radio transmitter that he accidentally dropped entering the building and returned to retrieve as Toney was entering. [13]

Chase Peterson meanwhile had another tiger by the tail: cold fusion. For more than three decades scientists had tried to create in the laboratory the same process that powers the sun—nuclear fusion. Unlike the "hot fusion" of the sun, however, cold fusion would occur at room temperature.

Cold fusion would be the holy grail of chemistry, offering the world an inexpensive, nearly unlimited supply of clean energy, relying on fuel found in ordinary saltwater. The breakthrough, if true, was "the most important development in a century," said physicist Phillip Morrison at the Massachusetts Institute of Technology. [14]

On March 23, 1989, the University of Utah stunned the world by announcing that two scientists had in fact discovered the grail, successfully creating a sustained nuclear fusion reaction in a bottle in one of the U's chemistry labs. "The breakthrough means the world may someday rely on fusion for a clean, virtually inexhaustible source of energy," said the U, which already had filed patents on the technology.

The two scientists were B. Stanley Pons, who chaired the department of chemistry at the U, and Martin Fleischmann, who held the same position at the University of Southampton, England, and was considered one of the world's leading electrochemists. Their breakthrough came after five and a half years of experiments.

Pons and Fleischmann wrote a ten-page manuscript describing the process, and scientific teams across the globe set to work to duplicate their feat. Unfortunately the results were not encouraging. Some scientists flatly said it didn't work. Others reported preliminary indications of cold fusion, followed by errors and ultimately little to no evidence of cold fusion.

What began as a red-letter day for the U, Pons, and Fleischmann, turned into an international embarrassment. On April 30 cold fusion was declared dead by the *New York Times*. Although that capsulized public opinion, a number of independent scientists continued to believe otherwise.

Peterson helped raise $5 million from the Utah Legislature to support Pons and Fleischmann's work, and the U set up a lab for them. The two scientists, however, refused to bring others into the lab or share their data with university colleagues. Their secretiveness led to their dismissal from the U. Both remained convinced of their findings, and as late as 2012 Chase Peterson himself insisted that the jury is still out on the efficacy of cold fusion. [15]

As Peterson juggled cold fusion, his defense of the agreement with Jim became more muted. Jim also grew weary of the controversy. On August 2, 1989 he sent Peterson a letter and issued a news release the same day. "My primary concern is that the gift be used to further the work at the University School of Medicine and to advance worthy medical teaching and research programs," Jim wrote.

"If it is unfeasible to fulfill your proposal and our agreement, I will certainly understand...My primary commitment at this time of my life is to commit my resources to medical advancements at the University." By then the $15 million stock gift had already grown to $16.3 million.

John Ward, a public relations consultant, helped Jim craft the letter and news release. "He really was being unfairly treated," said Ward. "It was the university, not Jim, that suggested the naming, showing him what the hospital and other buildings would look like with his name on them."

Ward said that Jim sent the letter hoping it would stir some action at the U. Rather than seek some kind of compromise, however, university officials began "running" from their agreement. "They came back to Jim and asked him to formally withdraw, in writing, from their offer to put his name on their facilities." [16]

Another issue arose. Abbott Laboratories—whose stock constituted Jim's gift—had operations in South Africa. Some university personnel suggested ownership of Abbott stock would violate the university's policy of not doing business in the country with the strict racial system known as apartheid.

While Jim waited for the university to respond, other interested parties hailed Jim's letter as a breakthrough.

"Utah business tycoon James L. Sorenson has given augmented, local meaning to the adage, 'All's well that ends well,' editorialized the *Salt Lake Tribune* on August 4. "Considering the recent controversy he found himself in, Mr. Sorenson's offer to forgo having the University of Utah School of Medicine named after him is as generous as was his $15 million donation to the institution."

It wasn't to be that simple. Jim had not finally made up his mind under what conditions he would leave his gift at the university.

After further verbal discussions with Peterson, the U president sent Jim a five-page letter that constituted the final attempt to come to terms. "We have concluded that it is not feasible at this time to name the School of Medicine and the Medical Center as specified in the May 22nd agreement." Instead, Peterson suggested the university establish the "J.L. Sorenson Institute for Medical Research." [17]

It was a proposal Jim had already turned down.

Jim responded by letter the same day, asking the university to return the shares of Abbott stock. In an accompanying letter to Peterson, Jim's final thought was "Perhaps 250,000 shares of a value stock is too much for the University of Utah to handle in one endowment. Please return it so that I can reallocate it to other charitable institutions that are in need."

Jim was chastened by the whole fiasco. "It appealed to my vanity. And that's when things started becoming unbalanced," he wrote. "The ugly public debate had soured the entire affair for me. The stress was greater than anything I'd experienced in business.

"...In the end, I blamed myself for the controversy. I'd spent a lifetime learning to balance elements around me as I worked to move forward. I should have recognized that my vanity was getting in the way. It knocked me off balance and left me unable to respond and control the situation." [18]

Chase Peterson's days at the university were numbered. In addition to the Sorenson donation, cold fusion was widely considered an embarrassment. The embarrassment became more acute the following year,

1990, when it was revealed that a $500,000 "anonymous" donation to further cold-fusion research actually came from internal university funds. Peterson acknowledged his mistake in disguising the funds, saying he did so to prevent jealousy from other campus departments.

In June the university's academic senate, comprised of faculty and some students, voted overwhelmingly to give Peterson a judgement of no-confidence. Soon afterward Peterson held a press conference to announce he would retire at the end of the 1990-91 academic year, ending his eight-year tenure.

A few months before he stepped down, Peterson had what would be the last word on the gift saga. He wrote that Jim's sons and daughters and the university would have been enlarged by Jim and Bev's name "if some of our colleagues hadn't become timid when a few others chose to misinterpret the gift.

"You are probably not perfect. I am certainly not perfect. But we both have moved some mountains, each in our respective lives, while critics watched." [19]

The university community paid dearly for its cavalier treatment of Jim. His stock gift, worth about $16 million when he retrieved it, soared more than 600 percent in value by 2012, to well over $100 million.

CHAPTER TWENTY-SEVEN

# JIM, BEVERLEY GENEROUS

## With Needy

On February 22, 1986, Emma Blaser Sorenson died in California at the age of 82. An era started to close for Jim. His father Joseph LeVoy Sorenson, who started as a plain man of the soil and rose to impressive heights, gave his son roots; beautiful, unconquerable Emma gave him wings. She was followed in death six years later by Joseph, who died on September 11, 1992 at 90 in Utah, where he lived with a daughter.

Jim was busy fending off petitioners, now that his immense wealth was public knowledge. Unfortunately the feeding frenzy further isolated him from some cherished friends who otherwise might have boosted the self-esteem he craved. Jim recalled getting together as mature adults with Willie Gamboa, a high school pal and fellow athlete at Lincoln Union High in California.

"He's one of the finest guys you could know," said Jim. "The last time we were together one of us said 'Let's do the weave'"—an old basketball drill. "We did it again. But now I don't keep in touch with people from the old days because everyone wants money."[1]

Petitioners to Jim rarely were as polished as University of Utah President Chase Peterson. But they get high marks for creativity.

"How long has it been since your wealth has brought you great joy and satisfaction?" asked Bob, a stranger, in a letter in August 1990. "I have a suggestion…Imagine what it would be like to completely change the life of a man and his family—to bring them happiness beyond belief."

"You watch me go into the mortgage office and write out a check to pay off my first mortgage in full. Then we go in and pay off my second mortgage in full. Then I go into a financial institution and set up some accounts. I set up a retirement account. I set up an account for my children's future…I set up an account that will provide me with a modest but steady income."

From there, Jim and Bob enter an auto dealership "and I buy my dream car right off the show room floor" as well as "a brand new family vehicle." Furniture is next, as Bob's wife picks out a new master bedroom set as well as a dresser and chest of drawers for their girls and another for their boys. Then comes a new dinette set, carpet, and draperies.

The shopping spree also nets a VCR and big-screen TV, freezer, new clothes for all, bicycles, Nintendo, a doll house, computer system for Bob and sewing machine for the Mrs., "cases and cases of our favorite foods and a side of beef for the freezer."

"Now we go home and look things over," continued Bob. A basement family room is finished, the driveway widened, leading to a new garage; the house is covered in aluminum siding to eliminate painting; the landscaping is improved and an automatic sprinkler system installed. Finally, the family vacations for two weeks in Florida, visiting Disney World.

Then Bob gets serious. "It is a dream that you could make come true for us. You are a man of great wealth. You have more than you and your family could ever possibly need…Wouldn't it make you feel good to help a family experience such joy?"

Bob says he recently lost his job in a budget cutback after eleven years. He's now working two other jobs and running a small home business, and his wife is a teacher's aide. The jobs still don't total the $35,000 he previously made.

"If your answer is yes, or if it is no, please call me and let me know." Bob ended by giving his phone number. Jim likely never called it.

Bob's letter was neatly typed. Two months later Jim received a handwritten one from Robert, who lived in Layton. "I woke up at 2:00 AM last night and your name came to me as clearly as one of my own childrens [sic]. I don't know you or you don't know me, but I need you and hopefully you can use me."

"My purpose in writing to you...is to meet you personally...and see if you can help me to find the success I'm searching for." Earlier in the letter Robert implored Jim by underlining these words: "Please don't throw this away. Keep on Reading." Near the end of the first of two pages, he underlined another sentence: "Please keep on Reading, as the Best is yet to come."

Robert explained that he had no college degree "but I'm very confident and capable and have always tried to do my best...Please find the time to bring your wife and come to dinner with me and my wife anytime you say...I've never met someone who is so successful as you and I can learn much from you.

"I await further word from you, please don't tell me No. Maybe both of us will be the recipients of meeting each other." Robert signed the letter, adding his phone number and address and this postscript: "Please Don't think I'm a Kook. I'm not."

In October 1990 *Forbes* named Jim the richest Utahn and 180th richest American, with a fortune estimated at $525 million. While gratifying his competitive nature, such public recognition also increased the pressure on him. Jim often said he found it easier to make money than to wisely give it away. Yet he had a soft heart and, when seeing genuine human need up close, many times pulled out his checkbook or wallet.

Jim seemed apolitical, and politicians were not among his favorite causes. One powerful Utah Republican who had legal problems met with Jim three times, asking for $10,000 to help pay attorneys. Jim did not give him a dime.

On the other hand, Salt Lake City Mayor Deedee Corradini, a Democrat who served from 1992 to 2000, charmed Jim, and he responded by contributing to her political war chest and to community needs she brought to his attention. Jim also contributed to Ross (Rocky) Anderson, another Democrat who succeeded Corradini as Salt Lake mayor. Such gifts helped the Sorensons maintain access to the local levers of power.

Jim and Bev also contributed to the campaigns of Republicans Michael Stewart, a Salt Lake County commissioner who ran unsuccessfully for governor, and Mitt Romney during his first campaign for President in 2007.

Many beneficiaries thanked Jim in writing for his generosity. None was more eloquent than Lowell L. Bennion, 82, an educator and outstanding humanitarian who founded the LDS Institute of Religion at the University of Utah as well as a boys ranch near Jackson Hole, Wyoming, and the first food bank and homeless shelters in Utah.

Bennion, who lived very modestly and drove dilapidated cars, thanked Jim for sending him "$1,000 for my personal use. I didn't need it... Your gift enabled us to help a number of elderly widows on low-income as follows: 1. Dental work in the home of two ladies; 2. Installation of a railing on front steps; 3. Purchasing and installing a swamp cooler; 4. Two sizable plumbing jobs; 5. Eye treatment, examination and glasses; 6. A television repair job; 7. Purchase of painting equipment for a paint job; 8. Purchase of window glass.

"Thank you. These were badly needed jobs and it gave us much pleasure to bless these women for you. Best wishes, Lowell." [2]

Jim was most open to appeals within his family. When a nephew was about to lose his home to foreclosure, Jim sent the mortgage institution $25,000. The president of the finance company wrote Jim to say the $25,000 gave his nephew "the ability to afford the mortgage on his home...I greatly admire your willingness to help..." [3]

His sister Eileen, in California, often wrote Jim or other family members about Jim, invariably calling him "My dear, amazing brother Jim." He sent her financial gifts through the years.

Gloria Sorenson was Jim's father's baby sister. As an infant, following the death of her mother in Idaho, Gloria lived with Joseph and Emma's family for several years in Yuba City, California. As an adult she married Richard (Dick) Backman and they settled on the east bench in Salt Lake City. Periodically they had financial challenges.

"When our new child Robert was born," recalled Gloria, "Jim came to the door. 'I hear you have a new baby boy,' Jim said. He gave me a $100 bill." The Sorensons gave the Backmans furniture as well, including a dining room set. [4]

That was part of a lengthy series of $100 bills he gave Gloria. On several occasions Jim gave Gloria envelopes with ten $100 bills. "He kept calling me down to his office for one reason or another, sometimes to identify old family photos. I had no idea who the people were. As I left he would give me another $100 bill or sometimes an envelope with ten of them." One time she and Jim were in different checkout lines at a grocery store. "He reached over and gave me $100."

The Backmans needed a new roof. "We didn't know how to pay for it," she said, "so I got up my courage and went down to his office. I told Jim our roof needed to be replaced." Jim was generous but also pragmatic. "He said 'OK , here's what you do. Get three bids on the job and bring them to me.'" Jim's suggestion made sense but it discouraged Gloria. Instead she borrowed the money from a financial institution.

Another relative named Ruth [not her real name] was masterful at winning Jim's sympathy. Her colorful appeals no doubt made him smile. At Christmas time one year, she sent him a letter with different- colored sad and happy faces the size of old silver dollars down the side. "Dear Jim," she began, " I was feeling [blue sad face] during the holidays trying to keep up...But I thought hey, can't let it get you down that you are always in the [red sad face].

"Your letter [bearing money] made me feel happy, cheerful, and in the [pink happy face]. I guess I'll never get all my accounts where they should be in the [black happy face], but you helped light up my life. So thank you, thank you for putting some [happy-face sunshine] in my day. I appreciate it so much."

Ruth suggested they play a game. "I'll give U a couple of deposit slips, and some day, sometime, any old day, any old time, you'll surprise me with a couple of bucks in the limp-along account. I'll never know when or what for, and I'll have eternal hope." His last gift paid for car repairs and a new kitchen disposal.

One letter from Ruth was somber. "I am literally dying of a terminal illness that is eating away at my well being. This cancer that is devouring me is called debt." Her husband had been out of work for three months and "I have been horrified with worry that I am going to lose my house." She asked for Jim's help, offering in exchange to take care of his and Bev's home and yard for the rest of her days.

Some time later Jim sent a check made out to Ruth's bank, paying off the $22,000 mortgage. "Dear Ruth," he said in a cover note, "Happy Day! Let's celebrate...[with family members] and all with the man upstairs. Stay out of debt. God bless, Jim."

Jim related better to his children as they reached adulthood than when they were younger. As they matured and grandchildren multiplied, he fretted over how to encourage and motivate without spoiling them. One practical approach was to give them cutting-edge technology to enhance their ability to learn, create, and communicate.

In February 1990 he wrote his eight children and spouses, asking if they would welcome having a state-of-the-art Macintosh computer network system in each of their homes. Would they be willing to take computer classes and practice what they learned? Family members responded enthusiastically.

"When we told Jenny her eyes lit up like sparklers," wrote son-in-law Ralph Johnson. "Your analogy to the piano is very well chosen and our plan is to arrange classes immediately for Shauna and the two oldest...thank you for your generosity."

Doug Smith, married to Carol, said "We have at least five members of our family who use computers and would like to receive training."

Jim Jr. wrote that "The network concept...if used by all family members, should greatly enhance the communication and organization within the family." Jim's wife Elizabeth and each of their children likewise wrote that they greatly welcomed the proffered gift.

Gail and Thom Williamsen's two grade school-age children handwrote their own thanks. "Grampa Jim, That you for given us a comper," wrote Travis. "I will learn more with a comper at home and in Math." His sister Natalie wrote that "I would like a computer because every day there is nothing to do. It will help me with math and reading too." [5]

Years earlier, when Gail was single, in her twenties, and living away from home, she received a dividend check from Jim. Her response offered an insightful look at him as a father. "...I really want you to know what a special man you are to me. Ever since I've been a little child, I've never wanted for anything. And I had a special sense of security just knowing you were my dad.

"I remember a time the family was driving through pouring rain in Vermont, looking for a place to spend the night. I must have been about 8 years old then. There was a worried look on your face, but I knew everything would be O.K. All the hotels we approached showed 'No Vacancy' signs, but dad found a nice comfortable place for us at the home of an older couple."

She continued:

> I know of no other person whom I love and admire more than you. Even when I was very small, I had a fear of bears. I thought that one might jump out of a bush and get me...They haunted me for a long time until I remembered one thing, My dad had a gun...No one could do harm to any of us without answering to you first! This is the kind of security I've felt growing up in our family...Moving here was scary at first...I had run out of cash, and things just didn't feel so secure as they were at home. Then I saw some familiar faces at the airport, and my dad filled up my pantry with the excuse that he "wanted to use up some tired travelers checks." I feel so extremely lucky to have such a "one in a million" dad...I just felt that I needed to let you know that this "thank you" is not just for the money. More importantly, it's for being the kind of father God meant fathers to be, for being a rock of stability, steering me in the right channels and taking over the wheel when I went down the wrong ones. Being away makes me appreciate you even more. [6]

Three decades later Gail expressed similar sentiments about her father to the author.

Among other letters from his children was one from Christine, their youngest child, when she was in her early twenties and married to Dale Harris, a medical student. "It was wonderful to have the opportunity to go to Europe with you and Mom...I really love you Dad and I hope you know that. I also love you for the times that you got tough and taught us the right things," wrote Chris.

"It's so wonderful to be in a home...We really appreciate the help you have given us financially. There aren't very many fathers who would give to their children like you've given to us...I appreciate all that you have done for me and Dale. Please know that I love you. You're a wonderful father." [7]

A third daughter, Shauna Johnson, sent Jim a Valentine's Day card in 1984. She enclosed a hand-written note that included these memories: "You used to call me 'Blondie'...The day they fired you from Upjohn's. I was seven and I knew it was very serious...You got out your medical books and explained the Facts of Life to me. (I was Seven.) Mom wouldn't talk about it... You held my hand all the way to the hospital when I cut my finger off...You gave me the little gold locket with a diamond chip inside and my wedding date inscribed on it."

In 1998 Jim was among five Utah men honored as Fathers of the Year by the Father's Day Council of Utah. They were called "exceptional fathers who have demonstrated the ability to make fatherhood a priority while achieving a high level of success in their chosen careers."

The other four honorees were businessman Kem Gardner, industrialist and future Utah Governor Jon Huntsman Jr., broadcast executive Bruce Reese, and state legislator Pete Suazo.

They were honored at a luncheon whose proceeds were contributed to the Juvenile Diabetes Foundation (JDF). A reporter explained that Jim "has been a key contributor to many Utah projects, including the Sorenson Multicultural Center in the Glendale neighborhood. He and his wife, Beverley, are parents of eight children. One of the Sorensons' grandchildren, Rachel Harris, 6, was recently diagnosed with juvenile diabetes." [8]

On the way to the luncheon Jim mentioned that he would donate $10,000 to the JDF. At the podium, however, he got wound up and challenged Jon Huntsman Sr. to match his donation of $500,000. Jon stood up, promptly accepted the challenge, and agreed to the match. On the way back to the office an aide congratulated Jim on his very generous pledge. Jim was startled to learn that his intended $10,000 had ballooned to a half-million dollars. But he donated it and Huntsman matched it. On a day when the JDF hoped to raise $250,000 for a good cause, Jim's enthusiasm helped them raise nearly $1.3 million.

### CHAPTER TWENTY-EIGHT

# NEW COMPANIES

## Launch, Fail

T he second half of Jim's career did not have the same professional luster as the first half. He would continue making his mark
not by what he accumulated but by what he gave away.

One problem was not that he had the formula wrong to continue winning as an entrepreneur, but that he often ignored it. To succeed, he told a
university group, ask, "How much good can I do? What's the value to human
lives?" Jim added that "I've been critical of some kinds of medical research
that does little for the quality of people's lives. If you have an idea that will
make things better, success will follow."[1]

With Sorenson Research Jim was involved in every facet of the company, directing operations day to day. He felt passionate about his creations,
which invariably made life better for others in significant ways. After the sale
to Abbott his personal involvement in the businesses he purchased was epi-
sodic, depending upon his interest in a particular industry and the stability of
an individual company.

What he needed most of all were first-rate professionals to help carry
the load. Jim had a hard time attracting top talent, however. He was not willing to pay competitive salaries, and had shafted some of those who helped
build Sorenson Research out of the fruit of their labors when it was sold. A

consequence was one business failure after another.

His mindset was revealed in a discussion with Jim Jr. When his son outlined a proposal to incentivize leaders of some Sorenson companies with stock options, Jim Sr. tried to dissuade him. "If you do that they won't need you anymore," he warned.

"That was the fear Dad had," said Jim Jr. "If they aren't reliant on what I pay them, I'll lose them."[2]

In the early days of Sorenson Research, Jim was forced to focus on and treat fairly his close colleagues because he lacked capital to compensate for any lack of effort. The only hope of success was to elicit the very best from each team member. In that electric, synergistic atmosphere, Jim made one great decision after another.

The stark difference in business outcomes during and after Sorenson Research reflected Jim's $100 million sale of Sorenson Research to Abbott Labs in 1980. He had the cash to play with, and play he did. "Jim's genius was as an entrepreneur, not in managing companies," noted Jim Larson, one of his top lieutenants.

As private individuals approached Jim for a handout, aspiring business partners also inundated him with proposals. "He was drawn in by one bad promoter after another," said Jim Jr. "Some were deliberate. Others were well-meaning but weren't equipped with the right background and abilities."

Jim invariably was told that his investment, married to their brilliant idea, was sure to make a lot of money. Perhaps feeling invulnerable after a long streak of successes, he left the comfort of industries he understood to sail in a variety of other fields—often ending up shipwrecked on the shoals. However, Jim was shrewd enough never to risk his taw, and the money he lost was a small fraction of the annual interest he earned on his wealth.

In 1981 Sorenson Development acquired the assets of a company called Stokermatic, which made heaters and automatic coal- and wood-pellet-burning stoves. Jim changed its name to Sorenson Energy Inc.—most of his companies carried the Sorenson name—and appointed a man named Duane Schow as general manager.

A news release, distilled by a local newspaper, said Sorenson Energy was about to introduce a new automatic auger-fed fireplace insert, and "results of market research indicate tremendous acceptance."[3]

Acceptance was not tremendous enough, however, and the company folded in 1987.

Other Sorenson enterprises that opened and closed in the early eighties included a retail furniture store, a store to rent and sell beta video tapes, and a company to sell long-distance carrier service. Jim enlisted friends to run the last company, Sorenson Telecommunications, which took off quickly. "Sales were going up like crazy," recalled company executive Jim Larson. "Jim couldn't quite figure out why losses were also going up like crazy."

Sorenson told Larson to find what was wrong. He did. For every $1 in sales brought in, the company was spending $1.10. That company folded after four years, with one of its managers suing Jim.

In 1989 Jim helped form an independent film and television company called Epperson-Dayton-Sorenson Productions Inc. Director Lyman Dayton, a relative of Beverley's, specialized in family films, Eric Epperson ran the company, and Jim supplied the several million in capital for their first movie, "The Dream Machine," starring teenage heartthrob Corey Haim. Four other films already were on the drawing boards when Machine was released in 1991.

Promoters assured Jim he would make $20 million. He did not. The film opened weakly and soon went to video. Most revenues came from foreign royalties, and it took more than ten years for Jim to recoup his investment. From then on, when he turned down proposals he didn't like or didn't understand, he often called them "another Dream Machine," the flop that killed his taste for Hollywood.

Conscientious about his hair loss as he got older, Jim apparently tried the hair-regrowth product Rogaine, manufactured by Upjohn, the pharmaceutical firm Jim worked for decades earlier. Rogaine was a liquid, and Jim and numerous other balding men and women found it trickled down the scalp rather than remain where it was applied.

That problem typically set Jim to thinking of a better approach. His answer was to dispense Rogaine in a foam rather than liquid. Jim repeatedly called his contacts at Upjohn (which merged with another company in 1995 to form Pharmacia & Upjohn), urging them to develop a foam.

Jim's idea eventually was adopted by the pharmaceutical firm, whose scientists produced the first FDA-approved hair regrowth foam. The company advertised men's Rogaine unscented foam as "our most popular, easy-to-use formula."

Meanwhile, Jim saw an opportunity for Sorenco, his company that produced personal-care products, to develop specialized shampoos and conditioners, not to replace Rogaine but to work in tandem with it. In 1996 Sorenco signed a contract with Pharmacia & Upjohn to produce these products, marketed under the name Progaine. Bob Kaelin, head of Sorenco sales, called the contract "an important part of our plan to reach annual sales of $40 million."

The partnership, however, was of short duration.[4]

During his career Jim started or acquired at least forty research, development, manufacturing and sales companies, in addition to the scores set up to hold, sell, or develop land. At least half of the non-land companies typically were operating at any one time in the last decades of Jim's life.

In addition to medical products, his first love, and those described above, a cross-section included manufacturing of clothing and selling it retail, farming and ranching, a bed-and-breakfast, a bakery, cosmetics and other personal-care items, vitamins, injection molding of medical devices, bioscience, genetic engineering, environmental testing, genomics and DNA, video-compression technology, and the list goes on.

All of Jim's businesses were privately held. With no legal obligation to answer to stockholders, their progress or demise happened largely out of public view.

A mammoth exception was an apparition that rose at 45th South in the early eighties. It was a full-size riverboat called the Jordan Queen, complete with a churning, fire-engine-red paddlewheel. The Queen had 40,000 square feet of space, including a 500-seat seafood restaurant. It was anchored to dry ground that was then flooded to make it appear seaworthy. The boat and pond, in the vicinity of the Jordan River, were the centerpiece of Sorenson Research Park.

The $2.5 million vessel was the brainchild of Garth Campbell, owner of a well-established inner city steak house called Diamond Lil's. Campbell, a hefty man six years younger than Jim, had also been a pharmaceutical salesman early in his career, which may have helped persuade Jim to take a ride on the river. A third partner was A. Paul Bruno, whose son Paul A. Bruno was general manager.

The restaurant featured an all-seafood menu, ranging from fried squid to crab cakes, and a variety of entertainment including minstrel singers, Dixieland bands, and a piano bar.

The Queen was only the start of their ambition. The men formed a company called River Queens, which intended to construct riverboat restaurants on rivers all across the country. The Jordan Queen was christened and opened to the public in October 1984.

Unfortunately the Queen's sailing was not smooth. Sold out for that Christmas season, the number of patrons dwindled afterward. Campbell blamed the slowdown on "the many restaurants (seafood) that opened, a slight recession, and employee problems (cooks)...I still believe, with imagination, and good management, it will pull out of it."[5]

The Jordan Queen closed as a public restaurant and in 1988 opened as a special-events facility. Sorenson Development became sole owner, hoping its good name would help revive the Queen. This second effort also failed, however, and the riverboat was torn down a decade later.

"We really didn't know the restaurant business," explained Sorenson executive Jim Larson. "We found out later that you get one or two chances at a restaurant, but that's all. We weren't set up right to give the customer the experience they were hoping for." [6]

"For the first time in my life I learned how many ways there are to lose money," wrote Jim in 1993. "In all of my previous business endeavors I ran lean, betting on myself and on my ideas...I always kept an optimistic attitude and expected good things to happen. After Sorenson Research was sold, I began betting on other people's abilities and ideas to succeed. For the first time, I began to experience some feelings of being confused, manipulated and even bewildered at times." [7]

In a revealing letter to a granddaughter, a wounded Jim—whose entrepreneurial genius was under attack—defensively struck out at individuals less bright than himself. "It seems like physical superiority is accepted in society, but not intellectual superiority or attainment," he wrote. "In fact we are often forced to play down our abilities in fear of arousing resentment." He added:

We are all born with a certain skeleton, size, and set of muscles. It is easy to accept the fact that we cannot run, throw, box, bat, or jump as well as those better endowed at birth physically—but just about everybody has a sneaking suspicion that they have not made the most of their minds; that they have allowed their brains to lie dormant; that laziness or fear or greed has prevented them from cultivating their mental powers to the fullest. So perhaps, Diana, when you achieve intellectually with excellent grades or speak and debate so beautifully, it is not your assumption of superiority that determines how others feel about you, but it is the other person's hidden sense of failing to live up to their own potential...So be your own self, stick to your value systems and enjoy what you have and what you are! Don't let other people get you out of your groove, out of your value systems and cheat you out of the joy of being what you are—a beautiful, lovely, maturing intellectual person.[8]

After the sale to Abbott, wrote Jim, "I began to grow companies that would provide opportunities for my family...I began to worry about the negative things that could happen in the lives of my children and grandchildren if they were to suddenly inherit a great deal without a work experience that balances the equation and puts money in the proper perspective.

"You can't really appreciate or enjoy anything without the effort and process of earning it...New companies and business opportunities were purchased, old ones were expanded and remodeled, and the children and their spouses were invited to assume leadership positions."[9]

The businesses, however, were bought because they appealed to Jim, not necessarily to members of his family. That was one factor that led to differences, especially between Jim and his sons-in-law. Another factor was his admitted penchant for interfering with the businesses over the heads of those tapped to run them.

During the eighties James Lee Sorenson was president and chief executive officer at Utah Biomedical Testing Laboratories and DataChem, an analytical environmental testing lab. He then found and licensed a video-compression technology that would lead to unprecedented success for the Sorensons. Doug Smith, who had a doctorate in physiology, joined Jim as a medical and environmental consultant. Jim and Ralph Johnson developed Sorenson Research Park.

Tim Fenton, who had the unenviable task of trying to turn around the Jordan Queen, led LeVoy's, the clothing firm. Joe Sorenson became president of SOREX Medical, a manufacturing and sterilization company. Thom Williamsen helped purchase land southwest of Salt Lake City and assisted with other development work. Gary Crocker stepped away from the Sorenson umbrella and led a number of companies, first as CEO of Research Industries

Corp, a publicly held firm. The youngest son-in-law, Dale Harris, continued as a physician and radiologist.

While trying to give his children and their spouses more responsibility for Sorenson businesses, Jim Sr. had a hard time letting go of the reins. He acknowledged the problem, saying "It's very hard after a lifetime to give up control, to quit being 'in charge.'" Jim's interference and the bad feelings it led to damaged his relationship with some children and sons-in-law.

Gary Crocker, however, along with Jim Jr., succeeded in rising above Jim Sr.'s peculiarities, and, like him, became entrepreneurial superstars.

Jim Sr.'s business failures were intriguing in that, despite the losses, his reported net worth continued to rise. It was based on hundreds of millions in real estate and, especially, his Abbott stock. Jim assiduously avoided cashing in the stock, for a good reason. As long as it was kept intact he owed no taxes on it. The stock spun off enough cash dividends to keep his ventures well oiled with capital.

Between 1980 when Jim acquired the $100 million in stock, and 2003, the stock split two-for-one five times. An Abbott company spokesman estimated that the value of Jim's stock in the latter year was 32 times greater than when he acquired it, or about $3.2 billion. More conservative estimates pegged Jim's stock value at a little over $2 billion.

The latter figure assumed that Jim then owned 52.4 million shares. The annual dividend return on that many shares was around $50 million. [10]

By then Jim had been appearing annually for two decades in *Forbes* magazine's annual list of the 400 wealthiest Americans. He loved being on the list and instructed his PR assistants to include every possible asset at its highest possible value when reporting to *Forbes*.

In 1984 *Forbes* estimated Jim's fortune at $150 million, followed in 1985 at $200 million. *Forbes'* rankings of Jim continued—1986, $375 million; 1987, $480 million; 1988, $360 million; 1989, $460 million; 1990, $525 million; 1991, $700 million. In each of those years *Forbes* named Jim as the richest Utahn. He continued to appear on the *Forbes* list for the rest of his life, in some years playing leapfrog for first place with his friend Jon Huntsman Sr.

Mega-wealth did not change Jim's lifelong habit of living far beneath his means. "Would you like to be a billionaire, or at least live like one?" asked Max Knudson, business editor of the *Deseret News*, who knew Jim well. "Dumb question, right? Money may not buy happiness, but you'd like the chance to find out for yourself.

"Oddly enough, the chances are good you already have. If you work hard at your job, are devoted to your family, pay your bills, avoid bad habits and take time to smell the roses...you're living like a billionaire. That is, if the billionaire's name is James LeVoy Sorenson."[11]

*Forbes'* ranking that year, 1999, of the world's known 465 billionaires, estimated Jim's wealth at $2.9 billion, $500 million higher than the previous year, placing him 172nd on the billionaires' list. (According to *Forbes*, Huntsman displaced Jim that year as the wealthiest Utahn, with a fortune of $3.2 billion.)

"Let's ponder that for a moment," wrote Knudson. "Of the 6 billion people on the planet, only 171 of them are wealthier than Jim Sorenson. "What to do with all that money? Buy a yacht? A jet? A mansion? An Island? An emerging Third World nation? At the very least, most of us would quit the daily grind to devote full time to spending our money and living like kings." Not Jim, however, who continued to report to his office daily for the rest of his life.

Knudson reported that, while Jim and Beverley had a large house in Holladay, south of Salt Lake City, they had none of the other usual perks of great wealth. "...at 78, he's much too busy starting and running new companies to waste time on high living."

Jim in fact flaunted his frugality. Early in his career as a pharmaceutical salesman for Upjohn, Jim routinely bought a couple pillows and rode the bus overnight to meetings in California, as his colleagues flew. With the money saved he bought pieces of ground.

Writing in 1993, Jim explained that he no longer took the bus. "But I do routinely fly in the coach sections of airplanes while using special senior citizen fares." He recalled one such flight in particular. "I was waiting in line to use one of my 'grandpa tickets' and another fellow fell in behind me doing the same thing.

"We ended up sitting next to each other and struck up a conversation about what a good deal the $100 special fares were. After chuckling about it, I introduced myself by saying, 'I'm Jim Sorenson.' The other fellow shook my hand and said, 'Pleased to meet you. I'm Ray Noorda." Noorda was the founder of Novell Corporation and also one of Utah's richest men.[12]

John Ward, a public relations specialist who helped Jim with a number of thorny problems, sometimes traveled with him. "He knew that I knew people at Delta Airlines," said Ward. "He had me call Delta and ask for [free] upgrades. They did it the first time, but the second time he asked, they checked him out and found out that he was a billionaire. They decided he could afford to pay for upgrades."[13]

Ward recalled one time when he and Jim were traveling in Europe. At the departure lounge for Lufthansa, "the German airlines had bags and snack food items you could put in them for the flight—sandwiches, cheese, crackers. Jim filled a couple of bags. Four days later he was still digging into the Lufthansa bag."

"I learned not to take him to a buffet; he would always overeat and feel sick the rest of the day."

Jim wore the same yellow windbreaker for decades, evidenced by numerous photos in family albums. He bought his suits at Mr. Mac's in Salt Lake, whose owner, Mac Christensen, was a staple on local television, hawking suits, "buy one, get one free." Jim also wore the same suits for decades.

The reasons he seemed to care little about his clothes may have been more than simple frugality. As a young man he had deeply resented being treated differently depending on the clothes he wore. In the U.S. Merchant Marine he went from a nondescript uniform as a recruit—including bellbottoms and white sailor hat—to a handsome uniform as an officer candidate at the Merchant Marine Academy in New York.

On the cross-country trip by rail from California he traveled first class, slept in a Pullman berth, with fresh white sheets each night, and ate three good meals each day.

A few months earlier he had taken a train to boot camp, packed into a stifling car with a horde of uncouth, stinking recruits. The difference in how he was treated—symbolized by his different uniforms—unsettled him. "I was the same guy who was in boot camp one week before where we were treated like cattle. Suddenly, overnight, I was treated very differently. The trip gave me my first glimpse of something that both troubled and motivated me for many years to come."

Jim continued for the rest of his life to run his empire from the same two-level cinder-block building in an industrial section of downtown Salt Lake City. The 1960s shag carpet on his office floor was not replaced until just before the start of the next century.

While strange to most observers, Jim's spending habits actually were not far removed from those of many other self-made men and women of great wealth. Two researchers who made a seminal study of the topic concluded that amassing a fortune seldom depended on "luck or inheritance or advanced degrees or even intelligence." More often it is "the result of hard work, perseverance, planning, and, most of all, self-discipline."[14]

The wealthy individual usually is a businessman "who has lived in the same town for all of his adult life...He has married once and remains married. He lives next door to people with a fraction of his wealth. He is a compulsive saver and investor. And he has made his money on his own." Jim obviously fit the mold.

Thomas Stanley and William Danko found seven common traits among those who successfully build wealth:

- They live well below their means.
- They use time, energy, and money efficiently in building wealth.
- Financial independence is more important than exhibiting high social status.
- Their parents did not provide "economic outpatient care."
- Their adult children are financially self-sufficient.
- They successfully target business opportunities.
- They began with the right occupation.

Jim would have identified with a wealthy Texan interviewed by the authors. He had a very successful business rebuilding diesel engines, but drove a ten-year-old car, wore jeans and a buckskin shirt, and lived in an average house in a lower-middle-class neighborhood.

"After he substantiated his financial success with actual numbers," they wrote, "this Texan told us: 'My business does not look pretty. I don't play the part...don't act it...when my British partners first met me, they thought I was one of our truck drivers...They looked all over my office, looked at everyone but me. Then the senior guy of the group said, 'Oh, we forgot we were in Texas!'"

Explained the Texan: "I don't own big hats, but I have a lot of cattle."[15]

### CHAPTER TWENTY-NINE

# SORENSON BIOSCIENCE

By the mid-nineties Jim felt panicky. After more than a decade of mixed results with his array of companies, operating under his holding company, Sorenson Development Inc. (SDI), he finally conceded the need to bring in top talent to lead them. He did not have to look far.

Jim, whose own higher education was at a two-year community college, had always been enamored with son-in-law Gary Crocker's two Harvard degrees. Far more than that, Gary had proved his mettle in the real world. In 1982, two years after engineering the sale of Sorenson Research, he founded his own medical device company, Research Medical, selling it fourteen years later for $240 million—more profitably than even the sale of Sorenson Research to Abbot Laboratories.

With Gary finally between jobs in 1996, Jim came calling again. "He had always wanted me to work with him, and there was a lot of stress because I wasn't working in the family business," said Crocker. "He told me I was wasting my life by not working with him."

Jim's persistence wore Gary down. His refusal to pay Gary the $1 million he owed him for selling Sorenson Research back in 1980 still smarted. This time Gary would come only on his own terms. After negotiating a handsome salary along with stock options in the companies he would be directing as vice-chairman, Gary joined SDI in 1996.

Once he had landed Gary, Jim went after another prize, Jim Jr. However, he too had been burned badly by his father and likewise harbored serious reservations about working directly under him. "I had a good relationship with Dad, but I needed to be very careful and get everything in writing," said Jim Jr. "He was very hard to work with day to day—dominant, impetuous, and very idiosyncratic."

On the other hand, Gary had plowed new ground with Jim Sr., in negotiating a high salary and stock options—compensation Jim Jr. too would receive. Jim Jr.'s other condition was that some SDI companies he led would offer employees stock options—which would be a first for Jim Sr.

"The biggest reason I joined Dad was because he was my father and I owed him that respect," said Jim.

Jim Jr. admired Gary's abilities and believed that, between the two of them, SDI would make better decisions in the future than in the past. They shared the title of vice-chairman, both answerable only to Jim Sr. At the top of SDI's organizational chart was Jim Sr. as company chairman, aided by executive assistant Gloria Smith. Centralized departments included finance and administration, human resources, public relations, and legal.

Reporting to Gary were Sorenson Bioscience, Sorenco, which manufactured personal-care products; and Sorenson Labs, which created medical devices. Jim Jr. directed Sorenson Vision and related companies, Sorenson Medical, and tens of thousands of acres of real estate.

Jim Jr. was leery of having an office too close to his father, and worked out of a nicer facility across town. Gary moved into an office in the same dingy cinderblock building at 2511 South West Temple that Jim Sr. had long occupied.

That was a serious mistake. Gary chafed under Jim Sr.'s scrutiny and his insistence that Gary be on hand during normal work hours. Close observers said Gary sometimes could not be found when Jim wanted to consult with him—a situation highly annoying to Jim. In addition, said one insider, Gary disliked the tenor of the weekly executive meetings with Jim Sr. and Jim Jr., complaining that there were "too many egos involved."

At any rate, the reorganization seemed to work, and the future looked good. Then one day, three months after joining SDI, Gary did not show up for work—then or ever again. He simply vanished off SDI's radar screen, with no explanation.

Asked about his unusual departure, Gary mentioned the $1 million commission he was owed but never received. Since that predated his signing up as vice-chair, however, it is doubtful that the unpaid commission was the major reason he jumped ship. Pressed on the question, Gary simply said "our operating styles were dramatically different."[1]

Gary's abrupt departure was a blow to Jim Sr. as well as to Jim Jr. A key reason why Jim Jr. agreed to join SDI was because Gary was already there to split the load. Jim Sr. needed his son now more than ever, and despite a more adverse outlook, Jim Jr. felt duty-bound to stay.

Jim Sr. tried but failed to get another family member to take Gary's place. Finally he stepped into the breach himself and had the presidents of the companies formerly assigned to Gary report directly to him.

It may be easier to understand why Gary, a new multi-millionaire on his own, left the Sorenson companies than why he took the vice-chairmanship in the first place. Jim Sr. could be notoriously hard to work for.

"Dad had a way of not recognizing or acknowledging the value that others brought to the table," explained Jim Jr. An example was when he and a brother-in-law, Ralph Johnson, along with another man, acquired several parcels of land in Bluffdale for a new development. Some of the parcels were contiguous to land owned by Jim Sr.

Ralph and Jim Jr. wanted to demonstrate the market for housing developments in the new area. They invited Jim Sr. to partner with them in hopes that they would prove their abilities and the market potential and gain the opportunity to co-develop the rest of Jim Sr.'s property. Though more amused than optimistic, Jim Sr. joined them as a fourth partner.

Each man put in $5,000 to get the venture, called Deer Mountain, off the ground. The new project was a remarkable success and within a short time returned more than $1 million to Jim Sr.

"Rather then give the other partners credit for creating this $1 million, Dad would find ways to explain how he himself played the key role," said Jim Jr. "He would rationalize by saying a portion of the project was on his ground: 'The $1 million profit was because of the better market that occurred. Your role was not all that important.'"

Minimizing the roles and ingenuity of the others discouraged Jim Jr. and infuriated Ralph. Sometime later, when Jim Sr. put the development of all his property in the vicinity under the direction of his son, Jim Jr. invited Ralph to join in the development opportunity. Still wounded by his father-in-law's belittlement, Ralph responded that he would join only if they—not Jim Sr—had control. Knowing this would never fly with his father, Jim Jr. then invited his brother Joe and another brother-in-law, Tim Fenton, to assist.

Jim Sr.'s pattern of rewarding others mirrored this attitude. "He didn't value the talent or offer someone an incentive for what they could do," said Jim Jr. "That was sad because as I look back, that was a big reason for the failure in all these companies since Sorenson Research...Ideas are cheap; you've got to have the skilled talent to implement them."

Jim Jr. and his mother Beverley both cited Jim Sr.'s psychological makeup to help explain his actions. "He was insecure, constantly driven for self-validation," said Jim Jr. "...he was both a loner and very, very self-centered. He [believed that he] had the best ideas and the best vision. I had to make a decision whether to be his son and have things I did be attributed to him, or change my name and live somewhere else entirely. I couldn't be anywhere in between."

He chose to be close to his father, personally and professionally. It was a choice that set Jim Jr. apart from most of his siblings and their spouses.

Jim Sr. had never been easy to live with as a husband, and was more difficult than ever during the last decade of his life. "As long as I've known him, fifty some-odd years, he has had an inability to know when he's hurt people," said Beverley in 1998. "He seems to feel threatened by everything right now."[2]

A big concern to her husband was the family trust that held hundreds of millions of dollars worth of Abbott Laboratories stock. Jim had assigned 90 percent of it to their children years earlier—long before anyone knew his estate would become so valuable—but continued to control it by controlling its eight voting shares.

Jim was now 77 and sensing his mortality. The question of what to do with the trust haunted him. If he tried to do anything but leave it to his children he risked legal action. Yet he ostensibly worried that leaving too much money to them would ruin them.

"He is so used to controlling everything but had to give up control to the kids years ago," explained Beverley. "He doesn't know how to let go, and there's a lot of anger inside him."

How did Jim get the energy into his eighties to juggle so many balls? He answered that and other personal questions for *Forbes* magazine.

First, he continued a lifelong daily regimen—jogging one mile and doing 80 pushups. For breakfast he ate raw carrots, tomatoes, oatmeal, and almonds. He prayed daily, relaxed by enjoying the beauties of nature, and read three to four hours each day. At the age of 66 he had become a certified scuba diver, and long after that he played squash twice a week.

His mentors were his father "for his work ethic and ability to find rhythm in life," and his mother "for her creative, innovative approach, and the way she challenged the status quo." The worst day of his life was the day his 11-year-old sister Carol was killed by a car. He didn't recall any mistakes, "only the opportunity to overcome problems."

The worst business idea is "following what other people say you should do instead of charting your own course." The best investment advice is to "invest in yourself and in your own vision." Young entrepreneurs should "be guided by your own real passions and convictions, not just by what you think might get you ahead in life."

The best part about being the boss is "lifting, expanding, and nurturing other people."[3]

Jim's best instincts for lifting and nurturing others were seen at Sorenson Bioscience. It was one of the smaller Sorenson companies and one of his favorites. The firm made pipettes and other disposable plastic liquid-handling products used in scientific research. The company, located in Midvale, was founded in 1981 as Multi Technology, Inc., and bought by Jim a decade later.

In selecting key personnel for his companies, Jim's longtime pattern was not to pay top dollar for experience, but to find someone less costly who Jim intuitively believed could be molded into the employee he needed to do the job. His instincts seemed better earlier in life before Jim became wealthy, but he retained the intuitive ability to choose wisely when he took the time to carefully think through a personnel decision.

In 1992 Jim hired West Price, a pleasant young man who stood a full head taller than Jim, to manage the final assembly of their products. Price's background was in inventory control; he had been working for a garage-door manufacturer. The following year he became director of Bioscience production and a member of the management team. In the summer of 1996 company president David Jeffs retired and Jim named Price, 32, as interim president.

The company had long been unprofitable and only survived because Jim poured his own money into it. Price explained, "I pulled our management team together and said 'We have a lot of debt to Mr. Sorenson. How can we make this a legitimate company?' We talked over ideas how to reduce costs. Then I went to Mr. Sorenson and suggested four or five things to make us profitable."

Jim liked what he heard and told Price to do what was needed to turn Sorenson Bioscience around.[4]

Price considered the company top-heavy, and recommended cutting several higher-paid personnel. Jim agreed. He suggested ending the contract with a company that supplied security guards, and no longer wearing smocks over other clothes. Price believed company employees could secure the premises, and tests showed the laboratory was as clean without smocks. Again Jim agreed. Both moves resulted in significant savings.

In September 1996 Jim began looking for a company president. The candidates were narrowed to three, two of whom had worked closely with Jim in other capacities, and Price, youngest of the three, who lacked a college degree and had worked least with Jim.

On a Friday afternoon Price was at home mowing the lawn when a call came from Jim's office. Jim's executive assistant Gloria Smith was on the line. "How soon can you get down to Mr. Sorenson's office?" she asked.

"I walked into his office; the lights were dim and he was on a Lazy Boy recliner," recalled Price. "I sat down across from him. He said 'West, I want to offer you the full-time job. I like how you are all working together. I want to keep all that going.'"

The two quickly became friends, Jim calling him "Youngster." At that time Sorenson Bioscience "truly was bankrupt," said Price. "We continued to operate only because he was the owner and we borrowed from him."

By the end of that year the company made money for the first time— $160,000 on $4 million in sales. February 1997 was the last time Sorenson

Bioscience borrowed money from Jim. "We could meet payroll and accounts payable, and worked with vendors to start getting them paid down," said Price. Profits doubled in 1997, enabling the company to start paying Jim back the $6 million he loaned it.

Then calamity. Corning Inc. was by far the company's biggest client, accounting for about 40 percent of revenue. Near the end of 1998 Corning asked Price to come to New York to meet with Steven Wood, vice president of Corning's Life Sciences Division. Wood's news was devastating. The company was going to end its contract with Sorenson Bioscience and produce and self-manage its laboratory products in Mexico.

"Here I was just two years into the job and we were losing our biggest customer," recalled Price. "I didn't know what to tell our team. Several times on the flight home I had tears in my eyes."

John Brophy was the other leader of Sorenson Bioscience. A colorful easterner from Philadelphia, he joined as vice president of marketing, responsible for developing new business. Jim made an exception in hiring Brophy, who had an extensive background and contacts in their industry, rather than someone less costly. Jim paid dearly for his choice. The small company Brophy left sued him and Jim for loss of their key man to a rival. Reportedly it cost Jim several million dollars to settle the suit.

Brophy, also young, was hired at about the same time as Price. He too was a head shorter than Price; they were a Mutt-and-Jeff team whose strengths complemented each other. Jim relished being around Brophy, a Catholic with thick auburn hair who he called "my outside guy."

While Price continued to pare costs inside, Brophy traveled widely in the U.S. and abroad, drumming up business. The combination worked and the future had looked bright. Now it appeared that Corning was putting a dagger in those dreams.

When Price returned from New York he sat down with Brophy and delivered the bad news. Then they made an appointment and dropped in on Jim. His reaction astonished them.

"West and John," said Jim, "this will be the best thing that ever happened to you!" As they waited for the punch line, Jim added "Mark my word. I want you guys to put a plan together to do what you do best—build and sell our products. You'll see that this will turn out to be a blessing in disguise."[5]

The two men anticipated they would be leaving Jim's office crestfallen. Instead they left it excited and energized. "It was a complete vote of confidence," recalled Price. They did as Jim asked and proved him right. Within a few years they blew past where they were when Corning was aboard. The average annual growth in the industry was about 3 percent; Sorenson Bioscience was averaging 11 percent.

By 2004 the company paid off its debts, including the millions owed to Jim, and was financing all of its own growth. By 2007 revenue was $20 million, rising to $30 million in 2011. Meantime, Jim was knocking down old facilities at the site and constructing new ones. Sorenson Bioscience became one of the most highly automated companies in its field.

There were high personal costs, however, for Brophy. He and his wife were going through a divorce—exacerbated by his frequent travel, including weeks at a time in Asia. In addition, Brophy was intent on getting sole custody of their two young children who were at home in San Diego. He lived there Friday through Sunday and in Utah the other days of the week, staying in a condo owned by Jim.

"Mr. Sorenson knew the names of my daughter Erin and son Colin, and really felt bad that all my travel had been so hard on our family," said Brophy. On one occasion Brophy arrived home in a taxi, jumped out, and, seeing his daughter in the yard, yelled "Erin!" She turned and ran screaming through the garage. "She didn't know who I was."

Brophy succeeded in gaining custody of the children, moving them and himself to Salt Lake City when Erin was 4 and Colin 2. California courts usually do not grant child custody to the father, and the legal process cost him around $350,000. Jim genuinely offered to pay that expense but Brophy did not take him up on it. He has since remarried.

Having been educated in Catholic schools, Brophy wanted the same experience for his children. Although there were a half-dozen or so Catholic grade schools in the Salt Lake area, the only one that seemed a possibility was Our Lady of Lourdes, attached to Judge Memorial High School. "I went down there but couldn't get them in; there was a long waiting list."

Returning to the office, he mentioned it in passing to Jim, who said nothing. Two hours later Jim said "John, go down to Our Lady of Lourdes. The pastor will meet you in the principal's office."

"Why, Mr. Sorenson?" asked Brophy.

"Because your kids are in that school," he answered.

Brophy never learned how Jim turned the key at the school for them but he never forgot it. Erin started first grade at Our Lady of Lourdes, and Colin kindergarten.

When Brophy and Price began attending Jim's weekly management meetings, they saw that some company leaders feared Jim, whose moods indeed could be unpredictable. Brophy, who hails from the City of Brotherly Love where Sylvester Stallone's Rocky Balboa repeatedly overcame the odds in the boxing ring, advised their management team that "when you fight somebody bigger than you, you don't stand back and let 'em punch, you pull 'em in close, where he can't get a haymaker off."

That's what their team did. They invited Jim to their quarterly staff meetings, and he came. It helped that, unlike in many of his companies, Jim understood what Sorenson Bioscience did—injection molding, the process used to manufacture catheters and other disposable medical products Jim had invented.

Jim took great pride in the diversity of Bioscience's workforce. The air hummed with more than a dozen languages from its 200-plus employees. Among countries represented were China, Russia, Taiwan, Vietnam, Laos, Cambodia, Tonga, Samoa, Mexico, and Romania. Some came from refugee camps and were extremely grateful to be working in a safe, pleasant environment at $9 an hour or more. Several employees were deaf; the company had an interpreter for them.

Jim loved to go onto the production floor and banter with employees. He would gather workers around him, give them a pep talk, and ask where they were from and how they liked their jobs. He seemed genuinely interested in them.

After the company started making money, Jim enjoyed personally handing out profit-sharing checks or cash bonuses of $50 or $100 to the several dozen workers on duty at any given time. He gave a stack of checks or cash to Price and Brophy to distribute to employees on other shifts.

"It was always like a barrel of monkeys being around Mr. Sorenson," said Brophy. "When he came over here he was always happy. Or if he wasn't happy at times he'd come in and say 'John, tell me a funny story.' He just wanted to get away from the rest of it, and when he left, he left happy."

Jim was often on the lookout for new employees, recalled Price. "I remember that one day he called John and me and said he'd just met a clerk at a 7-Eleven in Rose Park. He thought the kid could be a salesman and maybe we should hire him." Apparently they did not follow up on the suggestion.

Like Brophy, Price was impressed with Jim's humanity. Three of the four Price children were born while Price worked for Jim, and two had cleft palates—a daughter, Imogene, and son, Easton. "Mr. Sorenson often would point to his own lips and ask 'How is Easton doing? How does he look and how is he dealing with the [surgical] scars?'"

"My wife's favorite memory of Jim is when our management team first took over in 1996," recalled Price. "Mr. Sorenson took the six of us and our wives to dinner at Mulboons," a nice seafood restaurant. "Beverley was having some health issues and he was distraught. Talking to my wife Robyn, he broke into tears several times while describing what Beverley was going through. Robyn was touched by his concern for her."

Price and other team leaders hoped that if Sorenson Bioscience were sold again, they would be given an opportunity to acquire it. Unfortunately that did not happen. Soon after Jim's death in 2008, his family sold the company to Axygen BioScience for $20 million—far below its value.

In 2010 Axygen sold it and other subsidiaries to Corning for some $400 million. Axygen and Corning set the value of Sorenson Biosciences at $80 million—quadruple its sale price of just two years earlier. The company had come full circle from a decade earlier when Corning ended its contract with Sorenson Bioscience.

"This is still a good company," said Brophy, "but it is not what it was before. No one ever got rich working for Mr. Sorenson, but it was a great environment. We had a lot of freedom to be creative; he treated West and me like we were his own kids.

"I still miss Mr. Sorenson, and think of him every day."

A decade after the debacle of trying but failing to give a major gift to the University of Utah, Jim tested the waters of public philanthropy again. This time the beneficiary was the stately Cathedral of the Madeleine in the heart of downtown Salt Lake City.

The cathedral is an outgrowth of the Catholic Church's long history in Utah. While the state is commonly known as the headquarters of The Church of Jesus Christ of Latter-day Saints, two Catholic priests beat the Mormons to Utah by seventy years. They were storied explorers Francisco Atanazio Dominguez and Silvestre V. des Escalante. Today there are tens of thousands of Utah Catholics, and the center of their faith is the Cathedral of the Madeleine, in downtown Salt Lake City.

The cathedral, dedicated in 1909, had fallen into disrepair by the 1980s; the electrical and mechanical systems, the windows, and the organ all needed overhauling. The woodwork and seating also needed to be redone.

The Most Reverend William K. Weigand, of the Roman Catholic Diocese of Salt Lake City, headed a funding drive to raise $6.3 million for the needed repairs and upgrades. When Bishop Weigand announced the campaign in the fall of 1988 there was an outpouring of support from all quarters—individuals, corporations, and foundations, including the LDS Church's foundation. Jim and Beverley contributed $50,000 to the goal, which was reached in May 1990.

Jim's support should not have been a surprise to those who knew him well. Though a lifelong Mormon, he was increasingly ecumenical in his outlook. One of several books he wrote, coincidentally published in 1989 when helping to raise money for the cathedral, echoed phrases he often uttered in other settings. The title was *Just Love the People: The World is our Family.*

Meanwhile, a 1989 earthquake in San Francisco led leaders of the project to increase the fund-raising goal by $1.8 million to a total $8.1 million, to provide seismic upgrading.

The last money was not raised as easily as the first. At the end of July 1990 Jim and other key supporters met with Bishop Weigand over breakfast. Jim suggested, for starters, that each of them give a third more to the project than they had already given; for him that was nearly $17,000. Bishop Weigand wrote Jim the next day to say that, thanks to his "imaginative intervention," one other attendee pledged an additional $180,000 and a second one $30,000.

When the extended goal continued to prove elusive, at the last minute an anonymous donor pledged up to $500,000, about half of what was still needed—as a match to what others gave by June 30.

During the last week in May, half-page ads appeared in Utah newspapers, under this headline: "For Heaven's Sake, Don't Miss This Chance To Double Your Money."

In a cathedral flyer Bishop Weigand said "I wish I could reveal the donor's name so that he could receive the recognition and public thanks he deserves, but he prefers to remain anonymous." That was the shot in the arm the campaign needed. More than 600 additional donors took the offer to double their gifts, and the full amount was given before the end of July.

Only then was Jim revealed as the anonymous donor. "Mr. Sorenson's donation came at the right time and was very effective," the cathedral's rector, Reverend M. Francis Mannion, told the Associated Press. "It elicited the interest of lots of people who hadn't previously contributed."[6]

Among expressions of thanks to Jim was a hand-written letter in sky-blue ink from Joan M. on Center Street in Salt Lake City:

> As a newcomer to the area and a Catholic, I felt as though I might have two strikes against me... Your generous and ecumenical gift warms my heart and welcomes us. My husband and I contributed what we could upon reading of your not-to-be-refused offer. We will remember you in our prayers as we worship in our newly restored cathedral. It's the least we can do in appreciation not only for your gift which is tangible but for your spirit which unites us all. Thanks for dispelling a myth and creating a closer community.[7]

### CHAPTER THIRTY

# JIM A VOLATILE LEADER

J im was not a calm manager. Those who stayed with him long-term—from Beverley to several key assistants—found redeeming traits in him that helped counterbalance his capriciousness, need to control, and occasional explosive temper.

"He was a hard driver, didn't like to be in the box," said Jim Larson, Sorenson's chief operating officer, who was at his boss's side for a quarter-century, "I was trained to stay in the box. We had to figure each other out. I was conservative; he would accuse me of being too conservative. Later I was not conservative enough."

After joining Sorenson in 1982 as company controller, and experiencing Jim's volatility, Larson feared he had made a mistake and began looking for another job. Not finding one to his liking, he meanwhile discovered that "I kind of enjoyed being around him." He noted that Jim was not trained in the management of companies, but had "the greatest mind I've ever been around in terms of ideas" and a unique ability to see the potential in people to achieve the goals he set with them.[1]

Gloria Smith was another employee who knew Jim extremely well. She worked for Jim and his companies for forty years, the last fifteen as his executive assistant.

"My life with Mr. Sorenson was 24/7," she explained. "One day it would be out to the ranch, then down to [northern California] to the bed and breakfast. Things could change on the spur of the moment. I wouldn't get frustrated with any change, and because of that we had a great relationship." [2]

Not everyone in their office coped as well with Jim's mercurial disposition. "I told the girls on the front desk and other young people who came in that, if Mr. Sorenson gets upset, listen to what he's trying to tell you, not the tone of his voice," said Smith. She said it was not unusual for Jim to make an appointment, then decide he didn't want to see the person when he or she showed up—ironically the same discourtesy that soured him on selling to doctors.

"They could be sitting out in the foyer waiting. After awhile I would say 'Mr. Sorenson had something come up and can't meet with you today.' If it was someone he wanted to meet, I'd schedule something for another day. If it was someone he didn't want to meet, I'd say 'Leave your number and I'll get back to you when he's available.'"

One time he was traveling in Norway and forgot a medicine. Smith arranged with Jim's doctor in Salt Lake to have it compounded in Norway. "He'd call at three in the morning and say 'I need such and such,' then he'd ask what time it was here. I'd tell him and he'd say 'It's close enough to when you should be getting up anyway.'" Or he'd call at any hour of the night with more routine needs, such as fixing his fax machine in the morning.

A rabbi asked Jim to sponsor a Russian scientist named Natalya (pronounced "Natasha") Rapoport to immigrate to the United States. Jim interviewed Natalya, who had a Ph.D. and specialized in polymer chemistry. He gave $5,000 to the University of Utah to finance her research, for which she is now world-renowned.

Dr. Rapoport, who has since become an American citizen, specialized in the delivery of drugs to cancer cells using ultrasound. At this writing she is a research professor at the U and on the staff at the Huntsman Cancer Institute.

Jim believed an ancestor five or six generations ago may have been a tax collector from St. Petersburg. Dr. Rapoport accompanied him back to Russia to try to verify this. While there they ran afoul of Russian corruption, endemic in a society that was in transition after the breakup of the

Soviet Union.

When they checked into a hotel the desk clerk took their passports and later refused to give them back. Passports, especially coveted American ones, were sold on the black market. Natalya angrily leaped over the counter and, nose to nose with the clerk, said "I know you have the documentation. You give it to me right now!"

Jim put in a frantic call to Smith in Utah. "I want to come home *now*. I don't care what it takes. You get me and Natalya out of Russia." She did.

Natalya had enlisted Jim's help to sponsor Aleksey Blyumenfeld, a longtime friend and a leading microbiologist, out of Russia. Aleksey was a cowboy on the Sorenson ranch in central Utah during his first months in the U.S. He was then hired by the Sorenson companies as a chemist.

Despite all his accomplishments, Jim's self-esteem seemed fragile. "He wanted to be a person who people accepted and admired," said Smith. "He really struggled in life trying to be the one that everybody looked to, not so much for answers but for needing him."

Another insider close to Jim, Duane Toney, echoed Smith's sentiment. "Jim was really good at reading how people felt, especially about him," said Toney, age 28 when he began with Jim in 1987. Toney, a CPA, was with Jim for twelve years and played a key role in structuring taxes and other financial issues impacting the company as well as the Sorenson family.

"There were times when we were on the same page. Then there were times when he was very critical, very hard." After years of trying and failing to change Jim in any significant way, Toney decided he had two choices— leave the company or more fully accept Jim and serve him in every way possible. He chose the latter.[3]

"Jim noticed right away. My body language must have been different. He knew something had changed in me. He would call me to his office; sometimes I'd spend a couple hours there. He'd tell me who he was going to meet with and what he hoped to accomplish. Then the person would come in and I'd watch the interactions as Jim tried to achieve what he wanted.

"Some of his reactions were very kind, very friendly, and some of them showed pretty hard-core feelings. The big difference was how he thought the person was doing at the task he had assigned them." After an individual left such meetings, Jim would explain to Toney why he acted as he did and what he felt was accomplished. "He was trying to tutor me to help me manage the way he managed."

Toney came to believe that how Jim acted in those meetings, often including the anger when shown, was calculated in advance to achieve the result Jim wanted. Jim also was known to fire employees on the spot—and rehire some of them just as fast.

In fairness, it should be noted that Jim had a good rapport with office staff who saw him daily. Whether there or somewhere else, he often went out of his way to be friendly and personable with individuals at the lower end of the pay scale.

Jim relished fresh ideas and innovation far more than day-to-day management. He encouraged those around him to not only meet company objectives but to generate creative ideas to improve their respective companies or other Sorenson enterprises.

He probably would have resonated with a Dutch marketing and innovation consultant who wrote that "Cost cutting is essential to keep companies profitable on short term. But in the long run you cannot survive on doing the same things better and cheaper."[4]

Better and cheaper newspapers, he noted, could not stop digital news. Nor could better and cheaper postal services stop email, medical doctors stop nurse practitioners, or walk-in stores stop e-commerce.

Jim's own biggest successes, medical inventions, showed that to be true.


Another kindred spirit was legendary Steve Jobs, co-founder of Apple Inc. He was forced out of Apple in a power struggle in 1985 and returned years later when the company was nearly bankrupt. By 1998 Jobs had returned Apple to profitability—one of the greatest turnarounds in business history.

The Sorensons played a role in Apple's recovery. Apple's QuickTime 3.0, unveiled by Jobs in 1998, was powered by Sorenson Vision's video codec (coder-decoder) software. It was an outgrowth of video compression technology invented at Utah State University and licensed by Sorenson. Viewers with access to the Sorenson codec could download videos faster to their electronic devices, and the picture quality surpassed anything else on the market.

When Apple made QuickTime available to the public, the response was a record download by consumers that far surpassed any similar download to that time. It became the technology of choice for movies and movie trailers.

In 1997, at Job's direction, Apple unveiled the celebrated "Think Different" marketing campaign that helped turn his company around. It could well have been written to describe Jim:

> Here's to the crazy ones. The misfits. The rebels. The troublemakers. The round pegs in the square holes. The ones who see things differently. They're not fond of rules. And have no respect for the status quo. You can quote them, disagree with them, glorify or vilify them. About the only thing you can't do is ignore them. Because they change things. They push the human race forward...While some may see them as the crazy ones, we see genius. Because the people who are crazy enough to think they can change the world, are the ones who do.

The presidents of Sorenson companies did not have the luxury of being too wild and crazy. Jim held them strictly to account for progress toward mutually shared goals. With so many companies to oversee—more than forty through the years, including nineteen functioning at the same time—he had no choice but to put a lot of responsibility on their respective leaders.

"I had no board of directors. I didn't even have formal business schooling," he wrote, "so I made a lot of decisions by the seat of the pants. I never took a position that was immovable. I knew how to listen and how to encourage the ideas of my employees. I enunciated my ideas strongly, then I listened...Because I balanced hope with caution, I could make quick decisions."[5]

Jim continued a practice he followed most of his life, carrying simple three-by-five file cards in a shirt pocket. As a young man it was to track income and expenses; later it was to prioritize business tasks for him and his associates. "Through listing tasks and following through on them, I put myself and my attitudes to work in my teams' minds," he explained. "I got my teams to persist, to be courageous when they weren't courageous, to delve deeper than they knew they could."

He met one-on-one with company leaders to outline and explain what he expected of them and their operations. Those whose companies were struggling found themselves often in Jim's office.

"I didn't do a lot of desk pounding, but I was inclined to throw my whole body into an idea, into a convincing argument. I wanted others to see the smoke, feel the fire, and hear the roar. I used the 'emotional blow' to move the team, to refine the idea, to get the concept right...If I pounded the desk, it was carefully measured pounding. If I shouted, it was controlled shouting."

Jim's "controlled" pounding and shouting often came in weekly management meetings led by him and Jim Jr., company vice chairman. Also in attendance were Gloria Smith, Jim Larson, legal and financial advisors, and presidents of the primary Sorenson companies, who numbered six to ten depending on the era.

In the latter years company leaders included Don Wallace, Sorenson Real Estate Group; Pat Nola, Sorenson Communications; Matt Cupal, Sorenson Media; West Price, Sorenson Bioscience; Bob Tingey and DeeRay Nielsen, Sorenco; Jim Larson, White Sage Ranch & Farm; Steve Makert, Sorenson Mold; Dale Poplin, Tom Orsini, and LeVoy Haight, Sorenson Medical; Scott Woodward, Sorenson Molecular Genealogy Foundation; and Doug Fogg, Sorenson Forensics.

For many years the meetings were held in Jim's personal office at 2511 South West Temple. Later he had an elegant conference room constructed in the old LeVoy's clothing area. Jim commented that his family didn't like to come to the "schlocky side of town," and apparently felt they may be more keen to come to a handsome conference room. It was built and furnished at a cost of more than a half-million dollars to showcase Sorenson Vision technology. The room has an enormous boat-shaped cherry wood conference table, eighteen leather executive chairs, a projector and drop-down screen.

Weekly meetings were held on Tuesday from 10 a.m. sharp until noon. Presidents were required to submit a written report the previous Friday, containing their company's significant activities for the week, including financial progress, new project or investment proposals, and outstanding challenges. Jim Larson submitted a financial summary. Gloria Smith assembled the reports and gave advance copies to Jim Sr., Jim Jr., and Larson.

Jim Sr. typically began the meetings with light-hearted banter about the weather, the Jazz, the Church, his family, or something in the news.

His tone then got serious as he singled out companies that were "carrying the load" and those that were "dragging things down." The agenda listed a number of important items that required attention. However, it was not unusual for Jim to become fixated on something entirely different and guide the discussion down that alley instead.

When it was the presidents' turn, Jim sometimes placed a three-minute egg-timer shaped like a miniature hourglass on the table—a reminder to talk succinctly.

The presidents reported on their companies, one by one. Their presentations typically were followed by comments and questions by Jim Sr., focused on product ideas and promotions, and by Jim Jr. on the business models and the economics of the products, services, and operations.

Presidents learned early on that one thing they were never to say was "we can't do that." Jim would not tolerate defeatism, no matter how hopeless a goal might seem. Once an idea entered Jim's head it was almost impossible to dislodge it. He was tenacious and would cling to an idea, business or otherwise, long after most others abandoned it.

Jim also bristled if ever there appeared the slightest doubt that this was still *his* show. Pat Nola, head of Sorenson Communications, reported to Jim Jr. day-to-day. During one presidents' meeting he referred to Jim Jr. as "boss."

Jim Sr. stopped Nola in mid-sentence. "*Who* is your boss?" he asked Nola.

"Jim is," answered Nola, nodding toward Jim Jr.

"And who is Jim [Jr.'s] boss? pressed Jim.

Nola got the point. There was room for only one boss at the table, and Jim Sr. was it.[6]

As long ago as sixty years earlier when he was a Mormon missionary seeking converts in New England—and personally baptizing as many as the entire mission did the previous year—he quoted in his journal a philosophy he lived by the rest of his life:

The line between failure and success is so fine that we scarcely know when we pass it—that we are often on the line and do not know it...A little more persistence, a little more effort, and what seemed hopeless failure may turn to glorious success. There is no failure except in no longer trying. There is no defeat except from within, no really insurmountable barrier save our own inherent weakness of purpose. [7]

Jim did not micro-manage, and gave an executive great authority and a wide berth, IF his company was hitting its targets. If it was struggling, the Sorenson conference room was the last place a president wanted to be. Jim's comments could be extremely pointed, even harsh. Such exchanges were uncomfortable for their colleagues to witness and probably almost unbearable for the one in the hot seat.

"He saw himself as the refiner's fire," explained Duane Toney. "Not just the refiner, but the refiner's *fire*. When he got emotional you could see the flame in him light and then burn. Later, usually he'd calm down and you could see the flame decrease."

Invariably Jim would circle back, apologize for his sharp comments, and express confidence that the targeted president and company would turn things around. For presidents whose companies were performing up to expectations, Jim's comments were as laudatory as his other comments were negative. Jim often ended the meeting by saying "the best is yet to come."

Since most of the Sorenson companies were start-ups or were early in the product-development stage when Toney was there, there were numerous challenges and many stressful meetings.

Toney believed Jim had to be hard to accomplish all that he did. "I don't know of anybody else who created that many different businesses. He drove people to their best excellence. They didn't always like it, but they responded and they produced. I think the reason he could be a serial entrepreneur and create so many companies was because he was really good at getting the best out of people.

"He wasn't as productive when he was nice and lovable, as he would sometimes try to be. He thought there were times when he had to be in people's faces or at their rear...He tried all methods, but there were times when he had to really put the pressure on with great emotion."

Toney noted that Jim had a history of hiring people with a lot of latent potential at each stage of his career—at Deseret Pharmaceutical, LeVoy's, Sorenson Research, and at Sorenson Development. But Jim sometimes spent more time thinking of how to solve a company's problems than the company's leader spent. "Some of them would come to work at a comfortable time and leave at a comfortable time, and their company was sick," recalled Toney. Jim would keep thinking about those business problems at all hours of the day and night and apply whatever pressure it took to get the manager to solve the problems.

Jim's obsession with continuing to create enterprises right to the end of his life stood apart from most other men and women of great wealth. Victor Cartwright, one of his partners at Deseret Pharmaceutical, whom Jim split with decades earlier, observed of Jim when the latter was in his eighties, that he "never takes a vacation. He doesn't have any hobbies...He doesn't go on any cruises that I know of. He just liked to make money. That was his hobby."

Cartwright went fishing in Alaska once or twice a year for a quarter-century. "I said, 'Come on, let's go fishing up there,' He said 'No, I can't. Maybe next year.'" Next year never came. Cartwright opined that to build a huge estate, Jim had neglected his family.

Jim Sorenson Jr., however, said although his father was often away from home, he was a good father. "He taught all of his children the value of work and, I think, good virtues," said Jim. "Dad was always one to be immersed in his work, but his family was very important to him."[8]

Although some former Sorenson employees no doubt cursed Jim the rest of their days, unsolicited letters from others give evidence of admiration and even love for their former boss:

"Dear Jim," wrote one man, "It has been 20 years since I hooked up with the KG2000 product & I seriously doubt if ever any salesman & any product were better suited to each other. Thanks to your product line & my sales efforts my children all attended good schools, had their teeth straightened, saw the U.S.A. on various vacations, & attended college...Those were good years, Jim [1970s and early '80s] – Thanks."[9]

Another former colleague wrote, "Thank you so much for all your support and interest in trying to make something good happen at the University this past June. Even though the risks were high, we had to try to explore a new way...I'm forever grateful to you for your efforts. You are an honorable and kind person and should be appreciated more.[10]

A man named John wrote that "I want to thank you especially...for the many opportunities you've provided me over the last couple of years. I've learned more by working with you in this time than a small squadron

of Harvard MBAs could muster. In this way, you've prepared me for a successful life that will (I hope) last many, many more years.[11]

Aleksey Blyumenfeld the Russian cowboy sent this undated thank-
you card to Jim: "Dear Mr. Sorenson! April 14, 1995 I came in the USA.
This day at night I was in SLC. Same day April 14, 2005 I got American
citizenship. Ten years of wonderful experience. For all of that I thank you.
You did so many for me and my family. Your kindness and attention will be
forever in my heart. I pray for your health and prosperity."[12]


Early in 1994 Jim received a two-page hand-written letter from a
prominent developer he had offended years earlier. They were partners in
business deals that went sour. In frustration at the time, Jim, speaking to
others, called the man a "crook."

The accusation, which was false, haunted and tormented the man. "I
have felt feelings toward you for years," he wrote to Jim. "I must be able to
get them out of the inside of me...I have not been able to recover from your
remarks to [a prominent Utahn]."

"I cannot harbor any more thoughts concerning the statements about
my honesty. I in turn forgive you of wounding my very nature. I should
have forgiven you years ago. I hope you [have] continued great success..."

Jim responded generously that "It distresses me to learn that you have
carried so much resentment for me all these years...I know how resent-
ments can fester into anger and hate, until hate has cast a dark shadow on
your entire life...I am truly sorry for implying to anyone that you were a
*crook*. That was one of the times (and I'm sure there have been many in my
life) that I got off track and made a left-hand turn...

"I believe that true forgiveness comes when a person reaches a point
where he realizes that no one is really to blame for anything and knows
that whatever happens was necessary and right for his personal growth...
forgiveness is the highest, most beautiful form of love. In return you receive
abundant joy, happiness and peace. May the blessings of God rest upon you,
may His peace abide with you and may His presence illuminate your heart,
now and forever more."[13]

Jim sent a copy of the letter to the prominent Utahn to whom he had
called the developer a crook.

In May 2001 with his Holiness the Dalai Lama of Tibet and prominent advocate for the poor, Pamela Atkinson, also a Presbyterian Church elder, nurse and hospital administrator.

On the Lebanon-Israel border with (*from left*) assistant John Ward, son James Lee, and son-in-law Gary Crocker. Jim sponsored international conferences bringing together Christians, Jews, and Muslims.

Theodor "Teddy" Kollek was an Israeli and widely respected mayor of Jerusalem for nearly three decades. He worked closely with Jim to foster a wider dialogue in the Middle East involving Muslims as well as Christians and Jews. Courtesy *Deseret News Publishing Company*

Discussing the renovation of the Cathedral of the Madeleine with Catholic Bishop William Weigand (*left*) and Rev. M. Frances Mannion. Jim was a major contributor and bought newspaper ads encouraging other donors. Courtesy *Deseret News Publishing Company*

Reverend France Davis of the Calvary Baptist Church and choir, which performed one of Jim's songs.

Famed authors and journalists Tina Brown and husband Sir Harold Evans (*far left*) emceed the 2006 "Giant in Our City" event honoring Jim in Salt Lake City. Beverley is surrounded by Sorenson grandchildren, with Jim and Jim Jr. on the right.

LDS Church official Thomas S. Monson, later president of the Church, joins Abbott Labs CEO Miles White in honoring Jim as Salt Lake's 2006 "Giant In our city." White called Jim "one of the world's greatest inventors of medical devices."

Jon Huntsman Sr. and Jim were friends as well as Utah's two billionaires. They are at the ground breaking for the Sorenson Unity Center—a major expansion of the Sorenson Multicultural Center. Courtesy *Deseret News Publishing Company*

Major contributions to Southern Utah University are reflected in the J.L. Sorenson Physical Education Building *(left)* and the Beverley Taylor Sorenson Center for the Arts. Courtesy *Southern Utah University Photo Services*

Mexican President Vicente Fox thanks Jim for providing jobs for Mexican Americans.

A 1998 reception hailed the first of many volumes of Islamic writings translated into English. Jim and Bev helped fund the BYU project. Guests included *(left to right)* New York U. Professor Parviz Morewedge, BYU professor Daniel C. Peterson, BYU President Merrill Bateman, Beverley and Jim and their daughter Carol Sorenson Smith, son-in-law Gary and Ann Sorenson Crocker, and Jeffrey R. Holland, a member of the LDS Quorum of the Twelve Apostles.

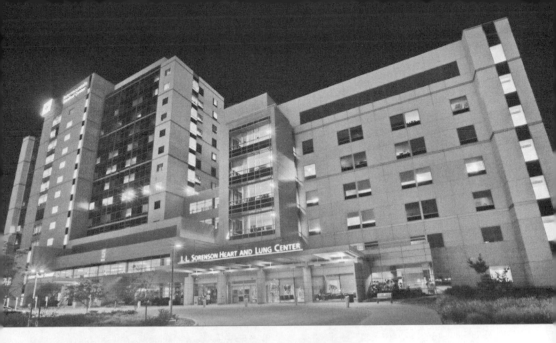

Major Sorenson bequests helped build IHC's flagship hospital complex with the J.L. Sorenson Patient Tower and the J.L. Sorenson Heart and Lung Center, pictured above. *Photos by Eric Roderick.*

Jim and Bev in a rare moment of relaxation.

With Gary Pehrson, CEO of Intermountain Health Care's Urban Central Region, in 2007. In back is the 15-story James L. Sorenson Patient Tower at the IHC medical center in Murray. Next to Jim in an atrium is a heroic-size statue of him with the inscription "Finding a Better Way." Courtesy *Deseret News Publishing Company*

Jim announces another million-dollar gift to honor three former medical collaborators, *(left to right)*, Drs. Homer Warner, Alan Toronto, and Reed Gardner. Courtesy *Deseret News Publishing Company*

Two features of the rebuilt temple are a traditional temple baptismal font, resting on the backs of twelve stone oxen, and a spiral staircase. Courtesy *Deseret News Publishing Company*

Sunstones for the rebuilt Nauvoo Temple were created in a Utah factory, here visited by Jim and Bev and two grandchildren, Sarah Smith Dunn and Robert Smith.

five computers, a new gym, Olympic-size swimming pool, boxing center, and playing field outside. Also included were parenting programs, a kitchen and meeting rooms, and resources for housing, food, and employment information provided by a dozen or so United Way service organizations.

At the dedication of the center, Jim spoke of his own family's years of living in Rose Park, when neighbor helped neighbor. "Families have been bruised and busted up," said Jim. "Fathers have been scared off or simply separated by an economy that is not as forgiving as it was forty years ago. So there is an even greater need for people to help each other, to walk across the street and extend a hand."

"I hope that this new building and all its facilities will be used in ways that will nurture the young, protect the old, and build a vibrant future for the Glendale neighborhood," said Jim. "By using the building for meetings, classes, special events, sports and just as a gathering place, I hope it will amplify the best efforts of community leaders."

Jim sought to bridge differences in the neighborhood. "Love people and they will love you. Fear people and they will fear you. Sow anger and you will receive anger. Sow appreciation and you will get appreciation. I hope this center can help teach such lessons,..."[5]

There is no way to know if the Sorenson Center led to fewer crimes in the area than there would have been otherwise. At any rate, the center was widely used.

Years later the recreation complex again beckoned Jim—this time as a crucial component of a solution to heal a deep church-state division in the city.

The battle began in April 1999 when the city council sold one block of Main Street to The Church of Jesus Christ of Latter-day Saints for $8.1 million. The Church used the land to create an ecclesiastical campus, joining the iconic Mormon Temple with church offices. As part of the deal the Church provided an easement allowing public access but establishing guidelines for behavior on the block.

Prohibited behavior included playing loud music, swearing, demonstrating, and sunbathing. The First Unitarian Church of Salt Lake City, backed by the American Civil Liberties Union, sued, saying the agreement violated First Amendment guarantees of free expression. The Utah district court ruled in favor of the LDS Church, but plaintiffs appealed to the U.S. Court of Appeals for the 10th Circuit.

In October 1999 the appeals court overturned the lower court ruling. That left the issue in limbo and the city—actually the state, which is more than sixty percent Mormon—sharply divided. The Church appealed to the U.S. Supreme Court. Before the high court could act, Salt Lake Mayor Rocky Anderson agreed to a land swap to solve the contentious issue.

Jim Sorenson entered the picture. On behalf of the Church he gave $500,000 in cash and 2.5 acres of land worth $886,000 to the city to expand the Sorenson Multicultural Center. The Alliance for Unity kicked in another $4 million. In exchange, Mayor Anderson and the city council agreed to the Church's restrictive terms, and the Main Street deal was finally settled.

"Without Jim Sorenson's help," Anderson told a reporter, "the Sorenson Center would have never become a reality. I think he really wants to leave this a better world, and he has made tremendous strides in doing that." [6]

Three years later, on December 13, 2006, Salt Lake City broke ground adjacent to the Sorenson Multicultural Center to begin construction of the Sorenson Unity Center. Both were part of what is called the Sorenson Multicultural Unity Campus.

The 26,000-square-foot unity center opened in 2008 and has multiple uses largely decided by local residents themselves through an extensive public-hearing process. The facility includes a 7,000-square-foot fitness center, adult education courses, a free, full-service dental clinic, drop-in child care centers, and a 150-seat performance space.

Some other features on the campus are a computer center, with separate training programs for youth and adults; free income tax assistance; a one-acre park, including community event space; and a 24-plot public garden which operated at 95 percent of capacity during the 2011/2012 fiscal year. Participants grow food for their own tables as well as to sell.

The Sorenson Unity Center has impacted and improved the lives of numerous residents. One of them is teenager Sujeit Chacon, who said "If this wasn't here, I would probably be like a lot of teens out on the street causing trouble. The other kids don't know what they are missing." She called the Sorenson Center "my second home."[7]

Chacon participated in campus programs for at least ten years—starting at the age of 6. She especially benefitted from the youth Computer Clubhouse, where she spent afternoons in technical and computer-based programs and, in 2009, appeared to be on the path to a college education and a future in engineering.

"The west side now has a first-rate facility compared to the best community centers in the state," said juvenile court judge Andrew Valdez. "... the Sorenson Unity Center is like music to my heart."

The Sorenson Legacy Foundation—whose board included Jim, Beverley, and the Sorenson children—donated $250,000 to fund the opening ceremonies of the February 2007 Deaflympic Winter Games. The Deaflympics are sanctioned by the International Olympic Committee (IOC) as the premier quadrennial winter competition for deaf athletes. The 16th Deaflympics brought athletes and officials from more than twenty countries to compete at world-class venues, including some used by the IOC for the Salt Lake Olympics in 2002.

Jim Sorenson Jr., a nationally recognized advocate for the deaf community, co-chaired the Deaflympic's honorary advisory board, along with I. King Jordan, president of Gallaudet University in Washington, D.C., the nation's premier educational institution for the deaf and hard of hearing.

In 2007 the Sorenson foundation also donated $1 million to Gallaudet's James Lee Sorenson Language and Communications Center. That brought to $4 million the total amount given by the foundation to Gallaudet to develop a center devoted to deaf people's language, culture, history, and community.

In 2006 Jim Sr. pledged $1 million in matching funds to refurbish the primary facility in Utah through which the YMCA serves children. The camp is in a spectacular Uinta mountain setting fourteen miles east of Kamas. It had twenty-five cabins, a lodge, stables, and athletic facilities that needed substantial overhaul.

Jim, who had a lifelong love of the out-of-doors, said "It is very important for kids to have the opportunity to hike in the woods, go fishing in a mountain stream, and do all the outdoor activities that contribute to a healthy mind, body, and spirit."

The Sorensons also provided college scholarships for Native Americans through American Indian Services. Joe Shirley, president of the Navajo Nation, offered the prayer in his native tongue at a black-tie "Giant in our City" evening honoring Jim in February 2006. Translated, he said in part: "Through his generosity...many of my people and children—those attending school—have made their mark in life. And because of this we [Joe and Vicki Shirley] weep of gladness."

Jim rescued another down-and-out group in June 2006. The Utah Legislature ordered cuts to Medicaid, the federal-state health program that serves the poorest of the poor, leaving 65,000 Utah adults without dental care.

Governor Jon Huntsman Jr. appealed to private citizens to help cover the gap, while House Republican leader Jeff Alexander unfeelingly said "We have no plans at this point to give any money to this. If there are any individuals in the state that feel a need to donate money to this, then great."

The greatest need was emergency dental care for 40,000 elderly, blind, and disabled Medicaid patients. Fortunately for them, an anonymous donor stepped forward with a gift of $1 million—given with the proviso that the Governor find other funds to match it. Individual Utahns called Huntsman's office to donate, and Intermountain Health Care covered the balance of the additional $1 million.

The $2 million total was enough leverage to draw another $4.8 million from Washington, saving the humanitarian program for that year. A week later the media revealed Jim as the anonymous donor. In a thank-you letter to him, Governor Huntsman wrote, in long-hand, "You are remarkable!" [8]

A month later the Sorenson foundation gave $100,000 to American War Heroes, to help military personnel injured in the Middle East in the nation's war on terror.

During 2007 the foundation donated $6 million to the University of Utah's David Eccles School of Business, for the James L. Sorenson interdisciplinary center for the study of discovery and innovation. The foundation also gave $6 million to Intermountain Healthcare for IHC's patient tower in Murray—bringing to $22 million the family's contributions to IHC hospitals since 2003.

Jim was a stand-alone philanthropist. Many major donors speak and give on behalf of their spouses as well as themselves, as it is generally recognized that money gained in one-earner families belongs equally to both spouses.

Jim's gifts were virtually always given in his own name and not that of Beverley or the Sorenson family. It was not until Bev stepped out of Jim's shadow during the last dozen years of their marriage—cheered on by their children and the Sorenson Legacy Foundation they led—that Beverley came into her own as an honored, even beloved public figure.

### CHAPTER THIRTY-TWO

# BEVERLEY SAVES KIDS

## With Art

J im Sorenson found his life mission by a wrenching experience—watching an 11-year-old boy die on an operating table when doctors lacked a medical device that could have saved him. Jim invented that and many other devices.

Beverley Sorenson found her mission in enriching the lives of children. At about the age of 12 she lovingly taught young children in Junior Sunday School; at 19 she was called to direct her congregation's entire children's program, called Primary. Her diary entries from those years are full of references to "the darlings."

Bev played the piano and was an excellent dancer, often performing on the stage. She taught the children to sing and dance and act out stories. Bev told an interviewer many decades later, "I can't go anywhere and see a little child without being drawn to that child in some way."

As an adolescent Bev's three goals were to attend college, become a kindergarten teacher, and save $1,000—for what purpose she didn't know. In 1945 she graduated in elementary education from the University of Utah and, through hard work while going to school, had salted away the $1,000. She used it to travel to and set up in New York City, where she landed a job teaching kindergarten at a private school.

She met Jim in the Big Apple, they were married, and eventually produced eight children of their own. Jim's resistance to her activities outside
their home limited Bev's involvement with other children in the church
and community. His demands, however, gave their own children something
very precious—a mother at home.

With six daughters and two sons, Bev had her own child laboratory,
where she put to work the nurturing skills learned as a teacher in church
and school, and as a college student. She was closely attuned to her children's individual needs, often praying for and with them.

Beverley worried about the lack of seatbelts in the little BMW Jim Jr.
and his bride Elizabeth Hodson were about to take on their honeymoon.
On the very day of the wedding in 1973 Beverley and daughter Carol drove
to an auto shop in west Salt Lake and had seatbelts installed in the car. Days
later, driving home from California, Jim and Elizabeth hit a patch of black
ice and pitched off the road, rolling into a ravine and totaling the car. The
seatbelts may well have saved their lives. "She was always spiritually in tune
with what we needed," said Carol.

The eight Sorenson children gave Bev and Jim forty-seven grandchildren, also a source of great pride and care. At one time Bev was particularly
concerned for a zoned-out 12-year-old grandson who was depressed and
doing poorly in school. She found it hard to get his attention as he tuned
out the world with earphones attached to a CD player blaring heavy metal
music.

That proved to be a catalyst that propelled Bev into what would be
her most important public contribution: putting the arts back into Utah's
elementary schools. With the nation's largest families and usually the largest class sizes in its elementary schools, effectiveness in the classroom was
especially important in the Beehive State. [1]

The arts had largely fallen by the wayside in many states, including
Utah, where, increasingly, the emphasis was on passing standardized tests
in the core subjects of reading, writing, and mathematics. The emphasis
was formalized at a national level when Congress passed the No Child Left
Behind Act of 2001. Congress's intent was to ensure that every child was
given a chance to succeed; one result was to dumb-down many classes and
too often teach for testing more than for understanding.

A lot of school administrators and teachers themselves came to believe they could not afford the time to incorporate arts into their curricula and still prepare students to pass the annual state-prescribed exams. Between 2007 and 2010 alone, about 70 percent of schools cut instruction time for non-core subjects including history, visual arts, language, and music. [2]

Bev Sorenson believed that one important thing lacking in the life of her grandson—and by extension in the lives of numerous other children—was exposure to the kind of uplifting music that filled the home she grew up in. She also knew instinctively that, rather than detracting from the learning of core subjects, music *enhanced* such learning. National surveys tended to bear her out.

She gathered education officials and arts experts around the large round wooden table in the Sorensons' kitchen, brainstorming what could be done to reintroduce the arts to Utah schools.

Someone pointed Bev toward Lincoln Elementary, an inner city school that inaugurated an unusual integrated visual arts program. The school principal hired a teaching artist to instruct students in visual arts concepts and collaborative art projects as an approach to combat escalating youth violence in the neighborhood.

Bev visited the school in the spring of 1994 and was awe-struck. "I saw all these children of all races, many of them at risk," she recalled. "The gangs and graffiti were terrible at that time; some of the children had brothers who had been killed in gangs."

Children indifferent to school in the past were discovering its value in their lives. Teachers told her the arts program increased the children's self-esteem and desire to cooperate with students of different cultural backgrounds. It was also helping them learn core subjects better.

"The art specialist was teaching them how to paint, how to do ceramics," said Beverley. "And they were *enjoying* being in school. They were learning principles, how to cooperate and how to share. It affected the whole community." [3]

Beverley was smitten. Her kitchen table became Ground Zero for reintroducing the arts into Utah's schools. Beverley and her team launched Art Works For Kids, a non-profit organization "dedicated to enriching the lives and improving the minds of children in Utah through high-quality, innovative and sequential arts education."

"Beverley's passion built a fire in everyone," recalled Lisa Cluff, Bev's highly capable special assistant and executive director of the organization. Art Works for Kids' first pilot program, between 1995 and 2000, focused on kindergarten through second grade at six elementary schools. Beverley financed the program, providing the salaries of arts specialists, grants for materials, and professional-development workshops for teachers.

The program integrated four artistic disciplines into the schools' course of study—visual arts, music, dance, and theater. By 2000 the positive impact on the six schools led Beverley to consider how to expand the effort. Utah had more than 500 elementary schools, and it seemed clear that the only way to reach a significant portion was to win the active support of the state legislature and education officials.

Beverley and her team crafted a five-year model—one year for set-up in a school and four years to expand the number of arts specialists and grade levels served. They presented it in the 2000 session of the Utah Legislature and Bev campaigned tirelessly among legislators, inviting them to her home for dinner meetings and to the schools utilizing the program.

In the face of intense competition for education funds, Art Works for Kids prevailed in the 2000 session, which allocated one-time funding for startup costs in twelve schools and promised four years of continuing funding, which Art Works would match. The twelve schools were chosen by Beverley and her colleagues to represent a broad spectrum of cultural diversity, location, and economic backgrounds.

After the first year, however, budget shortfalls led the legislature to stop funding the program. Beverley proceeded to fund it herself, establishing a system in which individual schools would raise money to match Beverley's.

She personally visited every school sponsoring the program, which grew to twenty-five by 2008. Beverley scored a major victory that year when the legislature passed a bill creating the Beverley Taylor Sorenson (BTS) Arts Learning Program, along with $16 million over a four-year period to help provide arts specialists in fifty-five schools.

Although the program is now administered by the State Office of Education, proponents of Art Works for Kids must still lobby legislators for funding each year.

Another essential component of Beverley's program is for colleges to prepare teachers to teach the arts. Beverley and the Sorenson Legacy Foundation have funded arts-teaching programs at the University of Utah, Utah State University, Southern Utah University, Brigham Young University, and Westminster College.

By 2012 Beverley and the Sorenson Legacy Foundation had committed more than $50 million directly to elementary schools and to higher-education institutions. Tangible evidence of her passion and generosity is seen from one end of Utah to the other. A $12 million donation to her alma mater, the University of Utah, enabled construction of an interdisciplinary art and education complex. A donation to Southern Utah University funded a new theater for its world-renowned Shakespeare Theatre program and an art museum and educational center.

Most impressive, to date, through her efforts, more than 100,000 Utah school children have received an arts-rich education.

The evidence is strong that these fortunate children have learned core subjects better because they were exposed to the arts at the same time. A cross-section of results:

- Midas Creek Elementary in Riverton—91% of students learned letter sounds when integrated with dance—including making the shape of the letter with their bodies—compared with 37% taught in the standard visual and verbal way.
- Davis Elementary in Vernal—music helped fifth-grade vocabulary scores increase from 68% to 95%. Between the two results, words and definitions were set to simple beats, using West African drum rhythms.
- Oakwood Elementary, Holladay—Average science vocabulary test scores improved from 19% to 94% when combined with dance and visual arts.
- Iron Springs Elementary, Cedar City—End-of-level test results for fourth-grade science increased a remarkable 22%. Throughout the year an arts specialist integrated visual art into core subjects.

Beverley's accomplishments were even more heroic given the health

challenges she faced through the years. In 1991 she suffered breast cancer. A lumpectomy and radiation treatments left her cancer-free but facing
other health problems, including vertigo.

Asked why she devoted much of her life and resources to arts education, Beverley believed she was led by God: "He wants us to give. He wants
us to love. He wants us to care. I feel I am doing something that's going
to make a difference...so many [children] don't have the opportunity, in
school or sometimes in their homes, to feel special...I look at every one of
those children and I see them as special and unique."

David Parkinson, the Sorensons' public relations manager who knows
the family well, believed that, ultimately, Beverley's impact on the world
will be greater than her husband's. "Her mark will be bigger than his," he
said.

That prospect probably did not figure into Jim's thinking, but it remained true that he was an unusually difficult spouse. He did not like
competition, especially from a family member. If a family initiative did not
carry his name, he tended to dismiss it as unimportant or, worse, bad.

"I was getting known, and that was hard on him," said Beverley. "Jim
always wanted to be the leader in everything. He gave me trouble about
the arts. He'd say 'Don't you know the arts are in everything?'" Sorenson
Family members believe that Jim from the start was intimidated by the
cultured, musical Taylor family Bev grew up in. [4]

"Dad had a drive to be the sole wage earner," said their oldest child,
Carol Sorenson Smith. "When Mom was involved in the workforce [in
cosmetics and clothing], she was competing with Dad. She wasn't trying to
be that way, but she could get the hearts and emotions of the children in a
way that he couldn't."

Carol empathized with her father as her mother's meetings around
the kitchen table became frequent. "Dad felt emotionally manipulated.
He couldn't go to breakfast in his own house, because she so often invited
other people to breakfast. She was entertaining all the people who wanted
to get to him—the people he needs relief from, and they're having breakfast
in his house."

Some of those who met at the Sorensons' report that occasionally Jim
would wander into the meeting room wearing only his underwear, perhaps

to show Bev and her guests what he thought of their discussions.

Jim needed and used the back escape from his bedroom, said Carol. "I remember one day he came down and I was the only one in the kitchen. He said 'Oh goodness, I can have breakfast!' Mom made the home their workspace, so you never left work."

Carol, speaking when her mother was still alive, emphasized, that "Mom is very giving and forgiving. She is truly good—that will ring through the eternities." [5]

For all his rough edges, Jim leaned on and loved the woman whose life he shared for more than sixty years. From the first time he met Beverley in New York, he said, he found they had something important in common, "a quality that might be called 'drive.'"

Beverley reciprocated love through all those years, doing her best not to let his put-downs keep her down. In their later years together she sought to understand better what made Jim the way he was. "[I] had been awed by his unorthodox mind and attracted to his drive and energy," Bev wrote in her own biography, "yet often embarrassed by his outbursts and humiliated by his behavior."

She came to believe Jim might have had manic depressive disorder, commonly called bipolar disorder, in which a person's moods swing unpredictably from very high to very low, and back again.

Bev saw "A Beautiful Mind," a 2001 biopic based on the life of John Nash, a Nobel Laureate in Economics. "I left the theater in tears, because I thought I had just seen someone like my husband on the screen," said Beverley. She apparently mentioned her observation to Jim, who brushed it off. An obvious difference was that, like the screen version of Nash, Jim was abrupt and volatile, but unlike Nash he did not claim to see people invisible to everyone else.

On one memorable occasion, Jim and Bev were among VIP guests of Utah Governor Scott Matheson, who invited them to view the progress of a project to rehabilitate the Jordan River. It connects Utah Lake with the Great Salt Lake. Guests were furnished with canoes in which to navigate the river. The others glided away, but Jim and Bev became stuck in the reeds. Struggling to break free, they tipped the canoe and both plunged into the river.

Rather than call for help, the two gamely struggled with the canoe, finally righting it. They got in and proceeded to paddle to Jordan Park, where a feast awaited. "We were greeted by the Governor as we got out and sat at the banquet," recalled Bev. "Dripping and covered in black bog."[7]

Daughter Gail Williamsen wrote a song about the misadventure, which ended with these lines:

Bev, she was dripping, not in diamonds and jewels,
But in seaweed and sludge and Jordan River gruel.
Jim, he was fuming, it was as simple as that
As he sat down to dinner next to Joe Rosenblatt.

Now faint hearts would exit before matters got worse,
But these two consider it par for the course.
In life we are tested not by how smooth we sail,
But by strength and demeanor when it comes time to bail.

O, Jim and Bev, they zig and they zag
Like divine syncopation or a Scott Joplin rag.
They're different, as different as night is to day,
But each needs the other in the very same way. [8]

A suit of Jim's showed how far Beverley would go to please him. He bought the tan corduroy suit in the 1970s and was wearing it on the roof of a new Sorenson Research building for a photograph that appeared in a Salt Lake newspaper.

Years later a niece staying with them was sorting through Jim and Bev's clothes to prepare a bundle to donate to Deseret Industries (DI), an LDS Church-owned charity. Among the items she threw into the stack was Jim's corduroy suit.

When Jim noticed his suit was missing he exploded. To him it symbolized all he went through with Sorenson Research. Beverley quickly drove to DI to retrieve the suit, only to find it had been sold. "I kept checking time after time at that DI and others in the region, hoping whoever bought it might decide to return it."

Months later she felt prompted to try once more. "I made it a real matter of prayer," said Bev. Her assistant Lisa Cluff called the local DI out-let again. This time there was a glimmer of hope. They did indeed have a tan corduroy suit. A grandson, Adam Fenton, drove Bev to DI, and they struck pay dirt. There was Jim's beloved suit. Bev was so thrilled that she gave them $100, and rushed home to surprise Jim.

That evening, as she set out their supper in the bedroom where they often dined at night, Bev hung the suit on the door in his line of sight. When Jim spotted it his eyes lit up. "That's my suit! That's my suit! That's my suit!"

Years later the suit and its story were on display at Jim's funeral.

### CHAPTER THIRTY-THREE

# DNA KINSHIP

## And World Peace

Scott Woodward was minding his own business, that is to say he was sleeping soundly, when the phone jarred him awake at 2:30 a.m. on that July morning in 1999.

"With four teenage sons, the first thing you think of in the middle of the night is that this can't be good," quipped Woodward. On the line, however, was Jim Sorenson, who he had never met or spoken with before.

Jim was calling from Norway, the land of his forefathers, where he was trying to identify family members and trace their paths.

"Do you know anything about DNA?" Jim asked.

"I purport to," answered Woodward, a nationally noted science professor at Brigham Young University who helped discover the first genetic marker for cystic fibrosis. He gently tried to explain the difference in time zones between Norway and Utah, but Jim was unconcerned.

"How much it would cost to DNA all the people in Norway?" asked Jim.

"I told him I'd think about it and let him know," explained Woodward. In the following days Woodward buttonholed Sorenson employees, asking one burning question: "Is this guy serious?"

Jim was. And, with Woodward's help, he was about to pioneer yet another global industry—tracing family roots through DNA. That is short for deoxyribonucleic acid, a molecule that encodes the genetic instructions that determine the development and growth of almost all living organisms.

A couple of weeks later Woodward met with Jim in his West Temple Street office. By then he knew what Jim had in mind—a dream that dwarfed every project or scheme of his that came before: World Peace. "Of all the things I've invented," said Jim, "this is the big one."

Jim believed if diverse peoples were shown that they were related by blood, they would beat their swords into plowshares and learn to live peaceably. After years of just going through the motions, trying to feel the emotional highs he felt when inventing medical devices, Jim was on a high again.

He had numerous detractors, however. It was commonly assumed that the most recent common ancestor (MRCA) of humans lived tens if not hundreds of thousands of years ago. Finding familial connections over such a vast time span seemed impossible.

However, less than five years after Jim's quest began, two well-respected academicians, one at Yale and the other at MIT, announced results of a groundbreaking study demonstrating that the most recent ancestor of all humans now alive apparently lived within four to five thousand years ago—from third millennium BC to first millennium AD. "While we may not all be brothers," said Joseph T. Chang, a Yale mathematician, "the models suggest we are all hundredth cousins or so."[1]

They arrived at that conclusion by constructing elaborate computer models that simulated human history under a number of assumptions, tracking the lives, reproduction, and movements of significant groups of people.

"No matter the languages we speak or the color of our skin," wrote the two men, "we share ancestors who planted rice on the banks of the Yangtze, who first domesticated horses on the steppes of the Ukraine, who hunted giant sloths in the forests of North and South America, and who labored to build the Great Pyramid of Khufu."

Their study was a stepping-off point for other genetic researchers, some of whom, by 2013, held that every person on earth has common ancestors within just the past thousand years.

DNA is the definitive tool to trace human genealogy. It is the build-ing block of life with hereditary material that is the blueprint for all liv-ing organisms. As humans, more than 99 percent of our DNA is like every other human's. But to a scientist's trained eye, microscopic "mark-ers" in our DNA prove we are related specifically to others having the same gene markers.

DNA, mused Jim, could be used to verify standard, often laborious methods of collecting information to document one's genealogy. Errors often creep into names taken from written sources. DNA can conclu-sively prove or disprove a familial link

Answering Jim's original question, Woodward said to analyze the DNA of all 4.6 million people in Norway could cost $500 million. "I don't think you can afford it."

"Oh yes I can!" answered Jim—a reply and ambition that unnerved family and financial advisors. [2]

Woodward convinced Jim it would make more sense to collect and analyze DNA samples from indigenous populations across the world, at a cost of about $50 million—one tenth the cost of testing all of Nor-way. Jim agreed, and hired Woodward to lead the effort. He left BYU to organize and direct the Sorenson Molecular Genealogy Foundation (SMGF).

In a letter to a friend, Jim wrote that "The vision of the Foundation is to promote peace among diverse cultures of the world by demonstrat-ing how closely we are all related using combined genetic and genealogi-cal data. To accomplish this vision, the Foundation is creating the world's largest correlated genetic and genealogical database." [3]

Jim saw other purposes. "We want to be able to cure diseases," he said. "The database is going to be the information goldmine of the future for preventive medicine."

Every cell of the body, except red blood cells, contains a complete set of chromosomes. A common way to gather DNA is by taking a swab from inside the mouth. The chromosome that was then most commonly used for genetic ancestry purposes was the Y Chromosome, the part of the DNA that determines the male gender and paternal lineage. It passes down from father to son, relatively unchanged over time. The mitochondrial DNA, found in both males and females, defines maternal lineage and is also commonly used for genetic ancestry.

Jim renovated warehouse space at company headquarters and created a laboratory, Sorenson Genomics, to analyze DNA samples collected from around the world.

Jim typically wanted to get the biggest bang for his buck out of the lab. "Mr. Sorenson made it clear that we (Sorenson Genomics) were to be more than just a lab to process DNA samples for his molecular genealogy foundation," said Doug Fogg, one of Jim's first hires and Sorenson Genomics' chief operating officer in 2013. Fogg, who helped recruit the lab's scientists and other managers, said Jim "expected us to figure out how to become an economically viable operation, and continually gave us innovative ideas." [4]

"Mr. Sorenson was never a respecter of persons," added Fogg. "He would always value individual comments and contributions. I can't tell you how many times he called me on the phone and said 'Doug, get your team in the boardroom.' We would bring in as many people as we could without disrupting operations.

"He would go around the table and simply ask everybody 'How are you doing? What do you do? Do you have any ideas to share with the group?' I think he was looking primarily for new products and services, not necessarily for process-improvement."

Sorenson Genomics has scored an impressive list of firsts in developing automated processing of DNA samples on a large scale—called "high throughput" by scientific organizations.

In September 2001 Sorenson purchased its first revenue source, GeneTree, based in San Jose, California. Beginning in 1997, GeneTree was the first company to offer DNA paternity testing services online. At the time, paternity of a child typically was determined through blood typing. Following the 2001 acquisition, all DNA lab testing for GeneTree was redirected to Salt Lake City.

The following year, 2002, Sorenson pioneered another new direct-to-consumer DNA company, called Relative Genetics. It was for genealogists who wanted to be certain they had identified ancestors correctly or were up against a brick wall with traditional research and hoped to get around it by establishing an ancestral connection through DNA testing and a matching database.

In 2007 Sorenson acquired Identigene, based in Houston, Texas. Identigene was the first company to commercially offer DNA paternity testing using STR technology, now the gold standard in the industry. Under the Identigene brand name, Sorenson launched the nation's first—and at this writing still its only—over-the-counter DNA paternity test kit, available today in major drugstores and pharmacies including Walgreens, Walmart, CVS, and Rite Aid. A consumer could purchase the kit for about $30, take a mouth swab sample, and send it to Sorenson Genomics, which would analyze and provide the DNA results for about another $130.

DNA activities occupied a substantial portion of Jim's time during the last two to three years of his life. "Every day was a new day with Mr. Sorenson," said Doug Fogg. "He had incredible foresight and ability to envision the future. Mr. Sorenson was way ahead of his time with this ancestral DNA initiative.

"We didn't know when we started where we were going. We just knew that he had a vision, and that if we would support him in that vision, we would go places. And we have."

Jim's enthusiasm wasn't always reciprocated. John Brophy of Sorenson Bioscience recalled one weekly managers meeting when Jim brought a guest, the late Jack Anderson, a family friend from Washington, D.C. and one of the nation's leading newspaper columnists.

"Mr. Sorenson was talking about what he wanted to do with this DNA research," said Brophy, "how he wanted to go into countries and collect samples, and basically prove we're all from the same mother—to bring everyone together."

Brophy continued: "I said 'Mr. Sorenson, you need to be very careful.' He thought you could just go into a country, like a Viking, without getting permission. I said 'You just don't go out and stick people. I know what you want to do, and you know what you want to do, but if people hear there's a company in Utah that's Mormon out collecting DNA samples...

'Mr. Sorenson, this kind of smacks of the 'Boys from Brazil' [a film about German Nazis who escaped to South America]. You have to be very careful. I'm a Catholic; there are 200 million Catholics and 10 million Mormons. Some people think the Mormon Church is a cult, and—'"

Jim exploded, jumping to his feet, face red as a beet. Anderson, himself shaking from advanced Parkinson's disease, grabbed his arm. "Jim, settle down! Listen to the man." [5]

Sorenson's DNA expertise was put to new use following the monster earthquake that struck off the coast of Indonesia the day after Christmas in 2004. The quake, one of the largest ever recorded, unleashed the deep-water tsunami which swamped fifteen coastal countries without warning, killing more than 230,000 men, women, and children.

Thailand was one of the hardest-hit countries, with deaths estimated at more than 8,000 and another 10,000 missing. A Utah businessman named David Rockwood, a friend of Jim's with deep ties to Thailand, brought Sorenson Genomics to the attention of Thai officials. That led to Sorenson's involvement in the disaster.

About forty forensic teams from different nations helped identify Thai victims and associate them with surviving family members. Sorenson Genomics, one of the few DNA labs internationally accredited for verifying human identity, was the only American DNA company involved that provided its services free of charge.

Jim volunteered hundreds of thousands of dollars worth of services to Thailand and its shattered families. A dozen scientists and lab technicians, led by chief scientific officer Lars Mouritsen, received about 500 swabs from tsunami survivors and nearly 1,300 body parts of victims, mostly teeth, hair, tissue, and bones.

It was painstaking work. By the end of May 2005 Mouritsen and his colleagues had analyzed specimens from 800 victims and compared them with more than 500 possible living relatives. The results of this work were provided to the Thai police to help in their efforts to repatriate the remains of tsunami victims. The Sorenson team succeeded in identifying about 100 of the victims.

The work of Sorenson Genomics was of interest to the Thai government for other reasons as well. The country suffered from a rash of kidnapping and murder, and wanted to build its own DNA expertise to help fight crime. Jim paid for a high-level Thai delegation to visit Utah and learn how Sorenson Genomics operated.

A year later, in June 2006, Jim started Sorenson Forensics, a division of Sorenson Genomics. Another Salt Lake company, Myriad Genetics, closed its forensics division to concentrate on developing and marketing cancer genetic tests. Sorenson created its own forensics division largely from the team that had been at Myriad.

The company tests forensic DNA casework samples from human remains sent from within and outside the U.S. The scientists at Sorenson Forensics also consult with state and local governments within the U.S. and with foreign governments who want to build or improve their own forensic crime labs. They have helped design and build labs in several African countries, including Senegal, Nigeria, and Zambia.

Sorenson Forensics, whose work would be familiar to fans of the long-running CBS Television series "CSI,"—Crime Scene Investigation—has made an excellent name for itself in the half-dozen years since its launch. By 2013 it was considered one of the top three private forensic labs in the country.

One heinous crime solved by the lab happened in broad daylight in the heart of Salt Lake City. Ten-year-old Anna Palmer was returning home after playing with friends in the late afternoon of September 10, 1998. She had reached her own doorstep when she was savagely attacked, beaten, and stabbed to death.

Salt Lake law enforcement ran out of clues and the crime became one of the department's most important cold cases.

In 2009 detectives asked Sorenson Forensics to examine the evidence, including clothes. Something else offered the clue they needed. "We determined that fingernails from the victim would be something that might yield...results," said Sorenson's Dan Hellwig, "and we took them into the lab and tested them." [6]

DNA analysts found that Anna, by fighting back, had gathered the evidence pointing to her killer. Her fingernails yielded the DNA of Matthew Breck, who lived just a block away at the time of her murder. By 2011 he was imprisoned in Idaho for a sex-related crime involving a child. In August of that year Breck, then 32, pled guilty to aggravated murder. He will spend the rest of his life in prison.

Sorenson Forensics made headlines in January 2007—just three months after opening for business—for apparently solving three Salt Lake City cold cases in a single week.

Michael Jones, 40, was arrested and charged with the slaying of 28-year-old Tara Cassandra Brennan in February 2004. She was strangled with a belt and stabbed in her car. Jones' DNA was found on the belt as well as on the butt of a cigarette. Three years later he was convicted of killing her.

Michael Waddell Johnson was charged with murder for the 1998 strangulation death of his former wife, Cathy Cobb, 40. Sorenson identified DNA on fingernail clippings taken at the time of Cobb's death as that of Johnson. In 2010 Johnson, then 65, was found guilty of the slaying.

In the third case, Dan L. Petersen, 44, was charged in the stabbing death of 14-year-old Tiffany Hambleton twenty-one years earlier. When Petersen came to trial in August 2007, the case took several bizarre twists. One of the twists unfortunately came from Sorenson Forensics. Lab director Tim Kupferschmid testified that more than one man's DNA was found on Hambleton's fingernails. The following day, however, he retook the stand and said evidence of a second man's DNA was inconclusive: "We couldn't say whether or not it was there."

Sorenson Forensics also found DNA from Petersen's semen on Hambleton—proving, as Petersen then admitted, that he had been lying to law enforcement when he said he did not have sex with the girl. A jury of seven men and three women, however, acquitted Petersen of killing Hambleton. [7]

Forty miles south of Salt Lake City, in Orem, was the scene of another vicious crime. In June 2010 a 19-year-old freshman from rural Utah was attending Utah Valley University. On a warm afternoon she walked just steps from her apartment complex and sat on a bank of the Provo River to jot in her journal.

As she finished writing and headed down the path toward her apartment, a muscular man with dark hair and tattoos on both sides of his neck stepped out of the bushes and pulled her into them. The 5-foot-11, 130-pound teen fought for her life as he wrapped a bootlace around her neck and choked her.

Blacking out briefly, she came to and continued to flail at him as he dragged her deeper into the brush. The man found a cinder block and smashed it against her face so hard that it broke in two. She was still conscious, so he picked up a boulder and hit her again, smashing her face and knocking her out. Then he raped her.

Miraculously, with horrendous injuries, the young woman lived to tell her story.

Law enforcement officials compared notes and learned that a career criminal, Shawn Michael Leonard, 34, had walked away from a jail work release program. Incredibly, he left his calling card—his jail identification bracelet—in the Provo River, lodged against a rock or branch. Leonard apparently threw the id bracelet in the river while washing blood off himself, assuming it would be carried to Utah Lake. He also used the same bootlace to bind the hands of a woman clerk when robbing a boutique later that day. He took the clerk's credit card and car.

A day and a half later police found Leonard in a tent in Juab County, camping out with equipment bought using the stolen credit card.

An open and shut case? Veteran prosecutor Donna Kelly took nothing for granted. "Whenever I start thinking that as a prosecutor, I think about this scene," Kelly told a crime-victims' conference, projecting a slide of O.J. Simpson tugging on a leather glove. Simpson, she reminded the audience, had blood on his socks from both victims, yet he walked free.

Kelly turned to Sorenson Forensics to make her case as airtight as possible. The lab examined the bootlace and found Leonard's DNA, as well as that of the coed and clerk on it. Case closed.

Shawn Michael Leonard was found guilty of attempted murder, among other crimes, and sentenced to life without parole. [8]

One reason Sorenson Forensics has been remarkably successful in cracking such cases is that it uses the very latest technology. Sorenson has solved many cases, for example, with Y-STR analysis, which seeks only the Y chromosome in men, linking blood, hair, or skin cells specifically to their male owners.

DNA evidence usually is so precise that even the worst criminals tend to plead guilty and hope for a bargain when facing it. Sorenson's Kupferschmid says the likelihood of an error in a match can be as low as one in sextillion—21 zeros. "Less than two percent of DNA cases go to trial," he said.

Even more important is the value of DNA in freeing someone wrongly accused of a crime. Early in 2014, for example, two men in Brooklyn, New York were freed after spending more than half their lives behind bars for a murder they did not commit. They were Anthony Yarbough and Sharrif Wilson, convicted in 1992 of murdering Yarbough's mother, 12-year-old sister, and another 12-year-old girl.

At the time of the crime Yarbough was just 18 and Wilson 15. Before DNA evidence absolved them in 2014, they had been in prison 21 years. The evidence that freed them was found on the fingernails of Yarbough's mother, who was 40 when she and the two girls were choked to death with electrical cords and stabbed multiple times.

To date, more than 300 men and women incarcerated in the United States have been exonerated by DNA testing, including 18 who served time on death row. They served an average of 13 years in prison before being released.[9]

Jim Sorenson was delighted that some of his DNA companies served the public and made money. His primary purpose, however, remained world peace, and he continued for the rest of his life to pour millions into the effort. In 2007 his genetic foundation had a database approaching 100,000 samples collected in 170 countries—90 percent of all countries—often in cooperation with local universities.

"We went to every tribal group in Mongolia, for example," explained foundation director Scott Woodward. "Almost universally, when we sit down with the elders in the community, explain that we're building a very large database that connects the people of the world, connects families together, they're intrigued, they're interested, and they almost always participate."[10]

The foundation in 1999 was the first company to offer DNA testing to trace family ancestry. By 2007, reported *Science* magazine, "At least two dozen companies now market 'genetic ancestry tests' to help consumers reconstruct their family histories and determine the geographic origins of their ancestors. More than 460,000 people have purchased these tests over the past 6 years, and public interest is still skyrocketing." [11]

In 2002 Jim had been diagnosed with prostate cancer, but kept going at a fast pace. Increasingly, however, the voice most often heard publicly speaking for the Sorenson companies was that of vice chairman Jim Sorenson Jr., who had long shared leadership duties with his father.

"When the foundation was formed eight years ago," he said, "...my father felt that if people had the answers to [who they were related to] they'd feel differently about one another and it would foster world peace and a greater sense of kinship." [12]

Did Jim Sorenson achieve what he set out to achieve? "Many others have joined what is now a billion-dollar [DNA] effort, and it will continue to grow," said Woodward.

"We may not yet have nations sitting down at the table together, but that definitely has happened in individual cases. We have seen it happen over and over. When people understand that they are probably connected, that changes the way they think about each other, and they treat each other better."

Thinking back to that 2:30 a.m. phone call from Jim in Norway, Woodward said "I learned that Jim made calls like that even in the *same* time zone." He added that "Other people had a hard time connecting the dots, but Jim knew exactly where he wanted to go."

Jim himself said simply, "People want to be connected."

### CHAPTER THIRTY-FOUR

# FOSTERING FAITH,

## Choosing Family Over Fame

J im had one more big dream. In a world torn apart by sectarian strife, use religion instead to pull it together.

In the late 1980s Jim was appointed a board member of the Utah chapter of the National Conference of Christians and Jews. Its mission is to fight religious prejudice and promote understanding and respect among religious groups.

"One day I looked around the table and said 'Where are the Muslims?'" He joined the NCCJ's national board and continued to press for inclusion of the faith claimed by about one in every five people on earth.

Once again Jim was ahead of his time. Before the horrific events of September 11, 2001, relatively few Americans likely had even considered the issue. Jim instinctively knew something must change. The three great mono-theistic religions springing from Father Abraham in the Holy Land must find common ground.

In the last decade and a half of his life, Jim's primary purpose was not making money. "I'm more concerned about basic human values and needs that are shaping the world my grandchildren are growing up in." Youth must be taught "that all human beings have worth...have inalienable rights, and... the ability and responsibility to make choices that respect those values."[1]

Jim put his muscle and his money behind a concerted effort to bring Islam to the table. In 1989 he funded the NCCJ's first international interfaith meeting of the three religions, called the International Scholars Annual Trialogue. Co-sponsor was the Journal of Ecumenical Studies, edited by Leonard Swidler, a noted religion professor at Temple University in Philadelphia.

Similar trialogues had been held in the past, sponsored by other organizations. They brought together leading scholars from each of the three Abrahamic faiths in regions where interreligious tolerance is essential to peace and stability. Academics and political leaders sat together to vigorously but civilly discuss issues facing communities in crisis.

Jim continued to underwrite the event annually, held in the United States, in Graz, Austria; or in Jerusalem, with some sessions at Brigham Young University's Jerusalem Center for Near Eastern Studies. The five-acre BYU campus on Mount Scopus opened to students in May 1988. Beverley's brother, Robert Taylor, who was head of BYU's study abroad program, oversaw the project.

Jim pushed the NCCJ to change its name to be more inclusive and accommodate Islam, no small task given that the venerable organization was founded way back in 1927. (In 1961 President John F. Kennedy said the NCCJ was doing more than "perhaps any other factor in our national life to provide for harmonious living among our different religious groups.")

Jim used an analogy from boyhood: "If there are three boys who want to play [marbles] and the third one isn't invited, there is war."

There were obvious hurdles to engaging Muslims. Jews and Christians have books of the Old Testament in common, and know each other relatively well. A huge cultural gap exists between them and Muslims. Islam as a whole has not fully embraced the Enlightenment, the cultural reformation of society in the seventeenth and eighteenth centuries, based on reason and scientific thought.

Riffet Hassan, 70, a Pakistani-American theologian and leading Islamic feminist scholar of the Qur'an, explained that "If Muslims were to exercise all the human rights granted to humankind by God, they would create a Paradise on earth and have no need to spend their time and energy dreaming about the 'hur' [splendid companions of the opposite sex] promised in the afterlife.

"Unfortunately, at this time the spectrum before us appears very bleak, as more and more human rights disappear under the pressure of mounting fanaticism and traditionalism in many areas of the Muslim world." [2]

Far from discouraging Jim, the challenges whetted his competitive instincts. He set about to court Islam.

Jim's initiatives sparked the interest and support of key figures, including Roman Catholic Bishop William Weigand of Salt Lake City and LDS leaders Gordon B. Hinckley and Thomas S. Monson among Christian leaders, and Theodor (Teddy) Kollek, mayor of Jerusalem, among Jews.

A prominent Swiss Catholic theologian, Hans Küng, observed in 1989: "No peace among nations without peace among religions, no peace among religions without dialogue among the religions." [3]

Kollek was widely esteemed. He was elected mayor of Jerusalem in 1965 and re-elected five times, serving for twenty-eight years. "Jerusalem is the one essential element in Jewish history," said Kollek, who transformed Jerusalem into a modern city. "A body can live without an arm or a leg, not without the heart. This is the heart and soul of it." The city, of course, is also holy to Christians and Muslims. [4]

East Jerusalem was controlled by Jordan from 1948 to 1967, when Israel captured it in the Six-Day War. Within hours of consolidating Jerusalem, Kollek saw to it that milk was distributed to Arab children. He advocated religious tolerance and reached out to the Arab community. Kollek continued to give Muslims access to Al-Aqsa Mosque and Temple Mount for worship.

Jim and Kollek were natural allies, and they forged a strong bond. In 1990 Kollek wrote Jim, reporting the impressions of an Israeli associate who visited Jim in Salt Lake City. "I was very moved to learn of your special love for Jerusalem and your impressions of our city and country," wrote Kollek. He invited Jim to visit Jerusalem and the Jerusalem Center, "one of the city's most beautiful buildings," six weeks later. [5]

Jim answered that he could not come at that time because of business and family commitments, but expressed interest in coming later.

Kollek visited Utah and several European capitals on a trip in 1991. Back in Jerusalem he wrote to say that "despite these [other] travels, the warmth and friendship I experienced during my visit to your part of the world have not dimmed...I did want to thank you again for the lovely breakfast you hosted at the Riverboat. I have fond memories from this occasion." [6]

One of Jim's trips to Israel was for a week in December 1992. Jim Jr. accompanied him, along with son-in-law Gary Crocker, Michael T. Benson, president of Southern Utah University; and an assistant, John Ward. They toured medical device plants and discussed potential joint business ventures; met with officials at two leading universities; spent a social evening at the Jerusalem Center with Kollek and other officials; and experienced violence on the West Bank as their cars were stoned on two occasions, once shattering a large window.

"Yet everywhere I went I met people who have more in common than their day-to-day conflicts will let them admit," wrote Jim. "Even the young people who threw stones at our cars. I'm convinced their actions are a product of the environment...not of any genetic disorder."

During a dinner in Jim's honor at the Jerusalem Center, he was pleasantly surprised to hear a hymn he had written, played on the center's magnificent organ by Mormon Tabernacle Choir organist Robert Cundick and sung by Jim Jr., who has a beautiful tenor voice. The hymn, called "I Do Believe," begins:

> Thou who knowest my ev'ry need,
> Guide me while I try to lead.
> Lead me, help me see so high,
> Thy compass spirit is nearby.

Jim said "this trip reaffirmed my belief that Christians, Jews and Moslems have a common background and underlying set of beliefs that can help them understand each other better."

Jim and his traveling companions proposed several initiatives to strengthen Israeli society, including teaching character education to the very young in public schools and forming youth sports leagues for adolescents of all races and creeds. Back home he met with Larry Miller, owner of the Utah Jazz, to discuss setting up a public sports program in Israel. He kept religious leaders in the U.S. informed of these activities.

Catholic Bishop Weigand of Salt Lake City, in a hand-written note, wrote "Thanks for the periodic information on the Trialogue, truly something important you are doing." [7]

"Jim," wrote Thomas S. Monson of the LDS Church's First Presidency, "you not only see problems, but you also create ways in which to solve them. I am impressed with your plans to improve the education of the young, the attitudes of adolescents and the ecumenism of adults of diverse backgrounds." [8]

In a letter written on Christmas Eve in 1992, Kollek thanked Jim for visiting his country and city, saying "You will be in my thoughts and prayers tonight when I am at Midnight Mass in Bethlehem." Kollek added this handwritten note: "Yesterday the Tabernacle Choir arrived in Jerusalem. We, the whole country is impatiently waiting for the concerts."

A year later the annual NCCJ Trialogue underwritten by Jim was held in Graz, Austria—a city where the three religious groups have lived in uncommon harmony for centuries. Among those Jim lined up to give presentations was Professor Daniel Peterson, a BYU scholar in Arabic and Islamic studies.

After that conference, Gordon B. Hinckley, also a member of the LDS Church's First Presidency, wrote Jim to say Professor Peterson "certainly writes enthusiastically of his participation in the trialogue in Graz. Thank you for what you did to make all of this possible." [9]

Late in 1995 the Sorensons hosted Kollek at their home. On the flight back to Jerusalem, he hand-wrote a note to them. "You all gave us a few unforgettable days, but the evening at your home, with all the many friends and your son's singing your song was no doubt the crowning event. We are now waiting with a prayer for the great event of the video transmission [using Sorenson technology] from Salt Lake City to Jerusalem...With respect, thanks & much love. Yours, Teddy." [10]

Jim kept religious leaders back home informed of his activities in the Middle East.

"I think this effort is a very important one," wrote Dallin H. Oaks, a member of the LDS Church's Quorum of the Twelve Apostles, "and that it is providential that you are involved in it and supporting it. Please keep up the good work..." [11]

"I am pleased to find that your conference in Jerusalem was a success," wrote Elder Hinckley. "You have done a significant thing in adding the Muslims to the gathering of Christians and Jews." [12]

In January 1994 the Trialogue conference was back in Jerusalem. "I hope that we can all remember just one principle," said Jim in welcoming guests the first evening at the Jerusalem Center. "It is the principle that still motivates me as I fund this great gathering. It is the principle of peace. "He continued:

> The children of Abraham are spread across the world—sometimes sep-arated by oceans and mountains, sometimes separated by tradition and dogma. But there is so much more that we have in common as broth-ers and sisters if we will but work to love each other and unite. Unite children of Abraham—all over the world—is the hope that brought us all here. As you continue your discussions this week and as you return to your homes, I hope and pray that you will keep this thought always with you. [13]

Jim's activities led to some light moments. Israel's leading newspaper, *Maariv,* ran a lengthy article on him, complete with a large photo. An Israeli official had it translated from Hebrew to English and sent Jim a copy. In giving his life story, the reporter told about the time Jim got inebriated as a teenager after drinking beer with friends. (It led to his father returning to church and taking Jim with him.)

*Maariv* said "Sorenson returned home drunk as Lot." The story of Lot is in Genesis 19. Lot's two daughters got him drunk with wine. Then, on suc-cessive nights, they lay with him "that we may preserve seed of our father." Each bore him a son.

The creative reporter also wrote that Jim had eight children who worked in his businesses but did not remain with them. "Sorenson admits this was not easy," wrote the reporter, "and in this he resembles a Jewish mother." [14]

Jim, ever the entrepreneur, returned from a trip to Israel with an idea. He had his assistant Gloria Smith make a yamaka—the skull cap, about the size of a small pancake, worn by Jewish men.

Gloria came up with a  black wool felt cap with gold braid on the top and bottom edges. Around the band were five symbols of peace, including the Jewish Star of David, the Muslim crescent, and Christian cross. In the middle of a weekly staff meeting, Jim summoned Gloria, who brought in the yamaka on a cafeteria tray.

Jim explained that while he was in Israel he went to the Western Wall, better known as the Wailing Wall, but was not allowed to touch the wall and say a prayer because he did not have a Jewish cap. Then he turned to John Brophy from Sorenson Bioscience.

"Do you see the idea, John?"

"I'm sorry, Mr. Sorenson, but I don't see it."

"I want to put a vending machine in at the Wailing Wall, selling Jewish hats!"

The idea, for some reason, never went further than that staff meeting.[15]

Jim succeeded in his quest to change the name of the National Council of Christians and Jews. In 1999 it became the National Conference for Community and Justice.

The Sorensons also donated to an ambitious project at Brigham Young University to have Islamic texts in Arabic and Persian translated into English. The first volume rolled off the presses in October 1997. By 2007 thirteen volumes had been produced, under the overall direction of BYU professor of Arabic Daniel Peterson. The project, said Peterson, was designed out of "respect" to the Islamic world and to break stereotypes that the peoples of the Middle East were just "wandering nomads and terrorists."

"My pursuit of peace clearly found its roots in my faith, the Church of Jesus Christ of Latter-day Saints," explained Jim. Interactions with other cultures and religions "did not detract from my core beliefs."[16]

Jim developed a personal relationship with a number of LDS leaders, notably Elder Hinckley, who became the fifteenth president of the Church in March 1995 upon the death of his predecessor Howard W. Hunter. President Hinckley met and corresponded with Jim and once gave him a health blessing in his church office.

President Hinckley, a visionary and creative leader, received the nation's highest civilian honor, the Presidential Medal of Freedom, at the White House in 2004. President George W. Bush said the LDS leader "has inspired millions and has led efforts to improve humanitarian aid, disaster relief, and education funding across the globe."

President Hinckley inaugurated the Church's Perpetual Education Fund (PEF) in 2001, to help lift young church members around the world out of poverty. Recipients between the ages of eighteen and thirty—most of whom have served missions—are loaned money to attend a college or trade school. After graduating they are to pay it back, to be used for other member-students.

Church leaders briefed Jim on the PEF two months before it was announced publicly, and he and Beverley responded by contributing $5 million.

On March 31, in general conference, Hinckley outlined the program. "Where there is widespread poverty among our people, we must do all we can to help them to lift themselves, to establish their lives upon a foundation of self-reliance that can come of training. Education is the key to opportunity."

He added that "We have enough money, already contributed, to fund the initial operation," gifts given "through the goodness and kindness of wonderful and generous friends."

John Carmack, an emeritus general authority, was called to direct the new program. He sent annual reports to Jim and Beverley and other "partners." By the end of 2002 the full program was introduced in Latin America and the Philippines. About 5,800 loans had been made at a cost of $3.9 million and the average loan was $675 for a year of school.

In March 2006 Carmack reported that 22,000 young men and women in 30 countries participated in the program during the previous year. The typed letter included this handwritten note across the top: "Jim, you were there first!"

By 2011 there had been 50,000 participants. Most of those completing the program were employed and earning 300 to 400 percent more than what they had made previously. [17]

Elder Hinckley's presidency was especially noted for building temples. More than half of existing temples were built under his leadership; as president of the Church he dedicated or rededicated eighty-seven temples.

The Church has tens of thousands of chapels across the world for Sunday worship. Temples, considered the "House of the Lord," are not open on the Sabbath. They are reserved for other days of the week when worthy members participate in sacred ceremonies that they consider essential for them and their families—both living and dead—to be together for eternity.

One of the most storied temples was the second one, constructed in Illinois in a small community on a wide bend of the Mississippi River. Early members of the Church fled there after being persecuted and driven out of Ohio and Missouri. The Church bought the small community and named it Nauvoo, interpreted from Hebrew to mean "beautiful city."

In the teeth of continued persecution—Church leader Joseph Smith and his brother Hyrum were assassinated in June 1944 by a mob in nearby Carthage—the Saints built a stately temple at enormous sacrifice. Less than two years later, in the dead of winter, with their lives constantly threatened, they began to cross the Mississippi toward a haven in the West, today's Salt Lake City.

By September 1846 the Nauvoo Temple was in the hands of their tormentors. For two years it stood abandoned, then was set ablaze, apparently by an arsonist, and gutted in November 1848. A tornado finished the destruction less than two years later.

Mormons had anticipated the rebuilding of the Nauvoo Temple for more than a century and a half. In 1998 President Hinckley began talking with Jim and Bev about helping to rebuild it. The Sorensons, after talking it over with their children, said they would be honored to make the donation.

Jim expressed the hope it would be a fully working temple, not just an attractive monument. President Hinckley responded to Jim that his "preliminary reading leads to the conclusion that it would be very difficult to make of it a working temple. However, this is not final..."

The Church Temple Department continued to study the matter and apparently concluded that the cost of rebuilding would be about $30 million. President Hinckley conveyed that figure to the Sorensons, who agreed to contribute it.

Jim turned to an assistant, Duane Toney, who consulted the company's law firm and concluded the donation could be made from Sorenson Development in two payments, $15 million in one year and $15 million in the next tax year. [18]

In closing the spring general conference on April 3, 1999, President Hinckley said "I feel impressed to announce that among all of the temples we are constructing, we plan to rebuild the Nauvoo Temple. A member of the Church and his family have provided a very substantial contribution to make this possible. We are grateful to him."

Jim was thrilled with the announcement, interpreting it to mean the new edifice would be a working temple. Six months later ground was broken for the temple.

On June 27, 2002, the extended Sorenson family was on hand for the dedication. Photographs taken on the temple steps show seventy-three family members—fourteen babies and young children, and fifty-nine adolescents and adults.

By 2007, five years of prostate cancer had taken a toll on Jim. Contrary to all his instincts he was forced to slow down. He maintained a full schedule, including office hours, until December 26. Starting in early January, Jim remained at home, with round-the-clock nursing care.

New Year's day fell on a Tuesday in 2008, so the company's weekly management meeting was moved to the next day. Jim's last meeting with those who would carry on his professional legacy was held in his upstairs bedroom at home in the Holladay suburb of Salt Lake City.

West Price, one of Jim's favorite company presidents, was the first to arrive. "Mr. Sorenson was on his bed. Looked thin," recalled Price. "He asked me to set up chairs in a half-circle around the bed. West did so, taking the first chair on the right.

When the others had arrived, Jim pointed to Price, who started to explain how Sorenson Bioscience did in the year just ended. After one or two sentences, however, Jim interrupted. "West, you have four children, and I think your youngest and oldest are girls, right?"

"Yes, they are."

"Wow, those must be beautiful girls," said Jim. "Have any of you ever seen his wife?" Then he asked about West's two boys: "Those must be two fine young men."

Jim proceeded to the next president. He seemed more interested in the families of his top leaders than he did in their balance sheets.

West was also the last to leave. As he got up to go, Jim grabbed his hand. "Tell that great wife hello for me, and stay after it kid."

Jim took special note of one other temple—to be built in Rexburg, Idaho, the place of his birth. In 2004 President Hinckley had asked the Sorensons to consider contributing $15 million over three years toward its construction.

"My response was that we would be pleased to give $5,000,000 in the year 2004, but we would need to review our situation in the following years," wrote Jim to the executive director of the Temple Department. Further donations for [the temple] will be considered with the input of my advisors, both family and business." [19]

Jim prevailed, and within three months the full $15 million had been donated. "This brings our total temple donations to $55,000,000 over a five-year period..." he reported. [20]

Ground was broken in July 2005 for the Rexburg Temple, which sits on a hillside visible for miles in the pastoral Snake River Valley. It rises nearly 169 feet, about the same height as the Nauvoo Temple. Over 200,000 visitors toured the temple before it was dedicated on February 10, 2008.

Neither Jim nor Gordon B. Hinckley attended the dedication. Each died the previous month within a week of each other, President Hinckley on January 27 at age 97 and Jim on January 20 at 86.

A short time before he passed away, the eight voting shares of Sorenson Development, a relatively small portion of Jim's personal fortune, was gifted to his family, while the rest was bequeathed to the Sorenson Legacy Foundation.

The irrevocable trust still held all the Sorenson Development stock which owned the Abbott stock, worth hundreds of millions of dollars.

As his life ebbed, Jim was concerned about the amount of wealth that would be transferred from under his control to that of his family. He worried that controlling that much money would ruin his children. He also worried that the global work of the genealogy foundation he had started—his own public legacy—would not continue to be funded.

Another drama unfolded during Jim's last days. He considered leaving as much as $400 million to the Sorenson Molecular Genealogy Foundation (SMGF), to carry on his dream of fostering world peace by linking families across the globe through their DNA. He was concerned about what would become of the vision and the work he had started when he was no longer there to champion it.

Jim Jr., who had worked closest with his father, sat by his bedside and reasoned with him. He urged his father to trust his family. "I reminded him that his children and their spouses were responsible people, and that he ought to trust his family with the  wealth he had given them." Jim believed his siblings would continue to fund the SMGF.

Days before he died on January 20, 2008, Jim chose family over further fame and his public persona. He gifted the voting shares of Sorenson Development to his children.

Jim had ended his autobiography, *Finding the Better Way,* by saying of his 47 grandchildren: "More than my millions, this is my greatest joy, my greatest hope, and the continuing accomplishment of my greatest goal."

About a week before his death, the eight Sorenson children reverently entered his bedroom. As they surrounded the bed, Jim brightened. "Ah, here is my legacy!"

# EPILOGUE

**M**illions of people across the globe experience less suffering—and many of them survival itself—because of Jim Sorenson. He was one of the world's greatest inventors of medical devices.

"If Jim was coming up today and not in the '70s," mused one former aide, "would he be as successful? I think he probably would have been more successful now. He came up in an era when innovation was very structured—R&D programs, trials, and tests. His type of creativity is exactly what happens today in the dot.com world, in social media. He was before his time."

However, Jim and his fellow inventors had one advantage not available today: the absence of strict regulation by the U.S. Food and Drug Administration. Many of Jim's most important inventions predate the Medical Device Regulation Act, signed into law by President Gerald Ford in 1976. The new law required that devices be approved by the FDA as safe and effective before they could be marketed to the public.

Federal regulators would not have stopped Jim, but they could have frustrated and inhibited his hands-on approach. If one of his devices was not working properly, Jim or a colleague was known to fly all night to a doctor or hospital, bringing whatever was needed to alter or repair the device on the spot—a response highly unlikely to satisfy FDA bureaucrats.

Since Jim's death, even the U.S. Supreme Court has underscored the value of DNA as he envisioned it when sparking a new industry. Jim pioneered and helped popularize the global use of DNA tests to link families together. By 2007 the Sorenson Molecular Genealogy Foundation (SMGF) had collected more than 100,000 cheek-swab samples in 170 countries, and was the first organization to offer DNA testing kits associated with extended pedigrees to trace family ancestry. More than 460,000 people had purchased kits by then. Since the beginning of SMGF, more than a dozen other companies have sprung up doing similar work.

In June 2013, the Supreme Court ruled 5-4 that police can take a cheek swab for an arrestee's DNA, calling it the twenty-first century's equivalent of fingerprinting.

Jim, however, was right to have concerns about the future of the genealogy foundation. In the years before Jim's death, Sorenson Development and the Sorenson Legacy Foundation (SLF) gave tens of millions of dollars to the SMGF. Following his death the amount of support declined. Jim Jr., his mother and a few of his siblings, tried to make a case for the family to continue to support what had meant so much to Jim in the later years of his life. Other siblings and their spouses were not supportive.

Beverley had a 50 percent allocation in bequests from the SLF; the eight children shared the other 50. Following his death, during Beverley's lifetime the support continued from Beverley's, Jim Jr's and a few other of her children's gifting allocations. That funding declined and later stopped when Jim Jr. left the Legacy Foundation and established the Sorenson Impact Foundation.

Jim Jr. was also one of three board members of the SMGF. He was able to find a home for the work that had begun that would carry it forward to a much more scalable future. In March 2012 the board sold the foundation's data base——100,000 names gathered from across the globe——to Ancestry.com, the largest online community and resource for family history.

The database was a valuable addition to the Ancestry.com DNA genealogy offerings and fulfilled Jim's dream of making the foundation's data base readily available throughout the world to connect people with their ancestors.

Jim's intuitive belief that all humans are connected in the relatively recent past has recently been underscored by some prominent genetic scientists, who hold that our most recent common ancestor (MRCA) lived just within the past thousand years.

Most other Sorenson companies likewise have been sold by the Sorenson Legacy Foundation, comprised of most Sorenson children, since Jim's death. Other firms are being liquidated over time. Notable companies still owned by the family at this writing include Sorenson Forensics, part of Sorenson Genomics, the one operating company still owned by the family. White Sage Ranch, Rosecrest, North Village, and Missouri Flats are all part of the real estate empire Jim amassed during his lifetime, and are still owned by the foundation.

Sorenson Media also continues, largely owned by James Lee Sorenson and the Sorenson Impact Foundation. Sorenson Research Park was subdivided and distributed to four individual family owners and a small company owned by the eight children.

Jim Sorenson was more than a genius inventor. He was a genius entrepreneur, who never lost sight of the fact that no innovation is of worth until it is in the skillful hands of those who can put it to its intended purpose. Doing so widely made Jim successful and very wealthy. His creations were far from random. Throughout his life Jim was a need-seeker, passionate only about pursuits that held real promise of making someone else's life or society itself better.

A testament to Jim's genius came from other professionals who witnessed it up close. Twice he left medical-device companies he created or helped create. Both times those who remained behind or acquired what he built did their level best to prevent him from competing against them in the future.

The CEO of industry giant Abbott Laboratories, in purchasing Sorenson Research for $100 million, insisted on a contract preventing Jim from producing new inventions for five years "because I could never start a company from scratch like you've done...Abbott has to be protected against what you might do again."

Deseret Pharmaceutical, founded by Jim and two partners in 1956, was the start of Utah's medical-device industry. Today the state has more than 110 such firms, along with some 5,000 tech-related companies.

Jim's entrepreneurial prowess led to significant contributions in a wide variety of industries as he launched dozens of businesses during his lifetime.

In his published autobiography, *Finding the Better Way,* he offered "nuggets of wisdom" that guided his own success. They include: Never stop growing, but maintain your balance. Find your rhythm and stay in it; pace yourself. Learn something every day. Study the tree and put your basket where the apples will fall. Think, then tell, then do. Never dwell on the negative. Have courage to bet on yourself. Don't sell yourself short. Find a "better way!"

Jim saw other important needs and thought large. The last couple decades of his life were largely devoted to nothing less than world peace.

He pursued it by becoming a leader in the National Conference of Christians and Jews and urging inclusion of the third great monotheistic faith, Islam. Jim led the campaign that succeeded in changing the organization's name to the more inclusive National Conference for Community and Justice.

He sponsored a series of three-party international conferences that brought together prominent Christians, Jews, and Muslims to discuss differences and possible accommodation on a variety of issues dividing them.

Jim was a loner at heart whose candor sometimes wounded others. He craved quiet but, with eight children at home, seldom found it there. As a young man in California he loved exploring the foothills of the high Sierras, especially in springtime. Starting as a young married man he spent many lunch hours hiking among the sagebrush on Salt Lake's east bench.

"Often my hikes in the mountains cause my thoughts to return to family," he wrote. "When my father died at age 90, I escaped to the mountains to find solace. I hiked for hours in solitude as I felt my grief. Other times in the mountains are joyous."

Jim was a philosopher who filled hundreds of pages with his unique approach to maintaining balance in all aspects of life, and what he saw as the immutable law of threes—essential everywhere, from the number of legs under a milk stool to the Christian diety of God the Father, Jesus Christ, and the Holy Ghost.

He couldn't sing a note but compensated by writing poetry that became lyrics in music written by others. On love, perhaps he revealed himself in writing that "To love deeply is a daring and courageous act. It's scary to expose tenderness, to give of yourself."

He also saw the potential for great wealth to harden a man's heart and cost him love. "I wonder if Hell is the loneliness of having everything and knowing that it's still not enough," he wrote. "I think of Howard Hughes in his last years, an expert at manipulating and using people to do his will.

"[Hughes was] a master at the art of exercising power, ending up a lonely old man, surrounded by hired servants and favor seekers and wondering why so few people loved him...I do not want people to be afraid of me, to obey me sullenly and begrudgingly rather than freely, out of love."

In his autobiography, Jim included just one sentence in bold face: *"True wealth comes through health and family and friends."*

Those who felt his love the most, or at times the absence of it, were members of his own family, starting with his highly accomplished wife, Beverley Taylor Sorenson. Through more than sixty sometimes tumultuous years, she encouraged, loved, and forgave Jim, and defended him to their children and others.

A popular Mormon aphorism is "No other success can compensate for failure in the home." Beverley made it possible for Jim to aim for one star after another, knowing she had his back at home.

At this writing their posterity includes eight children—all of them married and living in Salt Lake Valley—along with forty-seven grandchildren and more than sixty-five great-grandchildren.

Remarkably, Beverley, who passed away in May of 2013, was personally involved in the individual lives of their huge family, writing individual birthday cards and seeing that each one got a wrapped gift at Christmas. An annual ritual was holding a huge family Christmas party at Jim and Beverley's home and directing their eight children with their families to the individual rooms where a cornucopia of gifts awaited them. Tangible evidence of a life of accomplishment.

Jim remained in the chase right to the end of his eighty-six years. After he was diagnosed with prostate cancer six years previously, he quoted American philosopher Horace Kallen:

There are persons who shape their lives by the fear of death and persons who shape their lives by the joy and satisfaction of life. The former live dying, the latter die living. I know that fate may stop me tomorrow, but death is an irrelevant contingency. Whenever it comes, I intend to die living.

Near the end of his life, when asked why he did not take it a bit easier, he said "Because I want to leave something behind."

No one can doubt that Jim succeeded.

# APPENDIX

U.S. Patents awarded to James LeVoy Sorenson et al.

| Granted | Number | Abstract |
|---------|--------|----------|
| July 2, 1963 | 3,095,972 | Self-sealing sterile packaging and method. A packaging structure to store equipment such as surgical tools in sterile condition, which permits pulling off an end of a flexible sac or envelope for the tools as needed. |
| Nov. 17, 1964 | 3,157,277 | Sterile packaging (also see above). A sterile packaging structure which permits removal of the packaging from one part of the equipment during medical or other procedures while maintaining a sterile condition for the part still covered. |
| May 25, 1965 | 3,185,150 | Intravenous catheter placement unit. A sterile unit for making a venipuncture and changing from a needle in a vein to a tube leading to the vein without the need for touching any of the parts that actually enter the body. The unit may be simultaneously connected to an intravenous feeding set. |

| July 26, 1966 | 3,262,448 | Intravenous catheter placement unit. Improvements in a unit highly desirable for placing an intravenous catheter for parenteral infusions into the body. It embodies a plastic sheath that protects the catheter before and during its advancement. |
| January 10, 1967 | 3,297,030 | Catheter placement unit with removable cannulated needle. It provides a unit constructed so that the cannulated needle is completely freed from the catheter as the needle is withdrawn from the body of a patient at the same time as completion of catheter advancement. |
| June 13, 1967 | 3,324,853 | Intravenous catheter protector unit. Includes a needle-support means for protecting the patient and catheter from the pointed end of the needle. Needle support includes an elongated block having a lower surface attached to the patient and an upper surface with a groove to hold the pointed end of the needle immobile, protecting both the patient and the catheter. |
| September 3, 1968 | 3,399,674 | Catheter placement unit. Highly desirable for use with infants and or surface veins such as those on the back of the hand. Constructed so that the placement of the catheter in a body vein is extremely simple and rapid. During placement, the needle cannot turn or rotate relative to the catheter. |
| August 5, 1969 | 3,459,183 | Catheter placement unit with anesthetic. Unit includes a hollow needle and a flexible catheter in telescopic relationship and movable relative to each other. A unit can carry a supply of local anesthetic for application subcutaneously prior to venipuncture; a blood sample being obtained in the same receptacle that carries the anesthetic immediately after venipuncture. |
| August 26, 1969 | 3,463,152 | Catheter placement unit. (An enhancement of the invention immediately above. |

| April 14, 1970 | 3,506,014 | A brassiere with floating cup-supplementing breast supporting strip or panel means of which each breast supporting portion is separately adjustable from one central part of the brassiere. Each breast cup is separately and quickly adjustable through the cleavage of the brassiere without the necessity of removing any outer garments. The benefit to the wearer is uniformity in appearance of the breasts. [Patent awarded to LeVoy's] |
|---|---|---|
| February 2, 1971 | 3,559,643 | Catheter placement unit. For the sterile insertion of a catheter into a body lumen through an incised opening in the lumen wall for parenteral infusion and other purposes. Unit has no puncturing needle and provides extremely easy and rapid insertion of the catheter even under extreme conditions. |
| December 7, 1971 | 3,625,216 | A disposable bag for disposition between a source of suction and a container for collecting drainage from the body of a patient after severe wounding of or surgery performed on the patient. The bag and cover are discarded after use with a single patient or whenever desired, never being exposed to open air. |
| July 11, 1972 | 3,675,891 | Continuous catheter flushing apparatus. Provides continuous flushing of intravascular catheters in systems for monitoring conditions in the thoracic cavity during surgery, in cardiovascular diagnostic labs, etc. Equipped to limit flushing to a small amount of solution or for fast flushing with a much larger amount. |
| August 1, 1972 | 3,680,560 | Vacuum drainage-collecting apparatus with disposable liner. A new type of receptor for receiving drainage from a patient from a severe wound or excess of fluid. It includes a canister, a removable cover for the canister, a disposable liner-receiver for removable insertion in the canister, tubular means for connecting the interior of the liner through the cover to a tube leading from the body of a patient, and means to connect the canister and liner with a suction system. |

| | | |
|---|---|---|
| August 22, 1972 | 3,685,517 | Aseptic disposable drainage receiver. For receiving drainage from a patient after a wounding or surgery. The receiver includes a canister cover and flexible canister liner, means for connecting the canister and liner to a vacuum or suction system and the liner to a tube from the patient, and means to completely seal connections to the liner, so the liner and cover with its contents may be aseptically disposed of. |
| March 6, 1973 | 3,719,197 | Aseptic suction drainage and valve system. (Also see patent immediately above.) Foolproof valve prevents contaminated drainage from entering the suction or vacuum system of a hospital, regardless of carelessness or neglect of an attendant as to how full the drainage receiver may become. Automatically protects the main vacuum system of a hospital from contamination. |
| April 17, 1973 | 3,727,613 | Safety catheter placement assembly. Enables safe handling and placement with assurance against separation of the parts, and safe use of the needle as a stiffener for a catheter while advancing in a blood vessel lumen. The catheter and needle are positively but separably connected. Earlier catheters presented the danger of unintentional separation, which may result in blood spillage, resulting in injury or damage to the patient or attending physician. |
| January 22, 1974 | 3,786,810 | Placement apparatus for positioning an elongated element in a body lumen. The element may be connected to an apparatus for indicating or recording central arterial pulse wave-forms and other heart actions. The element is advanced relatively to a needle into a body lumen by pulling or pushing its sheath through an opening in the needle hub. It can monitor monitors venous or arterial pressure from the point of entry into a body lumen to the thoracic cavity at or adjacent to the heart. |

| February 4, 1975 | 3,863,634 | Aseptic suction system and valve for body fluids from either a living patient or a cadaver. Often in a hospital a single vacuum system is utilized which extends from floor to floor. Contamination of such a system results in a highly costly expenditure and time to de-contaminate the system. All parts of this system are plainly visible from across a room, whereby even a casual or careless inspection by an attendant indicates when flow of fluid from a body has stopped, and whether the fluid receiver should be removed and replaced with another. |
|---|---|---|
| April 1, 1975 | 3,874,369 | Method of monitoring venous or arterial pressure. Accomplished with the aid of an elongated element comprising a blood pressure-transmitting vehicle positioned in a body lumen. The element may be connected to an apparatus for indicating or recording central arterial pulse wave forms and other heart actions. Monitoring may be done during the advancement of the distal end of the element from the point of entry to its desired ultimate position, and thereafter. |
| April 15, 1975 | 3,877,428 | Variable infusion control device. A device for selectively controlling the rate of administration of fluids parenterally to a patient. The device provides attachment fittings which allow it to be placed at any point along a supply tube between a reservoir and the patient. The control valve achieves the precise flow rate through the use of a metering capillary having a variable effective length interposed between two fluid communication ports. |
| November 2, 1976 | 3,989,046 | Aseptic disposable rigid receiver for body drainage. Includes two or more sections, each equipped with means for interlocking with another section when snapped together to provide a fluid-tight joint. The collector may be disposed of, empty or full, in an aseptic manner or emptied and reused on the same patient. |

| | | |
|---|---|---|
| February 8, 1977 | 4,006,745 | Autologous transfusion system and method. Comprises at least two interconnected blood receptacles, the first of which is evacuated and connected to a suction device for aspirating blood. The second receptacle takes blood from the first by overcoming the vacuum in the first with a greater vacuum in the second, without interrupting the ability of the suction device to simultaneously aspirate blood. The second receptacle may comprise a transfer bag for reinfusion into the patient. |
| July 5, 1977 | 4,033,345 | Autologous transfer filter system and method (see immediately above). The second receptacle is selectively exposed to positive pressure to force blood through the filter assembly and expel the blood from the second receptacle into the transfer bag or patient. |
| September 13, 1977 | 4,047,626 | Autologous blood system and method. (An enhancement of patent 4,006,745 above) |
| March 21, 1978 | 4,079,738 | Needle-restraining apparatus. Used with a venipuncture device having a stylet needle that fits telescopically within a catheter. The invention prevents longitudinal movement of the needle through the catheter during the venipuncture process. |
| July 11, 1978 | 4,099,528 | Double lumen cannula. Mounted upon a hub and constructed to penetrate the human vascular system. The assembly has an interior cannula and, spaced from it, an exterior cannula. A bushing is normally situated in the space to facilitate venipuncture without damaging the tissue. After venipuncture the bushing is removable by withdrawing it through the hub. |
| August 15, 1978 | 4,106,621 | Combination needle cover and venipuncture device tray and method of using same. When opened it serves as a combination needle cover and venipuncture device tray from which the device may be withdrawn or inserted with one hand without having to apply any force to the package. |

September 30, 1980  4,224,943    Cannula and method for bidirectional blood flow. The cannula is constructed to provide a bifurcated flow path, each branch of the flow path independently communicating through telescoping cannulae and a venipuncture needle initially projecting beyond the exterior cannula to facilitate venipuncture. Thereafter it is removed from the venipuncture site to permit unobstructed simultaneous fluid flow in opposite directions through each of the bifurcated flow paths.

August 21, 1990    4,951,151    Image display system and method. Computer-operated projectors are positioned to project onto an uneven surface or relief map prepared to reflect a remote surface. If the remote surface is geographical, the horizontal scale is substantially larger than the vertical scale. A second substrate or movie screen and projector are positioned to provide related video images.

June 30, 1992    5,125,923    Laser surgical instrument. Embodied as a handpiece supportable on the wrist and forearm of a surgeon. The handpiece is connected by an umbilical cord to a remote console. An internal shutter mechanism is actuated by steady finger pressure applied by the surgeon. An annular aiming beam is projected through an aperture in a physical distance gauge to focus concentric with the surgical laser beam.

January 26, 1993    5,181,916    Surgical probe and smoke eliminator. A handpiece for use in a laser surgical procedure. It directs a surgical agent to a target area of a person's body which produces an unwanted smoke plume. The handpiece includes a probe for directing a surgeon, such as a $CO_2$ laser beam, and a smoke eliminator for suctioning the smoke created by the procedure.

| September 7, 1993 | 5,242,474 | Dual mode laser smoke evacuation system with sequential filter monitor and a vacuum compensation. Includes a sensor positioned at the surgical site to determine the need for evacuation. A vacuum pump draws smoke from the site through a system of conduits including an in-line filter. A sensor determines changes in the pressure drop across the filter, and is connected to vacuum pump to maintain a constant flow across the filter. |
| --- | --- | --- |
| November 29, 1994 | 5,368,017 | Apparatus for ventilating and aspirating the lungs of a patient. Delivers respiratory gases to the trachea and the congested lungs and breathing passageways. It includes a flexible catheter tube extended into and withdrawn from the patient's trachea. Enables a user to insert a flexible catheter tube into either lung of a patient in one smooth motion, without risk of contamination or infection. |
| November 21, 1995 | 5,468,239 | Apparatus and methods for using a circumferential light-emitting surgical laser probe. The burning laser comprises a conical surface at the distal end of a probe of the laser. The surface is designed to direct the laser light, which is emitted through the interior metal lumen of the laser probe, so that the laser light is redirected perpendicular to the longitudinal axis of the laser probe. The laser light is provided by a carbon dioxide laser which is attached at the proximal end of the laser probe. It gives a laser light emission that is polarized in a circular form about the laser device. This results in an approximately 90% efficient use of laser light emission. |
| May 7, 1976 | 5,513,628 | Apparatus and method for ventilating and aspirating. Accommodates a wide variety of commercially available suction catheters. The adapter comprises a catheter carrier and a manifold assembly that may be attached to a patient for an extended period, while the catheter is constructed as a single procedural use disposable device. The system effects an introduction of a catheter through a normally closed valve structure carried by the manifold assembly. |

| | | |
|---|---|---|
| February 4, 1997 | 5,598,840 | Apparatus and method for ventilation and aspiration. (An enhancement of the previous invention.) |
| August 11, 1998 | 5,791,337 | Apparatus and method for ventilating and aspirating. (An enhancement of the previous invention.) |
| October 26, 1999 | 5,972,317 | Composition and method for treating diseased nails. Used for delivering a medicament through nails, claws, hoofs, or other similar hardened tissue of dermal derivation. Includes a proteolytic enzyme component which facilitates permeation of substances through the hardened nail or keratin tissue, and a medicament component selected to treat a specific disease. The nail-permeable medication means is particularly useful for treating onychomycosis of the fingernail or toenail, and avoids the need for more drastic modalities, such as removal of the nail. |
| October 10, 2000 | 6,129,699 | Portable peristaltic pump for peritoneal dialysis. Existing systems have these disadvantages: Flow rates tend to be either fixed or irregular; flows are unidirectional; costs are prohibitively high for disposability; operation is excessively complicated, unduly limiting the home-care user. This system is small and light-weight. It has a micro-evacuator device wherein electronic circuitry enables regulated flow rates in alternate directions. It is an inexpensive, high-volume portable pump which can reduce health-care costs and enhance patient comfort and convenience. |
| May 22, 2001 | 6,234,992 | Portable peristaltic pump for peritoneal dialysis. (An enhancement of the previous invention.) |

| July 5, 2005 | 6,913,590 | Apparatus and method for peritoneal dialysis. For end-stage renal decline and failure, enabling ambulatory transfer of dialysate to and from the peritoneum of a renal patient. The system is unobtrusive and less restrictive of patient ambulation and orientation. It is sufficiently simple for use in a home-care environment. It may be designed to incorporate real-time, interactive or remote monitoring and regulation and visual or audible indication of system pressures, chemical balances and other important variables. |
|---|---|---|
| November 15, 2005 | 6,965,791 | Implantable biosensor system, apparatus and method. Includes an enzymatic sensor probe from which subcutaneous and interstitial glucose levels may be inferred. The assembly may be associated by direct percutaneous connection with electronics, such as for signal amplification, display, and storage. Irritation of tissues surrounding the probe is minimized due to ease of flexibility and small cross-section of the sensor. |
| June 5, 2007 | 7,228,160 | System, apparatus and method for inferring glucose levels within the peritoneum with implantable sensors. Includes an oxygen sensor from which glucose levels in the vicinity of the peritoneal cavity may be inferred. The sensor assembly may be associated with electronics, such as any or all of a DC power supply, an LED source of blue light, a photoreceptor for red light, a CPU, and transceiver, by a direct percutaneous connection. |
| June 19, 2007 | 7,232,425 | Apparatus and method for specific interstitial or subcutaneous diffusion and dispersion of medication. A medication discharge assembly useful in patient systems, includes a tubular element and a stylet. In a first, closed position, the stylet is seated within the tubular element and may provide a piercing point facilitating insertion of the tubular element to a treatment site. In a second, open position, the stylet is removed from the tubular element, and the element provides a travel pathway for a drug introduced to the tubular element at a proximate connection port. |

| April 6, 2010 | 7,691,326 | System for noninvasive extraction, secure handling and storage and facile processing of a [human] specimen. Includes in particular noninvasive extraction of buccal cells, specifically directed to capture of PCR-ready DNA from cheek cells. Invention includes a testing wand, a container which defines a storage region configured to receive and releasably retain the wand, a structure for sealing the storage region, and a fluid storage reservoir disposed within the container. [Patent applied for by Sorenson Genomics in 2002] |
| June 7, 2011 | 7,957,907 | Method for molecular genealogical research. A research and record-keeping system and method for identifying commonalities in haplotypes (sets of DNA variations that tend to be inherited together) and other genetic characteristics of two or more individual members of a biological sample. Especially useful in corroborating and improving the accuracy of genealogical data, and identifying previously unknown genetic relationships [Patent applied for by Sorenson Molecular Genealogy Foundation in 2002] |

# SOURCES

J ames LeVoy Sorenson himself was the most important source for
this book. I interviewed him a number of times over a six-month
period in 1998 when writing the first half-dozen chapters of *True
Wealth*. Then, seemingly uncomfortable with the breadth of my research,
which occasionally cast him in an unfavorable light, Jim stopped cooperat-
ing. He subsequently died in 2008.

Three years later I approached his widow, Beverley Taylor Sorenson,
asking for access to her late husband's private papers to put the book back
on track. To her credit, Beverley not only gave me unfettered access to his
papers, she agreed that I could and indeed should tell his story "warts and
all."

Jim Sorenson left behind a treasure trove of papers, organized chrono-
logically into about two dozen four-inch-thick black or white binders. The
binders include, notably, details of key inventions and patents protecting
them; Jim's entrepreneurial activities; other business and personal correspondence; his musings on a wide variety of topics; copies of contracts and
other agreements; and clippings from newspapers, periodicals, and other
public sources.

Additional loose leaf binders yield original correspondence from Sorenson to his parents and siblings when he was serving a two-year mission in New England for The Church of Jesus Christ of Latter-day Saints. His letters were hand-written starting in July 1942, then typed from that September through the balance of his time in New England.

Binders also include a half-dozen or so aborted attempts to write his biography or autobiography; a retrospective on his career; the history of Deseret Pharmaceutical; voluminous writings on his personal philosophy; and pages of poetry and music lyrics.

Through the years Sorenson cooperated to a degree with other writers seeking to tell his story. Some of their manuscripts—apparently never published, with one exception—are among his papers. The exception was his 109-page autobiography, self-published in 1993. Its title is *Finding the Better Way: The Life and Outlook of James LeVoy Sorenson.* He acknowledged seven writers who over the years helped gather and organize his thoughts.

Sorenson self-published several other books, including one with poetry or prose by himself and family members, called *Just Love the People: The World is Our Family.* Another similar, relatively short book is called *Loving Thoughts, Memories and Meditations.*

A final soft-cover volume, published by Bookcraft in 2001, explains his unique philosophy of life and is called *Finding True Balance: Great Balancing Acts of Life.*

Unless otherwise noted, quotations, narratives, and commentary attributed to Sorenson are from one of these sources or from the author's interviews with him.

Beverley Sorenson gave freely of her time in more than two dozen interviews prior to her own death in May 2013. These sessions took place at their home in the Holladay suburb of Salt Lake City, where Jim's papers were kept.

Beverley's own biography, *Look Beyond the Weeds: The Life of Beverley Taylor Sorenson,* was written with the help of Alison Armstrong Taylor and Tom Taylor, and self-published in 2012. Unless otherwise noted, quotes or summaries attributed to her in *True Wealth* are from my interviews with Bev or from her biography.

Professional colleagues as well as relatives and friends of Jim were also interviewed. Most are identified below in the endnotes of each chapter.

Finally, various medical authorities, both living and dead, were consulted. Especially helpful was the *Journal of the American Medical Association* (*JAMA*).

## PROLOGUE

1. Louise Gluck.

2. Miles D. White, keynote speech, James LeVoy Sorenson: A Giant in Our City, February 15, 2006.

### CHAPTER ONE
### TOUGH START FOR TEEN PARENTS

3. The early history of the Sorenson family in part is from documents compiled by family historian David L. Sorenson.

4. *Millard County Chronicle,* February 10, 1944.

5. History of Joseph Leonard Sorenson, by David L. Sorenson, 4.

6. This incident is found in a life sketch written by Joseph Leonard Sorenson and kept in a scrapbook by his grandson, James LeVoy Sorenson.

7. From the Ernest and Margaret Blaser Family History, undated, compiled by their children.

8. Joseph Smith 1:16-17, in the *Pearl of Great Price*, an LDS scripture.

9. Serialized novel appeared in the *Rexburg Journal*, including on January 7, 1921.

10. *Rexburg Journal*, circa 1916.

11. James LeVoy Sorenson overheard the conversation, referring negatively to his father. Found on p. 15 of an undated interview transcript in family files, called "More than Millions."

12. From a tape-recorded interview of Joseph LeVoy Sorenson in family files.

13. From a paper written by Joseph LeVoy, in family files.

14. From a paper written about her parents by Eileen when she was an adult.

15. *New West* magazine, December 1920.

### CHAPTER TWO
### "MENTALLY RETARDED"

1. "Tow Sack Tattler," unknown author, from Walter J. Stein, *California and the Dust Bowl Migration* (Westport, Connecticut: Greenwood Press, 1939), preface.

2. John Steinbeck, *The Grapes of Wrath* (New York City: Penguin Books USA., 1996 edition), 331.

3. Ibid, 77.

4. Marjorie Gordon, *Changes in Harmony: An Illustrated History of Yuba and Sutter Counties* (Windsor Publications, Inc, 1988)

5. *Deseret News*, see above.

6. Display ad is found in Jacqueline Lowe, Julia Stark, and Danae McDougal-Stewart, *Worth Keeping: An Architectural History of Sutter & Yuba Counties.* Locally published by unknown source, 1990.

7. *Changes in Harmony.*

8. Transcript of tape-recorded interview by David Sorenson.

9. Eileen Sorenson Smith, paper written in August 1977, found in family files.

10. "The Dyslexic Reader," published quarterly by the Davis Dyslexia Association International, Burlingame, California. Online at http://www.dyslexia.com.

11. Ronald D. Davis with Eldon Braun, "Adult Dyslexia and ADD: Effects in the Workplace," The Davis Dyslexia Association, 1998.

CHAPTER THREE
## A GIVING HEART

1. "Yakob Strauss" was committed to paper by Emma Sorenson in about 1976. Jim's sister, Eileen Sorenson Smith, has the original sheet with Emma's hand-written version.

2. Described in family papers written by Eileen.

CHAPTER FOUR
## BOY INNOVATOR

16. Interview with Gloria Backman, April 20, 2012.

17. Samuel Eliot Morison, *Oxford History of the American people* (Great Britain: Oxford University Press, 1965), 939.

18. From a paper written by Emma in 1985, called "Incidents From Emma Sorenson's Life," in family files.

19. Interview with William Gamboa, May 2, 1998.

20. 1939 and 1940 Lincoln Union yearbooks, pages 38 and 42 respectively.

21. Interview with Gloria Backman, April 20, 2012.

22. The history of the California cling peach industry is available in a number of books, including Frank A. Van Konynenburg, *75 Years of History with the California Canning Peach Association* (Lafayette, California: California Canning Peach Association, 1997).

23. Quote from LaFollette Committee and Elbert Thomas conclusion are both in Cletus E. Daniel, *Bitter Harvest, a History of California Farmworkers, 1870 - 1941* (University of California Press, 1982), 283-84.

24. "Women in the Fruit-Growing and Canning Industries in the State of Washington," Bulletin of the Women's Bureau, No. 47, U.S. Department of Labor, Washington, D.C., 1926.

CHAPTER FIVE
## BEVERLY BORN IN IDYLLIC FAMILY

1. B.H. Roberts, *The Life of John Taylor* (Salt Lake City, Utah: Bookcraft, 1963), 27-28.

2. *Deseret News*, January 3, 1882.

3. *Teachings of Presidents of the Church, John Taylor* (Salt Lake City, Utah: LDS Church, 2001), 82-83.

4. The following description of the martyrdom is from "An Eyewitness Account," by John Taylor, in family files.

5. *Doctrine and Covenants* 135:3, a Scripture of The Church of Jesus Christ of Latter-day Saints.

6. *Deseret News*, September 17, 1856.

7. Joseph Smith, *Teachings of the Prophet Joseph Smith*, ed by Joseph Fielding Smith and others (Salt Lake City: Deseret Book, 1938), 224.

8. Matthias F. Cowley, "Reminiscences of Pres. John Taylor," typescript of a speech at

the LDS University Breakfast Club, October 4, 1925. Church History Department Archives.

9. Julia Neville Taylor, "An interview with Ezra Oakley Taylor, Son of President John Taylor," the Family and LDS Church History Department Archives, microfilm, 2.

10. See Richard L. Jensen, "The John Taylor Family," *Ensign* (LDS Church monthly periodical), February 1980.

11. Roberts, *The Life of John Taylor*, 393, 399.

12. *Wilford Woodruff, Discourses of Wilford Woodruff*, ed by G. Homer Durham (Salt Lake City: Bookcraft, 1946), 208-18.

13. Richard L. Jensen, "The John Taylor Family," *Ensign*, February 1980.

14. Ibid.

15. J. Lewis Taylor (a great-grandson), compiler, *The Life of George Hamilton Taylor*, 2004, in family files.

16. The description of the Taylors' family life is from author interviews with Beverley Taylor Sorenson and from Alison and Tom Taylor, *Look Beyond the Weeds: The Life of Beverley Taylor Sorenson*, self-published, 2012.

### CHAPTER SIX
## FIRST LOVE

1. John S. McCormick, "The Great Depression," *Utah History Encyclopedia* (Salt Lake City: University of Utah Press, 1994).

2. *Look Beyond the Weeds*, 10.

3. *Deseret News*, March 29, 2005.

4. *The New York Times*, March 30, 2005.

5. *New York Herald Tribune*, April 4, 1963.

### CHAPTER SEVEN
## MISSION TRUMPS MEDICAL SCHOOL

1. Author interviews with William Gamboa and James Ragsdale, both May 2, 1998; Ken Bayless, April 23, 1998 at his office in Leesburg, Virginia

2. *Virginia Herald*, December 31, 1799.

3. James LeVoy Sorenson, *Finding The Better Way: The Life and Outlook of James LeVoy Sorenson* (self-published, 1993), 34.

### CHAPTER EIGHT
## CHAMPION BAPTIZER

1. Almost all of the information in this chapter is from original letters written by Jim to his parents and later compiled in a loose leaf binder.

2. Letter from Clara L.M. Davis, Nov. 9, 1942. Underlining in original.

3. This explanation is in family files.

4. *Doctrine and Covenants* 1:4-5.

5. Patriarchal blessing given by Herbert C. Prince, May 4, 1942.

6. *Finding the Better Way*, 35-36.

CHAPTER NINE
## WHIRLWIND COURTSHIP

1.  *Finding the Better Way,* 38.
2.  *Look Beyond the Weeds,* 64.
3.  *Salt Lake Tribune,* July 26, 1946.

CHAPTER TEN
## UPJOHN

1.  This and other conversations among Upjohn leaders about Jim in these pages are from Jim's notes, found in family files.
2.  Ibid.
3.  Sorenson interview by Maureen Ward in the early 1980s.
4.  *Look Beyond the Weeds,* 86, 90.

CHAPTER ELEVEN
## HIKING GOAT PASTURES

1.  Mark Twain, *Roughing It* (Chicago: American Publishing Company, 1872), chapter XIII.
2.  James L. Sorenson, writings in family files.
3.  From a transcript of an interview, in family files. The practice is not uncommon. A poll in 2011 by the National Endowment for Financial Education and *Forbes* found that 31 percent of couples with combined finances are deceptive about money: 51 percent hide cash, 54 percent hide purchases, and 30 percent hide bills. Survey released on January 13, 2011.
4.  Salt Lake County Recorder records. The Sorensons bought the land from Wilford and Jean Weight on June 13, 1950.
5.  Salt Lake County Recorder records.

CHAPTER TWELVE
## BOY'S DEATH SETS COURSE

1.  "We the Upjohn Company," published June 1946.
2.  Writings by Jim Sorenson in family files.
3.  *Finding the Better Way,* Prologue.

CHAPTER THIRTEEN
## DESERET PHARMACEUTICAL

1.  *Look Beyond the Weeds,* 70-71.
2.  James LeVoy Sorenson, unpublished manuscript he titled "More than Millions," 36.
3.  Interview with Gloria Backman, April 20, 2012.
4.  Interview with Carol Sorenson Smith, October 4, 2012.
5.  Letter to Mrs. Jessie Kunz, May 28, 1964.
6.  Hermelin obituary in the *St. Louis Post-Dispatch,* May 13, 2000.
7.  Deseret Pharmaceutical offering circular, dated September 10, 1956.
8.  Jim Sorenson letter to Keith-Victor Pharmacal, June 1956.

9. Victor Hermelin letter to Jim Sorenson, July 9, 1956.

10. *Deseret News,* March 19, 1957.

11. *Deseret News,* January 27, 1959.

12. Drs. W.L. Brown and C.P. Brown, "An Improved Face Mask," *Journal of the American Medical Association (JAMA),* April 25, 1914: 1326.

13. Dr. Joseph A. Capps, Major, U.S. Army, in *JAMA,* March 30, 1918: 70 (13): 910-11.

14. Dr. William C. Beck, president emeritus, The Guthrie Foundation for Medical Research, Sayre, Pa., in the *Association of PeriOperative Registered Nurses (AORN) Journal,* April 1992, Vol. 55, No. 4.

15. Lisa M. Brosseau, ScD, CIH, University of Minnesota, "Surgical Mask Performance," Institute of Medicine Workshop, August 2009.

16. "Shrewd, Very Shrewd," *Forbes,* March 1, 2004.

CHAPTER FOURTEEN
## FIRST DISPOSABLE SURGICAL MASK, CATHETER

1. Lawrence Meyers, M.D., "Intravenous Catheterization," *American Journal of Nursing,* November 1945, Vol. 45, Issue 11, 930-31.

2. *Salt Lake Tribune,* September 20, 1959.

3. "Value of Indwelling Catheters in Intravenous Therapy," *JAMA,* September 19, 1959; Vol. 171, No. 3.

4. Drs. Gustav Bansmer, Donald Keith, and Henry Tesluk, "Complications Following Use of Indwelling Catheters of Inferior Vena Cava," *JAMA,* July 26, 1958, Vol. 167, 1606-1611.

CHAPTER FIFTEEN
## SORENSON RESEARCH SOARS

1. Letter from Harold B. Lee to Jim Sorenson, June 21, 1961.

2. K. Pannier's background is from author interviews on July 9, 2012 with two sons-in-law, Todd Hyer and Arthur (Art) Sleeper, and K.'s four children, son Scott and daughters Norma P. Hyer, Sandy P. Sleeper, and Lisa P. Bradley.

3. *United States v. Byrum* – 408 U.S. 125 (1972).

4. Interview with Gordon's son, Valdon G. Reynolds, July 10, 2012.

5. *Finding the Better Way,* 16.

CHAPTER SIXTEEN
## LEVOY'S, RELIGION, MUSIC

1. Byron Russell related this to the author on May 30, 2013.

2. Interview with James Lee Sorenson, August 30, 2013.

3. Interview with Barlow Bradford, October 9, 2013.

4. Written agreement between Jim and the woman in Arizona, May 19, 1998.

5. Jackman-Sorenson royalty agreement, signed August 30, 1998, in Jim's papers.

6. Interview with Benny Richard Smith, August 23, 2012.

7. *Deseret News,* December 4, 1997.

8. Interview with Carolyn Muir, August 30, 2012.

9.   *Salt Lake Tribune*, October 21, 1968.

10.  *Salt Lake Tribune*, May 12, 1968.

11.  Jim's lesson notes for March 12, 1967.

12.  Jim's lesson notes for May 27, 1967.

13.  Don Lind in the *Church News*, April 15, 1967.

14.  Jim's lesson notes for July 2, 1967.

15.  Undated lesson note.

16.  *Look Beyond the Weeds*, 97.

17.  Dr. Edwin D. Starbuck, University of Iowa.

CHAPTER SEVENTEEN
## THE GREATEST MIND

1.   "Dr. Thomas Latta: the father of intravenous infusion," *Journal of Infection Prevention,* Vol. 10, Supplement 1, September 2009.

2.   Interview with Robert Hitchcock, August 25, 2012.

3.   Interview with Jim Larson, August 21, 2012.

4.   Interview with Reed Winterton, August 21, 2012.

5.   From Jim Sorenson's unpublished autobiography.

6.   *Finding the Better Way*, 67.

7.   Dr. James P. Orlowski, "My Kingdom for an Intravenous Line," *JAMA*, September 1984, Volume 138, No. 9.

8.   Patent 3,399,674, September 3, 1968.

9.   Ibid.

10.  Interview with John Brophy, August 25, 2012.

CHAPTER EIGHTEEN
## JIM, DR. HOMER WARNER TEAM TO MEND HEARTS

1.   Henry P. Plenk, *Medicine in the Beehive State*, 1940-1990 (Salt Lake City: Utah Medical Association, 1992), Introduction.

2.   The books, respectively, are Goodman & Gilman's *The Pharmacological Basis of Therapeutics*, McGraw-Hill; and Wintrobe's *Clinical Hematology,* Lippincott Williams & Wilkins.

3.   The 2007 and 2010 figures are from the "2011 Utah State Health Profile." The 2009 figure is from the Kaiser Family Foundation.

4.   Mark Twain, *Roughing It*, chapter 13.

5.   Paul D. Clayton, PhD, "Presentation of the Morris F. Collen Award to Homer R. Warner," *Journal of the American Medical Informatics Association,* Volume 2, Number 2, March/April 1995.

6.   Interview with Dr. Homer Warner, August 2, 2012.

7.   Ibid.

CHAPTER NINETEEN
## CARDIAC CATHETER OPENS NEW ERA

1.   Author interview with Reed Gardner, September 6, 2012.

2.  Homer Warner, Reed Gardner, Alan Toronto, "Computer-based Monitoring of Cardiovascular Functions in Postoperative Patients," *Circulation*, April 1968; 37 (4 Suppl): 1168-1174.

3.  Ibid.

4.  Dr. Deepak L. Bhatt, "To Cath or Not to Cath: That is No Longer the Question," *JAMA*, June 15, 2005, Volume 293, No. 23.

5.  Reed Gardner, Homer Warner, Alan Toronto, Walter Gaisford, "Catheter-flush System for Continuous Monitoring of Central Arterial Pulse Waveform," *Journal of Applied Physiology*, December 1970, Volume 29, No. 6: 911-13.

6.  G.J. Kuperman, R.M. Gardner, T.A. Pryor, *HELP: A Dynamic Hospital Information System* (New York, N.Y.: Springer-Verlag, 1991.

7.  Paul P. Clayton, *Journal of the American Medical Informatics Association,* Volume 2, No 2: March/April 1995.

8.  H.R. Warner, A.F. Toronto, L.G. Veasy, R. Stephenson, "A Mathematical Approach to Medical Diagnosis. Application to Congenital Heart Disease," *JAMA*, July 22, 1961; 177-83.

9.  Letter from Eric Skousen to the Sorenson Legacy Foundation, date unknown.

10. Dr. Brent James, dedication of Intermountain Homer Warner Center for Informatics Research, February 24, 2011.

CHAPTER TWENTY

# INVENTION SAVES, RECIRCULATES PATIENT'S OWN BLOOD

1.  Patent 3,680,560, filed November 26, 1968 and granted August 1, 1972.

2.  *Deseret News*, June 24, 1975.

3.  *The Watchtower*, October 15, 2000, p. 30-31.

4.  Patent 4,006,745, filed November 13, 1975 and granted February 8, 1977.

5.  "An Autotransfusor for the ER," *Emergency Room Medicine*, January 1978.

6.  Cost Containment report, Johns Hopkins, 1979.

7.  The first letter, dated June 8, 1977, was from Hella Kropf at Eurospital S.P.A., Trieste. The second letter, dated June 6, 1977, was from Alfred S. Cheng, hospital supply department, Harbour Commercial Building, Hong Kong.

8.  Perry Lane, transcript of remarks at staff meeting, June 1, 1977.

9.  Jim Sorenson, eulogy for Karl Arthur Pannier, Jr., May 31, 1977.

10. Interview with former LeVoy's employee and Jim Sorenson assistant Gloria Smith, August 14, 2012.

11. Interview with Doug Fogg, November 15, 2012.

CHAPTER TWENTY-ONE

# SELLING SORENSON RESEARCH

1.  Interview with Carol Sorenson Smith, October 4, 2012.

2.  Jim's letter to Ann is dated March 15, 1967.

3.  Harvard Business School, case 9-677-257, prepared by Gary L. Crocker under the direction of Associate Professor Steven C. Wheelwright, 1977.

4.  Jim Sorenson's unpublished autobiography.

5.  Interview with Gary Crocker, November 15, 2012.

6.  *Finding the Better Way*, 75-76, and other writings by Jim Sorenson.

CHAPTER TWENTY-TWO
## JIM TURNS HIS BACK ON FAMILY

1.  From Jim's notes of the meeting.
2.  Business Editor Robert Woody, *Salt Lake Tribune*, August 27, 1980.
3.  Patent No. 4,224,943, applied for by Jim on January 24, 1979 and granted September 30, 1980.
4.  Interview with Gary Crocker, November 15, 2012.
5.  Interview with James Lee Sorenson, March 13, 2013.
6.  Interviews with Scott Pannier, July 9, 2012 and April 25, 2013.
7.  Interview with Val Reynolds, July 10, 2012.
8.  Letter from Robert Schoellhorn to Jim Sorenson, dated May 18, 1981.
9.  *Bloomberg Businessweek*, March 31, 1991.
10. *Look Beyond the Weeds*, 101.
11. *Deseret News*, December 24, 1979.
12. *Deseret News*, Ibid.
13. *Deseret News*, Ibid.
14. Interview with James Lee Sorenson, March 13, 2013.
15. *Deseret News*, see above.
16. Interview by Cal Boardman, Utah Business Leaders History Project, University of Utah School of Business, June 9, 2010.
17. Interview with the neighbors' son, November 15, 2012.
18. *Look Beyond the Weeds*, 188.

CHAPTER TWENTY-THREE
## LURE OF THE LAND

1.  Interview with Carol Sorenson Smith, October 4, 2012.
2.  Interview with Don Wallace, August 14, 2012.
3.  Interviews with Don Wallace, August 14, 2012 and October 25, 2012.
4.  Interview with Brent Mathews, December 11, 2012.
5.  Emma Sorenson, hand-written letter to Jim and Beverley, October 21, 1977.

CHAPTER TWENTY-FOUR
## SORENSONS CREATE A CITY

1.  Herriman Historical Committee, Herriman, "A Few Moments in Time," brochure.
2.  *Deseret News*, March 25, 1999.
3.  Data from Onboard Informatics.
4.  Sorenson Group news release, June 30, 2008.
5.  *Finding the Better Way*, 92.

CHAPTER TWENTY-FIVE
## WHITE SAGE RANCH, FARM

1. Interviews with waitresses at the Garden of Eat'n, December 10, 2012.
2. U.S. Department of Agriculture, National Agriculture Statistics Service, 2010-11.
3. Interviews with the White Sage ranch and farm managers on December 10, 2012.

CHAPTER TWENTY-SIX
## UNIVERSITY OF UTAH GIFT FIASCO

1. Letter from Peterson to Sorenson, December 19, 1980.
2. Letter from Peterson to Sorenson, March 5, 1987.
3. Letter from Peterson to Sorenson, October 21, 1987.
4. Interview with Duane Toney, September 24, 2012.
5. *Salt Lake Tribune,* June 23, 1989.
6. *Salt Lake Tribune* July 12, 1989.
7. *Salt Lake Tribune* July 18, 1989.
8. *Deseret News,* July 27, 1989.
9. *Salt Lake Tribune* July 28, 1989.
10. Robert Woody, *Salt Lake Tribune,* July 29, 1989.
11. Warner letter to Jim, August 24, 1989.
12. Irving Giles, St. George, in the *Salt Lake Tribune,* August 11, 1989.
13. Interview with Duane Toney, September 24, 2012.
14. *Newsweek,* April 17, 1989.
15. *Deseret News,* May 31, 2012.
16. Interview with John Ward, formerly of Fotheringham & Associates, January 10, 2013.
17. Peterson letter to Sorenson, September 1, 1989.
18. *Finding the Better Way,* 87-88.
19. Peterson letter to Sorenson, January 8, 1991.

CHAPTER TWENTY-SEVEN
## JIM, BEVERLEY GENEROUS WITH NEEDY

1. Interview with James LeVoy Sorenson, April 30, 1998.
2. Lowell Bennion letter to Jim, July 17, 1990.
3. Letter from the president of Somerset Funding in California, written approximately July 8, 2000.
4. Interview with Gloria Sorenson Backman, April 20, 2012.
5. Family letters are dated between February 25 and March 1, 1990.
6. Letter from Gail to her father is dated July 12, 1982.
7. Letter from Chris Harris to her father is dated July 22, 1984.
8. *Deseret News,* June 11-12, 1998.

CHAPTER TWENTY-EIGHT
## NEW COMPANIES LAUNCH, FAIL

1.  Keynote speech on "Research in Action" to an engineering conference at Utah State University, May 2, 1990.
2.  Interview with Jim Jr., November 7, 2013.
3.  *Deseret News*, October 13, 1981.
4.  *Scope: Bio Med Gen Tech Utah Industry News*, April 1996.
5.  Campbell letter to Jim Sorenson, July 13, 1985.
6.  Interview with Jim Larson, August 21, 2012.
7.  *Finding the Better Way*, 82.
8.  Letter to Diana Johnson, March 3, 1992.
9.  *Finding the Better Way*, 80.
10. *Deseret Morning News*, September 7, 2003.
11. Max Knudson, *Deseret News*, August 29, 1999.
12. *Finding the Better Way*, 91.
13. Interview with John Ward, September 7, 2012.
14. Thomas J. Stanley and William D. Danko, *The Millionaire Next Door*, (Atlanta, Georgia: Longstreet Press, 1996) 1-3.
15. Ibid, 8.

CHAPTER TWENTY-NINE
## SORENSON BIOSCIENCE

1.  Interview with Gary Crocker, November 15, 2012.
2.  Interview with Beverley Taylor Sorenson, October 5, 1998.
3.  From a paper prepared by Jim for *Forbes* sometime in 2006.
4.  Interview with West Price, September 27, 2012.
5.  Interview with John Brophy, August 25, 2012.
6.  *Salt Lake Tribune,* July 20, 1991.
7.  Joan M., July 19, 1991.

CHAPTER THIRTY
## JIM A VOLATILE LEADER

1.  Interview with Jim Larson, August 21, 2012.
2.  Interview with Gloria Smith, August 14, 2012.
3.  Interview with Duane Toney, September 24, 2012.
4.  Gijs van Wulfen, "Operational Excellence will kill you," the FORTH Innovation Group, November 5, 2012.
5.  Jim's unpublished autobiography.
6.  Interview with Pat Nola, October 25, 2013.
7.  Credited to late American writer Elbert Hubbard.
8.  *Salt Lake Tribune*, September 7, 2003.
9.  Letter from "Dennis," December 7, 1989.

10. Letter from "Frank," November 23, 1990.

11. Letter from "John," December 15, 1992.

12. Undated letter to Jim from Aleksey Blyumenfeld.

13. Jim's letter is dated February 3, 1994.

14. Chapter 31, Crime vs. Basketball

15. 2011-2012 Annual Report of the Sorenson Multi-Cultural and Unity Center.

16. Blog sponsored by City-Data.com; postings on August 16, 2009.

17. "Overview of Gangs in Salt Lake County," by the Metro Gang Unit of police in county, on the web at http://updsl.org/divisions/metro_gang_unit/local_gangs.

18. Jim Sorenson, unpublished memoir.

19. From the brochure distributed at the Sorenson Center, June 28, 1996.

20. *Deseret Morning News*, September 7, 2003.

21. Sorenson Legacy Foundation at sorensonlegacyfoundation.org/grant_highlights/community.

22. Letter from Governor Huntsman to Jim, June 22, 2006.

CHAPTER THIRTY-ONE
## CRIME VS. BASKETBALL

1. 2011-2012 Annual Report of the Sorenson Multi-Cultural and Unity Center.

2. Blog sponsored by City-Data.com; postings on August 16, 2009.

3. "Overview of Gangs in Salt Lake County," by the Metro Gang Unit of police in county, on the web at http://updsl.org/divisions/metro_gang_unit/local_gangs.

4. Jim Sorenson, unpublished memoir.

5. From the brochure distributed at the Sorenson Center, June 28, 1996.

6. *Deseret Morning News*, September 7, 2003.

7. Sorenson Legacy Foundation at sorensonlegacyfoundation.org/grant_highlights/community.

8. Letter from Governor Huntsman to Jim, June 22, 2006

CHAPTER THIRTY-TWO
## BEVERLEY SAVES KIDS WITH ART

1. In 2007-08 Utah ranked 49th out of 50 states with the largest self-contained classes in elementary school, with 24.2 pupils; Michigan was 50th with 25.1 pupils. National Center for Education Statistics.

2. Anne C. Grey, "No Child Left Behind in Art Education Policy: A Review of Key Recommendations for Arts Language Revisions," *Arts Education Policy Review*, 111(1), 2010 8–15.

3. *Look Beyond the Weeds*, 177.

4. Jim Sorenson, unpublished memoir.

5. Interview with Carol Sorenson Smith, October 4, 2012.

6. *Finding the Better Way*, 40.

7. *Look Beyond the Weeds*, 162.

8. Ibid.

CHAPTER THIRTY-THREE
## DNA KINSHIP AND WORLD PEACE

1.   Joseph Chang, Statistician, Yale; Douglas L.T. Rhode, computer scientist, Massachusetts In-
     stitute of Techonology; and Steve Olson, freelance science writer, "Most Recent Common
     Ancestor of All Living Humans Surprisingly Recent," summarized in *Science News*, September
     30, 2004.
2.   Interview with Scott Woodward, April 17, 2013.
3.   Jim's letter was dated August 31, 2004.
4.   Douglas Fogg, interview on November 15, 2012.
5.   Interview with John Brophy, August 25, 2012.
6.   KSL-TV news report, November 17, 2011.
7.   The *Salt Lake Tribune*, August 22, 2007.
8.   *Deseret News*, April 26, 2012.
9.   The Innocence Project, founded in 1992 at the Benjamin N. Cardoza School of Law at Ye-
     shiva University, on the web at www.innocenceproject.org/about/mission-statement.
10.  *Deseret News*, October 23, 2007.
11.  "The Science and Business of Genetic Ancestry Testing," *Science*, October 19, 2007.
12.  *Deseret News*, October 23, 2007.

CHAPTER THIRTY-FOUR
## FOSTERING FAITH, CHOOSING FAMILY OVER FAME

1.   *Finding the Better Way*, 93-96.
2.   Riffet Hassan, professor of religious studies at the University of Louisville, USA, "A
     Muslim's reflections on a new global ethics and cultural diversity," lecture at a confer-
     ence in Amsterdam, November 8, 1996.
3.   Hans Kung, UNESCO Conference on world peace and religion, 1989.
4.   Quoted in *The New York Times*, January 2, 2007.
5.   Teddy Kollek letter to Jim, August 30, 1990.
6.   Kollek letter to Jim, July 18, 1991.
7.   Bishop Weigand letter to Jim, January 7, 1993.
8.   Thomas S. Monson letter to Jim, December 22, 1992.
9.   Gordon B. Hinckley letter to Jim, January 22, 1993.
10.  The card is undated.
11.  Dallin H. Oaks letter to Jim, February 5, 1993.
12.  Gordon B. Hinckley letter to Jim, January 25, 1994.
13.  Jim's remarks to participants in the International Scholars' Abrahamic Trialogue, Jan-
     uary 2, 1994.
14.  *Maariv*, February 9, 1994.
15.  Interviews with John Brophy and Gloria Smith.
16.  *Finding the Better Way*, 98.
17.  Church magazines, December 2011.
18.  Interview with Duane Toney, September 24, 2012.
19.  Letter to Ronald A. Rasband, August 16, 2005.
20.  Letter to Ronald A. Rasband, November 16, 2005.

# INDEX

## ABOUT THE AUTHOR

LEE RODERICK is a former television news director, AP reporter, newspaper bureau chief in Washington, D.C., and president of the National Press Club. His feature articles have appeared in *The Wall Street Journal, American Heritage,* and *Parade* magazine among other publications. Roderick holds a master's degree in International Relations from George Washington University. He and his wife Yvonne have six children and live in the Intermountain West. This is his seventh biography.

Back Cover: Jim on top of the first new Sorenson Research building, wearing his "lucky" tan corduroy suit. Decades later the suit was inadvertently given to a thrift shop and sold, much to his distress. After considerable searching by his wife Beverley, months later the suit was found and returned. Photo by *Salt Lake Tribune.*